THE
ADMIRALS

LEADERSHIP

THE
ADMIRALS

Canada's
Senior Naval
Leadership
in the
Twentieth Century

Edited by
Michael Whitby
Richard H. Gimblett
and Peter Haydon

DUNDURN PRESS
TORONTO

Copy-editor: Lloyd Davis
Design: Jennifer Scott
Printer: Webcom

Library and Archives Canada Cataloguing in Publication

Whitby, Michael J. (Michael Jeffrey), 1954-

The admirals : Canada's senior naval leadership in the twentieth century / Michael Whitby, Richard H. Gimblett, and Peter Haydon.

Includes bibliographical references.

ISBN-10: 1-55002-580-5
ISBN-13: 978-1-55002-580-4

1. Admirals--Canada--Biography. 2. Canada. Royal Canadian Navy--Officers--Biography. 3. Canada--History, Naval--20th century. I. Gimblett, Richard Howard, 1956- II. Haydon, Peter T. (Peter Trevor),1935- III. Title.

FC231.W44 2005   359'.0092'271   C2005-906318-1

1   2   3   4   5   10   09   08   07   06

  Canada

ONTARIO ARTS COUNCIL
CONSEIL DES ARTS DE L'ONTARIO

We acknowledge the support of the Canada Council for the Arts and the Ontario Arts Council for our publishing program. We also acknowledge the financial support of the Government of Canada through the Book Publishing Industry Development Program and The Association for the Export of Canadian Books, and the Government of Ontario through the Ontario Book Publishers Tax Credit program, and the Ontario Media Development Corporation.

Printed and bound in Canada.
www.dundurn.com

Dundurn Press
3 Church Street, Suite 500
Toronto, Ontario, Canada
M5E 1M2

Gazelle Book Services Limited
White Cross Mills
Hightown, Lancaster, England
LA1 4X5

Dundurn Press
2250 Military Road
Tonawanda, NY
U.S.A. 14150

THE
ADMIRALS

CONTENTS

FOREWORD *by Vice-Admiral R.D. Buck*   11

INTRODUCTION *by Michael Whitby*   15

PART I: CHIEFS OF THE NAVAL STAFF

1. Admiral Sir Charles E. Kingsmill: Forgotten Father   31
    Richard H. Gimblett

2. Commodore Walter Hose: Ordinary Officer,   55
    Extraordinary Endeavour
    William Glover

3. Admiral Percy W. Nelles: Diligent Guardian of the Vision   69
    Roger Sarty

4. Rear-Admiral Leonard Warren Murray: 97
    Canada's Most Important Operational Commander
    Marc Milner

5. Vice-Admiral George C. Jones: 125
    The Political Career of a Naval Officer
    Richard Oliver Mayne

6.   Vice-Admiral Howard Emmerson Reid   157
     and Vice-Admiral Harold Taylor Wood Grant:
     Forging the New "Canadian" Navy
     Wilfred G.D. Lund

7.   Vice-Admiral E. Rollo Mainguy: Sailors' Admiral   187
     Wilfred G.D. Lund

8.   Vice-Admiral Harry G. DeWolf: Pragmatic Navalist   213
     Michael Whitby

9.   Vice-Admiral Herbert S. Rayner: 247
     The Last Chief of the Canadian Naval Staff
     Peter Haydon

10. Rear-Admiral William M. Landymore: 275
     The Silent Service Speaks Out
     Robert H. Caldwell

PART II: COMMANDERS OF MARITIME COMMAND

11. Vice-Admiral Harold A. Porter, 1970–71   309

12. Rear-Admiral Robert W. Timbrell, 1971–73   321

13. Vice-Admiral J. Andrew Fulton, 1980–83   327

14. Vice-Admiral Charles M. Thomas, 1987–89   335

15. Vice-Admiral Robert E. George, 1989–91   341

16. Vice-Admiral John R. Anderson, 1991–92   349

Appendix I: Canada's Naval Commanders, 1910–2005   357

Appendix II: Career Summaries of the Flag Officers   360
                Included in This Volume

ABBREVIATIONS AND ACRONYMS   384

CONTRIBUTORS   388

ACKNOWLEDGEMENTS   394

BIBLIOGRAPHY   396

INDEX   403

FOREWORD

It was my pleasure and privilege to attend the Sixth Maritime Command Historical Conference in Halifax in 2002, the proceedings of which this volume records.

Canada's foremost naval historians presented a range of biographical and professional studies of the Chiefs of the Naval Staff and other influential Royal Canadian Navy senior officers from our founding in 1910, through the world wars and inter-war years, Korea and the Cold War, to our transformation in 1968. The scope of these scholarly enquiries is thus comprehensive; they are of sufficient depth and originality to provide us with genuinely new insights into an important part of modern Canadian history.

Most fascinating to me were the reminiscences of six of my predecessors, retired Commanders of Maritime Command, including Admirals Timbrell, Porter, Fulton, Thomas, George and Anderson. Their participation added a credible degree of relevance to the proceedings.

This volume outlines and examines the challenges associated with senior naval leadership within the sometimes fraught context of Canadian federal politics as well as period strategic geopolitics. It offers a valuable collection of case studies into the nature of leadership, from which present and future naval personnel (and, I would hope, those who aspire to a career in politics) can learn a great deal.

To paraphrase the novelist, while all happy admirals resemble one another, each unhappy admiral is unhappy in his own way. Perhaps more so in Canada than elsewhere in the Commonwealth or NATO, there has always existed a tension between the navy and governments of the day. This tension, I believe, has more to do with ignorance of our role and capabilities than any more sinister explanation, despite such unnerving (to Ottawa) precedents as the putting to sea of the fleet during the 1962 October Crisis.

My tenure was served in times of peace and war. Peace was better. For much of the time since September 2001, we have seen nearly the entire fleet serve a succession of arduous rotations as part of Operation Apollo, the first and most consistently applied response of Canada to the ongoing war on terror. Every sailor in a seagoing billet wears the ribbon. Every staff member and civilian employee has, to a greater or lesser degree, been affected, whether by greater workloads or neglected projects. Training, maintenance, refits, life-extensions, capital procurements, quality of life — all these have suffered. But despite everything, the United States Navy welcomes our ships as fighting units that can be relied upon, whether as fully integrated units within their Carrier battle groups, or as multinational task force leaders, or as amphibious assault group escorts, or in any number of other roles across virtually the entire operational spectrum. This is an achievement of which the whole navy can be proud, and it is a result of clear leadership whose strategic vision for the naval forces of Canada remained — and remains — sharply focused on making sure that our task group–based capability and effectiveness survive. For it is only by maintaining a medium-level navy, deployable around the world, that we can best serve the interests of Canada and Canadians.

In sum, I cannot say with hand on heart that I have been any "unhappier" than any of my predecessors, nor can I claim the opposite. We have all had successes and disappointments. And we have all had, by necessity, to confront our assumptions (monumentally self-evident to us) about why our country needs a navy, and thus justify our continued existence. This has always been an irony to me, given Canadians' warmly-embraced idea that we count and are involved meaningfully in the wider world. But this struggle will continue far beyond my time.

The torch will be taken up by the cream of our wonderful people — the properly trained naval officer, the steadfast non-commissioned officer and the well-trained rating. Their good work, in keeping with our finest traditions as well as new ways of thinking and doing, will at the end of the day persuade Canadians what a superb resource they have in their navy.

Vice-Admiral R.D. Buck
Vice-Chief of the Defence Staff

INTRODUCTION

The articles that comprise this volume were presented at the Sixth Maritime Command Historical Conference, held at the Canadian Forces Maritime Warfare Centre in Halifax over a two-day period in September 2002. Since the first conference — organized by Dr. Jim Boutilier in 1980 — naval personnel, veterans, students, academics and others interested in the Canadian navy have gathered every few years to discuss aspects of the service's history. The results have been exceptional, engendering a much wider interest and inquiry into an important Canadian institution. Most of the papers presented at these conferences have been published in various proceedings,[1] and they have contributed greatly to our understanding of the navy and served as a tangible reminder of the value of the MARCOM Historical Conferences.

Despite all the progress of research into Canadian naval history, it has long been recognized that insufficient attention has been paid to the *individuals* who served in the navy. The organizers of the 2002 conference determined to address that shortcoming by focusing on the select group of admirals who led the navy through its difficult evolution, three wars, and into the uncertainty of the post–Cold War era. An added advantage to this approach was that such inquiry would be of invaluable assistance to the naval history team at the National Defence Headquarters' Directorate of History and Heritage, which is in the midst of preparing the three-volume official history of the Royal

Canadian Navy (RCN). The result was a conference titled "Running the Navy," at which historians presented papers on the nine officers who had served either as Director of the Naval Service or as Chief of the Naval Staff. The achievements and significance of Rear-Admirals Leonard Murray and William Landymore — two officers who either did not rise to the highest appointment in the navy or held it only briefly — were of such magnitude that they were included as well.

Rather than simply have a series of academics espouse their views of the experiences of Canada's naval leaders, the organizers thought it would be particularly valuable for participants to hear first-hand from officers who had actually had the responsibility of running Canada's navy. In two truly memorable sessions, Rear-Admiral Bob Timbrell, Vice-Admirals Harry Porter, Andy Fulton, Bob George and "Chuck" Thomas, and Admiral John Anderson recounted the challenges and highlights of their service as Commander, Maritime Command. Their papers are included in this volume, and it is hoped that the combination of academic treatise and personal reminiscence will make a valuable contribution to our understanding of some of the individuals who had the honour to lead the Canadian navy.

Some will note, and rightly so, that we have not included all of the admirals who led the navy. Unfortunately, there was not enough time to cover them all, and there are always problems finding academics to write the necessary papers to "speak" for those who have passed on. Clearly, this volume would be enriched by telling the stories of Ken Dyer's troubled tenure as the Senior Naval Advisor for the first two years of integration and unification, and the way in which Ralph Hennessy and "Scruffy" O'Brien had to restore naval morale and a sense of purpose to the navy after the Landymore incident and the deep fleet cuts implemented by Paul Hellyer in his quest for reform. Many will remember the presence, often seemingly at the wrong moment, of Douglas Seaman Boyle. Also missing are Andy Collier and "Jock" Allen, both of whom had to lead Maritime Command through particularly difficult political times when budgets were tight and the ships getting older without prospect for replacement. That we were able to get so many of the former Maritime Commanders to come and talk about their days in command was wonderful, and their contributions have done much to further the course of Canadian naval history.

Introductions to published conference proceedings typically provide an overview of the papers presented at the event. In this case, however, the editors have decided to let the various papers speak for themselves. That said, readers will be intrigued by the fact that the papers sometimes differ in their interpretation of various issues, personalities and events; where one historian says Admiral "Bloggins" did this or was responsible for that, another will suggest that it happened another way entirely. Such disagreement is inevitable when weighing the role of individuals; it also makes for interesting reading and will perhaps raise a little controversy. That can be invaluable, and hopefully readers, especially students of the Canadian navy, will be motivated to conduct further research.

To further that end, this introduction will attempt to provide context to the careers of the flag officers that led the Canadian navy over its history. As far as the cultural background of those discussed and present is concerned, all but Walter Hose and Bob Timbrell were born in Canada, and their birthplaces represent all regions of the country except the north. None were francophones, but a number became bilingual. All were married with family. Their professional qualifications varied at a generational level. Before there ever was an RCN, Charles Kingsmill and Walter Hose had full careers in the Royal Navy (RN). Percy Nelles, Leonard Murray, G.C. Jones, H.E. Reid, Harold Grant, Rollo Mainguy and Harry DeWolf entered the navy through the Royal Navy College of Canada. Herbert Rayner, William Landymore and Bob Timbrell received their cadet training with the RN, while Andy Fulton was a graduate of Royal Roads. Bob George, "Chuck" Thomas and John Anderson were all products of the postwar, purely Canadian system; all obtained university degrees, and Thomas's subsequent MBA represented the only postgraduate experience. Of those represented here, Harry Porter was the only one promoted from the lower deck, as well as the sole qualified naval aviator, while Thomas was the only engineer. Their professional fates also varied: Kingsmill, Nelles and Landymore were fired, and evidence suggests that Mainguy may have been as well. Thomas resigned after becoming Vice-Chief of the Defence Staff. G.C. Jones died while on duty. Anderson was the only one included in this volume to rise to Chief of the Defence Staff.

That brief snapshot helps to define what our select group of naval leaders *were*. One can also gain insight into them and their careers by looking at what they *were not*. A vehicle that can be used to accomplish this is to compare and contrast their experience with their British and American counterparts. That methodology is apt, since throughout most of its history the Canadian navy has been closely associated and sometimes almost completely integrated with those two influential navies. Moreover, at various times the service has also defined itself by its relationship with either, or both, of those organizations. For most of the first four decades of its existence the RCN maintained strong links to the RN, relying upon its mother service almost exclusively for its equipment, training and doctrine. A stronger, more confident service emerged from the Second World War and even though it maintained complete independence it moved into relatively close orbit with the United States Navy, to the point that in the 1990s and into this century, seamless integration of our warships into USN task groups is heralded as a capability matched by no other navy, and one that the Canadian navy should strive to continue. Whether exercising with the RN's Atlantic and West Indies Squadron in the 1930s or with the U.S. Atlantic Fleet in the 1950s; whether fully integrated into the 10th Destroyer Flotilla in the English Channel or in the USS *Abraham Lincoln* Carrier Battle Group in the Indian Ocean; whether negotiating naval strategy at an Imperial Conference or in the Permanent Joint Board on Defense; the Canadian navy has been inextricably linked with either the RN or USN throughout its history. With such strong ties to such predominant allies, but without the strength in numbers or resources to match their strength and capability, it is intriguing to compare and contrast the qualifications and experiences of Canadian naval leaders to those of our two closest allies.

Command experience is the most basic qualification for senior naval leadership, and in that area the Canadian situation is vastly different from that of the RN or USN. In terms of individual ship command, whereas their American and British counterparts typically had capital ship experience under their belt, the largest ship commanded by a Canadian naval leader was a 16,000-ton light fleet carrier. However, even that "big ship" command experience was rare, and of the officers included in this volume, seven never commanded a warship larger than a destroyer. When wartime command experience is considered, just three—Walter Hose, Harold Grant and Rollo Mainguy—commanded anything as large as a light cruiser.

The contrast is even greater when one considers their experience commanding formations such as flotillas, squadrons and task groups. Of the officers in this volume, Kingsmill, Reid, Grant and Mainguy never commanded a permanently established seagoing naval formation in peace or war; a circumstance that would have made it virtually impossible for them to rise to the top of the RN or USN. Only G.C. Jones and Leonard Murray had seagoing commands as significant as a destroyer flotilla during major wars, although several Canadians later commanded national and international task groups during the first Persian Gulf War and in the war against terrorism. Apart from the NATO Standing Naval Force Atlantic, commanded at various times by a series of Canadian officers, including three future Maritime Commanders, Douglas Boyle, Lynn Mason and Greg Maddison, the largest force any led in peacetime was a carrier task group or escort formation.

Harry DeWolf's experience was typical. Although he is widely recognized as Canada's most renowned fighting sailor, his experience commanding formations of ships in either war or peace was almost negligible. Serving in the RN's Home Fleet in late 1943 as captain of the destroyer HMCS *Haida*, he once commanded the screen of a carrier sortie and was twice designated senior officer of the rear of the convoy on two Russian convoys. The latter was an important responsibility, especially given the fact that the convoys ran during perpetual Arctic darkness and were threatened by air, surface and sub-surface forces, but DeWolf had no strategic — and only limited tactical — control over his force. He led his largest peacetime formation when, in the rank of commodore, he was double-hatted as Senior Canadian Naval Officer Afloat and commanding officer of the carriers HMCS *Warrior* and *Magnificent*. But even then, the unit consisted only of the carrier, a cruiser and a couple of destroyers. DeWolf's experience was characteristic of the officers who rose to command the navy; they stood in stark contrast to their British and American counterparts, who had often commanded fleets on distant stations. For example, Arleigh Burke, who was Chief of Naval Operations when DeWolf was CNS, had commanded a destroyer squadron in war and a cruiser squadron in peace; and, as Chief of Staff in Task Forces 38/58, he had planned and often controlled the operations of the U.S. Pacific Fleet's fast carriers. Admiral of the Fleet Lord Louis Mountbatten, First Sea Lord when DeWolf led the RCN, had commanded a destroyer flotilla in war and the Mediterranean Fleet in peace. Interestingly, both Burke and Mountbatten had less command time at sea than many of the officers who rose to the top of their respective navies.

The fact that Canada's naval leaders have essentially been small-ship sailors has influenced their outlook far beyond their time spent at sea. Yet many of them rose to become the Commander, Canadian Fleet (CANCOMFLT) and took large formations of Canadian warships on major NATO exercises, often serving in operational command roles such as ASW Screen Commander, or taking a Canadian task force to places like Brazil and Argentina. Formation command was enormously important, and Canadian naval officers frequently excelled — how else would Canadians have earned sufficient trust and respect to be given command of a multinational task force during the first Persian Gulf War and again in the war on terrorism?

National and NATO formation command experience at sea was often the highlight of a Canadian naval officer's career, but many will claim that they were good because they had been good destroyer captains. Canadian officers have taken great pride in their ship-handling ability, and many — Murray, Landymore and DeWolf among those in this volume — were widely admired for that skill, which helped to give them the overall respect of the navy as they rose through the ranks. In contrast, the reputation of officers not known as skilled ship drivers, such as G.C. Jones and Percy Nelles, suffered.

The pride that Canadian officers took in handling their ships with skill and panache also coloured their attitude towards working alongside their "big navy" allies. Even though the RN and USN are larger and more powerful, Canadian sailors have taken great pride in showing that they can perform just as effectively at a ship-to-ship level. Reflecting upon his experience in the 1930s, when the RCN sub-flotilla exercised alongside destroyer flotillas from the prestigious Home Fleet, Leonard Murray observed "it was great fun getting on board the Fleet flag ship and being able to show them that in spite of their longer history, our people could keep up the game and be just as smart as theirs." That spirit survives to this day, and it continues to act as a measuring stick for Canadian commanding officers.

Besides losing out on the professional benefits that could be derived from leading significant seagoing commands, Canadian naval leaders also lost the opportunity to garner the publicity that usually resulted from success in battle while leading such forces. In other navies, winning a great victory at sea often translated into winning a great reputation. As just one example, the RN's Admiral Sir Bruce Fraser became forever known as the victor of the Battle of North Cape for his role in leading the forces that sunk the German battle cruiser *Scharnhorst* off northern Norway in December 1943. Although Fraser was a talented naval officer who had held important positions and would rise to become First Sea Lord after the war, North Cape defined his career and gave him a public persona. In contrast, within days of that battle, Harold Grant's cruiser HMS *Enterprise* and another British cruiser, HMS *Glasgow*, engaged eleven German destroyers in a long-running battle in the Bay of Biscay, sinking three and damaging others. It was an important victory, but although Grant was decorated for his performance and his actions were well publicized at the time, the success cannot be said to have had any lasting impact on his public reputation. Likewise, although Canadian naval figures won fleeting publicity for sinking enemy U-boats or destroyers, the fame never endured amongst the broader public.

There are other differences between Canadian commanders and their British and American counterparts that can be considered among the trappings and accoutrements that accompany success or even courage in battle. Canadians uttered no inspirational battle cries to match Admiral A.B. Cunningham's "Sink, burn, destroy; let nothing pass," Admiral Farragut's "Damn the torpedoes" or Halsey's "Hit hard; hit fast; hit often." Nor is there a descriptive phrase that summarizes the navy's role, such as John Paul Jones's "Go in harm's way" or Nelson's "No captain can do very wrong if he places his ship alongside that of an enemy." The most famous phrase in Canadian naval history — and perhaps the only famous one — is John Stubbs's courageous cry of "Get away, *Haida!* Get clear!" when Harry DeWolf stopped his destroyer to rescue *Athabaskan*'s survivors after she had been sunk by enemy torpedoes within miles of the enemy-held French coast. Stubbs, a well-respected officer, did not survive, and although his heroic gesture was well known within the postwar navy, there is no evidence that it reverberated in his country's psyche.

Like others, the Royal Navy, and especially the U.S. Navy, honour their leaders by naming ships or even entire classes after them; one needs to think only of the carrier USS *Nimitz*, the battle cruiser HMS *Hood* or the Arleigh Burke class of destroyers. In contrast, with the exception of the inter-war destroyers *Champlain* and *Vancouver*, Canada has avoided naming ships after national or naval personalities, and although the navy has named shore establishments after historic figures, that recognition would be unknown outside the services. This, and the lack of heroic *cris de guerre*, is reflective of our reserved national character; however, it does mean that the reputations of Canadian naval leaders have been neither enhanced nor perpetuated.

Probably the most significant difference between Canadian senior naval leaders and their British and American counterparts is that we simply do not know that much about them. Part of the reason for that is the general lack of recognition due to the reasons given above; however, there is another major contributing factor. Whereas it is common for senior RN and USN officers to write their memoirs or become the subjects of biographies, the same has not been true for Canadian flag officers. Only Jeffry Brock and Nelson Lay published memoirs, but both are of limited utility. Brock's are self-centred and of questionable reliability, while Lay's were intended as a "family" memoir and thus lack detail and sophistication. As for biography, with the exception of a sycophantic account of Leonard Murray's role in the Halifax riots, no Canadian admiral has been the subject of study beyond the biographical articles such as those that appear in this volume, and even those, until recently, have been few in number. Never have their stories been collected under a single cover.

The reluctance of senior Canadian officers to describe their experiences is hard to fathom, but a tradition of being a silent service based on the RN example seems to have taken hold early in the navy's history. As Richard Gimblett reveals in his article on Charles Kingsmill, Percy Nelles showed no hesitation in sanctioning the destruction of the private papers of the first head of the RCN, and other senior officers have sometimes followed suit by stripping their, or other's, files. Perhaps the practice of engendering a culture of silence and privacy has carried over into the writing of memoirs.

Canadian naval historians also deserve a share of the blame. Although they have been prolific since the 1970s and have earned solid reputations in the international naval history community, their work has concentrated almost exclusively on subjects related to policy, operations and equipment. As a result of that focus, and the reluctance of senior officers to reflect upon their careers, the Canadian public in general simply does not know much about them or their motivations.

It is fair to say, given the nature of their experience and their silence, that no matter what their accomplishments — and as the accompanying papers demonstrate, some were indeed great — Canada's senior naval leaders simply have not made any real lasting impression upon their country. There can be no blame or failure associated with that; it is simply a fact of the Canadian naval experience. Nonetheless, the lack of profile has not helped the navy's cause, especially in terms of influencing decisions or winning budgetary and policy battles in the corridors of power. It is there that Directors of the Naval Service, Chiefs of the Naval Staff, Commanders Maritime Command and Commanders of the Maritime Staff have had to persuade political leaders to support their programs and policies. It would be wrong to suggest that American or British naval leaders, even those of legendary status, won political battles as a result of their stature or the reputation of their service, but it is fair to say that they have had a better chance of doing so. Reputations carry weight in the hurly-burly realm of decision-making, especially when media focus is a factor. Largely unknown, Canadian naval leaders have not been able to bring much to the table in that regard.

Quite apart from the low public profile of the officers who lead the services, defence and the navy have never been major factors in political decision-making. One can debate whether or not Canada is a maritime nation, but it is clear that if we are, then there is simply not much awareness or recognition of that idea. The navy has never been a large blip on politicians' radar screen, and most have been unwilling to expend political capital in that area. Yet, ironically, those same politicians have been quick to deploy the navy as the initial response to an international crisis, such as the Korean War, the Persian Gulf War and the war against terrorism. Two entries from the diary of long-serving Liberal prime minister Mackenzie King provide good evidence of the place that military and naval budgets typically occupy in the overall government planning. Although King supported limited naval expansion in the late 1930s — with the Second World War on the horizon — and then funded significant emergency building programs during the war, he opposed measures that would result in an increased permanent postwar naval establishment. Through some deft, and at times disingenuous, stickhandling, the navy won its battle for cruisers and light fleet carriers, but even then King always had his eye on a return to peace — and with it, the restoration of the services to what he considered their rightful standing. When the minister of national defence Brooke Claxton argued a case for modestly increased estimates to the Cabinet Defence Committee in January 1947, King reminded him of the position of defence in the Canadian context.

> I then spoke of the necessity of all estimates before we decided what could be allotted for Defence, pointing out that Gardiner would want expenditures for agricultural purposes and for assisting farmers shipping food overseas etc. The Minister of Health and Welfare would want large expenditures for social services. E.[xternal] A.[ffairs] had put in large items for international conferences, delegations, etc. which were supposed to go to the keeping of peace and avoidance of war. The Minister of Finance [Douglas Abbott] would be expected to reduce taxation. I said we could only consider Defence in the light of those amounts. Abbott said he did not see how more than a certain figure which we mentioned could be allotted to Defence and the Chiefs of Staff were instructed to go over estimates again in the light of that statement.[2]

As exemplified by King's remarks, defence — except in times of significant international or national tension — has traditionally been a minor consideration in budgetary discussions, and as the junior service, the navy has probably suffered the most. That position has not been helped by the fact that our political leaders have never seemed to understand the navy and its requirements. Another King diary entry from April 1948 illustrates this point. After discussing the deteriorating international situation, specifically the threat posed by the Soviet Union, he enunciated his fears over the possible fate of Canada's aircraft carrier. "I cannot but shudder," he wrote, "each time I think of this enormous aircraft carrier which we are having brought out under the title of [HMCS] *Magnificent*. What Canada wants with the largest aircraft carrier afloat under a title like that, I don't know. It is just to invite an enemy's attack. I venture to say should war come soon, it would be about the first of the large vessels to disappear."[3] Perhaps if the carrier had been named HMCS *Percy W. Nelles* or the *Sir Charles Kingsmill,* he would have considered it more innocuous and less of a target. Nonetheless, although politicians could not be expected to know that *Magnificent* was actually dwarfed by the newest American carriers, the remark reveals an astonishing ignorance of naval matters.

But does the fault for that necessarily lie entirely with King? The aircraft carrier program had, after all, been the focus of much debate late in the Second World War, and King had been fully engaged in the process; indeed, it was he whom senior naval officers had to convince to support the program. That he reveals such unfamiliarity with the type of ship he ultimately approved — the most significant ships ever acquired by the navy — not only emphasizes how little the navy registered with him but perhaps reflects the quality of the naval advice the prime minister was receiving. Certainly, it is indicative of a major gulf between King and his naval advisors. It is evident from the papers in this volume that the problem did not only lie with King and his naval advisors, but that it has been a factor throughout our navy's history, and one that leaders of the future must be prepared to reckon with also.

Describing the impact of severe defence cuts in Great Britain in the early 1980s, one RN officer pointed a finger at his own service. "Perhaps in fairness," Commodore Michael Clapp wrote in his memoir of the Falklands war, "it was the Royal Navy, still by nature a Silent Service and at the time still a monastic and inward-looking organization with little contact with society, who never managed to explain its case satisfactorily or in sufficiently strong and unambiguous terms to the politicians and the press — and thus the public. Basically, few of us saw a need to. We knew and that was what mattered!"[4] Clapp's description may apply even more to the Canadian navy, and particularly to its leaders.

Canadian officers have been traditionally monastic in the sense that they have been inward-looking. Moreover, until relatively recently, they have not seen the need to engage the Canadian public.[5] Almost to a man, the reputation they cared about was that *within* the Canadian navy. And in almost every instance the officers represented in this volume had the respect of their service. Not all agreed with their decisions, there was plenty of competition in the promotion sweepstakes, and some just did not get along. But there was still a strong degree of mutual respect among them. And why not? They had all paid their professional dues in rising to the head of their service, and in doing so had helped to build a solid professional navy that serves their country well.

Sadly, the Canadian public knows little of that, and there have been consequences. It is doubtful that the state of affairs can ever be changed in a culture that seldom praises — or even recognizes — the role of individuals, especially those who lead such public institutions as the armed services. This volume will not change matters, but it will perhaps encourage the navy to celebrate those who have served it so well over the decades and to try to bring their accomplishments before the Canadian public.

Michael Whitby

NOTES

1   Boutilier, James A. (ed.), *The RCN in Retrospect, 1910–1968* (Vancouver: University of British Columbia Press, 1982); Douglas, W.A.B. (ed.), *The RCN in Transition, 1910–1985* (Vancouver: University of British Columbia Press, 1988); Hadley, Michael L., Rob Hubert and Fred W. Crickard (eds.), *A Nation's Navy: In Quest of Canadian Naval Identity* (Kingston and Montreal: McGill-Queen's University Press, 1996); P. Haydon and Ann L. Griffiths (eds.), *Canada's Pacific Naval Heritage: Purposeful or Peripheral* (Halifax: Dalhousie University Centre for

Foreign Policy Studies, 1999). Several papers from the 1990 conference were published in the *Maritime Warfare Bulletin*.

2 Mackenzie King Diary, 9 January 1947. The complete diary is available online at the Library and Archives Canada website.

3 Mackenzie King Diary, 9 April 1948.

4 Michael Clapp and Ewen Southby-Tailyour, *Amphibious Assault Falklands: The Battle of San Carlos Water* (London: Orion,1996), 11.

5 As just one example, in 1960 CNS Harry DeWolf decided to limit the celebrations involving the fiftieth anniversary of the RCN due to a lack of money, thus missing a great opportunity to celebrate the navy and bring its accomplishments before the Canadian public. The navy has learned, and plans to celebrate the navy's centennial have been underway since 2002.

Part I:
Chiefs of the Naval Staff

CHAPTER ONE

Admiral Sir Charles E. Kingsmill: Forgotten Father

Richard H. Gimblett

Charles Kingsmill in the rank of rear-admiral

Wh+en Charles Edmund Kingsmill was born on 7 July 1855, in Guelph, Canada West (now Ontario), there was little to suggest that he would become the first director of the naval service (DNS) of Canada and, as such, the father of the Royal Canadian Navy (RCN). The Dominion of Canada would not exist for another twelve years; the Upper Canadian establishment family from which he came had closer links to the Provincial (Land) Militia; and at any rate, the Royal Navy's (RN) preponderance at sea rendered the question of a Canadian naval service an abstract concept. At the time of his death eighty years later, in July 1935, the RCN that he had helped to establish in 1910 was in its silver jubilee year. Even if the celebrations were somewhat muted, and Kingsmill's vision of a proud, robust service remained unfulfilled, his legacy was of a solid institutional framework for the development of a truly national fleet finely tuned to Canada's aspirations, capabilities and limitations.

For a man who held such high office at a critical juncture, we know very little of Sir Charles — he was made a knight batchelor in 1918 for services rendered in the course of the Great War. He has never been the direct subject of secondary analysis, and although he figures prominently in Hadley and Sarty's comprehensive *Tin-Pots and Pirate Ships*, the few references to him in other episodic works tend to be either incomplete or incorrect.[1] The fault lies in part with Kingsmill himself. A proud but private man, he was very much the stereotype of the "silent service." He neither kept a diary nor left any private papers, as confirmed by the Assistant Naval Secretary in a memorandum to the Chief of the Naval Staff, Rear-Admiral Percy Nelles, in 1939 when the question of disposal of Kingsmill's records arose:

> I [the Assistant Naval Secretary] have gone through the box of correspondence of the late Sir Charles Kingsmill, CMG. I have segregated some of it for decision as to disposal as it may be of official interest and importance.
>
> The balance of the box comprises office copies of communications and private correspondence on a variety of subjects with a variety of people. The correspondence would be of value to anybody who would care to undertake to write the memoirs of the late Sir Charles Kingsmill, and some of it might be of interest to the Archives.
>
> I feel, however, that a dead man's private correspondence should not be disposed of where it would become public property as it reflects his private opinions, his private likes and dislikes, etc. Possibly it would be better to destroy this correspondence but it must be decided upon, please.
>
> There is no doubt that the late Admiral Kingsmill did not desire this correspondence to become a part of the official record of the Department, otherwise he would not have removed it from his office upon his retirement.[2]

Having served as flag lieutenant to Kingsmill for a period during the First World War, Nelles could claim some special insight into the former director's wishes. His response to the final question, "Do you not think that his wishes should be met?" was a simple "Destroy."

In consequence, Kingsmill tends to be forgotten in the chronicles of the RCN. In trying to assess him, it is necessary to turn to alternate sources and methodologies. Some useful clues from his professional career in the Royal Navy (RN) prior to his return to Canada in 1908 can be gleaned from the pioneering work of Andrew Gordon, *The Rules of the Game: Jutland and British Naval Command*, essentially a study of Kingsmill's RN contemporaries.[3] The ultimate test, however, is to consider his deeds as Director of the Naval Service, but this assessment is made difficult by the fragmentary state of the already concise records of the Department of the Naval Service. This chapter, therefore, shall look instead at the broad thrust of the early development of the RCN.

The accepted history is that the navy did not prosper during the years under Kingsmill, in part because he supposedly accepted its establishment as an imperial squadron.[4] An alternative assessment is offered: that Kingsmill actually was able to lay a remarkably sound foundation — both in fleet structure and the administrative staff headquarters to support it — upon which to build a rational Canadian naval service finely tuned to national aspirations, as opposed to the vision of a RN-in-miniature (not unlike the model of the Royal Australian Navy) preferred by the Admiralty and occasionally even by Canadian politicians. As can be appreciated from comparison to the present perilous state of the Canadian Forces, the failure of those other parties to appreciate the wisdom of Kingsmill's rational fleet structure was invariably driven by political motives having little to do with efficiency, and led directly to his dismissal in frustration early in 1920.

The Kingsmill family line in Canada can be traced directly to William Kingsmill, who was born in Ireland in 1794 of an ancient military lineage, joined the British Army in 1809, served under Wellington with the 66th Regiment of Foot in the Peninsular Campaign, came to Canada with that regiment in 1827, and resigned his commission in 1833 to take advantage of the free land grant available to retired officers and men. Going on to raise two regiments of foot during the Rebellion of 1837, he was made "a colonel in command of the Provincial Militia." By the time of his death in 1876, Colonel Kingsmill's two surviving sons were well established in the Ontario legal community, with strong links to the Liberal party in Toronto. The eldest of those sons was John Juchereau, whose own eldest son was Charles Edmund.[5]

Kingsmill's motivation for joining the Royal Navy, instead of pursuing either a legal or Canadian military career, is not recorded but can be traced to two possibly related events from his adolescence. Between 1866 and 1868, he studied at Upper Canada College under principal Frederick William Barron, then at "Dr Barron's school in Cobourg." That gentleman apparently passed on an interest in the RN not only to Kingsmill, but also to his own son, who became a Liberal member of Parliament (North Victoria, 1887–1891) and wrote "numerous papers and addresses favouring the formation of a Royal Can. Navy." In turn, *his* son, John Barron, joined CGS *Canada* "as first Can. cadet R.C.N., 1908."[6]

The lure of naval adventure probably was consolidated in young Kingsmill's mind by his grandfather's publication in 1869 of a pamphlet inspired by his visit to a 106-year-old survivor of the legendary battles of the Nile and Trafalgar, who was then living near Toronto.[7] Later that year, on 24 September 1869, at the tender age of fourteen, Charles Edmund joined the training ship HMS *Britannia* at Dartmouth, England, as a naval cadet.

Kingsmill's career in the RN can be characterized as interesting, but certainly not extraordinary. Neither, however, could he conceivably be styled a laggard.[8] His progression through the ranks was not far removed from that of his near and illustrious contemporary, Admiral of the Fleet Viscount John Jellicoe of Scapa. Jellicoe joined as a cadet three years after Kingsmill, in 1872, but was promoted to commander in the same year of 1891, and reached flag rank a year ahead in 1907 — Jellicoe's four-year catch-up equated roughly to his reduced time in the rank of sub-lieutenant, as well as the year or so that Kingsmill spent on leave on half-pay while awaiting appointments upon promotion to each of lieutenant, commander and captain. Jellicoe, however, had been "noticed" early, passing out of *Britannia* top of his term (Kingsmill was closer to the bottom of his), had continued to excel under various sponsors, and spent no time on half-pay.

There were other differences: Jellicoe specialized in gunnery, while Kingsmill qualified as a torpedo specialist; Jellicoe made important connections with the clique of naval officers associated with service in the Royal Yachts — both the gunnery specialization and Royal patronage are themes developed at length by Gordon in *The Rules of the Game* as important to the progression of "authoritarian" officers — and Jellicoe spent most of his time in the prized Mediterranean Fleet and even enjoyed rare junior Admiralty appointments.[9] Interestingly, Kingsmill also served in the Royal yacht *Victoria and Albert* for a short period (25 June–5 September 1877) upon completing his lieutenant's qualifying course at the Royal Naval College in Greenwich — the appointment was propitious, for although his selection was based simply upon availability and appears not to have coincided with any especial personage or event, it was enough to overcome his middling achievement in the course and ensure his timely advancement to lieutenant.[10]

Otherwise, in contrast to Jellicoe, Kingsmill's early and middle service was almost entirely on foreign stations.[11] But even after awaiting on half-pay the availability of such appointments, none of those positions he eventually filled were a signal of a career nearing termination. Indeed, important as the gunnery specialization and noteworthy service in the Royal yacht might have been to others, they served more to create opportunity than to guarantee special treatment.

Another contemporary was Sir Charles Henry Coke, who would be appointed to the RCN as Commodore of East Coast Patrols for a short period in 1917, after he was implicated in the loss of the *Lusitania* and dismissed from regular RN service.[12] Despite the latter's service in the RN gunnery school, HMS *Excellent*, and a longer period as a lieutenant in the Royal yacht, in point of fact, Kingsmill's career nearly perfectly mirrored Coke's.[13]

Having broached the issue, it is useful to pause briefly to examine the essence of Gordon's review of the "fundamentally different attitudes towards authority [within] the leadership mores of the late Victorian Navy and of the early career conditioning of the future admirals of the Grand Fleet," and to situate Kingsmill within that culture.[14] Building upon the archetypes described in Norman Dixon's unfortunately named but still quite useful *On the Psychology of Military Incompetence*,[15] Gordon describes two distinct officer types:

> The *authoritarian* … draws self-esteem from the status imparted by his rank and uniform. He defers naturally

to seniority and obeys orders to the letter,… is strong in sequential reasoning processes, suppresses his imagination, rejects information which conflicts with his (and his seniors') preconceptions, and is fearful of using his initiative.… He keeps an unblotted copybook and thus gains unhindered advancement in peacetime. But he is easily disoriented by the crises and dilemmas of war, and responds inappropriately or not at all.

The *autocratic* officer is approximately the obverse of the above. He tends to think laterally, rather than serially, and his convictions follow his instincts. He uses his initiative as a matter of habit. He is receptive to the possibility that his juniors might be right or his seniors wrong, and takes his career into his hands when he believes the latter to be the case.… His peacetime career ascent is often difficult because he lacks the docility convenient to his immediate seniors.… In wartime it falls to him to clear up the mess pioneered by the authoritarian who gained preference over him in the years of peace.

Gordon is quick to allow that "'incompetence,' in the detailed practical sense, finds fewer pegs in the Navy than [the Army]," if only because "the necessities and hazards of daily shipboard life demanded a higher degree of basic vocational competence."[16] He notes also that "most people seem to draw characteristics from both sides of the Dixonian spectrum." Indeed, while it is possible to identify a number of traits that would seem to place Kingsmill in the authoritarian camp — for example, his seemingly inappropriate reaction to the disaster of the Halifax explosion[17] and his occasional expectations of deference to his rank[18] — it is perhaps instructive that the casual image he chose to project for his official portrait upon promotion to flag rank (see photograph) is hardly that of the model stiff-collared Edwardian naval officer.

Within this cultural construct, there should be little difficulty placing Kingsmill in the autocratic school. In this sense, his service in the Royal yacht was little more than an anomaly, even as it takes nothing away from the political acumen he will be seen to demonstrate in establishing the Canadian naval service as a Liberal institution. One did not have to be a pure authoritarian to appreciate the value of political connections.

Indeed, a more important anomaly in his professional naval career serves to establish Kingsmill firmly as an autocrat: that he attended RNC Greenwich on two occasions beyond the standard "Subs" courses — the first time early in 1900, while still on half-pay upon promotion to captain, and the second in the fall and winter of 1904–05 for the newly established Captain's War Course before assuming command of the Atlantic Fleet battleship HMS *Majestic*. The significance arises not just from the fact he availed himself — and not just once, but twice, for whatever reason — of an opportunity the majority of his contemporaries would have forgone entirely, but also because the second of these occasions was at the time of the noted strategist Sir Julian Corbett's closest association with Greenwich. Corbett was developing the Captain's War Course as "a maritime programme, avoiding the twin dangers of 'blue water navalism' [and] conscriptionist homeland defence," and his specific historical case study in 1904–05 was the eerily appropriate *England and the Seven Years' War*, which "used a Clausewitzian analysis of a major conflict as a template for the development of contemporary strategy."[19] That Kingsmill studied the notions of the diffused essence of British sea power directly from Corbett, as opposed to the battle-fleet engagement theories of Alfred Thayer Mahan that were gaining popularity elsewhere, had to have been a major influence in his later method of direction for the fledgling Canadian naval service.

Besides his periods of advanced study at the naval college, another important influence from Kingsmill's RN experience upon his later Canadian command came from his periods of service on the Australia Station. There were two occasions, both in command — first of the 805-ton screw gunboat *Goldfinch* (February 1890–August 1891), and then of the 2,575-ton third-class cruiser *Mildura* (September 1900–December 1903). Although not the sole focus of his RN service career, and certainly not even the most exciting, these commands must have been made memorable by their respective circumstances. For a variety of reasons relating to their isolated strategic location on the periphery of the British Empire, the Australian colonies took an active interest in maintaining their maritime security by contributing directly to naval defence. Although the Royal Australian Navy (RAN) was not established as such until 1911, a number of preliminary steps towards its formation were being taken throughout the late nineteenth and early twentieth centuries, and Kingsmill could not have escaped becoming familiar with them. Indeed, his first period on the station coincided with the arrival of the Auxiliary Squadron approved under the Naval Agreement at the Colonial Conference of 1887,[20] and the second with federation of the Commonwealth of Australia in 1901 that served to rekindle interest in a national fleet.[21] Perhaps more significantly, from this latter period Kingsmill was bound to have encountered Captain W.R. Creswell, RN, then commandant of the Queensland Marine Defence Force. By the time Kingsmill returned to Canada in 1908 with the intent of becoming Director of the Naval Service, Creswell had been appointed Director of Naval Forces to the Australian Ministry of Defence. Again the record is sketchy, but there is evidence of a common approach between the senior Australian and Canadian naval officers at this time.[22]

One final point of interest in Kingsmill's RN service concerns the inference that his eventual successor as DNS, Walter Hose, "came to [his] attention" while the latter was a student at Greenwich.[23] Even if they were never together there, or apparently anywhere else, the search for other possible occasions of meeting did reveal a period in the winter of 1903 when Kingsmill was in command of the Channel Squadron cruiser *Scylla* at the same time that Hose was serving off Newfoundland in the cruiser *Charybdis*. Although the two ships were in different fleets, readers can nonetheless appreciate the coincidence, knowing the future hard times that both men would face.[24]

That brings us, then, to the circumstances of Kingsmill's retirement from the Royal Navy to return to Canada, which are important to understanding his later commitment to a particular vision of a Canadian naval service. In December 1905, he had just taken command of the recently completed pre-*Dreadnought* battleship HMS *Dominion* — one of the last of that type, and still very much a frontline vessel — when the Admiralty placed his ship at the disposal of the Canadian government to transport the remains of the Minister of Marine and Fisheries, Raymond Préfontaine, who had died in Paris early on Christmas morning, to Canada.[25] In accordance with protocol, the prime minister met the ship upon its arrival in Quebec. Sir Wilfrid Laurier usually was cool to imperial military officers — there is the famous occasion when he went so far as to warn one General Officer Commanding (GOC) the Canadian Militia, upon that officer's arrival in Canada, that he "must not take the militia seriously, for though it is useful for suppressing internal disturbances, it will not be required for the defence of the country, as the Monroe doctrine protects us against enemy aggression," and then promptly dismissing that same officer when he chose to take his duties too seriously.[26]

In the case of Kingsmill, there was no guarantee that his years of British service would not have subverted his Canadian-ness. Laurier, however, appears to have taken to him immediately, the ice perhaps having been broken in the knowledge that his uncle, Nicol Kingsmill, was a prominent Toronto lawyer — and good Liberal — with whom Laurier had had business dealings over the years. When Kingsmill and *Dominion* returned that August, Laurier readily accepted an invitation to dine aboard this "fair vessel of war."[27] A year later, at the time of the Colonial Conference of 1907, when Kingsmill called upon Laurier's secretary for an interview with the prime minister in London, the naval officer was instead invited, along with his wife, to dine privately with the Lauriers.[28]

Kingsmill had sought the interview to explain the outcome of the court martial into the grounding of HMS *Dominion* during the previous summer's visit to Canada. While departing Chaleur Bay on the evening of 19 August 1906 after a stop on passage to Quebec, the on-watch officer had misidentified a brush fire on shore for a lighthouse, causing the battleship to alter course early onto a sandbank. Little damage was done, and such incidents were not uncommon in those days before the widespread availability of modern and reliable aids to navigation. Both the captain and the navigator received severe reprimands for "grave neglect in duty" for not being present on the bridge at the time of grounding.[29] Press reports had Kingsmill being found guilty of negligence — a semantically similar but far graver offence — and he wanted to assure Laurier that those "are absolutely false … because I know Sir Wilfrid wrote personally to thank the Admiralty and would not like him to think that I were unworthy of his consideration."[30] His further assertion that he retained the confidence of Their Lordships, in that he had only recently been given command of the 14,000-ton battleship *Repulse*, involved some dissembling: that ship was a much older (1892) class of ship, indicating that Kingsmill's progress in the RN was clearly in abeyance. The prime minister seems to have accepted Kingsmill's account, and indeed may actually have found Kingsmill's circumstances fortuitous. Far from being a purely social visit, it appears that Laurier was actively assessing Kingsmill's suitability to head a nascent Canadian naval force.

Progress in that direction was proceeding slowly, but already was well advanced. As part of a general reform of the militia in 1904, the Canadian government had fully intended to establish a naval militia based upon the Fisheries Protection Service.[31] An Act Constituting the Naval Militia of Canada had been prepared for the 1904 session of Parliament but was not introduced, primarily due to the unexpected additional expenses that fell to the militia when it assumed responsibility for the garrisons at Halifax and Esquimalt from the departing imperial forces in 1904.[32] Although hardly a government priority, the naval militia project had remained alive. Indeed, Préfontaine had gone to London late in 1905 to discuss the issue with the Admiralty, and at the 1907 Colonial Conference Laurier allowed his minister of Marine and Fisheries, Louis-Phillippe Brodeur, to report that Canada was willing to proceed on naval matters "under the advice of an Imperial officer, so far as it is consistent with self-government."[33]

The catalyst for action came in 1908, when President Theodore Roosevelt offered that the United States Navy's Great White Fleet should stop in Victoria and Vancouver as part of its famous around-the-world cruise. With the RN's presence on the Pacific coast reduced to a token force, the episode highlighted the ability of any foreign fleet to enter Canadian waters at will. Laurier's protégé, Deputy Minister of Labour William Lyon Mackenzie King, recorded the direction in which official Liberal thinking was developing, noting in his diary after an interview with Laurier that the "situation reveals to me ... the necessity of our doing something in the way of having a navy of our own."[34] Coincident with a major commission of inquiry into improprieties in the administration of the Marine Department, the time was ripe for a major reorganization of the Department of Marine and Fisheries. Early that spring of 1908, Kingsmill was invited to take the appointment of Commander of the Fishery Protection Service (FPS) at an annual salary of $3,000.[35] With the concurrence of the Admiralty, the transfer was made effective 15 May 1908, and to facilitate it without provoking any of the constitutional problems that had accompanied militia GOC appointments, Kingsmill was promoted to rear-admiral before being placed on the retired list some months later — possibly so that he might return to service in the Royal Navy, in the event the Canadian appointment did not prove to his liking.[36] Confirming that a considerable upgrading in the status of the FPS was in the offing, the news was reported in the semi-official Toronto *Globe* under the banner headline: "Canada to Have Naval Militia. A Canadian Admiral Has Already Been Appointed."[37]

If Laurier did not fear Kingsmill to be a hidebound "The Sea is One" imperial navalist,[38] Kingsmill equally could not have hesitated at the prime minister's model for a Canadian naval service. Presuming that the general instructions governing the militia would have been understood to pertain, the underlying requirement was that it be not so much a fighting navy, but rather what we today would call an effective instrument for the enforcement of sovereignty. Clues as to the form it might take existed aplenty, and were readily available to Kingsmill, as his uncle Nicol was a prominent member of the influential Toronto branch of the Navy League, whose proposals on the subject had formed the basis of the draft 1904 Naval Militia Bill.[39]

Within a few months of his arrival in Canada, Kingsmill began to adapt these earlier ideas for the use of his minister in preparation for a debate on the naval issue early in the 1909 Parliamentary session. Dated 1 February 1909, Kingsmill's preliminary report on how "we should commence our work of assisting in the Defence of Our Coasts" is a clear exposition of the fundamental principles that would change only in detail through the remainder of his tenure.[40] Building upon the existing Fisheries Protection Service, he envisioned a gradual upgrade of its establishment so as to maintain the fleet's Canadian essence and focus on Canadian priorities. The major recommendations were the formation of a signal service connecting all of the important lighthouses, building a dockyard at Quebec, and starting a training establishment at Halifax from which:

> The men trained in the first year would be available to man a destroyer or a Scout [small cruiser] next year, and so on until we had sufficient officers and men well trained to man our proposed defence which should, in my opinion, be confined to Destroyers and Scouts for many a long day.

Continuing his counsel of moderation, Kingsmill noted the construction and upkeep costs of various classes of warships, warning that it would be far better for the government to continue for the time being with the development of the country, "as in that is our only hope of some day being in a position to defend our Coasts as they should be." By embarking on too ambitious a project, "a young and partly developed Country may, if not wreck itself, at any rate seriously injure its internal economy." At the same time, the Admiral noted, "to spend money on partial defence or rather inadequate defence is to waste it."[41]

Such was the framework for a Canadian navy that was debated late into the night of 29 March 1909, resulting in unanimous approval for "the speedy organization of a Canadian naval service in co-operation with and in close relation to the Imperial Navy, along the lines suggested by the Admiralty at the last Imperial Conference [in 1907]."[42] Although the debate had transpired at the height of the Dreadnought Crisis, Canadians did not see that the strategic situation should have changed. Three weeks later, Kingsmill presented a more detailed version of his plan to Brodeur, still recognizing the need to start small and recommending that "we must use the newly started Naval Service for the Protection of our Fisheries, in fact, that Fisheries Protection and Training go hand in hand" while developing the defences of the coasts.[43]

But the situation indeed had changed. When Brodeur, Kingsmill and their militia counterparts went to London that summer to discuss the development of the Canadian services, they were confronted with First Sea Lord Admiral Sir John Fisher's "fleet unit" scheme for dominion naval forces. This radical new strategic concept was for a much larger and clearly offensive force, consisting of a dreadnought battle cruiser supported by three unarmoured cruisers, six destroyers and three submarines.[44] Kingsmill figured prominently in the protracted negotiations that followed, supporting his minister in an attempt to keep the new Admiralty concept within the strict limitations of accepted Canadian naval policy.[45] As a compromise, the Canadians agreed to the loan of the cruisers *Niobe* and *Rainbow* for training purposes, pending construction of a fleet of oceangoing cruisers and destroyers. The precipitous acquisition of such large ships, however, could not be manned within the existing establishment of the Canadian Fisheries Protection Service; neither could such a fleet any longer be characterized as a naval militia restricted to Canadian coastal waters. Kingsmill was forced to crew them with some 600 officers and ratings seconded from the RN. Nationalists, especially French-Canadians, saw their naval force being subverted to imperial purposes, while imperialists now were convinced it would be an inadequate assistance to the RN. The "tin-pot" fleet that no one wanted became a contributing factor in the fall of Laurier's government in the 1911 general election.

The effort fared no better under the new Conservative ministry of Sir Robert Borden. Although he had been a nonpartisan supporter of the naval militia scheme as far back as 1901,[46] and then a co-drafter with Laurier of the final resolution of 29 March 1909, in the charged atmosphere of 1910–11 Borden succumbed to political opportunity and adopted a policy of contributing to the upkeep of the RN. The introduction of the Naval Aid Bill in 1912 led to the resignation of his Quebec lieutenant, F.D. Monk, quickly followed by the bill's defeat at the hands of the Liberal majority in the senate. Borden admitted privately that "Laurier had had the right idea in his program of 1903–1904 slowly to convert the Fisheries Protection Service into a fighting force."[47] It is difficult to assess the relationship between the Conservative prime minister and his admiral, but Ottawa was still a small enough town that Borden must have been aware of Kingsmill's Liberal connections, and one senses that their interaction was correct but distant.[48] That would explain why, in the fall of 1912, Borden renewed an appeal direct to the Admiralty for advice on a coast defence force. By that time, Fisher had been replaced by the less dogmatic Admiral Sir Francis Bridgeman, and

Borden received the much more balanced response of a scheme for torpedo craft flotillas to be augmented by seagoing cruisers.[49] But no progress had been made in this direction by August 1914, and in the opening days of the First World War *Niobe* and *Rainbow* were all that could hastily be put to sea in the search for German surface raiders.

Surprisingly enough, they contributed effectively to the roving RN squadrons that quickly put that threat to rest. With the German High Seas Fleet bottled up in the North Sea by Admiral Jellicoe's Grand Fleet, the Canadian war effort soon was directed to the Western Front. The Admiralty advice in October 1914 that "Canada should confine herself to contributions on land because warships could not be built quickly" was reiterated in the summer of 1915 with the admonishment that, "although a Canadian naval patrol service might not be without value, 'exaggerated measures of precaution were to be deprecated.'"[50] In anticipation of a German U-boat threat developing, Kingsmill chose to ignore this advice and established a series of East Coast Patrols by commissioning the vessels and crews of the Fisheries Protection Service into the RCN.[51] In a fashion not unlike the plans he had previously laid, the addition of converted yachts and a large number of anti-submarine trawlers and drifters gradually expanded this core force. When the U-boats did appear early in 1918, the RCN was not totally unprepared, and only three oceangoing merchant ships carrying supplies to Britain were sunk in Canadian waters.[52] By the time of the armistice, a Royal Canadian Naval Air Service was in the process of being formed with the assistance of the United States Navy; already the RN's Intelligence Operations Centre in Halifax had been established as a Canadian unit.[53] All in all, the record of Kingsmill and Naval Service Headquarters (NSHQ) in Ottawa in the First World War was one of effective command and control arrangements with the Admiralty, logical operational direction, and sound administrative oversight, all carefully managed to ensure Dominion autonomy while contributing effectively to the overall war effort at sea.

In August 1918, with the end of the war finally in sight, the British Admiralty charged Viscount Jellicoe to advise the dominion governments on their postwar naval requirements. Prime Minister Borden was now firmly opposed to the Admiralty's preferred policy of contributions to an Imperial Grand Fleet, on the basis these would likely "offend the newly awaked sense of nationhood which pervaded the people of Canada."[54] But a few months later, in February 1919, perhaps flushed from the recent allied victory, he suggested that "It might be possible for the Canadian Government to ... take over a fleet unit [of surplus RN warships] consisting, let us say, of a battleship, certain large and small cruisers, with the necessary quota of destroyers and submarines."[55] This sort of talk must have taken Kingsmill back a full decade, and again, in true "autocratic" style, he determined to stick to his principles, even if it meant going against his own government as well as the Admiralty.

This time, however, he had a proper naval staff at his disposal. To sidestep having to accept ships immediately from the Admiralty according to some "haphazard principle," he struck a naval committee to produce a series of "Occasional Papers" as a rational planning basis.[56] Eventually comprising some thirty-one memoranda prepared in the space of a few months, these were a major undertaking for any staff, but especially for one as small as that of NSHQ. Perhaps the most important of the staff analyses was the second, entitled "Proposals for Canadian Naval Expansion."[57] Clearly bearing the stamp of Kingsmill's inspiration, it envisioned the creation of a forty-six-ship navy, consisting finally of seven cruisers, twelve destroyers, eighteen anti-submarine patrol craft, three submarines and three tenders, all to be manned by 8,500 officers and men. Importantly, it saw the gradual buildup of the force over two seven-year building periods (1920–27 and 1927–34), timed to the capacity for Canadian crews to man the ships. It specifically rejected capital ships as being beyond the resources of Canadian shipyards to construct and the availability of the numbers of experienced senior Canadian officers required to command them.

Although this proposal became the basis of Jellicoe's report, the former First Sea Lord regrettably published his recommendations in terms of the immediate establishment along the old fleet-unit notion, advising that it eventually include battle cruisers and aircraft carriers.[58] Borden's initial impression upon reading the Jellicoe Report was that "the first chapter does not present anything new."[59] His earlier ruminations aside, it all was too bold an expansion of a navy that consisted of only a few trawler-size vessels and for which there existed no clearly demonstrable peacetime need, especially as the onset of a postwar recession was heightening concern over the accumulated war debt. The naval minister, Charles C. Ballantyne (notably, a former Liberal — Borden's was a Unionist ministry), appreciated that Jellicoe's minimalist "Plan 1" was not far removed from Kingsmill's own version, and obtained Cabinet approval for that. Apprehensive of the imperial undertones of Jellicoe's proposal, yet unable to appreciate the Canadian essence of Kingsmill's, the Unionist caucus generated a commotion that was, perhaps, not unexpected. Borden, conveniently, had gone on vacation for the occasion, and according to George Foster, the acting prime minister and the author of the original 1909 motion,

> Ballantyne went in with his modified $5m. per year programme sure of success, and gave it a good explanation & sat down beaming for results. Well, the Caucus knocked it sky-high…. Poor [Ballantyne] came out wilted & discouraged & mad….
>
> Next day … we found out the facts — that [Ballantyne] had sent … orders to dismiss most of the officials & had sent Kingsmill his letter of dismissal with the idea of scrapping the old if he could not get the new. Well, we had a talk over it, and ended with a compromise. (a) To give the Minister a free hand to reorganize by notice of discontinuance of present staff. (b) Accept two destroyers and one cruiser from [Great Britain] to replace the *Rainbow* & *Niobe* for training and protection purposes. (c) Keep up the College. (d) Defer Permanent Navy policy for the present.[60]

What part Kingsmill played in working out this compromise is not stated, but it was not inconsistent with his basic principles for institutional integrity. Yet neither did it allow for the growth for which he longed. He must finally have had enough, and if the price was to be his dismissal he did not protest it. By the end of the month he was gone, replaced by Captain Walter Hose. Similarly a former RN officer, although not a native Canadian, upon transferring to the RCN in 1912 Hose proved to be as alive to Canadian sensitivities as his predecessor. In these, Kingsmill had tutored him well, and also in the art of political survival — qualities that would help to preserve a viable institution against the attacks of intemperate governments and rival services, as will be demonstrated in the next chapter.

A passing glance at the RCN at the time of Kingsmill's death in 1935 would not seem to reveal a service proud or robust. With the RCN still only a shadow force of four destroyers, the Royal Naval College of Canada closed, and officers and ratings having by default to obtain the bulk of their training with the RN, Kingsmill could nonetheless rest easy with his legacy of an essentially solid institution. For one thing, the RCN did still exist, even if Walter Hose had had to weather harder times than Kingsmill ever had to contend with. For another, William Lyon Mackenzie King soon would be returned as prime minister, and he remembered the lesson learned from Laurier — and by extension from Kingsmill — of "the necessity of our … having a navy of our own." With the RN no longer the undisputed ruler of the seas, and with war clouds gathering in Asia and in Europe, King would see the navy as a primary focus for Canadian rearmament.[61] Moreover, Hose had passed the tiller of the naval service to Commodore Percy Nelles, the first truly "Canadian" leader of the navy, having been one of the original cadets, with John Barron, recruited by Kingsmill for training in CGS *Canada* in the summer of 1908. To be sure, there would be trials ahead, but the RCN did indeed enjoy a healthy foundation for future expansion.

That expansion would prove most rewarding when its proponents remained truest to Kingsmill's vision: that the navy existed not to serve as an imperial squadron but to meet Canadian national aspirations, whatever domestic or international dimensions those might entail, and that growth must be measured and kept within sustainable bounds. Faced with the urgency of global threats, first in the coming world war and again in the Cold War, future Chiefs of the Naval Staff occasionally would feel obliged to overreach those limits, and consequently the institution would suffer. They would enjoy their greatest success when they returned to their roots. Sometimes this would be in the knowledge of Kingsmill's intentions, but more often not. Even if the paternity might be forgotten, those instincts were ones bred into the bones of succeeding generations by the father of the RCN.

NOTES

1   Hadley & Sarty, *Tin-Pots and Pirate Ships* [complete references for commonly cited secondary sources are provided in the bibliography]. The best recent treatment is in Armstrong's *The Halifax Explosion and the Royal Canadian Navy: Inquiry and Intrigue*, but with that narrow focus Kingsmill is painted — possibly not inaccurately — as a fussbudget micromanager more interested in the fate of his son, who was attending naval college in Halifax, than in relief of the larger disaster. Although not a major figure in that work, it still is more than is provided in the official history, Tucker, *The Naval Service of Canada* (I): *Origins and Early Years*.

2   Assistant Naval Secretary to CNS [Nelles], 7 February 1939, DHH, Kingsmill BIOG file (typed copy by E.C. Russell from original on Library and Archives Canada [LAC], RG 24 [acc 1992-93/169], vol 116 [Kingsmill personnel file]).

3   Gordon, *The Rules of the Game*. As will be examined at length later in this paper, the book analyzes the action at Jutland against a study of the differing leadership styles of Admirals of the Fleet Sir John Jellicoe and Sir David Beatty.

4   The pertinent sections in neither of the two popular histories of the RCN (German, *The Sea is at Our Gates*, and Milner, *Canada's Navy*) are sympathetic to Kingsmill.

5   C.B. Koester, "Charles Edmund Kingsmill (1855–1935) Genealogical Sketch" (dated 9/3/92), Directorate of History and Heritage (DHH), C.E. Kingsmill BIOG file, provides indispensable family background.

6   Koester, "Kingsmill Genealogical Sketch"; Morgan, *The Canadian Men and Women of the Time*; and Wallace, *Macmillan Dictionary of Canadian Biography*.

7   Cited in Koester, "Kingsmill Genealogical Sketch." The veteran is identified only as "one Cordingley," and the pamphlet was entitled *Story of the Old Marine*.

8   Kingsmill's RN personal file is at the Public Record Office (PRO), ADM 196/19, 353-356, and ADM 196/38, 752 and 755; the RN Navy List, 1869–1920 (inclusive) provide some broad outlines.

9   Jellicoe biographical details can be found in Kemp, *Oxford Companion to Ships and the Sea*, 428–29. Other distinguishing traits of "authoritarian" Victorian naval officers, according to Gordon, were membership in the Society of Free Masons and a passion for Arctic exploration. There is no evidence that Kingsmill shared either of these.

10 National Maritime Museum, Manuscript Division, RNC Greenwich, "Results of Examinations, Acting Lieutenants, 1877," 11, Kingsmill Certificate, 18 April 1877. Despite his third-class standing, Kingsmill in fact placed second of nine on the course (ibid., 10a, "Order of Merit").

11 Kingsmill had experience on virtually all of the Royal Navy's stations (North America & West Indies, Mediterranean, East Indies, China, Australia, and the Channel) except for those of Cape of Good Hope and the Pacific.

12 Hadley and Sarty, *Tin-Pots and Pirate Ships*, 190–91.

13 MacFarlane, *Canada's Admirals and Commodores*, 50.

14 Gordon, *Rules of the Game*, 3. Although less precise because of changing circumstances, future students of the Canadian navy may find it interesting to apply Gordon's model against other Canadian naval leaders.

15 Norman F. Dixon, *On the Psychology of Military Incompetence* (New York: Basic Books, 1976).

16 Gordon, *Rules of the Game*, 177–78.

17 Armstrong, *Halifax Explosion and the RCN*, 85–89. Faced with a lack of information from Halifax authorities as to the extent of the disaster, Kingsmill chose to proceed there by rail for a personal inspection, rather than wait in Ottawa, as the Chief of the General Staff Sir Willoughby Gwatkin opted to do. While on the surface "inappropriate," this could be taken as an example of "lateral" thinking (especially knowing the frailty of the naval command and control arrangements in Halifax at that moment).

18 Kingsmill's admittedly scanty RCN personnel file contains evidence of at least two instances upon which he felt that others were not according him due respect: with his presence in Halifax frequently going unnoted, he ordered a Canadian Jack to be flown from the starboard signal yardarm of HMCS *Niobe*, or whatever vessel in which

he was embarked (DNS to C-in-C A&WI, 2 February 1917); and an apparent bureaucratic lapse in publishing his promotion to the rank of Admiral in the *Canada Gazette* (DNS to DM, 18 May 1917). While at first blush these might seem petty, they were not at all outside the bounds of standard practice for flag officers.

19 I am indebted to Professor Andrew Lambert for assistance in establishing these linkages. Quotes are from his "The Development of Education in the Royal Navy, 1854–1914"; also, Schurman, "Civilian Historian: Sir Julian Corbett," in *The Education of a Navy*, 149. Corbett, *England in the Seven Years' War*.

20 Preston, Canada and "Imperial Defense," 102–108 and passim.

21 Colin Jones, "'The View from Port Phillip Heads: Alfred Deakin and the Move Towards an Australian Navy," in David Stevens & John Reeve (eds.), *Southern Trident: Strategy, History and the Rise of Australian Naval Power*, (Crows Nest, NSW: Allen & Unwin, 2000), 160–73.

22 Nicholls, "William Rooke Creswell and an Australian Navy," and Sarty, "The Origins of the Royal Canadian Navy: The Australian Connection," 91–99 passim. Those familiar with the origins of the RCN and RAN will know that Creswell later had a change of heart, after the special Imperial Defence Conference in the summer of 1909.

23 Bishop, "Save Our Navy: Walter Hose, Rollo Mainguy," 121. Bishop earlier makes the incorrect statement (from admittedly confusing primary sources) that Kingsmill had been Director of RNC Greenwich; besides Kingsmill never having filled that position, by the time Hose took the war course it had been moved to Portsmouth.

24 In Greek mythology, these were the respective names of a sea monster and a whirlpool encountered by Odysseus on his return from Troy. The reference has come to symbolize "two dangers such that avoidance of one increases the risk from the other" (*Oxford Concise Dictionary* [8th ed.], 1089).

25 Lord Tweedmouth (First Lord) to Laurier, 27 December 1905, Laurier Papers, LAC, MG 26G, 104701-702. Acting as a conveyor of dead minister's remains was not a new duty to Kingsmill: as the commander (i.e., the executive officer) in HMS *Blenheim* in 1894, he had transported the body of the late Prime Minister Sir John

Thompson to Canada from England. The suspicion is that these duties fell to the ships in which he was assigned because of his position as a high-ranking Canadian in the service.

26 John G. Armstrong, "The Dundonald Affair," in *Canadian Defence Quarterly*, XI:2 (Autumn, 1981), 39–45. The quote is from Lord Dundonald, *My Army Life* (London: Edward Arnold, 1934), 191.

27 Laurier to Kingsmill, 10 August 1906, Laurier Papers, 112769.

28 Kingsmill to Lemaire, 29 April 1907, Laurier Papers, 124682-684; and Laurier to Kingsmill, 20 April 1907, Laurier papers, 124686. Kingsmill had married Francis Constance Beardmore of Toronto in October 1900.

29 PRO, ADM 1/7954, Report of Court-Martial, 7 March 1907.

30 Kingsmill to Lemaire, 29 April 1907, Laurier Papers, 124682-684; Laurier to Kingsmill, 30 April 1907, *ibid.*, 124686; and Kingsmill to Laurier, 1 May 1907, *ibid.*, 139926. See also *Canadian Almanac*, 1908, 475 (25 January 1907), 477 (5 March 1907), and 313, for press summaries concerning Kingsmill.

31 Gimblett, "Reassessing the Dreadnought Crisis of 1909 and the Origins of the Royal Canadian Navy," 35–53; and Gimblett, "'The Incarnation of Energy': Raymond Préfontaine, the Hydrographic Survey of Canada and the Establishment of a Canadian Naval Militia," in William Glover (ed.), *Charting Northern Waters: Essays in Commemoration of the Centenary of the Canadian Hydrographic Survey* (Montreal & Kingston: McGill-Queen's University Press, 2004).

32 The only existing copy of the draft bill appears to be in the Louis-Phillippe Brodeur Papers, LAC, MG 27, IIC4.

33 Canada, Parliament, House of Commons, Sessional Paper No. 58 (1908), "Proceedings of the Colonial Conference, 1907," Thirteenth Day, 8 May 1907, 476 and 488.

34 W.L.M. King Papers, LAC, MG26J13, Private Diary, 27 February 1908.

35 LAC, RG 2, Order-in-Council PC 2/1769, 13 August 1908.

36 PRO, ADM 196/38, 755, records his promotion date as 12 May 1908 and transfer to the Retired List on 12 September 1908.

37 *Toronto Globe*, 18 May 1908.

38 The need for unity of command had been the typical rationale

invoked against the creation of local colonial naval forces and in favour of contributions to the upkeep of the RN; although not nearly so widely held as is popularly believed, as recently as the 1907 Colonial Conference the First Lord of the Admiralty, Lord Tweedmouth had repeated "There is one sea, there is one Empire, and there is one Navy"; "Proceedings of the Colonial Conference, 1907," Fifth Day, 23 April 1907, 129.

39 Gimblett, "Reassessing the Dreadnought Crisis of 1909," 40.

40 Memorandum on Coast Defence, 1 February 1909, Brodeur Papers, Docket No. 5.

41 Kingsmill to Brodeur, 1 February 1909, Brodeur Papers.

42 Canada, Parliament, *House of Commons Debates*, 29 March 1909, col. 3564.

43 Kingsmill to Brodeur, 19 April 1909, LAC, RG 24, vol 3840, NSC 1017-1-1 (vol 1), "Defence of Coasts Generally, 1909–1939."

44 Confidential Papers Laid Before the Imperial Defence Conference, 1909, "Admiralty Memorandum, July 20, 1909," 30, Brodeur Papers.

45 Brodeur à Laurier, le 10 et le 26 août 1909, Brodeur Papers. For an overview of the negotiations, see also "L.P. Brodeur and the Origins of the Royal Canadian Navy," 25–28.

46 *Toronto Globe*, 14 February 1901, report of proceedings of the British Empire League annual meeting in Ottawa the previous evening.

47 Borden to Connaught, 24 March 1913, quoted in Roger Sarty, "Canadian Maritime Defence, 1892–1914," in *The Maritime Defence of Canada*, 20.

48 There is circumstantial evidence that the navy was seen as a Liberal institution. For one example, a sub-theme of Armstrong, *Halifax Explosion and the RCN*, is the crusade by the proprietor of the Halifax *Herald* (Conservative senator William Dennis) to divert attention from the Halifax Pilot Authority (the positions were patronage appointments) onto the Chief Examining Officer, Commander F.E. Wyatt.

49 "Protection of Trade Routes in Atlantic and Pacific," October 1912, LAC, MG 26H, vol 124, 66917. Less that two years later that advice would be changed slightly, in favour of a purely cruiser force: First Lord Winston Churchill to Borden, 5 May 1914, "Canada: Naval Defence of the Atlantic Coast," PRO, ADM 1/8369/47.

50 Goodspeed, *The Armed Forces of Canada, 1867–1967*, 73.

51 Hadley & Sarty, *Tin-Pots and Pirate Ships*, 121ff.

52 Sarty, *Canada and the Battle of the Atlantic*, 22.

53 Sarty, "The Naval Side of Canadian Sovereignty," in *Maritime Defence of Canada*, 67–68.

54 Henry Borden (ed.), *Robert Laird Borden: His Memoirs, Vol. II* (Toronto: Macmillan, 1938), 841.

55 Borden to Lord Milner, 18 April 1919, as quoted in Eayrs, *In Defence of Canada* (I), 151.

56 A published (if somewhat negatively slanted) survey of the work of the Naval Committee is in Eayrs, *In Defence of Canada* (I), 151–54.

57 "Occasional Paper No. 2: Proposals for Canadian Naval Expansion," 3 July 1919, LAC, RG 24, vol 5696, NSS 1017-31-2.

58 Jellicoe Report, passim.

59 Borden diary entry for 28 December 1919, cited in Eayrs, *In Defence of Canada* (I), 162.

60 Sir George Foster to Borden, 25 March 1920, quoted in *ibid.*, 163–64.

61 Sarty, "Mr. King and the Armed Forces: Rearmament and Mobilization, 1937–1939," in *Maritime Defence of Canada*, 110–37.

Commodore Walter Hose

CHAPTER TWO

Commodore Walter Hose: Ordinary Officer, Extraordinary Endeavour

William Glover

"Monday, 29 March, 1920: Hose here today. Is to replace Kingsmill. He is to take up reorganisation question immediately. Discussed matters with him."[1] So wrote George Desbarats, Deputy Minister of the Naval Service, in his diary. This simple entry marked the beginnings of an extraordinary endeavour — nothing less than the basic survival of the Royal Canadian Navy (RCN) — embarked upon by a heretofore rather ordinary officer, Walter Hose.

Captain Hose had arrived in Ottawa from Halifax to replace Vice-Admiral Sir Charles Kingsmill as the Director of the Naval Service (DNS) as a result of a crisis that was, in large measure, the making of the Conservative prime minister Sir Robert Borden's minister of Marine and Fisheries and of the Naval Service, Charles C. Ballantyne. Naval policy had been a political football since the original debate on the Naval Service Act. During the course of his premiership and the First World War, Borden, who had once loudly supported a direct cash contribution to Britain's Royal Navy (RN) rather than creating what one of his political colleagues had derisively called "a tin-pot navy," had come to recognize the importance of Canada having her own navy. At the Imperial Conference of 1917 he had been the architect of the proposal that eventually saw Admiral of the Fleet Viscount Jellicoe tour the Empire in 1919 and offer naval advice.

Jellicoe's three-volume report had been presented to the government on 22 December, and on 10 March 1920 Ballantyne tabled the first of them. Ballantyne secured cabinet agreement on a naval policy even more modest than the least expensive proposal advanced by Jellicoe. It was agreed that this would be unveiled before the caucus without ministerial advocacy. On Tuesday, 16 March, the caucus rejected it outright. The next day, Wednesday, Ballantyne decided to demobilize the navy, and gave orders to that effect to Kingsmill on Thursday. On Monday, 22 March, Desbarats recorded: "Papers have the story that naval service was being demobilized & great excitement. Minister sent cable to Jellicoe asking if Admiralty would present 1 light cruiser and 2 destroyers. Kingsmill away." The Conservative caucus, brought to its heels, was induced on 23 March to accept this as a basis for the navy. On 26 March, Desbarats recorded: "Minister in Montreal. Dept. in confusion owing to dismissal notice." Three days later, Hose arrived.

Kingsmill, after a career in the RN, had returned to his native Canada in 1908 to head what would become the Royal Canadian Navy. But in March 1920 he had clearly had enough. Indeed, after the 29 March diary entry, Kingsmill was mentioned only once more in Desbarats's diary.[2] To minimize the political damage of Ballantyne's impetuous actions, on 30 March Hose was appointed the Naval Assistant to the Minister, and on 1 July he became the Acting Director of the Naval Service. This was confirmed on 1 January 1921. But to all intents and purposes, Hose was the de facto head of the navy as of his arrival in Ottawa. Desbarats discussed all the important issues with him rather than Kingsmill.[3]

The frustrations of others at the wildly changing political fortunes and directions of the RCN were nothing new to Hose. Indeed, it had been his introduction to the navy. He arrived in Canada on loan from the RN to relieve the commanding officer of HMCS *Rainbow*, who had become "fed up" and wanted to return to England.[4] The month after Hose assumed command, Borden and the Conservatives defeated Sir Wilfrid Laurier's Liberal government in a general election; Canada's naval policy remained a political football, deadlocked between the Conservative majority in the House of Commons and the Liberal-controlled Senate.

Hose had been attracted to the fledgling RCN for two reasons. First, it seemed to offer better prospects for promotion. Second, "the work of assisting to build one of our Colonial Fleets appeals to me as most attractive as one is likely to see *results* from one's work in a far greater measure than in the Royal Navy, where one's work lies in [merely] keeping things up to the mark."[5]

Hose's assessment of his promotion prospects in the RN was almost certainly very realistic. His early career had been remarkably ordinary. His results in his examinations for promotion to lieutenant had been sufficiently mediocre that he spent twenty-seven months as a sub-lieutenant. By contrast, Andrew Browne Cunningham, the future victor at Matapan (who would rise to Admiral of the Fleet and First Sea Lord), seven years his junior in entry to the RN, had passed out tenth in his class and was promoted to lieutenant a bare fifty-four weeks after becoming a sub-lieutenant.

Their standing on those exams was also reflected in their respective appointments. Whereas Cunningham served in important theatres where he could be noticed by senior naval leaders, Hose had routine appointments in less important stations. Nor was Hose identified for early promotion. His general conduct, ability and professional knowledge were normally rated as "very good." Only twice was he described as having that most desirable of qualities — zeal — and only once was he "strongly recommended" for promotion.[6] At the age of thirty-seven, when Cunningham would be promoted to captain's rank, Hose at his own request retired from the RN and joined the RCN.[7] An "unimportant" appointment, one that doubtless had a profound influence on Hose's later decision, where results could be seen, was his time in Newfoundland working with the Fishermen's Reserve, where his work had been "favourably noted."[8]

During Hose's tenure as the head — de facto or de jure — of Canada's navy, he served under four prime ministers, observed four general elections and reported to five different cabinet ministers. The service that he passed to his successor, Percy Nelles, was much healthier than the one he inherited from Kingsmill, mired in confusion as a result of Ballantyne's actions. Throughout this thirteen-year period he had three enduring challenges. The first was the very survival of the navy.

The second was the problem of naval policy and, derived from it, the evolution of a naval service. The third was the day-to-day running of the navy and its administration. Each challenge had a variety of aspects and levels, and invariably they had to be addressed concurrently. In the memoranda and letters he wrote, and in his decisions and actions, we catch glimpses of a man who had a clear vision and who was not afraid to speak his mind directly. There is also an abiding interest in people, with perhaps a slight preference for the less favoured.

The immediate task facing Hose upon his arrival in Ottawa was to reorganize the navy following the debacle of the government's policy. Almost at once his directness was shown. Just before his arrival, Ballantyne had arrived at a compromise with his caucus colleagues that the RCN would accept the gift of a cruiser and two destroyers from the RN. However, the cruiser that had been selected was old and used coal for fuel. To Hose, this was unacceptable, but he was told it was a "done deal." His solution was to advise the RN that Canada would only be able to maintain fuel supplies of the sort that it actually used, and if a coal-burning ship was provided, then the RN should not expect to find stores of *oil* at Halifax for their own ships. Hose got a modern cruiser.[9] On 21 December 1920, HMCS *Aurora*, accompanied by the destroyers HMCS *Patrician* and *Patriot*, arrived at Halifax. Hose, as the Acting Director of the Naval Service, was there with the governor-general and the minister to meet them. However, this new little fleet was not to survive long.

The new year began with Hose's confirmation as DNS. It ended with the general election of 6 December 1921, in which the Liberals under Mackenzie King won a narrow majority government. On 10 January 1922, Desbarats "discussed with Hose rumour that Dept. is to be absorbed by Militia Dept. The Naval Committee will take it up tomorrow."[10] This set the stage for the challenge of the survival of the navy that lasted until 1933. It should be remembered that during this same time, the Canadian air force lost its fight for survival and was taken over by the militia. The challenge had three distinct components, the first two of which arose within days of each other. First, there was the basic survival of the navy in terms of budget support. Second, there was the battle of the reorganization occasioned by the new Department of National Defence, a struggle that turned on the independence of the navy from the militia and its right to offer advice directly to the government rather than through the militia's Chief of Staff. Third, there was the personal struggle of Hose to achieve equal standing with his militia counterpart as a Chief of Staff.

Through January and February 1922 there a series of meetings was held to discuss the proposed merger and to try to ensure that the navy was not swallowed up by the militia. On 14 February, Desbarats, Hose and Commander Stephens, the Assistant Director of the Naval Service, met with the Minister, George P. Graham (who was also Minister of the Militia,), to present the navy's views and concerns. They urged joint consultation with all the departments concerned. A week later, Graham wrote Desbarats with his proposals for the reorganization, and the next day, 22 February, Graham asked "for cut in estimates & information as to sum which could be cut."[11] On 28 February, Hose prepared a memorandum for Graham that proposed keeping the two destroyers in commission as training ships, closing permanent establishments and creating a volunteer reserve across the country.[12] On 7 March, the size of the naval appropriation was confirmed. Two days later, the new government's throne speech made specific reference to the formation of a new Department of Defence.[13] The naval estimates became the top priority as the government worked to present its first budget.

Initially, Graham wanted estimates prepared that kept *Aurora* in service and laid up the destroyers and submarines. Estimates along those lines were prepared and even tabled in the House of Commons. However, Graham refused to permit the navy to begin such a reorganization, thus creating a period of uncertainty. On 19 April, Desbarats "saw [the] Minister for [a] short time ... he is still undecided as to general naval policy and wants [an] alternative scheme submitted. Hose and Adams pressed on him scheme for doing away with ships forming a naval reserve." Finally, on 24 April, the reserve proposal was accepted.[14] Planning began immediately to pay off ships and retire personnel. However, Graham again refused to give authority to proceed with the plans until after the estimates had been presented in the House of Commons and the new naval policy described. This did not happen until 12 May. The requirement then became first to demobilize the permanent force no longer required, and then to create a volunteer reserve structure and begin to fill it in time to commence training in the summer of 1923.

While some may have questioned the wisdom of Hose's policy, now adopted by the government, he remained fully committed to it for the duration of his tenure as the head of the navy. His thinking was solidly grounded in the realities of Canadian life:

(a) If a Dominion is to spend money on the Navy, its people must be convinced that a Navy is necessary.

(b) In Canada a large majority of the people live far from the sea and do not visualize the necessity for safe sea communications.

(c) The first necessity therefore is to educate the people.

(d) The most effective method of educating the people is to bring the Navy to their doors, into the lives of families and friends.

(e) A small Navy is of no value as an educative measure as its personnel live in the neighbourhood of the naval bases; but a reserve force distributed across Canada would bring the Navy home to a great number of inland people; would be the only means of doing so within the appropriation available; would be a useful field of recruiting for the R.C.N.; would give the Director of the Naval Service opportunity to visit the Reserve Centres throughout the country and address Chambers of Commerce, Rotarian Clubs, etc., on the elements of Naval Defence.[15]

It is important to note that his vision of the service that was being created in 1922 was not static. He knew his bare-bones plan had to grow. He outlined his hopes to a retired RN officer in August 1922: "I have by no means lost hope as regards the future, and I hope within a couple of years to have an efficient reserve of at least 1,500 men organized and trained by the nucleus of the permanent force, and I still believe that from that we shall expand into a seagoing Service again."[16] At a minimum, the permanent force cadre had to expand in order to provide some career progression for the RCN personnel.

Otherwise, those in the service would leave in frustration and new people would not be attracted to join.

In 1924, Hose was presented with a personnel problem directly related to career progression. His solution may offer an insight into his own personality, and it certainly contributed to a dominant undercurrent of personality conflict that was prevalent during the tenure of his successor as Chief of the Naval Staff. The 1911 entry term comprised twenty-one cadets — the largest of the early years and a reflection of the promise of the RCN before it became stalled by politics. The First World War broke out while the officers were still under training. For the duration of the war, the Admiralty suspended examinations for the rank of lieutenant. As we saw with Hose and Cunningham, officers who had obtained first- or second-class certificates were able to use them to gain seniority in the rank of lieutenant. To compensate for this lost opportunity for gifted officers to advance, the Admiralty determined that standing on specialist courses could be used for the same purpose.

In the RN, the large majority of officers attended a specialist course; such was not the case for the RCN. Of the 1911 entry term, L.W. Murray did specialize as a navigator, and because of his standing was given six months seniority. His term mate, G.C. Jones, did not specialize; however, in 1923, he did attend the ten-month war staff course at Greenwich. On 4 August 1924, Jones wrote to naval headquarters: "Since my promotion to the rank of Lieutenant at least one officer has passed over my head, while several others have gained considerable time. During this period I was employed on services, which, I have been given to understand, were of importance. No opportunity occurred for me to specialise till 1923 and then my seniority did not permit." He asked that the war staff course count for the award of time for seniority. Although a certificate of merit with a standing was not provided, Jones argued that his course report — which read "Ability above average. Tactful, good tempered, and very cheerful. Very zealous and hard-working. A fine character" — would equate to a first-class certificate. Hose accepted the argument and recommended the award of six months seniority to restore Jones to the same seniority as Murray.[17] Hose later promoted the two rivals to commander at the same time. Jones presented an interesting argument to support his claim. The fact that it was contrary to

Admiralty policy may not have been a handicap in Hose's view, for it appealed to unique Canadian conditions. It may also have struck a responsive personal chord within Hose, who had not fared well in seniority from the lieutenants' exams, who had not specialized, and who had left the RN for better advancement opportunities in the RCN. But tinkering with individual cases would not solve the larger problem of ensuring a worthwhile career for new entrants.

In a letter of 30 July 1926 addressed to the prime minister, Hose was quite candid on the future needs of the navy:

> From time to time suggestions have been tendered by the Admiralty as to the development of Canadian naval forces and of our co-operation in Empire Defence.
>
> I find myself unable to concur with these suggestions in many important points for the following reasons:—
>
> 1. They are governed more by the idea of augmenting the sea-going forces available for operations in any theatre of the globe, which would be available to the Admiralty in a maritime war, than by important Canadian requirements.
> 2. They do not specifically meet the actual conditions of risk to Canadian interests, and it is these risks alone which can form an effective argument to convince the business interests of the country of the necessity of submitting to the taxation requisite for defence....
>
> In fact the stability of all our enterprises on land depends on the security of our communications at sea.[18]

That security was provided by the navy. However, that navy needed:

> 1. a minimum size of permanent force which can continue for any considerable length of time to function effectively

2. determination in advance of the composition of the naval force required to cover those risks which it may be considered should be guarded against

3. [a] school to commence the training of young officers.

Hose continued, "First of all it may be said that [the RCN] lacks all three of the above mentioned essentials." He then outlined what he thought was an essential fleet composition that had to be authorized by Parliament. He allowed that while the ideal would be to complete the program in five years, financial realities might dictate that it would be prudent to begin with one destroyer and one patrol vessel at a time.[19] King was returned to office in the election of 14 September. His choice for minister of National Defence was probably the ablest of those under whom Hose served: Colonel J.L. Ralston. In the course of 1927, Hose won approval both for the replacement of *Patrician* and *Patriot* and for the construction of two new destroyers. To fund the new ships, Ralston obtained from Cabinet an increase in the naval estimates of $1 million. By small steps Hose's navy was starting to grow to fulfill his vision for it.[20]

Hose wrote his letter of 30 July 1926 while many of the other challenges and questions affecting survival and policy remained unresolved. The most pressing issue was certainly the reorganization of the defence department, and relations with the militia. The act creating the new Department of National Defence received Royal assent on 28 June 1922. To allow time for organization and to effect a smooth transfer, it did not come into effect until 1 January 1923. However, on at least some important organizational details, the naval service was not kept fully informed. The Militia Department had consolidated a dominant position. One particular point that caused tension for five years was the title of the senior militia officer. An order-in-council of 24 November 1922 named the position "Chief of Staff, Department of National Defence." An accompanying organizational chart had the DNS reporting through the "Chief of Staff" to the deputy minister and through him to the minister — the position had previously been styled "Chief of the General Staff" and it had not been the sole avenue to the deputy minister.[21] This was totally unacceptable to Hose. Major-General MacBrien, the Chief of

Staff, soon objected to Desbarats, the Acting Deputy Minister, that Hose "seemed to be experiencing 'some hesitation in taking instructions' from himself." Hose quickly retorted that "he experienced 'no hesitation whatever in *not* taking instructions from the Chief of the General Staff.'"[22] Hose was not about to yield to an army officer a controlling voice in the development of naval policy and the evolution of his navy.

An important part of the campaign for equal status and for the development of policy was the ability to attend conferences as the naval advisor to the government. Throughout most of the 1920s the focus for the Canadian government at the imperial conferences was the evolving nature of national autonomy within the Empire. For Prime Minister King this meant staying clear of British-imposed commitments. Imperial maritime defence was an obvious issue on which dominion support would be courted, and therefore the presence of the naval advisor could be logically argued. However, the case had to be made on each occasion; R.B. Bennett, prime minister from 1930–1935, was particularly deaf to suggestions that Hose should accompany him.[23]

The politics of presence and being seen may well have been more important at the end of the day than the substance of the discussions, Hose's contribution, or the agreements reached. He does not appear to have been mentioned, for example, in the accounts of imperial conferences made by Dr. O.D. Skelton, King's principal advisor and undersecretary of the Department of External Affairs. When Hose returned from the 1923 conference, Desbarats noted, "Hose returned last night from Imperial Conference at London. Nothing much seems to have been done in Naval lines." To be there, Hose had been away from Ottawa for two and half months,[24] but in the official proceedings of the conference he was listed along with Major-General MacBrien as an advisor to the Canadian government.

A first step in rectifying the situation for the navy was to change the title of Hose's position from "Director of the Naval Service" to "Chief of the Naval Staff." That would then put him on an apparently equal level with the Chief of the General Staff. In addition, the Chief of General Staff title, which had been used prior to the amalgamation of the departments, should be restored. Graham, the minister who had advanced the objectionable organization, was not to be the minister who changed it. (In a cabinet shuffle on 28 April 1923, he was replaced by E.M. Macdonald.) Nor was he up to the task of removing the sources of tension. By the time of the 1926 election, "the Department of National Defence had reached a nadir of inefficiency."[25] However, relief was in sight. After the election, Ralston became the minister and MacBrien, exhausted by his running feud with Hose, resigned. In 1927, an order-in-council removed the "Chief of Staff" position, and the next year the Director of the Naval Service became the Chief of the Naval Staff. Responding to a letter of congratulations about the change, Hose wrote, "I am very happy about it myself as it means the end of the long struggle for recognition by the Department, and I may say the Government, of the proper status of the Navy in the Defence organization."[26]

Unfortunately, the struggle with the militia was not over. Desbarats's diary comment reveals the continuing tension with the militia, even under MacBrien's more moderate successor: "Discussed with Thacker title 'Chief of the Naval Staff' to which he does not object provided it leaves no chance of becoming senior appointment."[27] This attitude was far more important than any change in position titles or organization charts. The most dangerous attack from the army was yet to come.

In 1933, Bennett's Conservative government felt it necessary to reduce the defence budget significantly. Major-General A.G.L. McNaughton, the new CGS, took the liberty of forwarding his advice to the government without consulting Hose. His proposal would have reduced the naval estimate by $2 million. The balance remaining had in fact already been spent in the first part of that fiscal year. In response, Hose wrote a strong memorandum to the minister.

> I have, however, to protest most strongly against the tendering of advice by one Chief of Staff on matters of defence which affect the status of the Navy in the whole scheme of national defence....
>
> The fact that the Chief of General Staff has advised the Government and that this advice has not been made the subject of consideration by the Defence Council has the effect of nullifying the whole purpose of the above-mentioned Order in Council [P.C. 1252 of 20 June 1922].

In doing this it creates an absolutely impossible position for the Chief of Naval Staff and indicates a lack of confidence by the Government in him as a responsible officer to tender advice on national defence, even though the problem is one in which maritime security with its naval responsibilities is a vital factor.

In view of the advice which the Chief of General Staff informed me that he had tendered to the Government it is very difficult to avoid a connection between that advice and the proposals for reduction forwarded from the Treasury Board which are tantamount to the abolition of the Naval Service.[28]

Hose won his day in court, the right to appear in front of the Treasury Board and to preserve his budget. He won the day, and the naval estimate was reduced by only $200,000. In fact, the bulk of the balance came from elsewhere.

Hose retired at the end of 1933 and was relieved by Captain Percy Nelles. Before the 1935 election, Prime Minister Bennett moved McNaughton from CGS to become head of the National Research Council because the general had become a political liability. In 1922, in face of a severe budget cut, Hose had articulated a clear vision of a future navy and the necessary policy. He carefully shepherded his little "flock" of ships, and, as he had hoped, watched them grow, and his service expand. By the time he retired, the fleet had grown to four destroyers, including two constructed especially for the RCN. Under Nelles, growth would continue. The reserve force that Hose had created acquitted itself well in the Second World War, and many of the RCNVR personnel did, as Hose had suggested as a positive benefit of the reserve, join the expanding RCN after 1945. The rather ordinary officer in the RN who had transferred to the RCN in 1911 had indeed most emphatically succeeded in an extraordinary endeavour.

NOTES

1   Library and Archives Canada (LAC), Desbarats papers, MG 30, E 89, Vol 6, diary 1920 (hereafter Desbarats diary).

2   "20 May: Kingsmill left this PM for Victoria."

3   Desbarats diary, 1920.

4   Directorate of History and Heritage (DHH), 2001/12, Folder B, file 3, (hereafter "Hose papers"), "The Early Years of the Royal Canadian Navy," address by Rear Admiral Walter Hose, 19 February 1960, 2.

5   Cited in Michael L. Hadley and Roger Sarty, *Tin-Pots and Pirate Ships*, 71 [complete references for commonly cited secondary sources are provided in the bibliography]; Hose to Kingsmill, 5 May 1910.

6   Hose Personal file, Public Record Office (PRO), ADM 196/44. I am indebted to Dr Richard Gimblett for bringing this to my attention.

7   Details of Hose's career: Hose papers, Folder A, file 2, "Royal Canadian Navy Service Record: Walter Hose." Details of Cunningham"s career: SWC Pack, *Cunningham the Commander*, (London, 1974), Appendix 1.

8   PRO, ADM 196/44.

9   Hose papers, "Early Years," 12

10 Desbarats papers, vol 6, diary 1922. Professor Eayrs was able to interview Admiral Hose when writing the first volume of *In Defence of Canada*. He was also given access to Hose's diaries. The comparison of the extracts Eayrs chose to print with the bald notes of Desbarats's diary emphasize how unfortunate it is that the location of the Hose diary is now not known.

11 *Ibid.*, 22 February 1922.

12 DHH, 81/520/1440-5 vol 81.

13 Desbarats papers, diary 7 & 9 March 1922.

14 *Ibid.*, 19 & 24 April 1922.

15 Cited in Eayrs, *In Defence of Canada* (I), 171, Cdr. J.A.E. Woodhouse, Naval Secretary, 1927.

16 Hose papers, Folder C, file 11, Hose to Holme, 10 August 1922.

17 LAC, Personnel Record Unit, personal file George Clarence Jones, O-37330; Jones to Naval Secretary, 4 August 1924; Hose to Minister, 24 September 1924; Naval Secretary to Jones, 9 October 1924. Jones

and Murray were both promoted acting-lieutenant on 1 January 1917. Murray, who specialized in navigation, was confirmed on that date but Jones was confirmed on 1 June 1917. Agnew, who had been promoted acting-lieutenant on 15 February 1917 was confirmed with seniority 15 March after he specialized in navigation.

18 LAC, Mackenzie King Papers, microfilm reel C2718, frame 91015, 91022.

19 *Ibid.*, frames 91028–91033.

20 Desbarats papers, diary 1927: 24 February; 28 March; 11 June; 24, 28 October; 24 November; 6, 23, 26 December.

21 Eayrs, *In Defence of Canada*, 239–40.

22 *Ibid.*, 246.

23 *Ibid.*, 260–65.

24 Desbarats diary, 14 September and 2 December 1923.

25 Eayrs, *In Defence of Canada*, 256.

26 Hose to Brodeur, 29 March 1928, LAC, MG 30 E212, vol 3, file 28.

27 Desbarats diary 14 February 1928.

28 Hose papers, folder C, file 18, Memorandum for the Honourable the Minister, 23 June 1933.

Library and Archives Canada PA 206626

Vice-Admiral Percy W. Nelles

CHAPTER THREE

Admiral Percy W. Nelles: Diligent Guardian of the Vision

Roger Sarty

If good timing, persistence and hard work are the essence of good luck, Admiral Percy Walker Nelles had it by the boatload. He was the only qualified candidate for appointment as Chief of the Naval Staff (CNS) when that position became available in 1934. His predecessor, Walter Hose, left him with a well-developed program and, shortly after Nelles took over as chief, the government cracked open the coffers to allow implementation of certain aspects of that program. With the outbreak of war in 1939, the government proved willing to complete the program and to accept Nelles's recommendations for further expansion of the service. Perhaps this was his ultimate stroke of good fortune. Under wartime circumstances, persistence and dedication compensated for the deft touch and supple intellect needed to win the sympathy and confidence of those who wielded influence and power. A certain lack of these intellectual and emotional qualities would contribute to Nelles's removal as CNS early in 1944. The situation, however, was so unusual and extreme that one can fairly say that his luck had turned, and only after an extraordinarily long good run.

Nelles was born at Brantford, Ontario, on 7 January 1892. He came from a family of ambitious middle-class professionals and was raised in a military milieu.[1] His father, Charles Meklam Nelles (1865–1936), had served in the North-West Rebellion of 1885 as a young member of the volunteer militia.[2] He may have been working as a lawyer at the time of Percy's birth, but if so the military held a greater attraction.[3] In 1897 he took a commission in the Royal Canadian Dragoons of the permanent force and saw active service in the South African war, where he was wounded in an engagement at Oliphansfontein, near Rietfontein, on 7 July 1900.[4] Charles succeeded to command of the Royal Canadian Dragoons in 1912, and led the unit on its service in England and on the Western Front during the First World War. After leaving the front to command a base establishment in England, he returned to Canada in 1918 to serve as Inspector of Cavalry. He continued in the reserve of officers during the 1920s, with the rank of honorary brigadier.

Percy attended private schools — Lakefield Preparatory School, followed by Trinity College School at Port Hope. According to one newspaper account, in 1908, when Percy was sixteen, his father asked, "Well, what is it going to be: Royal Military College — or the Navy?"

Percy said simply, "You know, Dad, there's only one answer."[5]

Another press account explains that "during his childhood he played with boats on the Grand River because he did not want to go into the army, and he never had a moment's doubt that the navy was to be his life."[6] Charles wrote to the minister of Marine and Fisheries to "apply for the appointment of my son Percy Walker Nelles to be a Naval Cadet in the Canadian Naval Service." Charles added that "I am a Canadian by birth and my ancestors were United Empire Loyalists," a statement that might shed light on Percy's upbringing, and one source of the rather conventional, "Loyal Ontario" views of Canadian-British relations that he demonstrated in later life.

Strictly speaking, there was no Canadian Naval Service in 1908. Young Nelles's application had probably been inspired by the Laurier government's effort to organize the Fisheries Protection Service on military lines and develop it as a defence force. Earlier that year, the government had recruited Charles Kingsmill, a Canadian with long service in the Royal Navy (RN), to assume charge of the Fisheries Protection Service, and announced that cadets would be accepted for training as officers. Percy Nelles was one of only two youths to apply, and the only one from his year to continue.

Promotion within military forces normally reflects longevity as well as professional achievements, and Nelles's abilities were such that he was, throughout his career, senior among the Canadian officers recruited as cadets in the formative years of the service. Nelles's closest contemporary was Victor-Gabriel Brodeur, who became a cadet in 1909, the year after Nelles joined. Brodeur was the son of Louis-Philippe Brodeur, the minister of Marine and Fisheries and a leading player in the development of the Canadian naval service. The young Brodeur's strident Canadian nationalism, towards Britain in general and the RN in particular, could not have been in sharper contrast to Nelles's views. This difference manifested itself in the two men's physical appearance, which took the form of near caricature: Brodeur stocky and garrulous, while Nelles was slight and tidy of stature and had a careful manner. They represented the yin and yang of possibilities for Canadian naval development — as a branch of the RN, or as a more independent national service. These alternatives to some extent merged during the Second World War, when Allied decision-making increasingly shifted from London to Washington, and the Canadian navy, as an increasingly important component of the western alliance, grew from its British roots to become a more truly Canadian entity. Brodeur, as head of the Canadian naval liaison staff in Washington from 1940–1943, would be an essential source of information about British as well as U.S. intentions that allowed Nelles to successfully press for increased stature for the Canadian service.[7]

Nelles was appointed for training to the CGS *Canada*, an armed fisheries protection patrol vessel on the east coast. He transferred to the newly founded Canadian navy in 1910, and became a midshipman in HMCS *Niobe*, the large cruiser that the government had purchased from Britain to provide seagoing training for Canadian personnel. Although recruiting and ship acquisition for the service stopped when the Conservatives defeated the Liberals in the general election of 1911, training of the existing personnel continued, with British assistance. In December 1911, Nelles went to England, where he joined the battleship HMS *Dreadnought*, the first of the new, fast, all-big-gun capital ships, and namesake of a class of vessel. Nelles then joined the cruiser HMS *Suffolk* in early 1914, when she went out to North America as part of the cruiser squadron based at Bermuda to protect British interests in Mexico during its civil war.[8]

At the outbreak of the First World War in early August 1914, *Suffolk* rushed north to Halifax to protect transatlantic shipping. Nelles served in *Suffolk*, and then in HMS *Antrim*, another cruiser that carried out trade protection from Bermuda and Halifax, until April 1917, when he went to Naval Service Headquarters (NSHQ) in Ottawa as flag lieutenant to Admiral Kingsmill, Director of the Naval Service. Nelles remained in this appointment until Kingsmill's retirement in 1920, and then, after a short course in England, returned to headquarters for intelligence duties until early 1923. These sorts of extended staff appointments in Ottawa were unusual; indeed, Nelles may have been unique among the young RCN officers, who served almost exclusively in RN warships or trained at British establishments throughout the period 1914–1922.

Nelles's seniority, and some eight years of seagoing service by 1917, qualified him for the headquarters appointments, but there is also evidence that a problem with his eyesight had made him unfit for sea duty; the problem must have proved correctable, as he subsequently held other seagoing appointments.[9]

The two appointments at NSHQ gave the young officer a ringside view of the emergency expansion of the RCN in 1917–18, when it got by with small, hastily built anti-submarine craft after the RN and United States Navy (USN) proved incapable of supplying Canada with adequate assistance in countering transatlantic attacks by German submarines. Nelles was also present in Ottawa in 1921–22, when budget cuts by the new Liberal government under William Lyon Mackenzie King reduced the service to a training establishment for reservists. The only capable ships were two small destroyers, of British wartime construction, from surplus stocks. From 1923 until the spring of 1931, Nelles, like all RCN officers, alternated between appointments in Canada and in the RN, whose size and global commitments afforded opportunities for professional development and training not available in Canada.

During the late 1920s, Kingsmill's successor, Walter Hose, won the King government's support for the acquisition of larger, modern destroyers as the most practicable answer to Canada's naval needs. Serious tensions between the United States and Japan raised the possibility of a Pacific war in which Canada could not rely, as it had in the past, on strategic protection by Britain's fleet, which was now capable of dominating only the

Atlantic. The King government was not willing to pay the hefty premium needed to build destroyers in Canada's shipyards, lacking as they were in experience producing high-performance warships, but in 1928 it ordered the construction of two of the latest fleet-type destroyers in Britain.[10]

Nelles received command of HMCS *Saguenay*, the first of the new destroyers, when she was completed in May 1931. As the senior ship commander, he also became Senior Officer of the Canadian destroyer flotilla, which had now reached a strength of four vessels. The availability of this prestigious new command was Nelles's second great mid-career stroke of luck. In 1930, he had been serving as the executive officer in the British cruiser HMS *Dragon* when the commanding officer fell seriously ill. The ship was based in Bermuda and scheduled for a long cruise in South American waters, and no replacement captain was available. Nelles took command for the cruise, and did well. This was precisely the situation — an extended mission by a large warship operating on its own with no support — that the RN regarded as a compelling test of professional competence. Commodore Hose, impressed by the favourable British report, informed the deputy minister that Nelles, by right of proven ability as well as seniority, was Hose's logical successor as Chief of the Naval Staff, the new title for the professional head of the navy.[11] Hose arranged Nelles's postings — command of HMCS *Saguenay* in 1931–32, followed in 1933 by attendance at the Imperial Defence College and command of the navy's principal base in Halifax — to ensure that there could no question about his qualifications for the CNS appointment.[12]

In the urgency of Hose's communications recommending early promotion of Nelles from commander to captain, the minimum rank for selection as CNS, one can detect larger issues at play. Hose, like Kingsmill before him, had had a full career in the RN before transferring to the Canadian service, but he clearly appreciated that the increasing nationalism of Canadian defence and foreign policy now made the selection of an officer from the British service to head the RCN anathema on political grounds. Yet the underdevelopment of the RCN meant it had no choice but to co-operate intimately with the RN — Canadian security largely depended on it. Clearly, Hose was worried about the reaction in Britain if the senior position in the Canadian service should appear to pass to an unqualified Canadian on purely national grounds.

Despite Hose's pleas, financial cutbacks during the Depression forced the government to delay Nelles's promotion to captain until January 1933, more than two years after both Hose and the British commander-in-chief at Bermuda recommended it. Nelles became acting CNS in December 1933, and was confirmed, with promotion to commodore first class, in July 1934.

One of Nelles's first acts as CNS was to campaign for the development of naval shipbuilding in Canada. The two old, small destroyers in the flotilla, HMCS *Champlain* and *Vancouver*, were due for replacement. Destroyers were too complex for Canada's inexperienced industry, and too costly for any hopes to be entertained that the government might consider funding the development of the necessary capacity. Nelles therefore suggested, as a measure "for assistance to industrial recovery" from the Depression, that *Champlain* and *Vancouver* should be replaced by two sloops to be built in Canada. Sloops were as large as the latest destroyers, like the new *Skeena* and *Saguenay*, but slower, less heavily armed, and in practically all respects less technically sophisticated. The cost would be $3 million per vessel, about 50 per cent more than building in the UK, but would provide substantial employment and revive Canada's small and impoverished shipbuilding sector.[13] Nelles urged that a start should also be made in production of smaller coastal types of warships, similar to the anti-submarine and minesweeping trawlers that had had to be mass-produced in 1917–18 to meet the U-boat threat on the east coast. These proposals were hopelessly optimistic, given the government's fiscal circumstances. The entire naval budget for fiscal year 1934–35 was $2,222,000 — the austerity level set at the full onset of the Depression in 1932–33, and barely sufficient to sustain the existing cadre-strength service.

Circumstances, however, were changing. The British Admiralty had previously regarded Hose's concept of an all-purpose destroyer force with little enthusiasm. What Canada needed were cruisers — much larger and more expensive than destroyers, but highly capable for all naval tasks, especially the reinforcement of the British trade defence forces that would operate in the ocean areas adjacent to Canada's coasts in the event of war. If Canada were unwilling to procure cruisers, then vessels less complex and heavily armed, like sloops, would suffice for basic patrol and trade-defence operations close to the country's seaboards. With the darkening international scene in the mid-1930s and the resulting demands on Britain's greatly reduced navy, however, the Admiralty became willing fully to support the buildup of a Canadian destroyer flotilla. In 1935, the British government offered to transfer two recently built vessels, near sisters of *Saguenay* and *Skeena*, to replace *Vancouver* and *Champlain*, for $1 million apiece — less than a third of the actual cost of the ships, and a fifth or less of what would have been required to build them in Canada.

In the fall of 1935, Mackenzie King's Liberals returned to power, against the backdrop of international crisis resulting from Italy's invasion of Ethiopia. King reluctantly reconciled himself to the need for rearmament. With very limited support within his own party, he embarked on a cautious program that emphasized home defence and gave priority to the air force and navy over the army. Canada's dispatch of a large land force to Europe in 1914–1918 had produced enormous casualties that had necessitated conscription, a measure that had badly divided the country — and the Liberal party in particular. The government's first substantial step was to double the naval estimates for fiscal year 1936–37 to allow for the purchase of the two destroyers offered by Britain. These joined the Canadian fleet, recommissioned as HMCS *Fraser* and *St. Laurent*, in February 1937. In the following year, Canada purchased two more destroyers of the same class on the same favourable terms. These were recommissioned as HMCS *Restigouche* and *Ottawa* in June 1938. Thus, the navy finally had the flotilla of six destroyers that Hose had recommended, more than a decade and a half before, as the bare minimum required to provide a covering force for one coast only.[14]

Nelles never ceased to remind the government that the bargain-basement solution offered by the Admiralty for the destroyers by no means met the country's naval needs, not least because the RN itself was short of vessels and the British shipbuilding and other heavy industries were already overburdened by the demands of rearmament. As he remarked in a personal letter to Captain V.-G. Brodeur in March 1937, he saw the destroyers purchased from Britain as a "very good stop gap until we can work our blessed country up to the price of and/or building in Canada, plus having sufficient time to construct to our requirements."[15] It would take a good deal of persuading, and Nelles's determined efforts for the construction of vessels as large as sloops yielded extremely modest results. In 1937, the government placed orders for four Basset-class minesweepers — modest coastal types, which, with the elevated wages in Canada as compared to Britain, cost approximately $350,000 each.

In May 1938, Nelles reported to the deputy minister that his further "investigations" of the Canadian shipbuilding industry convinced him that it would be possible to construct not only sloops, but also destroyers. He appreciated that the undertaking would require a great deal of assistance from Britain: "designs, specifications and working drawings ... key [building] personnel, certain materials and finally the entire armament of the ship." Further, it would not be feasible to build only one or two destroyers, as no Canadian plant was producing the special high-tensile steel required for the hulls, and it would be necessary to make a long-term contract to secure production. The costs would be higher than he previously estimated — perhaps 75 per cent greater than British costs, for a total of $6 millions per ship — and "we would have to face the fact that the first destroyer delivered would not measure up to the English production." Nevertheless, he concluded, "I believe we, in Canada, will be forced to embark on warship construction in our own country.... The more ship building the Naval Service can give to Canadian firms in peace the better fitted these firms will be when the emergency arises." Nelles also warned of the navy's shortage of a vast range of equipment and stores — ammunition of all kinds, anti-submarine nets for ports, armament outfits for civilian craft earmarked for defence duties on mobilization — and pressed for early procurement, including arrangements for manufacture in Canada wherever possible.[16]

The urgency of Nelles's tone came from the gravity of international events. Japan had invaded northern China in 1937, and in March 1938 Nazi Germany had seized control of Austria — aggression that suggested that war could break out at any moment in Europe and on the Atlantic. There was also a serious possibility of a two-ocean war between the western powers and Germany, Italy and Japan. The weight of Canada's re-armament program had been on the Pacific coast, and in July 1938 the Chiefs of Staff warned the government that large preparations had to begin on the Atlantic as well. This effort would require the navy to more than double its strength because of German naval expansion, which featured fast, heavy-gun vessels that were well suited to long-distance commerce raiding. The U-boat force, moreover, had been reborn.

In July 1938, Nelles declared that Canada could no longer avoid the procurement of cruisers: two were required on each coast.[17] This was a standard that dated back to the ill-fated Laurier scheme of 1909–1911, and Canadian naval officers had never deviated from it. There was no mystery about the standard: the cruiser was the smallest class of warship that, with long endurance, considerable armament and large crew, could independently exercise control over large expanses of ocean; two per coast would ensure that one could constantly be maintained at sea in times of crisis. Hose's advocacy of the destroyer as an all-purpose warship had in fact amounted to the employment of destroyers as mini-cruisers. The destroyer had the greatest striking power among the smaller classes of warships because it shared much of the technology and armament carried by cruisers. By building up the cadre service of the 1920s as a destroyer flotilla, Hose had been consciously protecting the professional skills of the personnel so that they could, whenever political circumstances made the acquisition of cruisers possible, compete with the challenges of operating the large warships.

Nelles was never sensitive to the Liberal government's wariness that very large warships might revive the bitter divisions, via the naval debates, that had created the political fault lines for the conscription crisis. He did realize, however, that his call for cruisers was a whistle in the wind, given financial constraints and the huge challenge the service would face in trying to man ships whose crews, at approximately 500 personnel, were fully three times larger than those of the newly acquired destroyers. Nelles, like his mentor, found the answer in further development of the destroyer type. Late in 1938, the RN commissioned its first new Tribal-class destroyers, which at nearly 2,000 tons displacement were 25 per cent larger than existing fleet destroyers such as those in the RCN; the ships also carried a heavy-gun armament of eight 4.7-inch guns, double that of the previous types. This was close to the firepower of a small cruiser, and adequate to engage any but the heaviest long-range enemy surface raiders. The Tribals, moreover, unlike cruisers, were suitable for anti-submarine warfare, and thereby could meet both of the principal threats to Canadian waters.[18] Early in 1939, in the wake of the Munich crisis of the previous fall, Nelles recommended that Canada immediately begin construction of two Tribal-class destroyers per year, lay down at least eight minesweepers and anti-submarine vessels as the first instalment of the scores of ships required for the auxiliary coastal patrols, and accelerate the procurement of ammunition, auxiliary vessel armament, and harbour defence equipment.[19]

Once again the government shied away from the steep costs of production in Canada and the political difficulties that might arise from close defence industrial co-operation with Britain. The naval estimates for fiscal year 1939–40, although increased to $8.8 million, made no provision for warship construction or manufacture of other naval equipment. Once again, there was a cheap, partial solution: the purchase of another early-1930s-vintage fleet destroyer from the RN, which entered Canadian service as HMCS *Assiniboine* in October 1939.

The government did, however, quietly admit that the small size of the Canadian service left no option but intimate co-operation with the RN, despite the prime minister's public declarations that the country was bound by no commitments to support Britain in a future war. In 1938–39, Mackenzie King sanctioned full co-operation by the navy in British mobilization planning, in particular including arrangements with the Commander-in-Chief, America and West Indies that would effectively integrate the British cruisers based at Bermuda with the Canadian destroyer force. Among the arrangements were plans for the RCN to organize the sailing of merchant ships in transatlantic convoys from Halifax, under the direction of the Admiralty and the Bermuda command, in the event that Germany showed evidence of again attempting an unrestricted U-boat campaign against Allied ocean trade.[20]

When on 21 August 1939 the British government dispatched the first warnings of apprehended war, the RCN, with the government's approval, mobilized in lockstep with the RN, even as Nelles raced back from leave in Colorado. The destruction of the liner *Athenia* by *U-30* on 3 September, the day Britain entered the war, brought the Admiralty to order an ocean convoy. On 16 September, HX-1 sailed from Halifax under the escort of two British cruisers of the America and West Indies station — and, for the first twenty-four hours of passage, through coastal waters in which U-boats were known to concentrate, by two of the RCN destroyers.

The King Government had balked at passing the order-in-council prescribed by the 1910 Naval Service Act to place the Canadian fleet under Admiralty control in wartime. Nelles insisted the original order-in-council was essential until the government assured him that its updated version, which promised "close co-operation" between the RCN and the RN, merely used language more suitable to Canada's national status to signal full acceptance of British control: "it is most desirable that we have one Officer and Staff only directing naval operations at sea on the America and West Indies Station and the most suitable person is the Commander-in-Chief of the Station. To have more than one person and staff directing operations will cause confusion, delays and will not produce the efficient effort necessary." Canada, he explained, simply did not have the warships needed to assert a more independent posture: "four destroyers cannot defend our East Coast and focal areas [of shipping offshore]. The Commander-in-Chief has therefore stationed two eight inch cruisers to add to our efforts."[21]

The issue of command became a controversial one in the fall of 1939. Because of the threat the powerful German surface raiders posed to the convoys, the Admiralty dispatched the 3rd Battleship Squadron to Halifax to supply more adequate heavy-ship escort. The commander of the squadron, Rear-Admiral L.E. Holland of the Royal Navy, established his headquarters ashore and arranged for the escort of convoys, including the destroyers and aircraft allocated for the purpose by the Canadian east coast headquarters. In November, Nelles dispatched a complaint to Admiral of the Fleet Sir Dudley Pound, First Sea Lord at the Admiralty, asking for the withdrawal of Holland's headquarters. The presence of such a senior British officer at Halifax effectively usurped the authority of the Canadian Commanding Officer Atlantic Coast (COAC), Captain H.E. Reid, RCN, who was just as capable as Holland of generating detailed escort orders on the basis of the general direction from America and West Indies in Bermuda. Pound rightly doubted that an officer of the rank of captain had the necessary experience for transatlantic deployments of major fleet units, and responded that Holland would simply move onboard one of his battle-ships to exercise his command. Nelles, one suspects, was the source of a face-saving compromise, whereby Holland moved onboard a large yacht, provided by the Canadian government and moored alongside at Halifax, so that the admiral would have the full advantage of landline communications, which were much more effective than even a large warship's radio communications.[22] It would appear that the demand for Holland's removal came not from Nelles, but rather from the nationalistic Reid, who had the support of the equally nationalistic minister of National Defence, Norman Rogers. Later, Nelles would criticize Reid's "anti–Royal Navy" views, "which seem to give him a strange inferiority complex."[23]

Nelles's greatest efforts during the early months of the war were to press for a substantial beginning in shipbuilding. This included the full program he had presented in early 1939 — the two Tribals and twenty-two escort vessels and minesweepers — plus as many as forty-six additional escorts and minesweepers to complete the auxiliary coastal patrol. The need was more than self-evident, especially given the early offensive by the German U-boat and surface raider forces. Aside from the seven destroyers on strength once *Assiniboine* joined the fleet in the fall, and the four small Basset-class minesweepers, there were available only about a dozen civilian ships that had been taken up by the navy and given a light armament, which was all that these vessels were capable of carrying. Nelles forcefully compared these meagre resources to what had been necessary in 1917–18, when Canada had had to build up an auxiliary patrol of more than a hundred vessels in the face of a similar German threat.[24] It was a telling argument in light of the fact that the government had justified its pre-war rearmament program by promising it would provide adequate security against raids on the coasts by modern submarines, warships and aircraft.

To Nelles must also go a large part of the credit for rapidly revising and improving the auxiliary patrol shipbuilding program in September 1939. Only at that time did the naval staff learn of two new British designs — a telling commentary on the weakness in defence industrial liaison between the Canadian armed forces and the British services. A delegation of the Canadian Manufacturers Association, organized on a semi-official basis by industrialists in response to the government's hesitancy in searching out orders, had returned from the United Kingdom in August with basic blueprints for a coastal anti-submarine vessel of 900 tons. It was known as the "whale-catcher" type because it had been based on commercial fishing vessel designs that could be readily produced by non-naval shipyards. The delegation also brought drawings for the Bangor-class fleet minesweeper of 600 tons, a simplified naval design. Nelles quickly recognized that these vessels were ideally suited for Canadian circumstances. They were larger and more capable than the existing Basset-class minesweepers and trawler-type anti-submarine designs, but basic enough to be produced by Canadian yards without the extensive British technical assistance that the Admiralty warned could not now be spared.[25]

Nelles had a prolonged confrontation with officials of the Finance Department, who during the fall and winter of 1939 engaged in a determined effort to trim back demands, which they feared would bankrupt the country, from all three armed services. At one point Nelles, at the end of his patience, blasted that to let the accountants dictate the war effort so fully "is simply not facing our problem and is analogous to the ostrich burying its head in the sand."[26] The prime minister himself ultimately intervened on the side of the navy in February 1940. He had personally made adequate public commitments to provide for home defence during the late 1930s; he also understood that shipbuilding and the navy's program, which emphasized support for the RN's America and West Indies station, perfectly matched his government's desire to focus the war effort on industrial production and, as much as possible, North American military commitments, to avoid the dispatch of large numbers of troops overseas.

The prime minister's support produced even more than Nelles had asked for. Starting in February 1940, the War Supply Board began to place orders with shipbuilders for a total of sixty-four whale catchers — including ten ordered and paid for by the Admiralty — and twenty-eight Bangors. This was the maximum production that, estimates of the Depression-racked industry's capacity suggested, could be achieved over a two-year period.[27] Nor was that all. The government approved the conversion of three fast passenger liners, the Canadian National Prince-class ships, into armed merchant cruisers, as well as the Tribal-class destroyer program. The big Tribals were clearly beyond the immediate capacity of Canadian yards, which, given the paucity of help that British firms could offer, meant they would have to be built in Britain. The Admiralty was extremely reluctant, given the other pressures on industry and the difficulties in producing the Tribals as compared to somewhat smaller more conventional destroyers. Nelles, however, single-mindedly pressed the point, and hulls for two Tribals, which would later commission as HMCS *Iroquois* and *Athabaskan*, were laid down in the UK in 1940. In accordance with the two per year called for in Nelles's pre-war program, two more were laid down early in 1941; these would commission as HMCS *Huron* and *Haida* in 1943.[28]

Nelles explained to a visiting senior British officer that it was essential to procure the largest destroyers possible during the war and fully integrate them into the Canadian service so that they "could not be wiped off the slate by whatever Canadian Government is ... in power" when the armed forces demobilized with the return of peace.[29] Clearly, Nelles was haunted by the memory of how, in 1921–22, the Liberals had quickly reduced the navy to a skeleton force. Looking ahead, Tribals that had been operated by Canada in wartime and — he hoped — gave the service some measure of glory would not be so vulnerable to postwar cost-cutting. For similar reasons, in November 1939 Nelles quickly agreed to the Admiralty's request that fifty RCNVR officers with yachting experience should be sent for small vessel service with the RN.[30] They might have early opportunities to join dramatic operations in combat theatres and thereby help build up the fighting tradition that the service had not been able to acquire during the First World War.

Combat opportunities came much sooner than anyone could have predicted. At the end of May 1940, four of Canada's destroyers rushed to the United Kingdom in response to the British government's appeal for help as the German offensive in the west sliced through France. The RN, in the wake of heavy losses in the Norwegian campaign, urgently needed additional destroyers to protect the home islands against invasion, and to protect shipping that would shortly be exposed to U-boats and aircraft operating from bases in France, close by the sea approaches to Britain.

After hair-raising operations close to the French coast to evacuate British and Allied troops, the Canadian ships engaged in intense anti-submarine operations to protect convoys immediately west of Ireland as they arrived from Canada, Gibraltar and the South Atlantic. Canadian losses were heavy: *Fraser* sunk by collision during the evacuations from the French coast; a replacement destroyer provided by the British, HMCS *Margaree*, sunk by collision while on convoy duty; and *Saguenay* so severely damaged by a torpedo attack that the ship was out of action for three months.

All the while, during the fall and winter of 1940, the U-boats operated farther and farther west as defences in British waters gradually became more effective, and the Canadian government began to press Nelles to bring some or all of the destroyers home to cover Canada's exposed coast. Nelles not only held firm to the overseas commitment, but he scheduled the rotation of destroyers — which returned to Canada for refit — so that four were always on service in British waters, even when that meant that only one ship was available at Halifax.[31]

During the fall of 1940, Nelles also successfully urged the government to respond generously to the Admiralty's plea for help in providing crews for some of the fifty First World War–vintage destroyers that Britain obtained from the United States in the destroyers-for-bases agreement. Canada took over six of the old destroyers, a commitment of over 900 trained personnel. The government's expectation was that all of the ships would be employed for home defence, or, better still, some might be sent overseas to allow the return of the four more capable River-class to Halifax. Nelles pointed out that Canada had taken over the U.S. ships on behalf of the Admiralty, and that if they were not to be deployed as the Admiralty intended, the RCN might have no claim to the vessels. Thus, the four most capable of the ex-U.S. ships proceeded overseas early in 1941, while the RCN also continued to maintain four River-class in British waters. At that time the Admiralty asked for further manpower assistance: could the RCN provide crews to deliver the ten corvettes building in Canada on British account? The ships sailed to Britain with Canadian crews as they were completed between January and April 1941, and Nelles quickly agreed to a British request as the last of the ships arrived that the crews — a total of more than 500 personnel — remain with the vessels permanently; all ten were recommissioned into the RCN.

Very shortly, the chance arose for the RCN to take a much greater place as a national service in the naval war than had been remotely conceivable, and the service grasped it skilfully. In April 1941, as the RN was able, in part because of the Canadian and U.S. assistance, to extend anti-submarine escorts of convoys well to the west of Iceland, the U-boats began to head to the Grand Banks of Newfoundland, where convoys could be more readily located and were weakly protected. The Admiralty asked Canada to take a major share of the responsibility for a new escort force, based at St. John's, Newfoundland, to provide anti-submarine defence for convoys between Newfoundland and Iceland. The RCN destroyers and corvettes serving in British waters would be transferred to St John's, but in addition, newly completed Canadian-built corvettes would have to be committed in strength to this role rather than to their intended deployment to cover Canadian ports and coastal waters. Nelles responded that twenty new construction corvettes could be provided within a matter of weeks, but asked that a Canadian officer be appointed to command the new force. Admiral Pound accepted, even though at least half of the ships based at St. John's would be British, provided that Commodore L.W. Murray, a senior RCN operational commander in whom the RN had confidence, would be assigned. Nelles readily agreed.[32]

Murray, who took up the appointment in June 1941, assigned ships of his command to transatlantic escort duties under the orders of the Commander-in-Chief Western Approaches, the senior British commander in the Battle of the Atlantic, whose headquarters were at Liverpool in the United Kingdom. The Admiralty hoped even further to extend Western Approaches' direct control over Canadian ship deployments to Halifax, the home port of the Canadian navy's principal resources, which looked increasingly important to the Allied effort as the U-boats pushed west. The Canadians had forestalled the extension of Western Approaches' control to Halifax by creating Newfoundland and its seaward approaches as a new command separate from the Atlantic Coast command, and assigned the Newfoundland area to Murray. The effect of this division between the Canadian headquarters at Halifax and St. John's was that the Newfoundland command received only the ships allocated to it by Canadian authorities: the British Commander-in-Chief Western Approaches did not have a direct line by which he could suddenly call up additional ships from Halifax. Canadian ships based at Halifax could only be deployed by the Commanding Officer Atlantic Coast, now Rear-Admiral G.C. Jones, and British authorities could approach Jones only through NSHQ in Ottawa.[33]

The surviving documentation is silent as to why NSHQ created the separate Newfoundland command, although it made perfect sense in administrative terms. The Canadian navy was responsible not only for the contribution of ships to the transatlantic escort force but also for the local naval defence of the whole of Newfoundland and Labrador. With Murray's appointment to St. John's, he became the logical officer to oversee local arrangements. Indeed, there was no other rational choice, given the intimate interrelationship between local defence and shipping defence; the U-boats could just as readily strike in the near approaches to Newfoundland ports as at convoys and shipping offshore. Still, one cannot help but notice that the creation of the Newfoundland command firmed up Murray's status as a Canadian national commander, and safeguarded Canadian national control over operations on the Atlantic coast, even as Murray received his prominent appointment as a front-line commander in the Battle of the Atlantic under the direction of the British commander-in-chief at Liverpool. Certainly, Nelles had a leading hand in making the new arrangements. With the great expansion of the navy in 1940–41, he evidently was becoming more assertive about the development of the RCN as a national service vis-à-vis the RN than he had been in November 1939, when he had been surprised at the questions the Minister and Captain Reid had raised about the status of the Rear-Admiral Third Battle Squadron at Halifax.[34]

Certainly, national interests, as well as awareness of the desperate need for American assistance, made Nelles fully receptive to British and American proposals during the summer of 1941 for the USN to take over convoy escort west of Iceland and overall command in the western Atlantic. The objective was to relieve British escorts in the western Atlantic to allow the RN to concentrate in European waters to help ensure Britain's survival and ultimate victory, which was clearly in the U.S.'s national interests. Admiral E.J. King, Commander-in-Chief of the U.S. Atlantic Fleet (CINCLANT), was also determined to ensure that the U.S. Navy received strategic command authority, and was in no way subordinate to the RN.

The RCN was a subordinate but key player in these arrangements because the USN did not have sufficient numbers of warships suitable for anti-submarine escort, and therefore needed the Canadian part of the Newfoundland Escort Force (NEF), some ten destroyers and twenty-five corvettes, to remain on the run west of Iceland. On the self-interested principle that U.S. ships should not be mixed into British commands, the U.S. Navy Department made clear that it would also respect the integrity of the NEF, which would remain intact under Commodore Murray. Murray would only receive general direction from a U.S. admiral — Commander Task Force 4, later CTF 24 — at the new U.S. base at Argentia, Newfoundland.[35] More than ever, the NEF would be a distinctly Canadian force. Nelles therefore welcomed the new arrangements. So, too, did the Canadian government, which in the spring of 1941 had been enormously relieved to have the Canadian fleet return from British waters and concentrated close to home.

As luck would have it, the withdrawal of most British escorts from Newfoundland and the entry of the Americans in escort arrangements, coincided with a major new push by the U-boats west of Iceland. Several convoys, some escorted by small Canadian groups of only four or five warships — most of them newly built corvettes with incomplete equipment and poorly trained crews — suffered heavy losses. Nevertheless, the British and Americans, who had no readily available reinforcements, pressed Canada to take a still-larger share of the burden. Nelles responded to the crisis by pouring in all of Canada's new construction corvettes, increasing the strength of the NEF to some sixty destroyers and corvettes by the end of December 1941[36] and leaving the Canadian coast with little immediate protection. The additional numbers, however, in no way made up for the Canadian ships' lack of training and equipment; indeed, the rush to sea of newly built ships exacerbated these problems. As the German offensive shifted south to the Mediterranean in November and December and the USN was able to relieve some of the pressure on the Newfoundland force, NSHQ made arrangements to allow RCN warships more time in port for training and for repairs and upgrades.[37]

The training and repair scheme immediately came apart. As a result of the United States' formal entry into the war after the Japanese attack on

Pearl Harbor on 7 December 1941, early in January 1942 the U-boats made a strong offensive into the coastal waters of Newfoundland, Nova Scotia, and along the U.S. coast. At this same time, the USN had virtually to withdraw from North Atlantic escort in order to meet the Japanese offensives in the Pacific, and to escort U.S. troopships that carried American land and ground forces to the battlefronts in both the Atlantic and Pacific. The RCN therefore had to fully maintain its NEF commitment, while also deploying additional escorts to protect a new series of coastal convoys between Newfoundland and Canadian ports, as well as to north-ern-U.S. ports. As additional RCN escorts from the 1940 and 1941 build-ing programs were completed in 1942, they therefore had to be quickly pressed into operations; there was no margin to upgrade the training and equipment of the corvettes that had been hurried to sea in 1941.[38]

Nor were these the only difficulties. At this very time, the newly cre-ated infrastructure to support the fleet was overstretched to the breaking point. In the spring and summer of 1941, when organizing shipbuilding orders to follow on from the initial escort programs, the Canadian gov-ernment, on the advice of British and U.S. authorities, had focused on merchant ship construction, at that time Britain's most pressing need. Only as existing and new shipyards were being filled up with merchant ship orders did specific advice arrive from Britain about the need to sub-stantially reconstruct the corvettes to make them more suitable for transatlantic operations, and to build a larger new type, later known as the "frigate," specially designed for open-ocean anti-submarine operations. Frigates were much more challenging build than corvettes, and the design was still under development in Britain; Canada did not receive sufficient technical information to begin to organize production until the end of 1941 and the beginning of 1942. Also during 1941, the British govern-ment, whose own shipbuilding and repair yards were overwhelmed, had to ask that Canada's east coast shipyards undertake the repair of as many British merchant and warships as possible. The navy and the Canadian Department of Munitions and Supply had co-operated in developing new ship repair and naval base facilities on the east coast, but the sudden, unanticipated shift of the focal point of the Atlantic battle from the east-ern and central ocean to Canadian and U.S. waters took place when these facilities were still in the early stages of construction.[39]

During 1942, Nelles, under pressure from both the British and Americans, and with the full support of the government who saw that a large-scale effort in the North Atlantic and in North American waters clearly met national interests, continued to stretch the RCN's resources to the breaking point. In only two instances did Nelles defy Allied direction. In the spring of 1942, when four of the only twelve tankers in Canadian service were torpedoed off the U.S. coast because of the USN's unwillingness to organize coastal convoys, Nelles on his own initiative redeployed four to six escorts to run tanker convoys from Halifax to the Caribbean; at that time, refineries at Halifax and Montreal were running critically short of key types of crude oil. The Canadian initiative in fact helped to encourage the U.S. to hurry the organization of coastal convoys, and opened the way for the RN to deploy more of its ships in U.S. waters for tanker protection. In July 1942, when U-boats began to make sustained attacks in the Gulf of St. Lawrence and the St. Lawrence River, Nelles — also to the displeasure of the British and Americans — authorized the removal of a half dozen ocean escorts from the ocean routes for St. Lawrence convoys.[40]

At that very time, during the summer of 1942, British, U.S. and Canadian shipping authorities were making arrangements to shift much traffic from the St. Lawrence to New York. The RCN not only participated in these arrangements, but accepted full responsibility for the escort of UK-bound ocean convoys sailing from New York.[41] This role was a logical development of the RCN's prominent place in the Atlantic war, one that both the navy and the Canadian government now regarded as a foremost national commitment. During the fall of 1942, even as Nelles — and Cabinet — agreed to the Admiralty's pleas for the commitment of sixteen RCN corvettes to support the Anglo–U.S. landings in North Africa (Operation Torch), NSHQ began to take measures to consolidate national control over the fleet. In particular, Nelles transferred Murray, now a rear-admiral and the RCN's most prominent operational commander, from St. John's to Halifax, which had become the focal point of the war in the western Atlantic, and shifted Rear-Admiral G.C. Jones, the RCN's best administrator, to NSHQ to reorganize the national headquarters. At the same time, Nelles ferociously resisted British and U.S. efforts to transfer the RCN's responsibility for the analysis and promulgation of U-boat intelligence in the western Atlantic to the U.S. Navy Department in

Washington. The naval staff also won the government's support for a very large expansion of the frigate construction program.[42]

In December 1942, Nelles then received what he regarded as a body blow.[43] Because of successful Canadian and U.S. efforts to strengthen shipping defence off the North American coast, the U-boat force had returned to large-scale mid-ocean attacks on convoys, and two large convoys escorted by small, ill-equipped RCN groups lost a quarter or more of the merchant ships. These and other disasters to British escorted convoys, and the menace of a UK imports crisis, resulted in an Admiralty initiative to reassert unified British control over the whole of the North Atlantic, effectively displacing the Americans from convoy control west of Iceland. The Admiralty called for the redeployment of the exhausted RCN Newfoundland groups to British waters for retraining, repair and employment on the run to Gibraltar in support of Torch, to free up more capable British groups to reassert the British presence west of Iceland. Nelles complied, but had the full support of the government in asserting that the North Atlantic escort role was a foremost Canadian commitment, and that the RCN groups should be returned to Newfoundland no later than the spring of 1943.[44]

During the bleak early months of 1943, when convoy losses on the North Atlantic continued to soar and the Admiralty and the USN searched urgently for solutions, Nelles led a determined campaign for greater recognition of Canada's role. While he continued to press for the NSHQ to be allowed to retain the crucial U-boat intelligence role, Nelles also protested vehemently to Admiral King about how U.S. operating authorities failed to consult Ottawa whenever they reassigned important Canadian warships. Informed by Rear-Admiral Brodeur in Washington of important and fast-moving deliberations by British Admiralty representatives and the USN to make command arrangements in the Atlantic simpler and more efficient, Nelles and his staff made the case that the RCN should replace the USN as the command authority in the northwest part of the ocean. This offered Admiral King a method of escaping the complications of the North Atlantic run by turning over the whole area to the British Commonwealth, thereby bolstering the case for full USN control in other theatres that were more important to American interests. Equally, the RN saw in Nelles's proposal a means to end U.S. control of convoys west of Iceland, which, in view of the USN's redeployment of most of its escorts to other theatres in early 1942, had become an awkward anomaly.[45]

The establishment of the Canadian Northwest Atlantic theatre on 30 April 1943, under the command of Rear-Admiral Murray at Halifax, was the crowning achievement in Canada's assertion of its status as a significant maritime power. Murray was the only Canadian officer in either world war to command an Allied theatre of operations. Moreover, by the time he took command, the RCN mid-ocean groups assigned to the Gibraltar run, as well as the corvettes that had operated in the Mediterranean, had returned to the north Atlantic to consolidate the fleet.[46]

That fleet, however, still largely included the unimproved corvettes of the 1940 program. Because of the pressures of merchant ship construction — and repair — the first frigates would not be complete until the summer of 1943 and would not be available in significant numbers until 1944. In supporting the creation of the Canadian command, the Admiralty had, of course, effectively regained control over the RCN's Newfoundland-based mid-ocean groups, and was dependent upon increasing the efficiency of those ships for the effective protection of UK imports. Western Approaches Command embarked on a campaign to press NSHQ and the Canadian government to more adequately support the Newfoundland- — and Halifax- — based groups with improved equipment and more regular and complete refits. Impatient at the slow response of NSHQ, and unsympathetic to the pressures on Canadian industry that British needs had created, the senior officers at Western Approaches helped discontented officers in the Canadian ships bring the sorry state of the fleet directly to the attention of the minister, Angus L. Macdonald.

Macdonald, who had taken up the new portfolio of minister of National Defence for Naval Services in August 1940, had consistently supported Nelles and the naval staff, but had on several occasions balked at what he had seen as their unimaginative and elitist attitude that favoured the regular navy at the expense of the volunteer reservists who formed the bulk of the Atlantic escort crews.[47] Macdonald, who had previously paid little attention to, or even understood, the technical issues of fleet development, thus launched his inquiry into the state of the fleet that would in January 1944 result in Nelles's quiet removal from the CNS appointment and his reassignment to an ill-defined flag-rank appointment to supervise RCN forces based in the UK.[48]

There was more than a little irony in the timing of Nelles's departure. Even as the minister undertook his inquiry in the fall of 1943, the naval staff won the co-operation of Munitions and Supply in giving top priority to modernization of the 1940 corvettes, and the Admiralty assisted by finding U.S. dockyard space to help with this program.[49] The four RCN Tribal-class destroyers under construction in the UK had been commissioned, and British manpower shortages had resulted in the Admiralty making available to the RCN two large cruisers and two escort aircraft carriers. The major warship force that had always been the RCN's objective was thus taking shape.[50] Nelles, in short, albeit as a result of the unforeseen circumstances of the Atlantic war, had achieved all of the objectives of the service, and more. The irony was that he lost his position largely as a result of the shortcomings of Canadian industry when one of his first acts on becoming CNS in 1934 had been to alert the government to urgent naval shipbuilding needs.

NOTES

1   Nelles's grandfather, according to newspaper sources, was Samuel Sobieski Nelles, DD, LLD (1823–1887), a Methodist clergyman who had succeeded Egerton Ryerson as president and chancellor of Victoria College during its early, impoverished years at Cobourg, Ontario. Samuel Nelles did much to improve the college's academic standing and finances and, shortly before his death, presided over its federation with the University of Toronto. See *Hamilton Spectator*, 18 May 1940, Canadian War Museum (CWM), *Hamilton Spectator* collection, box 90, file 101; Toronto *Globe and Mail*, 11 January 1945, *ibid.*, file 102. The main published accounts, George MacLean Rose (ed.), *A Cyclopedia of Canadian Biography* (Toronto: Rose, 1888), 363–64, and *Dictionary of Canadian Biography, Vol XI: 1881–1890* (Toronto: University of Toronto Press, 1982), 640–42 disagree as to the number of children and do not give their names.

2   Canada, *Militia List, 1900,* 26, 186.

3   Rose, *Cyclopedia*, 364, states that the only son, without giving a name, was working as a lawyer in Tilbury Centre (now amalgamated into Chatham-Kent) in 1887.

4   *Militia List, 1900*, 26; Canada, Department of Militia and Defence, *Supplementary Report ... Service of the Canadian Contingents during the War in South Africa 1899–1900*, Sessional Paper 35a, 64 Victoria, 1901, pp. 88, 105.

5   *Hamilton Spectator*, 14 June 1951, CWM, *Hamilton Spectator* collection, box 90, file 102.

6   *Globe and Mail*, 12 January 1945, CWM, *Hamilton Spectator* collection, box 90, file 102.

7   Douglas, Sarty and Whitby, *No Higher Purpose* [Complete references for commonly cited secondary sources are included in the bibliography], 218–19, 621–26.

8   The information on Nelles's career to 1934 is drawn from his personnel file, Library and Archives Canada (LAC), NPRC, O-540990.

9   Kingsmill, 30 June 1920, LAC, NPRC, O-54990.

10 Sarty, *Maritime Defence of Canada*, 86-90.

11 Vice-Admiral V.H. Haggard, 21 October 1930, CNS to Deputy Minister, 11 December 1930, Kingsmill personnel file.

12 CNS to Deputy Minister, 23 February 1932 (two memoranda); same to same, 24 October 1932, Kingsmill personnel file.

13 CNS to Minister, 2 February 1934, LAC, RG 24, vol 3840, NSC 1017-10-17.

14 Sarty, *Maritime Defence of Canada*, 110–13.

15 Cited in Whitby, "The 'Other' Navy at War," 13.

16 CNS to deputy minister, 31 May 1939, LAC, RG 24, vol 3840, NSS 1017-10-18.

17 Joint Staff Committee, "A Review of Canada's Position with Respect to Defence, July, 1938," 22 July 1938, LAC, RG 24, vol 2693, HQS 5199-B.

18 Michael Whitby, "Instruments of Security," 1–3.

19 CNS, 16 May 1939, LAC, RG 24, vol 3840, NSS 1017-10-18; see also CNS to Minister, 3 Feb. 1939, NAC, I.A. Mackenzie Papers, LAC, MG 27 IIIB5, vol 29, file 189-31.

20 Sarty, "The Origins of Canada's Second World War Maritime Forces, 1918–1940," in *Maritime Defence of Canada*, 281–82.

21 CNS to Minister, 12 September 1939, LAC, RG 24, vol 3842, NSS 1017-10-23.

22 The main papers are in Directorate of History (DHH), 81/520/ 8000, "HMS *Seaborn*." For a full account see Douglas, Sarty and Whitby, *No Higher Purpose*, 51–52, 65–68.

23 CNS, December 1942, H.E. Reid personnel file, LAC, NPRC, 0-61610.

24 For example, CNS to deputy minister, 16 November 1939, LAC, RG 24, vol 3841, NSS 1017-10-22.

25 Sarty, "The Origins of Canada's Second World War Maritime Forces, 1918–1940," 287.

26 CNS to Deputy Minister, 16 November 1939, LAC, RG 24, vol 3841, NSS 1017-10-22.

27 Order-in-Council PC 438, 7 February 1940, copy in DHH, 81/520/8200, "Shipbuilding 1939–45," pt 3.

28 Sarty, "The Origins of Canada's Second World War Maritime Forces, 1918–1940," 287; Whitby, "Instruments of Security," 3–4.

29 *Ibid.* Dreyer to Secretary of the Admiralty, 31 January 1940, Public Record Office (PRO), ADM 1/10608.

30 CNS to Minister, 2 November 1939, DHH, NHS 1700-193/96.

31 On Canadian Second World War operations see Douglas, Sarty and Whitby, *No Higher Purpose*; Milner, *North Atlantic Run*; and Sarty, *Canada and the Battle of the Atlantic*.

32 Signals, 20–31 May 1941, LAC, RG 24, vol 3892, NSS 1033-6-1, pt 1.

33 Admiralty to Commander-in-Chief, America and West Indies (C-in-C AWI), 2004b/25 June 1941; C-in-C AWI to Admiralty, 1931q/26 June 1941, PRO, ADM 116/4387.

34 Douglas, Sarty and Whitby, *No Higher Purpose*, 183–89.

35 Stark to Commander-in-Chief Atlantic Fleet, 17 July 1941, file A16-3, Suitland, Maryland, Washington National Records Center, National Archives and Records Administration (NARA), RG 313, Cinclant Red, 1941, Secret, box 156.

36 Flag Officer Newfoundland War Diary, December 1941, DHH, NSS 1000-5-20 pt 1.

37 Douglas, Sarty and Whitby, *No Higher Purpose*, 293–303.

38 *Ibid.*, 373–401.

39 Tucker, *Naval Service of Canada (II)*, chapters 2, 5–7; Kenneth S.

Mackenzie, "Shipyard for the Freedom of the Seas," (unpublished narrative, DHH, 2000/5); Hennessy, "The Rise and Fall of a Canadian Maritime Policy, 1939–1965," 54–65. Smith, *Conflict Over Convoys*, 58–63, highlights the British ship repair problems that placed pressure on Canadian resources.

40 Fisher, "'We'll Get Our Own,'" 33–39.

41 Secretary Naval Board to COAC, "Rearrangement Convoys East Coast of North America," 3 August 1942, DHH, 81/520/8280B, pt 3.

42 W.G.D. Lund, "The Royal Canadian Navy's Quest for Autonomy in the North West Atlantic: 1941-43," in *RCN in Retrospect*, 146–49; Catherine Allan, "A Minute Bletchley Park: Building a Canadian Naval Operational Intelligence Centre, 1939–1943," in *A Nation's Navy*, especially 169–71; Milner, *North Atlantic Run*, 183; Tucker, *Naval Service of Canada, (II)*, 74–76.

43 CNS, "Reference-Despatches 264 and 265 from Prime Minister of United Kingdom to Prime Minister of Canada...," [nd — late December 1942], LAC, RG 24, vol 6796, NSS 8375, pt 4.

44 Secretary of State for External Affairs to Dominions Secretary, telegram 3, 9 January 1943, in John F. Hilliker (ed.), *Documents on Canadian External Relations Vol. 9: 1942–1943*, (Ottawa: Department of External Affairs, 1980), 359.

45 Naval Member Canadian Joint Staff (Washington) to CNS, 26 January 1943, LAC, RG 24, vol 11969, 222–24; Commander-in-Chief, U.S. Fleet to CNS, 31 Jan. 1943, reproduced in Commander in Chief, U.S. Atlantic Fleet, "Administrative History of the U.S. Atlantic Fleet in World War II," vol I, 1946, pp. 476–77, DHH mfm.

46 Douglas, Sarty and Whitby, *No Higher Purpose*, 626–30.

47 For example, Macdonald's determined resistance in late 1940 to the naval staff's recommendation for wartime expansion of the regular officer corps that would largely exclude ratings from receiving commissions and give little consideration to the claims of officers of the reserves: Naval Secretary to COAC et al, 27 January 1941, LAC, RG 24, 5586, NS 1-24-1 pt 4; DND Press Liaison Office, Release No. 586, 17 Jan. 1941, DHH, NHS 1900-120/1; Naval Council minutes, 29 Apr. 1941, LAC, RG 24, 4044.

48 Milner, *North Atlantic Run*, chapter 9 and *The U-Boat Hunters*,

pp. 3–96; Zimmerman, *The Great Naval Battle of Ottawa*; Mayne, "A Political Execution," 577–93; Mayne, "A Covert Naval Investigation," 37–52; Mayne, "Bypassing the Chain of Command," 7–22.

49 Figures compiled from Macpherson and Burgess, *Ships of Canada's Naval Forces* (1981), 68–91; and Macpherson and Milner, *Corvettes of the Royal Canadian Navy 1939–1945*, 89–126, indicate that 41 of the 65 short-forecastle corvettes of the 1940 and 1941 programs had either been rebuilt or were in progress by January 1944. See also Michael A. Hennessy, "The Expansion, Modernization and Maintenance of the RCN's Principal ASW Forces 1943, Parts I and II", DHH, 2000/5.

50 Tucker, *Naval Service of Canada (II)*, chapter 3; Sarty, "The Ghosts of Fisher and Jellicoe," 143–70.

Captain Leonard Murray

CHAPTER FOUR

Rear-Admiral Leonard Warren Murray: Canada's Most Important Operational Commander

Marc Milner

By any measure, Rear-Admiral Leonard Warren Murray was the most important operational commander in the Canadian navy's first century. Given the way war at sea seems to be headed, he may remain unique. From 15 June 1941, when he assumed the duties of Commodore Commanding, Newfoundland Force, until 12 May 1945, Murray exercised command over fleets of hundreds of warships and aircraft of several nationalities engaged in the key naval campaign of a total global war. He was also the only Canadian ever to command an Allied theatre of war in the great wars of the early twentieth century. It is difficult to conceive of any Canadian doing this again.

To a very considerable extent, Murray, like all those who have greatness thrust upon them, was a survivor who happened to be in the right place at the right time. In his case, that was both a blessing and a curse. It was a blessing because Murray was one of a small cadre from the Royal Naval College of Canada (RNCC) class of 1912 — the first class of its kind — to survive in the service until 1939. That class suffered a mortality rate of nearly 20 per cent in the First World War — probably the highest of any entering class of young officers in Canadian naval history. But that small cadre of survivors also proved to be a curse, because

Murray and G.C. Jones, the classmate who was a hair's breadth ahead of him in seniority by the late 1930s, shared a bitter personal animus. At a time when the Royal Canadian Navy (RCN), like its parent service the Royal Navy (RN), still operated on the basis of cliques built around rising stars, the division of the Canadian navy into Jones and Murray camps served to check the accomplishments both of the service and of Murray himself.[1] It also meant that when crisis descended upon Murray at the pinnacle of his career, his only option was self-imposed exile in England. As Wilf Lund has observed, Murray's story is one of "challenge, battle, success and, ultimately, pathos."[2]

Leonard Warren Murray was born in Granton, Pictou Country, Nova Scotia, on 22 June 1896, the second of four children, and grew up along the shores of Pictou Harbour. It was there, in 1906, that he saw his first warship, HMS *Berwick*, when the cruiser's picket boat landed crewmen near his home. Ironically, Murray's first naval command a few years later was that same picket boat. When the first class of the RNCC was enrolled in 1911, Murray was among them: at fourteen, the youngest, too. He graduated third — two ahead of Jones — among the nineteen cadets to complete the course in late 1912. It was a small basis upon which to build a navy: smaller still if you consider that two-thirds of the class were paymasters and engineers.

By 1913, Murray and others of his class, including Jones, were onboard *Berwick*, now the flagship of the Americas and West Indies Squadron under Admiral Sir Christopher Craddock, for their sea training with the RN. When that finished in early 1914, all the Canadian midshipmen were sent home — literally — there being no duties for them in the moribund RCN. When war came in August 1914, the RCN's idle midshipmen were mustered locally: all the Maritimers went to Halifax, except young Murray, who was ordered to Ottawa for duty. That assignment probably saved his life. When Craddock stopped in Halifax in 1914 en route to confront Admiral Graf von Spee's powerful squadron in the South Pacific, he chose the top midshipmen available (Arthur Silver and Walter Palmer) and two others by lot (Malcolm Cann and Victor Hathaway) to join him in the flagship, HMS *Good Hope*. Three others joined HMS *Suffolk*. Silver, Palmer, Cann and Hathaway all perished at the Battle of Coronel in November, when *Good Hope* was destroyed. There but for fortune went Murray. Another classmate, Maitland-Dougal, died in command of a submarine later in the war — a service Murray declined to join. For Murray, then, the First World War was the "bloody war" that all young naval officers toasted as a means of clearing their path to the top. The "sickly season" followed soon after, and Murray survived that, as well.

What saved Murray in 1914 was a temporary appointment, as a cipher officer, to Ottawa, where he watched the initial stages of the war and gained experience in naval administration, operations and defence of trade. Duty in HMCS *Niobe* blockading New York, gunnery officer for the Gulf of St. Lawrence patrol boats, a short stint in HMCS *Rainbow* in the Pacific, and troop convoy duty on HMS *Leviathan*, where he served as assistant navigating officer, followed. It was not until early 1918 that Murray finally received an overseas appointment, when he joined the battleship HMS *Agincourt* of the Grand Fleet. There, owing to illness in the wardroom, Murray soon became both acting first lieutenant and navigating officer: a huge responsibility for an acting lieutenant, but one he handled superbly by all accounts. By then, however, Jones already was an acting lieutenant-commander in command of the destroyer HMS *Vanquisher*.

In the decade after the war, Murray held a series of appointments in the RN, which kept him from leaving the service during the "sickly season" following the near-collapse of the RCN in 1921–22. This RN time served him well later on. Murray made some abiding friends and impressed them with his ability. After a brief navigation course in 1919 he went to the cruiser *Calcutta*, commanded by Captain Percy Noble, which he joined on her commissioning from the builder's yard. *Calcutta* was "a happy and efficient ship," and Murray later claimed that he learned how to deal with the men and achieve that state of bliss from Noble.[3] In 1920, Murray returned to the RCN as navigating officer of the cruiser *Aurora*, which, unfortunately, did not survive the great budget and service cuts of 1921. During that posting he married Jean Chaplin Scott in the Stanley Presbyterian Church in Westmount, Quebec, on 10 October 1921.

By 1922, Murray was not only married but at home in Canada on half-pay, seriously considering leaving the RCN to take up employment in a large manufacturing business. While his appeal to Ottawa to be transferred to the RN for service was processed, Murray obtained a master mariner's certificate in marine insurance and waited. Ottawa approved the temporary reassignment and the RN found a use for him, so Murray stayed in the navy.[4]

For the next six years, 1923 to 1929, Murray served almost exclusively in the RN. His initial appointment was as second navigating officer of the battleship HMS *Revenge*, commanded by Captain S. Merrick, and in May 1923 he became assistant to the master of the [Atlantic] Fleet (assistant fleet navigator) aboard HMS *Queen Elizabeth*. From there it was a logical step to the "big ship" navigation course at Portsmouth, which he "passed with ease" and stayed on as an instructor in navigation, fleet tactics and manoeuvres for a brief spell. By then he was marked as a gifted navigator and, according to many of his contemporaries, the best ship handler of his class.[5]

A short stint in command of the RCN barracks in Halifax in 1925 was soon followed by six months as navigating officer of the battle cruiser *Tiger*, which he left, with a glowing endorsement, to attend the staff college at Greenwich. It was at Greenwich that Murray's insight into convoys is first recorded. During a joint amphibious exercise he was tasked, as naval commander-in-chief, with organizing the convoys and their escort. When his plans for a thirty-six-ship convoy were tabled, he was sharply criticized by the deputy director of the college for planning convoys of suicidal proportions. "Yet in 1940," Edward Kemp wrote in 1945, "when Murray was Deputy Chief of the Naval Staff, he found it necessary to group as many as seventy ships in a convoy — and the officer commanding the escorting forces ... was the officer who had been Deputy Director of the Naval Staff College."[6]

After the heady days at Greenwich, Murray was promoted to commander on 1 January 1929 — the same day as G.C. Jones — and took charge of the RCN's west coast establishment at Esquimalt. Although he had responsibility for running the command and making mobilization and war plans, it must have seemed like rustication. So, too, his brief episode in Ottawa in 1931, although this was tempered by the certainty that he was in line to command one of the RCN's new River-class destroyers. Jones had already commanded HMS *Vanquisher* during the war, plus HMCS *Patriot* and *Patrician*. Ronald I. Agnew, the other contender from the class of 1912, had commanded *Patrician* and *Vancouver*. By this stage, the battle for succession was fairly joined, with Murray and

Jones clearly out in front of Agnew by one year's seniority in the rank of commander. But Murray had never commanded a ship. In 1932, he finally got *Saguenay*; the same year, Jones took command of *Skeena*.

The next few years proved to be crucial in the struggle between the two rivals. The change in command of the RCN from Commodore Walter Hose to Commodore Percy Nelles may well have been decisive. Hose seems to have liked Murray. His last evaluation (an "S206" in the form of the day) of Murray, completed at the end of December 1933, rated him nine out of a possible ten in professional ability, zeal, power of command, reliability and initiative. As for judgment, Hose rated Murray only seven, commenting, "His failing lies in letting his heart run away with his head somewhat." On the whole, Hose thought rather well of him: "A level headed officer who has the ultimate interest of the service at heart in all his activities, whether service, social or sporting..."

His first S206 prepared by Nelles ten months later is rather less glowing. Murray received a bare pass — five out of ten — from his new CNS on professional ability, zeal, initiative and reliability — and, significantly, a failing grade of four on power of command. Judgment, too, slipped from a seven to a six. Only as an administrator did Nelles think that Murray was better than mediocre — a seven. "I do not think that this officer is a sufficiently strict disciplinarian," Nelles observed, "with either officers or ratings. This I attribute to a dislike of hurting humans rather than to any weakness of character."[7] Although Murray continued to get outstanding assessments from RN officers, Nelles's tone never wavered, and he never got more than a grudging pass from his own CNS.

In the end, Murray had little chance to prove himself as a ship driver. His command of *Saguenay* lasted just two years, the only time — apart from a very brief stint as captain of *Assiniboine* (discussed below) — that he commanded his own ship. In 1936, after two years as commander-in-charge at Halifax, Murray returned to the RN, where, as executive officer of the old battleship *Iron Duke*, he worked for the experimental and gunnery staff at Portsmouth. From there the obligatory Imperial Defence College (IDC) course followed in early 1938. His confidential assessment from the IDC was positive but guarded. "In comparison with the other officers of the Dominion Navies, he has shown himself to be most exceptionally well informed on the Naval service," the commandant, an air marshal, wrote — which makes one wonder about the comparison group. His powers of expression were "in no way inferior … to Captains of the Royal Navy," and despite his "naturally quiet" but "very pleasant personality," it was reckoned that he could fill any naval staff position "with great ability" — an assessment Nelles might have agreed with.

Whether Nelles accepted the IDC recommendation for "accelerated" promotion is another matter.[8] Murray was, nonetheless, promoted to captain immediately after the IDC on 2 August 1938, his first promotion under Nelles's regime. Significantly, Jones, at home in command of *Ottawa* and Captain (D) of the Canadian Flotilla, was promoted to captain on 1 August. From that moment, Jones always enjoyed seniority, and to a considerable extent the course of assignments was set for the war that followed.

In late 1938 Murray returned to Ottawa as Director of Naval Operations and Training, a task he was now well suited for. Jones, with seniority and much more command experience, remained in Halifax in command of the destroyer flotilla. Murray was therefore involved in much of the immediate pre-war planning. This included liaison with the Flag Officer, America and West Indies Squadron — now Rear-Admiral S. Merrick, whom Murray knew well from him time in *Revenge* — and travelling across Canada to meet the retired RN officers who would be mobilized for RCN service. The organization of NSHQ in the event of war also was a major concern. Murray recalled later that it was "a matter we'd considered generally, in fact we made out a mock-up of it on the back of an envelope one day…."[9] By his own account, it was Murray who got naval mobilization going on 21 August 1939 — the day the Admiralty mobilized for war, and weeks ahead of the Canadian declaration — because Nelles was out of town on leave. When Nelles returned, they put the draft organization into action, and Murray was elevated to the post of Deputy Chief of the Naval Staff (DCNS). Murray's experience suited him well. He had, after all, been at headquarters in 1914 when that war started. Moreover, much of his sea time in *Niobe* and *Leviathan* and with the Gulf of St. Lawrence patrols had involved trade protection and small ship work.

Murray later claimed, in a 1970 interview, that he spearheaded the charge towards a small-ship anti-submarine navy from the outset. The crucial event was the sinking of the liner *Athenia* on 3 September, which seemed to suggest that the Germans would immediately wage another unrestricted submarine campaign. "[T]he Prime Minister was very concerned," Murray recalled of those days, "and we were able to impress on him that this kind of anti-submarine war was one that our small Canadian Navy was best fitted to compete in. We got his approval for anything that could be done and there was never anything to stand in our way."[10]

It is significant that Murray used the term "we": he certainly never claimed that he alone set the mould. But he was DCNS during a formative period, and it was under his direction that the initial plans and appropriations for the "Sheep Dog Navy" were made. It was Murray and the deputy minister who made the case before the Finance Committee of Parliament in February 1940 that the budget should be increased from $8.5 million to $111 million in order to finance the expansion program consisting chiefly of small auxiliary vessels. According to Colonel J.L. Ralston, the minister of National Defence, the RCN were the first to "justify everything [they] asked for. And the first people who have gone away with what they asked for."[11]

Over the spring and summer of 1940 the nature of the war changed, and Murray became deeply involved in the initial stages of the rapidly evolving Canadian-American defence partnership. These American contacts would later serve him well. By the time Murray left Ottawa to replace Jones as Senior Officer, Halifax Force, the initial stages of RCN expansion were well underway: nearly 100 auxiliary warships, corvettes and Bangor minesweepers were on order. This was the fleet that Murray would ultimately command in war. It was perhaps providential that he should be instrumental in its inception as well.

In October 1940, Murray raised his pennant as commodore over the flotilla leader *Assiniboine* in Halifax Harbour. He actually took over from Commander Cuthbert Taylor, who was given temporary command so that Murray and Jones would not have to exchange the honours directly. By then, the rest of the destroyers were overseas, helping to guard Britain from invasion by a German army now poised on the coast of France. *Assiniboine* was still alongside in Halifax because she had collided with the Dartmouth ferry, an incident that seems to have earned her captain the sobriquet "Jetty" Jones.

Murray's time in *Assiniboine* — and in Halifax — was short, which was probably for the best since Jones was now ashore as Commanding Officer Atlantic Coast (COAC). In any event, there was not much for a commodore to do at sea in small ships, and Murray's time was largely spent working with the Permanent Joint Board on Defence (PJBD). During this brief interlude in Halifax, Murray also renewed his friendship with Commander James Douglas "Chummy" Prentice, RCNR, whom he had first met at the RN staff college in 1927. The Canadian-born Prentice had retired from the RN in 1934 to take up farming in British Columbia. The two men shared many ideas about the nature of the war and how the new Sheep Dog Navy might be used, for Prentice soon found himself Senior Officer, Canadian Corvettes under Murray. This was the beginning of a tight working relationship that was to last until the spring of 1944 and have a profound influence on the fortunes of the RCN.[12]

In January 1941, *Assiniboine* finally went overseas, and Murray with her. There he soon discovered that his "seniority as Commodore 1st Class wasn't workable at sea," so he moved ashore as Commodore Commanding Canadian Ships (CCCS). Murray's brief sojourn in the UK from January to June was filled with high-level meetings, working with and for the Canadian high commissioner, helping to settle the issue of command relationships in Newfoundland, and — most importantly — renewing old acquaintances.

The most important event, however, was an invitation in the late winter of 1941 for Murray to attend a series of naval staff meetings at the Admiralty, at which the problem of the westward expansion of the U-boat war was discussed. Over the winter of 1940–41, the RN pushed its escort system farther and farther west, only to have the Germans move just beyond their limits and continue to attack unescorted convoys. By March 1941 they managed to get anti-submarine escort out to roughly 35° West, leaving a gap between there and local RCN escort out of Halifax. If a 1970 interview with Murray is to be believed — and in the absence of other documentation, there is no reason to doubt it — he was instrumental in persuading the British that the solution to the gap in anti-submarine escort of North Atlantic convoys was a Canadian base at St. John's, from which the bulk of the burgeoning fleet of small RCN vessels would operate. "I had just come from St. John's about a month and a half before," Murray recollected, "and was able to give them the low down about the situation there, about the anchorage and so forth."[13] After confirming with Admiral Nelles the RCN's willingness to make the commitment, Murray went off to see Admiral of the Fleet Sir Dudley Pound, the First Sea Lord, whom he found in the midst of the Bismarck chase. Pound immediately accepted the idea of the RCN closing the gap in transatlantic anti-submarine escort of convoys, and recommended that Murray be appointed to command the new force.

Murray is rather modest in his 1970 interview about his role in all this: "This is what comes of being in the right place at the right time." In a 1946 letter to Louis C. Audette, a Montreal barrister and confidant but also one of his erstwhile escort commanders, Murray was more candid. "If I had not gained the confidence of the Admiralty in 1941," he wrote, in part out of bitterness over his recent treatment following the Halifax VE-Day riots, "Dudley Pound would not have asked Ottawa to appoint me to the Newfoundland command, but would have sent out a Flag Officer of their own.

"This is not surmise," he added in brackets. "I know, I was there."[14]

It is also possible that Murray would not have assumed command of the new force had the newly appointed Commander-in-Chief Western Approaches Command not been his old captain from *Calcutta*, now Admiral Sir Percy Noble. As Murray recalled, the experience was "a very close connection indeed, which was very helpful."[15] As Commodore Commanding Newfoundland Force (CCNF), Murray initially worked under Noble's operational control, and so he spent a week with him before leaving for Newfoundland, where he arrived on 15 June 1941. With Murray at St. John's, the two soul mates intent on building happy and efficient organizations now commanded at either end of the North Atlantic run.

Waiting for Murray at St. John's were the first fruits of the building program which he had initiated and which he was now to lead in the first real wartime operational assignment of the RCN — the Newfoundland Escort Force (NEF). Prentice had brought them up from Halifax at the end of May and already was running them ragged with exercises afloat and ashore. About two weeks later, Captain Roger S. Bidwell, RCN, arrived to serve as Chief of Staff and the key members of the Murray team were set for several years. To a very considerable extent the job — protecting trade convoys between the Grand Banks and Iceland — and the fleet were of his making, so it is not surprising that he retained a proprietary interest in both from the outset.

Murray quickly put Prentice to the task of training the escorts as they arrived, rough-hewn, from Halifax. Crews were trained in the basics of ship-handling at sea and how to kill U-boats efficiently with their rudimentary equipment. Indeed, the emphasis of all of Prentice's efforts under Murray was on U-boat killing.[16] We can only assume that Murray shared his views, since this writer at least has found scant evidence of Murray's own ideas on tactics and doctrine. Certainly, Prentice ran the only operational training groups in Murray's commands from the time he joined NEF in 1941 until NSHQ forced operational training out of Murray's grasp in Halifax three years later. Perhaps this was because, from the outset, Murray used his training group as a thinly veiled support group. It was Prentice's group that reinforced convoy SC-42 when it was threatened in September, and sank U-501 in the process — the first known victory over an enemy warship in the history of the RCN.[17] For Murray, and for the Sheep Dog Navy he helped create, it was a milestone event, and he and Prentice spent the next two years and more trying to repeat it.

According to Murray himself, "for about three months I was running it [NEF] entirely to my satisfaction, without any trouble...." And then the Great Powers intervened. In August 1941, Britain and the United States divided the world between themselves, thrusting Murray and his command into the embrace of the still-neutral Americans. Although Murray did not like the new arrangement, he had enough sense to get along and ease the new U.S. Navy (USN) commander, Rear-Admiral A.L. Bristol, into the task. Murray would contend that the Americans learned about the convoy system from him and his staff, and there is no reason to deny his claim. But serving under the Americans also meant that Noble's writ no longer extended to NEF, and since the USN was not particularly interested in nurturing the RCN, Murray and Prentice were left to their own devices in the development of NEF. This proved to be a cause for concern at Western Approaches Command, which suggests that not everyone trusted Murray's — or Prentice's — grasp of the tactical situation at sea.

NEF convoys, now the slow variety as USN destroyers took charge of the fast ones, came under heavy attack in September and October 1941, revealing serious shortfalls in equipment, training, leadership and doctrine. To compensate, escort groups were enlarged, which led to the collapse of Prentice's training group. The fleet was stretched by increasingly bad weather and a decision by the Anglo-Americans to move the mid-ocean meeting point farther east to free RN escort for the UK–Gibraltar route. By mid-October, Murray's staff was complaining that his ships were logging too much sea time. Captain E.B.K. Stevens, RN, Captain (D) at St. John's, protested that "a grave danger exists of breakdowns in health, morale and discipline," while Bristol warned the British that the NEF was on the verge of collapse.[18]

There is little doubt that Murray, reflecting that "can-do" attitude that so often is the bane of the Canadian forces, drove NEF hard in the fall of 1941. It would appear that he had something to prove. Indeed, when he complained to Nelles in October about the deleterious effect that Jones's manning depot in Halifax was having on his operational fleet, Murray observed — with considerable prescience — that "The reputation of the RCN in this war depends on the success or failure of the NEF." Not everyone shared his views: certainly not Jones, whose job was to man the fleet and get it to sea. When Murray sent escorts to Halifax for repairs — just about the only place they could go — in the fall of 1941, Jones's staff stripped them of experienced personnel to disperse amongst the rest of the expanding fleet, and poured raw recruits back aboard to send to NEF. In perhaps his most sharply worded memo, Murray attacked Jones's staff, describing them as "pirates" and charging them with "lack of breadth of vision." He demanded that the manning policy be changed, and in early November submitted a long, closely-typed four page foolscap memo to NSHQ outlining the damage done to his ships by the policy and Jones's people.[19]

But not everyone, and certainly not the naval staff, shared Murray's belief that the success of the RCN in the war depended on the success of his command. In early December, Murray was informed that the manning policy would remain unchanged: he would have to make do. Nonetheless, the RCN pushed every available oceangoing escort his way, so that by early December Murray — promoted to rear-admiral on 2 December (again one day after Jones) and now Flag Officer, Newfoundland Force (FONF) —

had about 75 per cent of the RCN's disposable strength. This eased the strain, and plans to re-establish an operational training group were underway even as the Japanese attacked Pearl Harbor.

The fall of 1941 represents a crisis point in Murray's career, and it is worth a little reflection. The Newfoundland Escort Force was very much his "baby," but he also clearly saw it as the premier operational role for the RCN in the war. In that, Murray displayed remarkable forethought. What is not yet clear to historians is how that vision was seen in the rest of the RCN. We do know that while Murray fought the U-boats, Jones worked to commission the escort fleet and get it to sea as quickly as possible, and that in this he was supported by Nelles and the naval staff. The impact on NEF was sufficient to elicit from Murray some of the most strident language he ever used in official correspondence. Significantly, most — if not all — of his concern in October 1941 was over what would today be called quality-of-life issues, primarily the exhaustion at sea of the key officers charged with safe handling of vessels, and indeed of entire crews. These concerns seem to have been met by the influx of new escorts that Jones's hothouse in Halifax generated throughout the fall. If so, the cause also became the cure. Perhaps, Murray's tirade in October simply reflects the tension and lack of trust between the two antagonists: a relationship that would cloud the RCN story until the end of the war.

Murray's ongoing concern for operational training is clear, as evidenced by Prentice's group in the summer and the plans in early December 1941 to re-establish it. He also supported Commander H.S. Rayner's idea to concentrate the RCN's long-range destroyers into two support groups, so that convoys under attack could be reinforced. Unfortunately, Murray was denied permission to remove destroyers from close-escort groups, not least because, under the USN's CTF-24 (Admiral Bristol), he was a provider of escorts, not an operational commander. But the establishment of support groups, especially for the Grand Banks area, with its unique tactical conditions,[20] remained a recurring theme for Murray — and Prentice. Without the designated resources to provide such groups, or even the authority to operate them, Murray's persistence with a training group that could double as a local reserve was a stroke of brilliance. It speaks well of Murray that he deployed Prentice's group on what the local American admiral decried in mid-1942 as "freelance" operations, typically in support of Canadian-escorted convoys in trouble in the fog-shrouded waters of the Grand Banks. When the RCN became seriously overextended in the late summer and Murray was once again forced to abandon Prentice's group, within a few weeks the Anglo-Americans established "Western Support Force" at St. John's to do exactly the same thing. Murray's apparent understanding of those unique conditions on the Grand Banks may have been his most valuable operational and tactical insight of the Atlantic war.

Significantly, however, the primary function of Murray's training groups was always U-boat killing, which was reflected by their exercises and operational orders. This contrasts sharply with Western Approaches Command's emphasis on safe and timely arrival of the convoy. Indeed, when operations around transatlantic convoys heated up again in the summer of 1942, senior RN staff officers complained about the failure of Murray's escorts to adhere to the tenets of the Western Approaches Convoy Instructions, which admonished escorts to concentrate on defending the convoy first. The idea of Canadians charging madly about the ocean looking for trouble while their convoys suffered became the dominant theme in postwar British accounts of the Battle of the Atlantic.[21] This impression was formed during Murray's tenure in command. In that respect, he was absolutely correct about NEF laying the foundations of the RCN's reputation in the war. Unfortunately, it was not a good one, and the British pointed directly to Murray and his staff in St. John's as the cause.[21]

The same assessment seems to have been held by Murray's own chief, Vice-Admiral Nelles, who completed an S206 on Murray when he moved to Halifax in the fall of 1942 to replace Jones as COAC. It covered Murray's tenure as FONF and s anything but flattering. "An above the average officer," Nelles concluded, using a curious construction which seems to fall short of saying "above average." Numerical scores for initiative, zeal, reliability and administrative ability are all six — up one thin point from 1934! Only Nelles's rating of Murray's ability to command jumped, from four in 1934 to six in the summer of 1942. In judgment, surely a rather important characteristic in a flag officer, Murray's scored only five — down a point since 1934, and hardly a ringing endorsement from his service chief. The same can be said for Nelles's final written comments. Murray was "inclined to be over impressed with his own importance and ability" and "pro Royal Navy even to the detriment of the R.C.N., which is regrettable since he owes ... his present station and rank to the R.C.N."

Nelles nonetheless was flattering about what Murray had accomplished at Newfoundland as an administrator. "As the first Naval Officer and in particular the first R.C.N. Officer in command in Newfoundland the cards were stacked against him from the first. He overcame all prejudice and attained respect for the R.C.N. and himself." Perhaps for these reasons — and unquestionably for simple reasons of seniority and experience — Murray was appointed COAC on 18 September 1942.

Murray's S206 was not a vote of confidence, and hardly the kind of endorsement one might expect for a newly appointed senior commander. But Nelles had a very small pool from which to draw if the RCN intended to keep all its senior commands in Canadian hands. Ronald Agnew, the only other sea officer of the class of 1912 apart from Jones and Murray to make flag rank, had filled in behind Murray as Captain (not Commodore) Commanding, Canadian Ships in the UK in 1941. For whatever reason, the RCN never called him back. Agnew stayed overseas with the RN for the balance of the war, commanding an escort carrier in the Far East, and only made it to commodore upon retirement in 1946. The most capable and available sea officer of the class of 1913, Commodore H.E. Reid, filled Murray's post in Newfoundland in October. Reid was decidedly less tolerant of the British, and may have been selected by Nelles for that reason.

As things turned out, Murray took over in Halifax just as the RCN's fortunes at sea took a sudden and rather catastrophic tumble. In late August and early September, twelve ships and two escorts were sunk in the Gulf of St. Lawrence. With the fleet already stretched beyond endurance, the only solution was to close the St. Lawrence to oceanic shipping at the end of September. This may have made sound operational sense, but it was political dynamite, and the government had its feet put to the fire by the public for the navy's inability to keep the country's main artery open.[23]

Tactical defeat in the mid-ocean — Murray's old command — followed by the end of the year. Between July and the end of 1942, fully 80 per cent of losses to shipping in the mid-ocean affected the 35 per cent of convoys that were under Canadian escort. The trend did not go unnoticed, especially by Admiral Sir Max Horton, the tough, no-nonsense submariner who replaced the rather genteel Percy Noble — Murray's soul mate — as C-in-C Western Approaches in November. Horton soon fixed his steely gaze on the struggling Canadian escorts in the embattled mid-ocean. In mid-December, the British asked the RCN to remove them, citing lack of training and leadership as the key reasons for the heavy losses to Canadian-escorted convoys. The RCN flatly rejected the idea that there was anything uniquely Canadian in the loss rate. The real cause was lack of modern equipment and the frequent failure of the British destroyers assigned to Canadian groups to sail with their convoys due to mechanical problems.[24]

In general, Murray agreed with the Ottawa staff assessment that the British were wrong about the problems in the RCN. He was "loath to believe that convoys escorted by C [Canadian] groups have fared worse than those convoyed by B [British] or A [American] groups." He also dismissed the Admiralty's claim that the RCN was still untrained, since Canadian mid-ocean ships "have not been without success in destruction of submarines." If there were problems in the mid-ocean, Murray believed the blame could be equally shared by NSHQ and the British. The latter had failed to supply reliable and well-equipped RN destroyers to Canadian groups. Responsibility for shoddy maintenance standards and the overextension of the fleet — which prevented the maintenance of permanent escort groups in the mid-ocean — Murray laid squarely at the feet of the Canadian naval staff.[25]

Murray's complete disavowal of any responsibility for tactical failure of his recent command cannot have won him friends in Ottawa, and it makes his recent S206 seem like a fair assessment. Moreover, his argument that the RCN's skill at sinking submarines was evidence that they were, indeed, trained is both true — to a point — and suggestive of the very problems which the British saw. Certainly, over the summer of 1942 the RCN enjoyed more than its fair share of U-boat kills in the mid-ocean: three in July and August.[26] As suggested, this was the emphasis of Prentice's training groups in Newfoundland in 1941 and 1942. Unfortunately, after September 1942 the RCN briefly stopped sinking U-boats, while the crisis in the mid-ocean was about its inability to defend convoys. Murray's solution to the crisis was predictable: re-establish Prentice's training group in Halifax to mitigate the worst effects of NSHQ's bungled expansion policy, to meet the fundamental requirement for an effective operational training establishment, and give COAC a reserve he could manage.

In early January 1943, the Canadian cabinet agreed to the removal of Canadian escorts from the mid-ocean, and, to a considerable extent, naval expansion based on small ships was in political tatters. This seems to have been the low point of the war for Murray. In late December, when the issue of the efficiency of the Sheep Dog Navy was debated by the war cabinet, Colonel J.L. Ralston, the minister of National Defence, opined that if the war ended now "we would have to hang our heads in shame."[27] The issue did not die over the winter, as the government — itself on the ropes for its delay in getting Canadians into the fight — sought to salvage something from its "everything short of fighting" war effort. There was little that the modest escort fleet could do to save the government from an angry electorate. In 1942 the navy admitted tactical defeat in the Gulf of St. Lawrence and urged the government to close Canada's busiest shipping route amid howls of protest in the press and the House of Commons. Now, at the end of the year, operations in the mid-ocean had faltered, too. The navy and government kept the collapse in the mid-ocean under wraps for over thirty years.[28] By the spring of 1943, J.J Connolly, the executive assistant to the naval minister, confided to his diary that, "If we were to start over again, we would build convoy [escort] destroyers."[29]

By the spring of 1943, Canadian escorts were back in the mid-ocean, and in April the emphasis shifted to taking the offensive against the U-boats. Although Canadian escorts by training and inclination ought to have been well placed to participate in that shift, circumstances dictated otherwise. Murray certainly shared the government's zeal for making headlines by sinking U-boats. He and Prentice prepared an elaborate inshore offensive in early 1943 to meet the expected onslaught of U-boats into the Canadian zone in the spring, but the U-boats never came. The British defeated them in May, and then with American help harried them on the eastern side of the Atlantic for the balance of the year, inflicting a crushing defeat. The RCN, now well equipped and trained to defend convoys, lacked the necessary modern kit to make them prime U-boat hunters, and so they were virtually shut out of this part of the Atlantic war.

The great triumph of the spring of 1943, however, was the establishment of the Canadian Northwest Atlantic (CNA) Command with Murray as its first commander-in-chief.[30] In his 1970 interview Murray describes this development as both natural and perhaps inevitable. The RCN grew, local USN involvement shrank, and when the Americans "withdrew their control, I found myself Commander in Chief of the Canadian North-West Atlantic, a job which was almost exactly what I'd been doing in Newfoundland before the Americans moved in, but in this case I did have control of the aircraft cover."[31]

The truth of the matter is rather more complex. While Murray endorsed the proposed change in command as early as 1942, the driving force behind the ultimate establishment of the CNA was Ottawa. It was driven by the obvious muddle of commands in the northwest Atlantic — nine separate ones in late 1942 — but also by the tactical defeats in the St. Lawrence and in the mid-ocean late in that year. The RCN needed to be consolidated in home waters and modernized, and it needed to get a handle on operations off its own coast. It now fell to Ottawa to make an important Allied operational commander out of a man in whom Nelles had little real faith.

The issue gets even more complicated when one considers that senior Allied officers — both British and American — held similar opinions of virtually all senior Canadian naval officers. The final command arrangements worked out at Washington in March 1943, during the crisis of the Atlantic war, nearly collapsed over the inability of the Anglo-Americans to resolve who was going to be left to deal with the Canadians. The British were not happy with the establishment of a separate Canadian operational theatre, while the USN refused to allow its forces to operate in the new zone under Canadian command — a decision that was to be modified later.[32] As Alec Douglas has observed, the case for a separate Canadian theatre was successful because the Canadians demonstrated that they had the ships, the aircraft and the command and communications apparatus needed to operate a theatre. Murray, by his own reckoning, slipped into the new command because he was on the spot.

The establishment of the Canadian Northwest Atlantic Command at the end of April 1943 is nonetheless a watershed in both national and Canadian naval history. For the first time ever, an Allied theatre of war was commanded by a Canadian, and the remarkable development of the Sheep Dog Navy had carved out a niche in the northwest Atlantic that Canada could call its own. Murray had been deeply involved in the origins of that fleet and in the establishment of its operational role. Although these accomplishments were not uniquely his, perhaps no one could claim a more proprietary role. Murray could take justifiable pride in this accomplishment. Moreover, the care and attention he devoted to his small ships and their largely reservist crews — a subject too little explored by historians — probably had a great deal do to with the ability of the Sheep Dog Navy to stay at sea and do its job.

On 30 April 1943, Murray assumed operational control of convoy operations and naval and air anti-submarine operations in a zone stretching from the Gulf of Maine to Baffin Island via the eastern tip of the Grand Banks. He also controlled RCAF anti-submarine patrols to the limit of their aircraft's endurance — which pushed his control of some operations out to the mid-ocean. It was an astonishing accomplishment for Canada and its armed services, and Murray commanded it competently for the balance of the war.

To some considerable extent, Murray's story after the autumn of 1942 is one of professional success tempered by an uneasy relationship with his superiors in Ottawa, especially with Jones. This is a complex story and one not fully understood. In time, Jones's people at Halifax gravitated to Ottawa, and Murray brought his from St. John's — especially Prentice, who became Captain (D), Halifax in December 1942. Although Jones's principal task as Vice Chief of the Naval Staff (VCNS) in 1942–43 was to effect a major reorganization of NSHQ, Jones was also responsible for the "Staff Branch," which included the directors of Naval Intelligence, Operations, Plans, Signals and Trade — and ultimately Murray himself.[33] Murray ran the fleet, Jones ran the navy. The RCN, its seems, from late 1942 onward was a house divided.

In 1943, the RCN's emphasis was on consolidating the fleet in home waters, modernizing the escorts and taking the war to the enemy. Only the first part proved easy: it was accomplished by the spring. Murray and Prentice developed an elaborate scheme to launch an inshore offensive against U-boats, including some innovative tactics, in the Canadian zone in 1943 that in many ways anticipated the more famous

British offensives of the year. But the U-boats failed to come. In the meantime, modernization of the fleet got underway, although little was completed that year. As a result, the RCN possessed few ships capable of participating in the great offensives against the U-boats that characterized 1943. And even when Canadian hunter-killer groups got into the fray in the eastern Atlantic, they failed to sink U-boats. Little went well for the RCN in 1943.[34]

Nelles eventually came under intense fire from his minister for mishandling expansion, for the equipment crisis and for failing to deliver victories that the government could trumpet. Nelles was eventually sacked, and Jones replaced him in early January 1944. Curiously, in his 1970 interview, Murray professed virtually no knowledge of the equipment crisis and no certain awareness that Nelles had lost his job over it.[35]

The subsequent story of Canadian Northwest Atlantic Command, and Murray's role in command of it, remain to be fully explored by historians, but a few trends are evident. For example, the changing nature of the war at sea soon made Murray's new command too small to be fully effective. Command arrangements worked out at Washington in March 1943 dealt with a form of U-boat warfare — based on freewheeling surface manoeuvrability of wolf packs — that soon collapsed. The CNA was a coastal zone sandwiched between the USN's Eastern Sea Frontier to the south and the broad expanse of the Atlantic restored to Western Approaches Command. This arrangement allowed a single commander — Horton in Liverpool — to fight the climactic convoy battles of the war against huge packs of U-boats, and assumed that the inshore zones were secondary theatres dealing with lone hunters. However, by the end of 1943, U-boats were forced to operate submerged most of the time, and the mid-ocean became a transit area to the new primary theatres inshore. Murray's zone, in particular, remained a major operational area for U-boats in 1944 and 1945 — one of the few that the early schnorkelling U-boats could reach easily. But the crucial approach routes — often revealed by Ultra intelligence — now lay outside his operational control. Murray was permitted to send his aircraft out to the mid-ocean on searches, but not his surface forces. Instead, British and American naval groups trolled the edges of the Canadian zone, intercepting U-boats in comparatively good water conditions and sinking them while Murray watched.[36]

And so, although his command was under constant threat and attack, Murray seldom had his own resources to deal with the threat. By 1944, NSHQ clearly preferred to push its hunting forces overseas, where the U-boats were more plentiful and headlines were to be made sinking them. This trend is evident from the moment Jones took over as CNS in January 1944. Within days Murray was admonished to find and kill U-boats, while NSHQ sought ways of getting its ships into the offensive on the eastern side of the Atlantic. That meant sending most disposable forces overseas, leaving Murray with few extra of his own.[37] In early 1944, Murray fully endorsed this policy. The threat west of the Grand Banks was so slight that he preferred to deal with it by using an aggressive escort policy and occasional detachment of escorts for hunting purposes.[38] This was the kind of intelligent use of limited resources that Captain C.D. Howard-Johnson, RN — director of the anti-U-boat Division at the Admiralty and one of the RCN's most trenchant 1942 critics — considered extremely useful and "of great assistance."[39] All of this was clarified by pressure from NSHQ in March 1944 to move work-up training out of Halifax to a new base in Bermuda. Murray protested with a recurring theme — that by taking away the ships under training, Ottawa would take away his only reserve for hunting U-boats. In early 1944, Murray finally lost that battle, while at about the same time Chummy Prentice left Murray's side to command EG-11, a group of River-class destroyers, during the forthcoming invasion operations.[40]

Murray finally got a proper support group in July 1944: the frigates of EG-16. This was an important start, but they were never enough to respond effectively to U-boat attacks in his vast zone, nor was it sufficient to intercept and attack U-boats as they moved westward. That was done very largely by USN forces, often operating upon information provided by Murray's command. Throughout 1944 and 1945, USN hunter-killer groups, some with escort carriers included, prowled just outside the CNA. In part because of this distant cover, Murray's appeals for more RCN support groups and even an escort carrier to help him defeat U-boats in the Canadian zone fell largely on deaf ears. It says a great deal, nonetheless, about increased American faith in the RCN generally that their destroyer escort groups (but never ASW carrier groups) were, by 1944, routinely assigned to Murray's command for searches.

Throughout the summer and fall of 1944, Murray was content to nurture the fleet, assemble support groups and send them overseas. It was not until late October, with the formation of EG-27, that the CNA got its second support group. That gave Murray a little more flexibility; however, by then he relied primarily on radar-equipped aircraft to simply suppress U-boats in his zone. By the time his few hunters got to the "flaming datum," the U-boat was either long gone or was lost in the confused sonar conditions of the Canadian inshore.

On the whole, the reaction of Murray's command to the new schnorkelling U-boat in 1944–45 seems to be a model of sound judgment and common sense. With few resources at hand and terrible sonar conditions, Murray adopted a policy of maximum harassment of U-boats. He knew that the war was not going to be won off the coast of Canada, although the success of daring U-boat captains — like Dobratz, who attacked BX-141 in the mouth of Halifax Harbour in January 1944 — clearly galled him. Perhaps the worst that can be said for Murray at this stage of the war — and it was not unique to him — was that so little seemed to work inshore that he was content to simply fill the water with noise and keep the U-boats moving until either the war ended or the RCN got lucky.[41] Certainly, Captain (D) Halifax, now W.L. Puxley, RN, complained to the bitter end that training standards in the command were poor, and that searches for attackers were hurt by faulty plotting practices. Unfortunately, the war ended before Murray's command got lucky.

The best measure of Murray's success as C-in-C CNA was not how well he fared finding guerrilla U-boats in a complex ocean, but in the orderly and unfailing routine of convoy escort. In the spring of 1944 the RCN — essentially Murray — assumed responsibility for the close escort of all main transatlantic trade convoys between New York and Great Britain. This was no mean feat, and one in which Murray exhibited immense pride in his 1970 interview. The largest convoy of the war, HX-300 with 167 ships, was escorted by one frigate and six corvettes. "[W]hen it came 'round the corner at Nantucket," Murray recalled, "I pointed it on a rhumb line course nine miles north of Tory Island, on the northwest coast of Ireland, and they held that course all the way. They were never disturbed and there was no reason to change that course."[42]

There is little evidence in what has been written so far that the fissure of the navy between Jones in Ottawa and Murray in Halifax in the last two years of the war seriously affected Murray's command of the CNA. Battles over resources were to be expected; however, the tension remained. This emerged most clearly following the VE-Day riots in Halifax on 7–8 May 1945, in which naval personnel were heavily implicated. The Halifax *Chronicle* accused Murray of criminal negligence for failing to control his men.[43] The crisis eventually brought the acting prime minister, J.L. Ilsley, to Halifax on 11 May. The next day, Murray was relieved of command and Jones appointed in his place as C-in-C CNA. On 13 May, Jones in turn appointed a board of inquiry under Vice-Admiral Victor Brodeur and two others junior to Murray, Rear-Admiral H.E. Reid and Commodore A. Hope, RCN. Shortly afterwards, Isley announced the establishment of a Royal Commission of Inquiry under Justice R.L. Kellock.

Murray expected more from his service than he got in the aftermath of the VE-Day riots. He protested the inadequacy and impropriety of the naval inquiry because most of the members were his juniors, but he trusted in the Kellock Commission to exonerate him. "I can assure if justice is done," he wrote to Captain Roger Bidwell on 15 May, "and I have no reason to expect it will not be … the name of the Royal Canadian Navy is going to stand very much higher than ever before."[44] By late May he was not so sure about either, and advised Jones that if either inquiry went against him he wanted a formal court-martial. Jones offered him nothing. No report of the Brodeur inquiry has ever been found: it would seem that they were all destroyed.[45] Murray was left to the tender mercies of the press, the Kellock Commission and the government.

In truth, the Brodeur inquiry was in an impossible position. A finding in favour of Murray would exonerate him — and perhaps be seen as a whitewash. To find against him would have given Murray grounds for demanding a court-martial, something Jones could not allow. Murray probably knew this, but his anxiety over a fair hearing was only heightened by the actual conduct of the Kellock Commission. It seemed to put the navy on trial, but never — to Murray's satisfaction — looked closely at the shortcomings of the mayor of Halifax and his council. By late June, Murray expected the worst, and at the end of July his fears were confirmed. Justice Kellock's principal finding was that the chief cause of the Halifax VE-Day riots was a failure of naval authorities to control their personnel.[46]

The Kellock Commission saddled Murray with the blame for the riots, and the RCN and the Canadian government just washed their hands of him. In 1967, Murray confided to a friend that Jones should not have allowed Cabinet to dismiss him so abruptly from his post as C-in-C CNA. "Nelles," he contended, "would not have done so, and his own resignation would have been on the table if they had persisted against his judgment."[47] His dream of a court-martial also fell apart. There were not enough senior admirals in the RCN to do so, and establishing such a court would have required the politically incorrect expedient of bringing in British admirals. Jones would not have countenanced it anyway, and Murray knew that. Later, from his self-imposed exile in Britain, Murray explained to Louis Audette, "Perhaps the greatest service I did towards the RCN was to leave Canada when I did instead of staying to fight it out with the then CNS — that would have split the R.C.N. into small pieces."[48] He officially retired from the navy on 16 March 1946.

In retirement, Murray earned a degree in maritime law and was called to the bar in November 1949. He practised briefly in London, but when Jean's health began to fail he moved to a village in Sussex, where he was very active in local politics, eventually running unsuccessfully for office in 1965. After his wife's death, Murray married Dr. Nina Sergeivma Shtetinin Seaford Warwick, the granddaughter of a tsarist admiral, in 1963. Among his several return trips to Canada was one in May 1970, when he unveiled the Sailor's Memorial in Point Pleasant Park, Halifax, and — decked out in his wartime blues — took the salute of the march-past of 700 sailors on the twenty-fifth anniversary of victory in the Battle of the Atlantic. During that visit he also sat for an interview with an official historian. Murray maintained an active life until his sudden death on 25 November 1971, at the age of seventy-five. His ashes were interred in the Naval Vault of St. Paul's Church, Halifax, on 17 September 1972.

Whether a fight between the Murray and Jones factions would have split the navy at the moment of its greatest triumph, we will never know. But we do know that Murray was wrong in his belief that not confronting Jones and the government in 1945 was the greatest service he had ever done for his navy — or his country. His service to both was more profound than that. For thirty-four years he pursued a naval career through times that killed or drove from the service most of his classmates. By 1939, he was poised to play a crucial role in the largest and most complex naval campaign in history, and in the end to assume operational control over the core of Canada's crucial contribution to it. Despite the carping of Allies and his own CNS at the time, and some historians since, Murray clearly possessed the administrative skill, the sea-smarts and personal decency to keep the motley collection of reservists who made up his command at sea doing their job. The blend of happiness and efficiency he found in Calcutta in 1919 seems to have been the hallmark of his operational commands in the Second World War. As Nelles opined in 1934, Murray was not a driver or a strict disciplinarian. Nor was he weak of character; he just disliked "hurting humans." Murray's old mentor, Percy Noble, was of the same mould. He was sacked in November 1942 and replaced by a hard-nosed submariner who drove his people to victory. Murray got promoted and a more important job. Maybe Prentice, a hard driver and a bit of an eccentric, acted as Murray's alter ego during those crucial middle years of the war. How the RCN might have fared had Murray been more of a Horton than a Noble we will never know. He was not, and the RCN did remarkably well. That, perhaps, is enough.

NOTES

1   Vice-Admiral Harry DeWolf once described himself to the author as a "Jones man," and spoke of others as being in the Murray camp. See the quote in Cameron, *Murray the Martyred Admiral*, 230, attributed to the *Report of the Royal Commission of Inquiry into the Halifax Disorders May 7th–8th, 1945* (Ottawa: King's Printer, 1945), "Wardroom chatters held that the two regarded one another frostily, to such an extent that in loyalties the Royal Canadian Navy had Jones officers and Murray officers."

2   Lund, "Rear Admiral Leonard Warren Murray, CB, CBE, RCN: A Study of Command and Leadership in the Battle of the Atlantic," 297–308.

3 Edwards, *Seven Sailors*, 160 [complete references for commonly cited secondary sources are included in the bibliography].

4 The RN had just gone through its own major reductions, dubbed the "Geddes Axe" after the Chancellor of the Exchequer who forced it through, so it is curious that the RN would accept a Commonwealth officer for service. One suspects, however, that Murray's salary was still being paid by the RCN, so the RN got an extra officer for little cost.

5 Kemp, *Seven Sailors*, and interview with Vice-Admiral H.G. DeWolf. The assessments in his personnel file from various RN ships and establishments during this period are all "excellent."

6 Kemp, *Seven Sailors*, 168.

7 Murray S206s for 29 December 1933 and 31 October 1934. Copies from personnel file courtesy of Roger Sarty.

8 Murray personnel file, "Confidential Report on Captain L.W. Murray, R.C.N." [n.d.], copy courtesy Roger Sarty.

9 W.A.B. Douglas Interview with Rear-Admiral L.W. Murray, May 1970, Directorate of History and Heritage (DHH), Biog M.

10 Murray interview, 35.

11 Murray interview, 38.

12 This intriguing relationship is discussed in passing throughout the author's two books, *North Atlantic Run* and *The U-Boat Hunters*.

13 Murray interview, 40.

14 Murray to Audette, 6 October 1946: copy in the author's collection.

15 Murray interview, 42.

16 See the discussion in the author's *The U-boat Hunters*, 8–11.

17 HMCS *Ottawa* has since been credited with sharing the destruction of the Italian submarine *Faa de Bruno* with a British destroyer in 1940. However, the destruction of U-501 remains the first uniquely Canadian victory at sea against the enemy.

18 See Milner, *North Atlantic Run*, 80–81.

19 See Milner, *North Atlantic Run*, 85–86.

20 Because of the presence of fog, U-boat packs were able to press home attacks on convoys well within the range of land based air power in the western Atlantic: something they could not do in the eastern Atlantic.

21 See especially Chalmers, *Max Horton and the Western Approaches*, 147, where the Canadian method of convoy defence is described as the "cowboy" form: keeping a portion of the escort to ride "herd" on the convoy while outriders keep the U-boats "well stirred up." Donald Macintrye, a trenchant critic of the RCN, described their convoy battles as "wild and confused" in his memoir *U-Boat Killer*, 78.

22 See Milner, *North Atlantic Run*, chapter 5.

23 See Hadley, *U-boats Against Canada*, especially chapters 4 and 5.

24 "How about giving us a few decent destroyers in the C groups, Maxie [Horton]," Captain R.E.S. Bidwell, FONF's Chief of Staff wrote bitterly on the report of proceedings of ONS 154, which lost fifteen ships while the British request was being debated in late December, "instead of the discarded sweepings you're giving us now?" As quoted in Milner, *North Atlantic Run*, 210.

25 As quoted in Milner, *North Atlantic Run*, 199.

26 See Prologue of Milner, *The U-Boat Hunters*.

27 Angus L. Macdonald Diary, 23 December 1942, Public Archives of Nova Scotia.

28 The crisis over the transfer of escorts out of the mid-ocean was first brought to light in the author's 1979 MA thesis at the University of New Brunswick, "Canadian Escorts in the Mid Atlantic 1941–1943."

29 As quoted in Milner, *The U-boat Hunters*, 37.

30 Vice-Admiral G.C. Jones succeeded Murray as C-in-C CNA following his dismissal in May 1945.

31 Murray interview, 48.

32 See the correspondence between Vice-Admiral Moore (the VCNS) and Admiral of the Fleet Sir Dudley Pound (the First Sea Lord), 9 March 1943, Captain S.W. Roskill Papers, Churchill College, Cambridge, Rosk 5/14.

33 Tucker, *The Naval Service of Canada (II)*, 422.

34 See the author's "The Royal Canadian Navy and 1943: A year best forgotten?"

35 This is a significant gap in his memory — if indeed that is what it is. At a time before the details and significance of the equipment crisis had been exposed by historians, Murray may simply have been being coy about such a touchy subject: this is the charitable

interpretation. The interview contains enough information and detail that is lucid to suggest that memory was not a problem. The only other possible reason for Murray's apparent lack of awareness about such key developments — that he simply did not know — raises a whole host of difficult questions indeed.

36 This problem was later solved under NATO, when the CANLANT zone extended into the mid-Atlantic.

37 He created a small group of aged Town-class destroyers (W-10) to reinforce convoys in the Grand banks area, but it was blown apart by winter gales, and the ships — already slated for decommissioning — soon disappeared.

38 FONF to C-in-C CNA 09 1701Z/3/44, DHH, 81/520 NHS 8440, Support Groups — General.

39 As quoted in Milner, "The RCN and the Offensive Against the U-boats, 1939–1945," 32, DHH, 2000/5.

40 Significantly, Prentice came back, after a long convalescent leave, to take command of the Bermuda training base in 1945. See Milner, "HMCS *Somers Isles*."

41 See Milner, *The U-boat Hunters*, chapter 6.

42 Murray interview, 50–51.

43 Vice-Admiral Andrew Fulton, who worked briefly for the *Chronicle* immediately after the war, claims this was no accident. The editor of the paper was apparently a close personal friend of Jones and was in routine telephone contact with the CNS denouncing Murray's activities even before the riots.

44 As quote in Cameron, *Murray the Martyred Admiral*, 230–31.

45 Information courtesy Vice-Admiral Nigel Brodeur.

46 Cameron, *Murray the Martyred Admiral*, 121.

47 *Ibid.*, 230.

48 Murray to Audette, 6 October 1946.

CHAPTER FIVE

Vice-Admiral George C. Jones: The Political Career of a Naval Officer

Richard Oliver Mayne

A youthful-looking Commander George C. Jones

The 14th of January, 1944, was a solemn day for two British officers on loan to the Royal Canadian Navy (RCN). "[T]he bombshell has at last exploded ... GC has reached his goal and I expect all is in a turmoil," wrote one, while the other felt equally frustrated that "GC Jones took over as Chief of the Naval Staff, which he had been scheming for some time."[1] This was how Captains Massey Goolden and Eric Brand greeted the news that the naval minister had replaced Vice-Admiral Percy W. Nelles with Rear-Admiral George C. Jones. In contrast, for the nation's media it was only logical that Nelles was going overseas, where his experience (they assumed) was wanted; they hailed the move as a sign that the RCN was gearing up for the anticipated invasion of Europe.

Like Brand and Goolden, however, other officers did not share the press's depiction of the new CNS as the benevolent Admiral "Tiger" Jones.[2] They, too, saw Jones as a carnivore, but their view was that he had spent his career hungering for the top slot in the navy's hierarchy. As such, Nelles's replacement represented Jones's latest and biggest meal rather than a promotion from the minister, and this belief has left the Admiral with the dubious legacy of being both a political and careerist officer. Put another way, the term *careerist* defined Jones as a man who valued his own career requirements before the needs and welfare of the service. Subsequently, Jones is often portrayed as someone who not only manipulated situations so that he would stay ahead of his rivals, but also engineered a year-long whispering campaign against Nelles that was designed to clear the way for his own advancement to CNS.

Although new sources show that this interpretation of Jones is deserved, it should be measured against a naval community in which outmanoeuvring colleagues for promotion was simply a fact of life. And so, while being highly motivated and excessively competitive with his peers certainly made Jones a predator, the manner in which he clawed his way to the top — and then defended his turf once there — indicates that he just happened to be the fiercest amongst a number of tigers. But Jones's overly ambitious nature produced mixed results as CNS. On the one hand, he was a shrewd administrator whose skills resulted in remarkable gains for the RCN. On the other, he was an autocratic leader who bestowed undue power upon his office. An argument will be made, therefore, that Jones was an extremely capable officer, but his personal ambition caused more problems for the navy than it solved.

Aside from his reputation as a careerist, many found it difficult to get along with Jones. He was often described as a "tyrant" or "a sort of cold figure," who was "never one to be polite if he could avoid it." Most gave the admiral a wide birth in the halls of Naval Service Headquarters (NSHQ). That rudeness did not always endear Jones to others at NSHQ, where a common joke held: "Isn't it wonderful? CNS spoke to me this morning. He told me to get the hell out of his way." Such tales about Jones's temperament were nothing new to those who had served with him before he became CNS:

> He was a very capable officer…. The only thing you
> had to watch was his terrible temper. I ran afoul of it
> once … I made the unfortunate error of going to his
> cabin to take certain work in which he had required to
> be up-to-date by that day, and I just got the word,
> "Sir" out of my mouth and … his precise words were
> for me to, "Shut my f——ing mouth and get out." This
> so enraged me that I was very tempted to, as of that

date, to desert, because I had never had anyone speak
to me that way or ever since … that left a bit of a scar
with me for some years afterwards.[3]

Others had similar experiences, and even the naval information
directorate responsible for publicity was forced to admit in a press
release that "Jones is credited with a sharp 'bark' but an unbounded
enthusiasm for his men modifies his 'bite.'"[4] This was true. When Jones
felt he had gone too far with his disciplinary tactics, he would apologize.
Moreover, he rewarded his subordinates for their hard work with gen-
erous leave periods. But he was also relentless, telling them that he
would double their punishment if they were even "one minute adrift."[5]
There were, of course, worse tales, all of which indicate that the CNS was
not generally well liked.[6] What is perhaps more compelling, however, is
that accounts of him in the earlier part of his naval career seem to
describe an entirely different man.

From the moment the fifteen-year-old cadet began his studies at the
newly created Royal Naval College of Canada (RNCC) in January 1911,
until his time as a lieutenant in the mid-1920s, it appears that Jones was
ambitious but good-natured. While he may not have been the top student at RNCC — generally ranking fourth or fifth in a class of approximately twenty students — he thoroughly enjoyed life at the college,
which he later felt was the "healthiest" and "happiest" part of his life.
Others agreed, as one individual thought Jones was "always bright and
sometimes brilliant.… His laugh was infectious and his smile a dream,"
while seven years later another recalled that, "during his time at the
College, Lieutenant Jones infused much admiration into our hearts. It is
quite evident that this admiration had anything but died." And so in his
early years he was a likable, hard-working man whose only appreciable
flaw was a "shyness" at mixed social functions — which he either left
prematurely or simply "disappeared for most of the time."[7]

These comments were consistent with the progress of his career.
Once he graduated from RNCC, Jones saw service on a wide range of
British warships, and by the end of the First World War he was the first
lieutenant of the destroyer HMS *Vanquisher*.[8] The immediate postwar
period brought further success. In 1920, he became the first officer

from the original class of RNCC cadets to command a major Canadian warship when he was appointed to the destroyer HMCS *Patrician.* Two years later, he took over her sister ship *Patriot.*[9] With two commands under his belt it appeared he was outperforming his colleagues, especially since none of them had yet been given a crack at the "heavies." These accomplishments impressed his superiors, and one observed that Jones was "tactful, good tempered, and very cheerful…. A fine character."[10] Hardly consistent with the later accounts of his personality, it would appear that something happened to Jones that altered his attitude towards the service.

Life in the small interwar RCN officer corps was highly competitive. Government cutbacks and neglect led to a navy that offered few chances for promotion, the more so because, as one report observed, "officers' prospects are very poor, owing to the lack of important appointments." This created a cutthroat environment in which every single day of seniority was prized as if it were the key factor that made the difference between a plush job and eventual promotion or a stagnant career. Such a state of affairs had a tremendous impact on morale, and at least one individual complained that the officer corps's infighting "will eventually undermine naval discipline to such a stage that a complete abolition [of the service] will be a saving grace." While an extreme interpretation, this type of criticism was reflective of a naval community where "everyone knows everybody's business and relations."[11] Simply put, chronic attempts to gain seniority over peers caused much bitterness between some of Jones's former classmates.

It is common knowledge that Jones's chief competitor throughout his career was L.W. Murray and that this relationship developed into what was perhaps the most intense, hate-filled rivalry in the RCN's history. What is less well known is that another officer, R.I. Agnew, played a pivotal role in triggering the Murray–Jones feud. Whether it was a question involving travel claims, seniority or promotions, the documentation on Murray and Agnew leaves little doubt that both knew how to use naval regulations to their advantage.[12] Jones, on the other hand, made little effort to proactively manage his career throughout these early years. For instance, after both Agnew and Murray had passed their navigation course in 1920, Agnew immediately drew attention to the administrative order that granted additional seniority for "specializing" (a term used to describe qualifications, such as gunnery or navigation, that gave officers the distinction of being experts in a particular field). So, too, did Murray, but Agnew went so far as to write the incoming Director of the Naval Service (DNS), Walter Hose, asking that he be made the executive officer of one of the RCN's destroyers. While fully within his rights to do so, this type of proactive career management created a situation whereby Jones was falling behind his competitors.

Murray's additional six months of seniority for his navigation course did not seem to bother Jones as much as the fact that Agnew had surpassed him in the *Navy List*, a document that listed seniority and therefore acted as a barometer by which to measure an officer's potential for advancement. Realizing that trouble was brewing amongst his tight-knit family of officers, Hose observed in July 1920 that, "as regards Jones having just learned that Agnew is now his senior having completed his N [navigation] course. No N appointment vacant and he [Jones] is suitable for destroyer command." If giving Jones his first command was Hose's way of easing tensions between these officers, his decision to make Agnew the *Patrician*'s first lieutenant under Jones in August 1921 was clearly a mistake. That this arrangement did not last long suggests the two men were unable to work together. This was not entirely their fault, since Agnew's appointment had created an odd situation where he had more seniority as the executive officer than Jones had as the ship's captain.[13] Nevertheless, such incidents began to wear on the young lieutenant, and by the mid-1920s he seemed to have realized that merit alone was not enough to guarantee advancement in the service.

Acting as a harbinger of things to come, Jones wrote a carefully crafted letter to headquarters in August 1924 asking that he be granted additional seniority. Unable to specialize because of his two destroyer commands, Jones convincingly argued that "it appears unfair that in a small service I should be penalized owing to being employed on services [his two commands] that other officers were not considered suitable for." Eventually, Hose — who was now the CNS — took this matter up with the Minister on Jones's behalf. How much sway the letter carried is a mystery, but there can be little doubt that Jones believed it had done some good. Both he and Murray were promoted on 1 January

1925, while Agnew remained a lieutenant for another two and a half months.[14] The politician within Jones had surfaced, and he now understood why the college had stressed that "ambition and competition here [in the navy] as elsewhere are secrets of success." Since his colleagues were aggressively managing their own careers, Jones realized he would have to do the same. The difference between him and his rivals was that he would become the most efficient and ruthless career manager of them all.[15]

Although Agnew would remain forever his junior, it is evident that Murray was maintaining a slim advantage throughout the early 1930s. While Jones was undoubtedly disturbed by the outgoing CNS's decision to make Murray an acting captain for a short stint in 1934, his fortunes were about to change.[16] Unlike others, the new CNS was not as impressed with Murray, who, after receiving unprecedented scores of nines (out of ten) on previous performance reports, was suddenly getting fours and fives from Nelles. His comments that he did not consider Murray "a sufficiently strict disciplinarian" indicate Nelles wanted officers like Jones, who were fair yet strict.[17] And so, while Murray had prospered under Hose's reign, Nelles arguably had selected Jones as his favourite.

For many, this assumption was confirmed when Jones was promoted to captain on 1 August 1938, while Murray was not confirmed in the same rank until the next day. Indeed, the twenty-four hours of seniority seemed to act as a bizarre message from NSHQ that Jones was winning the neck-and-neck race with Murray. Moreover, this development further fuelled rumours that he was manipulating his career progression — so much so, in fact, that one officer claimed Jones had convinced Nelles to grant him the extra seniority because he had taken the Imperial Defence Course, a qualification Murray was lacking.[18] In reality, it is difficult to determine whether Jones was simply Nelles's preference or if he had influenced the CNS as he had done with Hose in 1924.[19] But evidence of his political machinations during the Second World War is much more conclusive.

Having taken the destroyer HMCS *Ottawa* from the west to the east coast in 1939, Jones was made Captain (D), which gave him administrative control over the escort forces in Halifax during the opening months of the war. Over the next two years, he would be made a commodore, and while still commanding the destroyer *Assiniboine* he would be given the title of Commodore Commanding Halifax Force, thereafter becoming the Commanding Officer Atlantic Coast (COAC), the top Canadian operational appointment on the east coast.[20] The war was clearly providing Jones with ample opportunity to advance quickly, and he pushed his own endurance, as well as that of his subordinates, to the limit. This may explain why some felt that they represented the rungs on his career ladder.[21]

In the strange mystique of the navy, sailors often find ways to even the score. In Jones's case, resentment towards his ambition manifested itself in the form of the unflattering nickname "Jetty" Jones that, according to naval lore, had two possible origins. One version had it that, as Captain (D), Jones sent other ships to sea while his own remained alongside the jetty. Certainly, under his command it was reputed that the *Ottawa* had become an extension of the jetty known as "O" block, and a more elaborate tale held that some disgruntled sailor had painted "JETTY JONES" on the *Assiniboine*'s side after he took over that ship. While the latter account was most likely apocryphal, such recriminations against Jones were unfair. Sailing schedules reveal that he did go to sea, and that extended stints alongside were easily explainable. The other origin of his nickname can be traced to a collision between the *Ottawa* and a Halifax ferry in April 1940.[22] In reality, Jones was not involved in that incident. The Board of Inquiry clearly indicates that Commander E.R. Mainguy, who had taken over from Jones ten days earlier, hit a tug called the *Bonsurf* instead of the ferry. The fact that scuttlebutt attributed this to Jones, rather than the more likable Mainguy, serves as a powerful example of his unpopularity.[23]

Nevertheless, there was a grain of truth to these stories. Naval records indicate that Jones was a poor ship-driver, a point that was further emphasized by one of his seniors, who remarked, "He was a very nervous fellow ... it took him an hour and a quarter to get the ship alongside, whereas it took me about five or ten minutes!"[24] Instead, his real strength lay in staff work, and this was what mattered to Nelles, whose reward was to tell the naval minister, Angus L. Macdonald, that Jones should be appointed a rear-admiral effective 1 December 1941. Whether through hard work or manipulation, Jones was clearly Nelles's favourite, as Murray's promotion was again dated the following day.[25]

Jones's bureaucratic skills also came in handy seven months later, when Nelles sought Macdonald's permission to move him so that he could help with an administrative crisis at NSHQ.[26] Although the new Vice-Chief of the Naval Staff (VCNS) would not take over until 9 October 1942, his presence at NSHQ was immediately felt and, according to the Secretary of the Naval Board, had this change not occurred, "the whole organization would have collapsed."[27] Ironically, the man whom Nelles would entrust to plan another reorganization was himself on the verge of collapse. Swearing the only witness to secrecy because he was "anxious only to finish out the war in harness," Jones had had a heart attack in March 1942.[28] To use a modern phrase, he was in every respect a workaholic whose health was secondary to his sense of duty. Indeed, his superior administrative abilities and unparalleled work ethic created a magnetism that attracted a small group of officers — the so-called "Jones men" — who were fiercely loyal to him.[29]

Key governmental officials were equally impressed, as the naval minister's executive assistant found that he was a "young, energetic type of man who will bring great credit to the service." Having lived in the same Halifax neighbourhood in the 1920s, it was even reputed that besides being one of his bosses at NSHQ, Angus Macdonald was also an old and trusted friend.[30] But as was so often the case, excessive ambition and his political nature masked Jones's admirable qualities. Only one step away from achieving his ultimate goal, and with connections that afforded him the opportunity and confidence to undermine the CNS, he initiated a campaign that whittled away at Nelles's base of political support.

Testimony from the director of the Operations Division, Captain Horatio Nelson Lay, makes it clear that the VCNS was pushing his own agenda in March 1943. During that month, Lay claimed Jones was "a bit red in the face" after Nelles discovered that he was discussing the fleet's training deficiencies with Macdonald behind his back.[31] Lay was a confirmed "Jones man," and it is highly suggestive that he was emphasizing the exact same training issues to Prime Minister Mackenzie King — who also happened to be Lay's uncle — that the VCNS was pressing on Macdonald. Put another way, while Jones was busy shaking the minister's confidence in Nelles, Lay was sending the same message to King, who observed in his diary that "I rather share his [Lay's] opinion of Nelles as not being any means a man large enough for the task in hand."[32]

Lay's account also was consistent with events. Since early February 1943, Macdonald had been defending the navy against a recently retired Royal Canadian Naval Volunteer Reserve (RCNVR) officer named Andrew Dyas MacLean. Knowing a good story when they saw one, both the press and official Opposition were fascinated with MacLean's allegations that there was a dangerous morale problem in the navy because the permanent force "discriminated" against reservists. As a former secretary to Conservative prime minister R.B. Bennett and the editor of a Toronto publishing company, MacLean was a powerful adversary and an embarrassment to Macdonald, informing Canadians that the minister was failing to properly supervise his own department.

While Jones disliked MacLean and disagreed with his allegations, this scandal provided him with an opportunity. Not only was Macdonald suspicious of Nelles, believing that the CNS was not telling him all that he needed to know, but he also became more interested in the navy and its problems.[33] As a result, at a pivotal moment, Jones was feeding the minister information that was intended to pit Macdonald against Nelles,[34] and this led to some interesting antics at NSHQ. For example, during a private conversation with another officer, Nelles apparently snuck over to his adjoining door with the VCNS's office and abruptly yanked it open. Unable to hear Nelles's footsteps through the keyhole, an unsuspecting Jones fell into the room. Undoubtedly, Nelles's realization that his VCNS was going to the minister had changed their relationship, and there is evidence that Jones was cut out of the CNS's inner circle.[35] In Jones's defence, however, he may have felt obligated to report problems that Nelles was apparently glossing over. In fact, the VCNS had once scolded an officer for refusing to bypass a superior, stating that "it was his duty to represent this fact to a higher authority however distasteful this course might be."[36] While this logic might have influenced Jones's rationale, his actions during the confrontation over the fleet's modernization leaves little doubt that he was undermining Nelles's authority.

Macdonald read a report, sent to him in confidence by Lieutenant-Commander William Strange, RCNVR, the assistant naval information officer at NSHQ, who observed that there was serious dissatisfaction within the fleet because they were trying to fight Germany's U-boats with antiquated anti-submarine equipment on their ships.[37] Having just survived his ordeal with MacLean, the news that there were rumblings within the fleet devastated Macdonald. Already suspicious, the minister now feared that his naval advisors were involved in a "cover-up" and so decided not to share Strange's report with Nelles or his staff. According to Strange, however, Jones was not only aware of his report but had also offered to look into these matters on the minister's behalf by travelling to the UK.[38]

While Macdonald opted to send his executive assistant, John Joseph Connolly, on the secretive fact-finding mission to St. John's, Londonderry and London, the VCNS still saw an opportunity to stoke the fire and announced that he was going on an "inspection trip" to the Maritimes.[39] Arriving on 7 October 1943 and leaving on the same day that Connolly departed for Londonderry, Jones took the minister's executive assistant to see the command's operational commander, Commodore H.E. Reid, RCN, and his Captain (D), J.M. Rowland, RN, whose comments confirmed his suspicions on modernization. While this is suggestive, the strongest evidence that the VCNS was participating in the executive assistant's secretive investigation can be found in a letter Connolly wrote to Macdonald in which he stated that he had "talked to GC Jones" about the difficulties he was encountering in St. John's.[40] Unlike the rest of the naval staff, therefore, Jones understood what was transpiring, yet apparently said nothing to Nelles when he returned to NSHQ.

Connolly returned from his trip with information that cast the naval staff in a negative light, and the stage was set for a bitter showdown between Macdonald and Nelles throughout November and December 1943. Macdonald's opening salvo consisted of an "anonymous" memo that Connolly had received while overseas.[41] This document, which was in fact written by the mastermind behind Strange's report — Commodore G.W.G. Simpson, RN, who held the key position of Commodore (D) Western Approaches at Londonderry — explained how NSHQ had botched the upgrading of the RCN escort fleet. Most staff members were naturally outraged, but there was one lone voice that did not respond with anger. "I ... do not consider it damaging criticism of our whole repair organization," Jones told Nelles on 12 November, continuing, "Rather, I interpret it as constructive criticism, containing suggestions for improving." This was typical of Jones's behaviour throughout the confrontation. He kept his distance from Nelles and only haphazardly participated in the naval staff's defence, and while he never overtly sided with Macdonald, he secretly passed documents to Connolly that strengthened the minister's case.[42]

Despite his attempts to conceal these activities, some officers realized that Jones was relying on his "political pull to reach the top." Word of his efforts had even spread to the west coast, where Rear-Admiral Victor Brodeur was calling Jones's careerist tactics the "gangsterism of GC." Closer to the centre of power, the Director of Trade, Captain Eric Brand — actually serving in NSHQ at the time — observed that the VCNS "was a great politician ... he never did anything without thinking how it was going to affect him ... he had quite a hand in the Nelles business — just quiet remarks [to the minister]." Brand was distressed that Jones was manipulating the confrontation for his own purposes and took it upon himself to stop the VCNS before it was too late. He went to see Nelles and then Connolly, but both men seemed disinterested in his revelation about Jones, and so Brand gave up, believing that "the pressure against Nelles was too strong."[43] In reality, Brand did not understand that, while Jones's shenanigans may have been annoying, Nelles had to worry about the larger problem of dealing with an actual politician.

Faced with a minister afraid of a public scandal that would dwarf the earlier MacLean affair, Nelles was asked to admit that the naval staff was fully culpable of failing to brief Macdonald on the RCN's modernization problem. Macdonald was on a witch hunt, and Nelles knew it. Although recent research identifies many more examples than the ones Nelles would cite, the CNS defended his officers by illustrating that the Naval Board had informed Macdonald about their difficulties in modernizing the RCN. There was more. Nelles had also tried to enlist Macdonald's support in getting other government agencies, such as the departments of Munitions and Supply, Finance, Labour, and National Select Services to help the RCN out of its dilemma by building more shipyards.[44] Could Nelles have done a better job of explaining these highly technical matters to his civilian master? Perhaps, but this did not change the fact that he had played a powerful trump card in the Minister's "blame game" that suggested Macdonald's ignorance was his own fault.

Even Connolly was forced to concede that the CNS had the better hand. Providing strong evidence that the real crisis was not about equipment shortages, but was instead a political struggle for survival, the executive assistant emphasized to Macdonald in a key memo on the CNS's future that "some day this story will be out. Unless you have strong action to point to, your lot will not be easy.... The Navy knows one rule well — the Captain bears the responsibility for his ship [and] I am unable to escape the conclusion that you must move the CNS."[45] Apparently, in Connolly's eyes, that responsibility conveniently stopped at Nelles. Macdonald was not so naïve, as the Naval Act clearly placed him at the top of the navy's hierarchy, and so folding became an option as the minister contemplated resignation.

Whether or not the escort fleet possessed modern equipment had become irrelevant. What really mattered was that there was a disgruntled seagoing element that believed the fleet was substandard and, despite Nelles's powerful evidence to the contrary, Macdonald was influenced by Connolly's interpretation of their cause. Moreover, impressing the importance of the situation upon the minister, Connolly had emphasized that the "whole business will get to the men at sea.... What will they say if no effective action is taken?... Drastic action is *expected*.... If it does not come many ... will be let down." Images of discontented sailors, their unhappy relatives and vengeful voters gave Macdonald good reason for concern. After all, the perception of incompetence was just as dangerous to his political career as a situation based on fact. However, having found a way to remove Nelles without attracting outside curiosities, Connolly had managed to slip an ace up the minister's sleeve.[46]

Intended to save the minister, Connolly's plan was to transfer Nelles overseas under the guise of supervising the RCN's contribution to the upcoming invasion of Europe. Had the so-called "equipment situation" become public knowledge, as Connolly believed it inevitably would, Macdonald would have spun the transfer by claiming that he had actually fired Nelles. Whether this Machiavellian plan would have fooled anyone is speculation, but what it shows is that Nelles's removal was both a smokescreen and a political execution, designed in its entirety to make him the scapegoat in any future scandal.[47] Despite Brand's accusations, therefore, Jones's meddling was not an essential factor in the actual decision to replace Nelles. In fact, Connolly had organized the transfer so quickly that the usually astute Jones was caught totally off-guard by the news that he had just become CNS. "Oh no! I'm down here for a meeting of the Canada–United States Defence Board — I'm running around in circles," Jones told a journalist who had tracked him down in Washington, adding, "I can't comment on these changes until I've had a chance to talk things over with the minister."[48]

Brand was also wrong to place Jones at the centre of what he called the "skids under Nelles party," or the "underground movement." Although Jones took advantage of their handiwork, other officers — who were either disciples of the reserve discrimination campaign or supporters of the modernization complaints — had long been circumventing Nelles in an attempt to capture Macdonald's attention. As a result, Jones's interference simply formed part of this larger tapestry. While the CNS's removal was serving a political agenda, it is hard to believe that Nelles could have survived much longer with so many groups undermining his authority; the more so because their collective efforts had led Macdonald to conclude that Nelles did not have "the power, the personality [or] the respect of his officers."[49] Perhaps it was time for a change, as Nelles's relaxed demeanour and lenient style had not quelled the disgruntled elements in the navy. In contrast, Jones would keep a tight rein on the service, and there were few naval officers who would dare challenge his autocratic control.

Jones, unlike Nelles, was a shrewd administrator who knew how to work with politicians and felt comfortable in their world. But there was a politician who felt uncomfortable around him: the prime minister once wrote in his diary that "Jones is a type which should be dismissed from the service." For Mackenzie King, there seemed to be two sides to this enigmatic personality. When it came to dealing with politicians, Jones was described by King as "a very pleasant fellow," but his attitude towards naval personnel was "much more a disciplinary than is really necessary.... I saw several evidences of his quick temper which discloses anything but a fine nature."[50] Nor was the prime minister alone in his assessment, as it seemed that Jones's political masters got Dr. Jekyll, while others in the navy felt that they had to contend with Mr. Hyde.

A purge of the officer corps left little doubt that things were going to be different during Jones's watch. As soon as he became CNS, plans were laid to dismiss from the navy more than twenty-five retired RN officers who were living in Canada and had been taken into the RCN at the start of the war. Nor were they the only ones, as scores of Royal Canadian Naval Reserve (RCNR) officers — men who had had merchant marine experience prior to their enlistment — were also targeted for release. Moreover, to keep it secret, the American naval attaché in Ottawa reported to his superiors that the RCN had organized these "forced retirements" to be "camouflaged ... in piecemeal groups, rather than in any considerable number at one time, this to avoid repercussions from Parliament and the press."[51]

Although one officer stated that Jones had once "said that no Reserve officer would take command as long as he was around,"[52] his decision to purge the RCNR was based on a legitimate desire to rid the navy of troublemakers. For instance, while most NRs were excellent officers who had filled a real void earlier in the war, Jones had had to deal with a number of complaints while he was COAC from "responsible citizens" of Halifax regarding "excessive drinking by some Naval Officers," which was apparently "assuming mob proportions." It is doubtful that NRs were the only ones drinking to excess, and at the time, Jones defended his officers. In private correspondence with Macdonald, however, he hinted that there was a small faction of NRs who were behaving in an unruly fashion.[53] Two years later, he would have none of it while he was running the navy.

Although replacing "inefficient" officers could be easily justified, releasing the individuals with RN backgrounds was more problematic. This group consisted of professional, experienced and often high-ranking men whose only sin was to have been RN officers prior to joining the RCN at the onset of the war. As with others, the first of the five British captains released from the service, Massey Goolden, was extremely bitter about his forced retirement:

> They are glad to be rid of me. I know them so well, their methods, likes and dislikes, their real inferiority complex (I speak of the most senior [Canadian] officers only) and their policy of using the RN as long as it suits their suds and does not interfere with their own ambitions. No two senior officers trust each other, they have

less loyalty among themselves than they have from us if only they could see that and not be always under the impression that we want to usurp their jobs ... how can the service function smoothly and efficiently with GC [Jones] LM [Murray] RR [Reid] and that despicable creature VB [Brodeur] intriguing and jockeying for their own suds.... Most of the pully-hauley work is even now being done by RN (ret) [retired] officers.[54]

Given that Jones had once observed that "this officer carries out his duties to the very best of his ability at all times," and later that he was being released "through no fault of his own," it is understandable why Goolden felt so betrayed. But while many different excuses — such as "clashes of temperament with [Canadian] officers" or that "all the old fellows are returning to their farms in England" — were used to justify the purge, Jones had his own nationalistic agenda for authorizing the dismissals.[55]

Unlike many of his permanent force colleagues, Jones was a staunch nationalist who was unwilling to copy RN mannerisms and ideals. Some suspected that his anglophobia was the product of an unpleasant experience with the RN during his interwar training, as the CNS was "quite bitter regarding the continued attitude of lofty superiority on the part of the British Navy towards the Canadian Navy."[56] While Jones may have disliked how the RN treated Canadians, he was grateful to the retired British officers who served with the RCN. As the war progressed, however, he thought that younger Canadian officers should be given the chance to prove themselves in positions of responsibility. Consequently, the new CNS's decision to replace British officers wherever possible represented the first step in his desire to further "Canadianize" the service. But before he could continue with his aim of distancing the RCN from the parent service, Jones had to focus on stabilizing the situation in Ottawa.

Two months of intense infighting had left NSHQ in a state of chaos and so the CNS's first real challenge was to restore Macdonald's confidence in the navy. To facilitate this, Jones immediately authorized a new administrative body called the Deputy Minister's Advisory Committee (DMAC), designed to streamline the channels of communication between Macdonald and his advisors. This organization, which was to consist of every member of the Naval Board except the CNS and the minister, allowed Jones to avoid one of the key mistakes Nelles had made. For example, during the confrontation, Nelles had stressed to Macdonald that "it was my particular care to keep you informed of every conceivable thing or happening, even to things that are of no consequence." This was true, but by doing so Macdonald suffered from an overabundance of information that made it difficult for him to separate the wheat from the chaff. By harvesting staff proposals, therefore, the DMAC ensured that only vital issues would be passed on to Macdonald for consideration.[57]

Jones's political astuteness also helped to alleviate the minister's anxiety over reserve officers' complaints of discrimination at the hands of the permanent force. Believing that the issue was largely artificial and the product of a small but vocal element, Jones did not agree with Connolly's plan to quell the apparent dissatisfaction by giving the reservists special representation on the Naval Board, but nor he did not block the move. His decision not to resist Connolly and Macdonald on what he considered a valueless board position was undoubtedly the right one. Once he learned that the disgruntled reservists had greeted the appointment of the Chief Staff Officer Reserves with "great satisfaction," the minister lost interest in the subject.[58]

The same was true also for modernization, and it could be argued that Jones was reaping the benefits of what Nelles had sown. The seeds for recovery already had been planted throughout 1943, and by the time of Nelles's dismissal 70 per cent of the corvettes had either been modernized or were in the process of being upgraded. By May 1944 another 13 per cent were allocated to the shipyards, at which time Jones promptly announced that the corvettes' modernization crisis was over. In reality, the CNS was just telling the minister what he wanted to hear. While helping him become CNS, the political battle over modernization had been fought one year after the actual operational crisis. It was an operationally stale but politically tender matter, and Jones knew it. In fact, it should never have become an issue in the first place.

One of the major reasons that the RN had been able to upgrade was the RCN's willingness to cover the Allies' operational demands throughout 1942. Therefore, the RCN's most senior engineer, Rear-Admiral G.L.

Stephens, was not too far off the mark in his assessment that "we have been straining every nerve to keep our ships running and provide escorts, [while the] Admiralty have kept their ships at home and modernized them." Put another way, the Canadians were dependent on supplies of British equipment, so there was little chance of fully modernizing the fleet throughout 1942 because the RN had naturally given priority to its own ships. When the RCN finally began upgrading in early 1943, Nelles's three-pronged plan — which included a short-term solution of asking for British assistance, a mid-term reorganization of the existing east coast refit structure, as well as a long-term proposal to build more shipyards — obviously achieved miracles. Most of the fleet was upgraded in less than a year.[59] More importantly, with the arrival in large numbers of the River-class frigates, Jones could give Macdonald the hard truth in May 1944, that "the fact must be faced that the Corvette, which has given excellent performance in the Battle of Atlantic, must now be regarded as superceded by modern ships."[60]

The state of the fleet's training system had also been a key issue. It, too, had improved throughout 1943, but Jones wanted to make it even more effective. Ever since he had been COAC, Jones saw the RCN's inadequate training facilities as one of the most serious impediments to efficiency. When the British decided early in 1944 to abandon their training base in Bermuda, he was quick to apply pressure on Macdonald to take it over. Macdonald did so, and once cabinet approval was obtained, the RCN finally possessed a first-rate warm-weather base.[61]

By the spring of 1944, Macdonald could rest easy. From his perspective, Jones had exorcised the ghosts of 1943. Even though Macdonald's original fears were largely apparitions in there own right, Jones ensured that the spectre of a parliamentary inquiry into the state of the fleet's equipment would no longer haunt the minister. More than any other factor, therefore, it was Jones's early actions as CNS that caused the adversarial atmosphere at NSHQ to finally fade away. This was important. Without a healthy relationship between the minister and his naval advisors, there was little chance that the headquarters would function properly. But there was another reason why Jones, who became a vice-admiral in early May, wanted Macdonald to focus on the RCN's future rather than rehashing its past.

Like his predecessor, Jones sought more than just an escort force — which consisted of smaller vessels such as the corvettes and minesweepers — by the end of the war. Getting the government's permission to acquire larger warships for a balanced postwar fleet had never been easy. In fact, it was only through some brilliant politicking of his own that Nelles got the ball rolling at the first Quebec Conference in August 1943, when he managed to secure cruisers, fleet destroyers and eventually escort aircraft carriers from the British.[62] Discussions over the summer of 1944 regarding the RCN's contribution to the Pacific war offered Jones his chance to mould the postwar navy. The problem was that he faced a prime minister who was not only cost-conscious and noncommittal but also angry that Nelles had successfully outmanoeuvred him. Overcoming King's anticipated resistance to his plans for both the Pacific war and the post-hostilities navy would prove a formidable test of Jones's political skills.

At the 12 July meeting of the Naval Board, Macdonald rejected a plan to create a sizable Pacific Fleet of over 100 ships that would operate with British forces. He was right to be cautious. This paper fleet, which would form the basis of what Jones wanted to sell to the government, was not what it seemed. Originally presented to the naval staff in a 28 June memo by the Director of Plans, this proposal was actually a carbon copy of one that the Admiralty's Military Branch had sent to Nelles, now serving as head of the Canadian Naval Mission Overseas (CNMO) in the United Kingdom. As a result, when Jones confirmed the Canadian modification to these figures, which was to add six fleet destroyers and possibly replace the escort carriers with two light fleet carriers, he was in fact tacitly approving a British request that would not be sent officially for another three weeks. There was more. The naval staff also appeared cautious by placing a limit on the number of personnel that would be sent to the Pacific. In reality, they were being clever: the ceiling of 25,000 represented only the seagoing personnel. Once the estimated 40,800 shore-support personnel were factored into the equation, the naval staff was actually proposing that 70 per cent of the RCN's total strength should be used in the Pacific, indicating that there was a large hidden attic above this house of cards' so-called "ceiling." Coincidentally, this figure matched British projections that also called for the RN to send 70 per cent of its fleet to the Far East.[63]

When the final version of the British proposal was brought to Macdonald's attention, he correctly predicted that it would never get past King, and so argued that allocating 50 per cent of the RCN's total strength was a more realistic target. Jones, however, pushed for the original estimate, and in late August he sent a cryptic message to Nelles indicating that the political winds were favourable, albeit "unlikely to exceed seventy percent of present total." Although King made it clear three days later that he would not accept large military commitments at the upcoming Quebec Conference on Pacific strategy, Jones never told the CNMO as much. His failure to do so was unfair to Nelles. As CNMO, Nelles was the key liaison between the RCN and RN, so he would later look foolish when the government cut the navy's figures, but Jones's actions were not meant to be malicious. In fact, Jones would assure the British at Quebec that he agreed with their proposal, which in turn solicited a promise from the First Sea Lord that he would "be as helpful as possible [and] will do whatever we want."[64] Moreover, the CNS advocated a 70 per cent commitment level at the 13 September cabinet meeting, and to King's chagrin, "Jones was seeking to work in an extra aircraft carrier."[65]

Despite intense pressure from Macdonald and the other defence ministers, King remained steadfast in his desire to send only a token force to the Pacific. Worried that the navy's plans were foundering, Jones pitched a smaller fleet to Cabinet in early October. What happened next is highly suspicious. Having returned to Ottawa after commanding the Canadian-crewed escort carrier HMS *Nabob*, Nelson Lay went to see King, and by doing so put him in a difficult position. "Matters are being focused to the point where Nelson may be told ultimately that it is his uncle who is responsible for not permitting the air carrier side of the navy," King wrote in his diary on 9 October 1944, after which he concluded, "I must leave the cabinet itself to decide what is to be done...."

This was exactly what Jones and Macdonald wanted, as it was King who represented the main opposition to their plans. With King abstaining, the vote on the navy's commitment level in the Pacific was carried in Cabinet two days later. Although it cannot be proven that Jones had used Lay as he had done in the spring of 1943, it is interesting that the CNS told Connolly that he had personally just "saved the navy." On the following day, Jones modified his view by noting that "a Minister alone could do it ... a service man, no matter how hard he tried could not *sell* the proposition."[66] The truth rested between these two extremes.

Macdonald and Jones were a formidable team, and the fleet that Cabinet approved represented a significant victory for the navy. Although it was approximately half the original size, the loss of fifty-three escort vessels was inconsequential compared to what had been gained. All of the larger units were earmarked for the Pacific, and it was agreed that the RCN should acquire two light fleet carriers and eight Crescent-class destroyers from the British. Jones's primary goal had been to create an exclusively Canadian task force, and he finally was being given the ships to do it. But while Macdonald and Jones were "greatly pleased" with their achievement, the British were not.[67]

It was always the RN's hope that the RCN would operate with their forces in the southeast Pacific, and both Jones and Macdonald had aggressively pushed this agenda to King. Eventually realizing that the prime minister would never yield on what he considered an imperial escapade to recapture British colonies, Jones recommended that Macdonald drop the matter and acquiesce to northern Pacific operations.[68] Politically, this was a wise choice — especially since King was both angry at and suspicious of the navy's obstinacy — but the Admiralty was confused by a decision that was "not as understood at Quebec." Perhaps feeling a little betrayed, they hinted that the transfer of the carriers and fleet destroyers was now in jeopardy.[69]

King's attitude had forced Jones and Macdonald to make tough choices, and both men found themselves in an awkward situation. In order to acquire the carriers and destroyers, they needed the RN officially to offer them to the Canadian government, after which King and the cabinet would formally have to accept them. The stumbling block was the RN's rider on southeast Pacific operations, which of course was at cross-purposes with King's stated policy. Caught between the prime minister's wishes and the RN's stipulation, Jones and Macdonald decided that they would overcome King's resistance first and worry about the Admiralty later. Consequently, the resulting communication blackout with the British was largely their own fault, as repeated pleas from Nelles for updates were regularly ignored. That left the RN with an uneasy feeling, yet despite his efforts to get solid answers from NSHQ, it was Nelles who paid the price. Although Jones had indicated to the CNMO in late August that the RCN would likely contribute a large fleet capable of southeast Pacific operations, the prime minister was told through Lay that it actually was Nelles who was responsible for the drive to serve in this area. This diverted attention away from Jones and Macdonald, as King was presented with a new target through which he could direct his anger towards the navy's shenanigans over its Pacific policy. Believing he had come home to clarify the RCN's position, Nelles soon discovered that he was being forced into retirement.[70] Once again the victim of a political agenda, Nelles left the navy in January 1945, while Jones and Macdonald traveled overseas to repair the damage that King's interference had caused to the negotiations with Admiralty.

Having learned in late November that the Admiralty had placed the transfer of the carriers and Crescents before the British cabinet, Jones believed that the discussions with the RN would not be as difficult as first thought. The problem was that, while Jones and Macdonald were in transit to the UK, the Admiralty reverted to their previous position. Telling Macdonald that this was yet another example of "perfidious Albion," Jones was certain that they had walked into a British trap designed to put the minister on the spot. Whether real or imagined, this incident only served to excite the CNS's anglophobia. However, realizing that the Canadian cabinet would never accept the RN's conditions, he used his political savvy to save the deal. Despite his personal feelings towards the RN, he wanted the carriers and Crescents, and was willing to do whatever it took to acquire them under Canadian terms. In order to foster a sense of kinship with the British, the CNS even was willing to adopt their vernacular because, as he told Connolly, "our accent probably annoys them as much as theirs does us." After a series of tense negotiations, the British finally yielded — and, had Macdonald had his way, Jones would have received "the VC [Victoria Cross] for work beyond the call of duty."[71]

Although the war would be over by the time these ships were in RCN hands, Jones still had ambitious plans for their employment. According to his view of the future, the RCN would be organized into a task force of light fleet carriers, cruisers, and two destroyer flotillas with a personnel level of 20,000 men. Moreover, believing that the RCN's function in the postwar world would revolve around hemispheric defence, Jones advocated closer ties with the USN rather than the RN. He also warned that the Soviet Union represented the next great threat to Canada's security.[72] Unfortunately, his navy never saw the light of day. In large part, this was due to post-hostilities cutbacks, but the admiral's personal ambition also played a role in undermining his own achievements.

Throughout his two years as CNS, Jones ruled the navy's administration with an iron fist. Unlike his predecessor, who valued the role of the Naval Board as the minister's advisory body, Jones disdained the committee system and subsequently created an unofficial organization that restricted the board members' ability to present ideas to Macdonald. Breaking with protocol, the CNS had participated in DMAC meetings, and by doing so turned it into a Naval Board without a minister. As such, the actual Naval Board was only convened sporadically and, having become a rubber stamp, its primary function was to seek the Minister's approval for DMAC decisions regarding naval staff proposals. For his part, Macdonald accepted Jones's administration, especially since fewer Naval Board meetings meant that he could devote more time to cabinet affairs. This setup gave the CNS considerable power, but it worked reasonably well because Jones never abused the Minister's trust.[73] The same cannot be said for his relationship with Douglas Abbott after he took over the naval portfolio in April 1945.

Within weeks of assuming his new cabinet post, the inexperienced naval minister had to contend with the VE-Day riots in Halifax. Angry that the city's liquor stores and drinking establishments were closed, citizens and sailors alike got carried away while celebrating Germany's defeat. Characterized by looting and acts of lewdness, the riot was a public-relations disaster, with most of the blame falling upon the Commander-in-Chief Canadian Northwest Atlantic (C-in-C CNA), Rear-Admiral Murray. Naturally, Murray understood that he had to accept responsibility for the actions of his subordinates, but he was also concerned that another factor had led to his dismissal. Jones had usurped the commander-in-chief appointment on 12 May 1945; worried that the riots were being used as a means to finally settle their longstanding feud, Murray made an impassioned plea that he only wanted "to finish up this war cleanly at sea, [and] I am not gunning for your job, now or later." While robbing Murray of the distinction of being the only Canadian to command an operational theatre,[74] Jones's actions indicate that he was actually more interested in personally containing the damage that the riots had caused to the navy's reputation.[75] Nevertheless, Jones's decision not to replace Murray immediately with another officer made him a powerful admiral, and there was more to come.

Spending most of his time in Halifax, Jones designated the Assistant Chief of the Naval Staff, Commodore H.G. DeWolf, his point man in Ottawa. Although his title was changed unofficially to Acting CNS, DeWolf lacked the recognized authority to maintain the routine at NSHQ because Jones had left the position of VCNS vacant when he became CNS. References to the "CNS" being "directed" to take action or to contact Jones on various issues by the officers on the DMAC provide testimonial to DeWolf's conundrum. Moreover, since the Naval Board was never convened after June 1945, DeWolf did not have an effective link to the Minister and often was forced to rely on long-distance communications to get Jones's approval. This led to an administrative meltdown at NSHQ, which was described by the American naval attaché as follows:

> Naval Service Headquarters is in a state of confusion.… Vice Admiral Jones has spent nearly all of his time at Halifax.… Mr. Douglas Abbott has devoted about one day a week to his office at NSHQ and has spent the remainder of his time indulging in political manipulations and in other matters. The result has been, with no responsible head functioning at Naval Service Headquarters, senior officers on duty here have remained in a state of confusion with no idea as to the policy of the Canadian Navy, the reason principally because no policy has apparently been formed. The result is that Naval Service Headquarters are beginning to lose the best of their officers through resignation.[76]

Although Jones abolished the C-in-C CNA position and then appointed Rear-Admiral Cuthbert Taylor as COAC in September, he continued to fixate on Halifax. This was an important issue, but with neither a VCNS nor a Naval Board, nor by this point a fully functional DMAC, the naval staff was not receiving sufficient direction. As such, the trouble it had coping with governmental policies on demobilization — not to mention reduced spending — resulted in much instability. It is unfortunate, therefore, that an admiral with such grand plans for the postwar service had overextended his reach, and in so doing set the navy on a rudderless course that would not be adjusted until his successor reestablished the Naval Board's bearing in February 1946.

Perhaps the ultimate tragedy was that Jones's health could not compete with his personal ambition and hectic schedule. On 8 February 1946, the Carleton Coroner announced that Jones's hypertension had caused a massive heart attack. For at least one naval officer the diagnosis was more basic: Jones had simply worked himself to death at the age of fifty.[77]

The only CNS to die in office, Jones represented both the best and the worst that the RCN's second generation of officers had to offer. Possessing a healthy dose of ambition and industriousness from the start of his career, Jones soon discovered that he could play the political game better than others, which gave him a tremendous edge in a highly competitive service. A product of his environment, Jones became an ardent careerist whose demeanour, natural ability and acumen allowed him to advance quickly. Rightly or wrongly, he further refined his skills by conducting a whispering campaign against Nelles throughout 1943, and as CNS he created an organization that gave him unprecedented powers and control over the navy. Such activities sullied his reputation with many in the service, but it would be a mistake to assume that his politicking always was detrimental. Jones was a shrewd, hard-working administrator whose understanding of the political world allowed him to advance an impressive plan for a truly Canadian postwar task force. Had it not been for his excessive personal ambition, Jones would have been remembered as one of the best administrators in the naval service, determined to finish the balanced fleet that Nelles had started. Instead, he was a cryptic and complex man who left the navy a mixed legacy. Providing a rare glimpse into his inner thinking, Jones once stated that he had three maxims:

> "External vigilance is the price of safety."
> "The Lord is on the side of the strong battalions."
> "Nothing matters but victory."[78]

This is a good epitaph for Jones. The problem is determining whether these words summarize his attitude towards his own career, or if they were directed at his desire to see the service mature into a blue-water navy that would protect Canadian interests. The answer, it would seem, is that it was a little of both.

NOTES

1   Massey Goolden Diary, 16 January 1944, Directorate of History and Heritage (DHH), Biog G; Eric Brand Diary, November 1943, DHH, Brand Papers, 81/145.

2   Lamb, *The Corvette Navy*, 136. [Complete references for commonly cited secondary sources are included in the bibliography.]

3   Interview with Lieutenant-Commander D.A.J. Higgs by Hal Lawrence, DHH, Biog H.

4   Office of Director of Public Information, Commodore George C Jones (career summary) 17 July 1941, DHH, Biog J.

5   Higgs interview.

6   Goolden Diary, 24 October 1943; Gow, *Alongside*, 19, 50; K.F. Adams Memoir, DHH, 89/19, 42; Narrative Summary of Interviews by Hal Lawrence, Lieutenant-Commander A.A. Beveridge interview, DHH, 90/86; Interview with Admiral Collins by William Glover, 4 February 1992, Victoria, BC and Interview with John Wade by William Glover, 4 February 1992, Victoria BC, DHH, Glover Papers, 97/8; Interview with Angus G. Boulton by Hal Lawrence, DHH, Biog B; Goolden diary, 24 October 1943; Katherine Roberts to Roger Sarty, 19 December 1991, DHH, Jones file, Biog J.

7   *Sea Breezes*, December 1914, I:1, 6: and June 1921, II:3, 1–2; Commodore W. Hose to H. Steele, 15 April 1921, Library and Archives Canada (LAC), NPRC, 0-37330; Gow, *Alongside*, 19.

8   Office of Director of Public Information, Commodore George C Jones (career summary) 17 July 1941, DHH, Biog J; V.G. Brodeur interview, "In the Beginning," in *Salty Dips* (6), 44; *Jane's Fighting Ships, 1919*, 72, 105, 138, 139.

9   *Sea Breezes*, June 1921, II:3, 1; Macpherson and Burgess, *The Ships of Canada's Naval Forces, 1910–1993*, 190–203; RNCC (1911–1922) Class List, 1 March 1968, DHH.

10 Hose to Minister, 1924, Jones personnel file.

11 Lieutenant V.G. Brodeur, "Present RCN Naval Organization," [nd, circa 1922] DHH, Brodeur Papers, 79/19, Folder 2.

12 Milner, *North Atlantic Run*, 93; Lund, "Rise and Fall of the RCN," 33–37.

13 Agnew appointment notification to HMCS *Patrician*, 17 August 1921; Hose memo, 20 July 1920; Agnew to Hose, 27 July 1920, LAC, NPRC, O-1290, Agnew personnel file.

14 Appointment List, Jones, Murray, and Agnew personnel files, LAC, NPRC; *RCN Navy List*: January 1917, September 1917, January 1918, May 1918, June 1918, March 1919, June 1928; Jones to Naval Secretary, 4 August 1924, Jones personnel file. *Sea Breezes*, December 1917, I:4, 4; Murray to Commanding Officer, HMCS *Aurora*, 3 November 1920 and other various correspondence on Murray personnel file. Various correspondences on Agnew personnel file. I am grateful to Bill Glover for drawing my attention to the fact it was Agnew who had surpassed Jones on the naval list.

15 The best academic account on Canada's naval defence in the interwar era remains Sarty, *The Maritime Defence of Canada*. For an excellent summary of relations between officers in this period see Lund, "Rise and Fall of the RCN," particularly chapter 1; German, *The Sea is at our Gates*, 59–61; Office of Director of Public Information, 17 July 1941, DHH, Jones file. Gow, *Alongside*, 19; Katherine Roberts to Roger Sarty, 19 December 1991, DHH, Jones file.

16 Hose to Minister, 15 December 1933; proposed officer appointments May 1931–June 1933; Murray Appointment List, Murray personnel file; Jones Appointment List, Jones personnel file. Hose left little doubt as to who was ahead when he wrote in December 1933 that Murray "is the senior of the two Commanders 'D' by one place in the Naval List, [even though] the actual dates of seniority being the same."

17 S206, 29 December 1933 and 31 October 1934, Murray personnel file.

18 Lund, "Rise and Fall of the RCN," 36.

19 Lay to Marc Milner, 8 October 1981, LAC, Lay Papers, MG30E420, vol. 1–16; Milner, *North Atlantic Run*, 93; Captain Eric S. Brand, Interview by E.C. Russel, 22 February 1967, DHH, Brand Papers, 84/145, Vol. 7, 6.

20 Jones and Murray personnel files. Officially, Jones and Murray were cordial in their exchanges, but it was obvious that their dislike for each other was growing.

21 Higgs interview; Jones (career summary) 17 July 1941, DHH, Jones file.

22 German, *The Sea is at Our Gates*, 92.

23 "Board of Inquiry into the collision between HMCS *Ottawa* and Tug *Bonsurf*," 15 April 1940, LAC, RG 24, vol. 11, 106; Boulton interview, 10–11; "Jetty Jones," September 1969, DHH, Biog J; Interview with Commodore R.I. Hendy by Hal Lawrence. DHH, Biog H; Interview with Rear-Admiral H.N. Lay by Hal Lawrence, DHH, Biog L; various sailing schedules, DHH, 81/520/8000, box 76, file 1.

24 V.G. Brodeur, "In the Beginning," *Salty Dips* (6), 58.

25 Walter Gilhooly (Director of Naval Information) to DSSD, 22 December 1941, and NSHQ fleet signal, 22 December 1941, Jones personnel file. Lay interview by Lawrence; Lay interview by Mark Yeo, LAC, Lay Papers, MG 31E420.

26 *Niobe* newsletter, no. 6, 1 November 1942, in *Salty Dips* (4), 19; NSHQ to FONF, Naval Message, 31 July 1942, Murray personal file; Appointment List, 25 September 1942, Reid personnel file; Douglas, Sarty and Whitby, *No Higher Purpose*, 537–538.

27 Pennington's comments recorded in Goolden Diary, 28 October 1942.

28 William Slater to R.C. Hayden, 14 October 1959, DHH, Jones file, Biog J.

29 Lay to Milner, 8 October 1981, Lay Papers, vol. 1.

30 J.J. Connolly to Edward Connolly, 15 January 1944, LAC, J.J. Connolly Papers, MG32C71, vol. 1; Halifax Telephone Directory, 1925–1933, National Library of Canada; Interview with Vice-Admiral D.A. Collins by Hal Lawrence, DHH, Biog C, 36. Lay interview by Lawrence, DHH.

31 Lay, *Memoirs of a Mariner*, 148.

32 King Diary, 29 March 1943, DHH, 83/530, 185: 231; King Diary, 05 April 1943, DHH, 83/530, 185: 255.

33 Naval Board Minutes, February 1942–April 1945, DHH, 81/520/1000-100/2. Macdonald's sudden interest in naval affairs can be detected in his much improved attendance record at Naval Board meetings from this time onwards; Jones minute note, 26 January 1945, Connolly Papers, vol. 3–10.

34 Jones to Nelles, minute on Lay to Jones, 22 March 1943, LAC, RG 24, vol. 3996, NSS 1057-1-35, Vol.1.

35 Lund, "Rise and Fall of the RCN," 36.

36 As quoted in Whitby, "Matelots, Martinets, and Mutineers," 89.

37 Strange to Connolly, "Certain Conversations with Senior RN officers at Londonderry," [Strange memo], 13–15 July 1943, Connolly Papers, Vol. 3. Other accounts on the effect that the lack of modern equipment had on the fleet include: Douglas, Sarty and Whitby, *No Higher Purpose*; Douglas, "Conflict and Innovation"; Milner, *North Atlantic Run* and *U-boat Hunters*; Zimmerman, *The Great Naval Battle of Ottawa*; and Sarty, *Canada and the Battle of the Atlantic.*

38 Nelles to Macdonald, 26 November 1943, Public Archives of Nova Scotia, Macdonald Papers, MG2, F276/39; Strange to Adams, 21 September 1943, DHH, E.C. Russel Papers, 91/298; Interview with Mr. John Connolly by Lieutenant-Commander T.R. Daly, 26 January 1945, DHH, 1700-196/96D.

39 NOIC St. John's War Diary, FONF Monthly ROP, October 1943, DHH, 81/520 NSS 1000-5-20, vol. 4; Sydney Monthly Reports, DHH, 81/520 NSS 1000-5-21, vol. 2; *Stadacona* War Diary, DHH, 81/520 NS 1000-5-13, vol. 20; Jones personnel file; Connolly diary, 8 October 1943, Connolly Papers, vol. 2–6; Nelles to Macdonald, 26 November 1943, Macdonald Papers; FONF, Halifax War Diaries, August 1943, War Diaries, DHH.

40 Connolly Diary, 07 October 1943, Connolly Papers, Vol. 3; Connolly to Macdonald, 8 November 1943, Connolly Papers, Vol. 3, "Equipment on RCN ships part 1" [n.d., 1943]; Connolly to Ida Connolly, 9 October 1943, Connolly Papers, Vol. 1; Connolly to Macdonald, 9 October 1943, Macdonald Papers.

41 Connolly to Nelles, 10 November 1943, Macdonald Papers.

42 Simpson to Horton [n.d.], Connolly Papers, vol. 3; Jones to Nelles, 12 November 1943, Macdonald Papers; Griffiths to Nelles, 16

VICE-ADMIRAL GEORGE C. JONES

November 1943, Macdonald Papers; Johnstone to Nelles, 13 November 1943, Macdonald Papers; Connolly interview by Lieutenant-Commander Daly, 26 January 1945; Connolly to Nelles, 10 November 1943, Macdonald Papers; minute note, Jones to Connolly, on SCNO (L) to Secretary of Naval Board, 29 October 1943, DHH, 81/520 NSS 1000-5-35, vol. 1.

43 Goolden Diary, 24 October 1943, 11 December 1943; Brand interview; and Brand Diary, vol. 7, 27, 35–36.

44 In fact, only two weeks before receiving Strange's memo, Macdonald had attended a Naval Board meeting that discussed a report by Captain Edmund Johnstone, who stressed that these problems were "so urgent and of such vital importance ... that [the proposed] steps be taken at once to effect a radical change in the existing conditions." It is clear that the minister had forgotten about Johnstone's memo, as well as the July Naval Board meeting when it was discussed. After Nelles reminded him about its recommendations in November, Macdonald wrote a note to Connolly to "get this" report. See Mayne, "A Political Execution"; Naval Board Minutes, 27 July 1943, DHH; Nelles to Macdonald, 26 November 1943, Macdonald Papers.

45 Connolly to Macdonald, 30 November 1943, Connolly Papers, vol. 3.

46 Interview with Lieutenant-Commander Hill by J.J. Connolly, April 1943, Macdonald Papers.

47 Connolly to Macdonald, 30 November 1943, Connolly Papers, vol. 3.

48 Montreal *Gazette*, 15 January 1944.

49 Connolly Diary, 5 February 1945, Connolly Papers, vol. 2–8.

50 King Diary, 14 September and 19 October 1940, DHH, 83/530. Thanks to Roger Sarty for drawing my attention to King's October Diary entry.

51 List of RN officers on loan to RCN and RN (Retired) officers serving in RCN. DHH, 81/520 4000-100/14, Personnel A–Z (Prior 1950); Various Naval Lists, 1944, DHH; U.S. Naval Attaché report, 9 February 1944, US National Arcives and Record Administration (NARA), RG 38, Reg. 4303-I, File E-3-e.

52 Boulton interview, 7.

53 Jones to Macdonald, 8 June 1942, Macdonald Papers, F883/3; 6 June 1942, F883/4.

54 Goolden Diary, 26 May 1944.

55 Jones's minute on Mainguy to Jones, 24 January 1944, S206 (by Jones), 12 August 1942, Goolden personnel file; Goolden Diary, 26 May 1944; US Naval Attaché report, 9 February 1944, NARA, RG 38, Reg. 4303-I, File E-3-e.

56 *Ibid.*

57 Nelles to Macdonald, 27 November 1943, Macdonald Papers, F276/39; Naval Board meeting, 24 January 1944, DHH; DMAC, 28 and 31 January 1944, 3, 4 and 23 February 1944, DHH; "Miscellaneous Papers on the History of the RCN," Naval Historical Section, August 1960, DHH, 75/496; Connolly Diary, 12 September 1944, Connolly Papers, vol. 2–8.

58 As quoted in Connolly to Macdonald, 14 July 1944, Connolly Papers, Vol. 4:12; Jeffrey to GA Youle (Naval Historical Section), 9 December 1947, DHH, 81/520 HMCS *Bytown*, 8000, Vol.2.

59 Stephens to Nelles, 26 November 1943, Macdonald Papers, F276/37. See early confirmation of the success in "Minutes of Combined Canadian, United Kingdom and United States Committee to Examine Repair Problem for Warships and Merchant Vessels on the East Coast of Canada," 12 August 1943, DHH, Repair and Refits, 8780.

60 Naval Board Minutes, 14 February, 1 May, and 23 June 1944, DHH; Command of the Honourable Minister, Appointment Sheet, 9 May 1944, Jones personnel file; "The Modernization of Armament and Equipment," DHH, 8060.

61 See Milner, "HMCS *Somers Isle*."

62 See Sarty, "The Ghosts of Fisher and Jellicoe."

63 For a better understanding of the role that naval planners played in shaping the composition of the fleet see Douglas, "Conflict and Innovation in the Royal Canadian Navy."

64 Jones to Macdonald, 17 August 1944, LAC, RG24, vol. 5685, file 3-18; Connolly Diary, 16 September 1944, Connolly Papers, vol. 2; Jones to Nelles, 28 August 1944, DHH, CNMO files, 1650-1: Cabinet War Committee meetings, 31 August 1944, LAC, MG 26 J4; King Diary 1944, DHH; Tucker, *The Naval Service of Canada (II)*, 444, 466–67.

65 Cabinet War Cabinet Committee, 13 September 1944, LAC, MG 26 J4; King Diary 13 and 14 September 1944, DHH.

66 Connolly Diary, 12 and 13 October 1944, Connolly Papers, vol. 2.

67 Deputy Minister Advisory Committee, 8 September 1944; Naval Board Minutes, 18 September 1944, DHH; King Diary, 5 October 1944, DHH.

68 Sarty, "The Ghosts of Fisher and Jellicoe," 160–61.

69 12 October 1944, Connolly Diary. DOP to ACNS, 13 October 1944; CNMO to NSHQ, 16 October 1944, DHH, CNMO file, 1650-1.

70 King Diary, 9 October 1944, DHH; Nelles to NSHQ, 18 September 1944; Nelles to NSHQ, 2 October; NSHQ to Nelles, 4 October; Nelles to NSHQ, 5 October 1944; NSHQ to Nelles 13 October 1944, CNMO Files, DHH, 81/520 1650-1.

71 CNMO to NSHQ, 14 January 1945, DHH, CNMO files, 1650-1; Connolly Diary 18, 26, 28 January 1945, Connolly Papers, vol. 2–11.

72 Chief of Staff meeting minutes, 25 June 1945, LAC, RG 24, vol. 619, 1818-13; Jones to Major-General M. Pope, 4 January 1945, LAC, RG 24, vol. 8185, NSS 1818-2; U.S. Naval Attaché report, 3 August 1945, NARA, RG 38, Reg. 4303-I, File E-3-e; Eayrs, *In the Defence of Canada* (3), 327.

73 DMAC meetings 1-32, DHH; Naval Board minutes, DHH; Lay, *Memoirs of a Mariner*, 147–48.

74 I am grateful to Mike Whitby for pointing this out to me.

75 Lund, "The Rise and Fall of the RCN," 76.

76 Glenn Howell US Intelligence Report, 23 July 1945, DHH, 92/184, Folder 8, USNA RG 38, REG 23371.

77 Death Certificate, 27 February 1946, Jones personnel file; Naval Board minutes, February to July 1946, DHH; Lund, "Vice-Admiral H.T.W.Grant: Father of the Post War RCN," 193.

78 Connolly Diary, 27 January 1945, Connolly Papers, vol. 2.

Captain H.E. "Rastus" Reid

CHAPTER SIX

Vice-Admiral Howard Emmerson Reid and Vice-Admiral Harold Taylor Wood Grant: Forging the New "Canadian" Navy

Wilfred G.D. Lund

Vice-Admiral Harold Grant inspecting sailors on HMCS *Sioux* during the Korean conflict

The three Chiefs of the Naval Staff (CNS) who led the Royal Canadian Navy (RCN) during the first challenging decade of the postwar period were Vice-Admirals Howard Reid, Harold Grant and Rollo Mainguy. Their careers and activities reveal quite different personalities who, while having fairly similar naval backgrounds, took dramatically different approaches in "running the navy."

The history of the RCN may be described as sinusoidal, a series of abrupt ups and downs.[1] In September 1945, the historical path abruptly achieves an almost vertical downslope from the high wartime plateau. The primary characteristics of the post–Second World War period are instability and uncertainty. The RCN's ambitious plans to build two air-craft-carrier task groups to fight in the Pacific evaporated in the blasts of the atom bombs that suddenly ended the war. These plans were also a stratagem devised by Vice-Admiral Percy Nelles to ensure the survival of the RCN after the termination of hostilities. Nelles had ridden the tiger after the First World War, when Prime Minister Mackenzie King cut the navy to the point of extinction.[2] Nelles's "big-ship" navy plan survived the coup that ousted him, and it was continued by his successor, Vice-Admiral G.C. Jones, articulated in a policy paper, "The Continuing Royal Canadian Navy," that became the postwar planning blueprint.[3] The plan proved politically impractical.

As Canada's wartime military structure began to implode with demobilization, the spectre of the RCN's possible extinction re-emerged. The fear was well placed, as Mackenzie King had "smoked"[4] the RCN's big-ship navy ambitions and was determined to curb the reckless inclinations of the "Imperial navy" men and restore sanity to defence spending.[5] He ordered his newly appointed minister of National Defence, Douglas Abbott, to pare all three services to the bone.[6] Abbott focused firmly on demobilization and took no interest in postwar defence planning.[7] While Abbott announced optimistically that the RCN would possess a "good, workable little fleet [that] can easily be expanded if need be," the reality would be considerably different.[8]

The services now found themselves virtually excluded from policy development. The war was over and Mackenzie King cut them adrift in his determination "to get back to the Old Liberal principles of economy, reduction of taxation, anti-militarism."[9] This set the tone. The wartime coalition forged between the military and the Department of External Affairs shattered over the form of postwar policy. Peace presented External Affairs with the long-awaited opportunity to seize the reins. While the military wanted firm commitments, External Affairs demurred, and planning for postwar force levels became virtually impossible.[10] The services entered the period of the "interim force," wherein a deadline of 1 September 1947 was set, by which the forces were to be demobilized and stabilized. The navy's active fleet composition was set at a light fleet carrier, a cruiser and eight destroyers in commission with full peacetime complements, and a personnel ceiling of 10,000.[11] These numbers were entirely notional and "dictated by expediency rather than by strategic requirements or consideration of commitments which the RCN might be required to fulfil in connection with Hemispheric or Commonwealth defence."[12]

As Nelles predicted, the RCN was about to engage in another postwar struggle for survival.[13] By March 1946, 346 of 404 ships had been paid off and personnel reduced by 83 per cent — to 15,234 from 92,529 just one year before. These personnel were largely employed in decommissioning duties, and there were sufficient personnel to man only the carrier, HMCS *Warrior*, which was fitting out in Belfast. Even this could be accomplished solely by holding over a number of "hostilities-only" personnel. A second carrier, HMCS *Magnificent*, was being built in the UK. All other fleet units were non-operational in "care and maintenance." Many of these ships were in need of modernization or replacement.

The ceiling was soon to be cut to 7,500, and the navy would actually bottom at 6,800 on active strength. The permanent force numbered only 3,800, of whom 95 were officers,[14] and many were due to retire.[15] Few permanent-force officers, and virtually no ratings, had been recruited during hostilities. In fact, the RCN personnel structure had to be completely rebuilt, expanding 200 per cent to attain the 10,000 target. This number would prove to be 1,500 short, given the commitments. Owing to the shortage of trained personnel, the fleet itself had virtually ceased to function. With current projections, it would be capable of training only and no operations. As a consequence of inadequate funding, the navy was barely on life support.

The RCN was adrift in the doldrums of the interim-force period when G.C. Jones died in his bath on 8 February 1946. His long absences from Ottawa to deal personally with the politically sensitive issue of compensation for damage caused by sailors during the VE-Day riots in Halifax exacerbated the malaise. Jones had given little attention to the postwar plan.

The Naval Board went eight months without meeting.[16] The Naval Staff and Deputy Minister's Advisory Committee (DMAC) continued to function, but a certain lethargy crept into "A" Building on Cartier Square. A clubbish atmosphere prevailed where the secretaries served tea, and Buster — Captain Sam Worth's bulldog — had the run of the offices. In Jones's place, the Assistant Chief of the Naval Staff (ACNS), Commodore Harry DeWolf, supervised the day-to-day operations of the headquarters. That was his style, and DeWolf recalled Jones "as a great delegator of authority and he would rely on you to do the job and get it right. His mind was way up there [in high politics], not on the day-to-day problems of the navy."[17] With respect to Jones's legacy, DeWolf said, "I don't remember that he had any firm picture where the navy was going."[18] These were the circumstances of the RCN when Rear-Admiral Howard Emmerson Reid was suddenly and unexpectedly called to take over the watch.

"Rastus" Reid presented a stark contrast in style and personality to the enigmatic Jones.[19] He was born in Portage-du-Fort, Quebec, in 1895. At the age of fourteen years and eight months he was enrolled in the second term of cadets to attend the Royal Naval College of Canada (RNCC), which graduated in 1913.[20] The influence of the RNCC on Reid and his generation's cohort cannot be overstated. Until 1922, the RNCC was the cradle of the navy, and Commander A.E.A. Nixon, RCN, was mentor to the fledgling naval officers.[21] Nixon taught cadets the values of loyalty, self-discipline and persistence. He emphasized the Nelsonian credo of service above self and kindled a spirit of camaraderie in the "band of brothers."[22] Brooke Claxton was accurate in characterizing the RCN senior officers as "an extraordinarily homogeneous group," and it was for good reason.[23] Above all, Nixon instilled in the cadets a tenet preserved in the seamanship notebook of Cadet — later Rear-Admiral — Hugh Francis Pullen: "To be an officer you must be a seaman and to be a good officer you must be a gentleman."[24] Five of the six postwar CNS's graduated from the RNCC. They shared a common notion of the character of the RCN. This was tempered by the "lean years" of the 1920s and 1930s, when the tiny "family navy" struggled for survival.[25] The paramount objective of preserving the navy — its ships, customs and traditions — was passed from senior to junior as a sacred trust. Comprehending the depth of this commitment is vital to understanding the motivation of the officers who led the postwar navy.

Reid flourished at the RNCC. In spite of his youth and diminutive size, he was an aggressive hockey player described as "full of fire on the ice."[26] When Reid graduated, he went to the Royal Navy (RN) and embarked upon the traditional apprenticeship to learn his profession. He served in RN destroyers during the First World War and survived the sinking of HMS *Attack*.[27] Reid followed the normal pattern of alternating appointments between the RCN and RN during the interwar period. He qualified as an "old China hand," having served twice on the China Station, commanding the destroyer HMS *Sepoy* during his second tour. He also commanded the RCN destroyers *Patriot, Fraser* and *Skeena*.[28] While in command of *Skeena*, he precipitated one of the pre-war "incidents" by attempting to apply RN routines to noncomplying Canadian sailors. Nelson Lay, Reid's executive officer, interceded and the incident was quietly resolved and never reported, becoming just another "unmutiny" in the history of the RCN.[29] Reid was married at age thirty-eight in 1936 to Miss Edith Houston, daughter of a prominent Vancouver businessman. He was promoted to captain at the beginning of the Second World War, one of only four executive-branch officers at that rank, and appointed Commanding Officer Atlantic Coast (COAC) in Halifax. Reid held progressively important appointments, first as COAC, then Vice-Chief of the Naval Staff (VCNS) and finally Commodore Commanding the Newfoundland Escort Force (CCNF), and he was intimately involved with the wartime expansion of the RCN.

While COAC, Reid had a fractious confrontation with Rear-Admiral L.E. Holland, the British admiral commanding the Third Battle Squadron based in Halifax. The RN was inclined to treat the RCN as an adjunct squadron and Reid, no retiring violet, objected. A dispute arose between Reid and Holland over local command and control responsibilities.[30] Personal relations between the two men had previously been poisoned by Holland's derogatory remarks about Reid.[31] The dispute rose to the highest levels. On constitutional grounds, the Admiralty was obliged to accept a compromise offered by NSHQ and it directed Holland to remove his flag to a commissioned yacht, HMS *Seaborn*, in Halifax Harbour. As a result of this dispute, Nelles observed on Reid's personal report that he was "anti-British."[32]

That characterization was incomplete. While VCNS, then Commodore Reid represented the RCN as the Canadian naval member during the tough negotiations of the Permanent Joint Board on Defence (PJBD) to develop the Canada–United States defence plan, ABC-22. The Montreal meeting of the PJBD in mid-April 1941 was a "first-class row" later referred to as "the Montreal Disagreement."[33] There the Canadians bravely faced a frontal assault as the Americans demanded strategic control of Canadian forces. General Pope wrote, "Actually, it was largely a naval battle, with

Commander Forrest Sherman [USN] on the one side and 'Rastus' Reid on the other, firing broadsides at each other that would have commanded any man's respect."[34] In the end, the Canadians extracted an agreement from the Americans that military co-ordination would be on the basis of "mutual co-operation."

Reid was promoted to rear-admiral in December 1943 and served as the naval member of the Canadian Joint Staff in Washington until his appointment as the Chief of the Naval Staff in February 1946. He had never aspired to be CNS.[35] He had had a long, tiring war and was simply waiting out his time when Jones's death thrust greatness upon him. His mind was more on hunting and fishing, his favourite pursuits, than the challenges of building the postwar navy in a time of uncertainty and financial restraint. He took the appointment only until 1 September 1947, the end of the interim force. His private secretary, Lieutenant D.A. Collins, remarked that Reid had had administrative appointments during the war, but the role of CNS "wasn't something that his life had prepared him for; certainly he came into something he had no part in preparing."[36] Collins described him as "a real sailor's sailor, abrupt, intelligent, intelligently lazy, perhaps without — because he was no longer interested, really — a vision of what lay ahead for the navy in terms of what we were building for the future."[37]

Reid brought casualness to the office at a time when energy was needed and he delegated "to the point of laziness."[38] His presence and style reinforced the clubbish atmosphere at naval headquarters. He applied a simple, common-sense approach to resolving the important postwar decisions and he avoided stressful situations. The navy avoided the controversy with External Affairs that the other two services experienced because Reid had served with Lester Pearson in Washington and they were able to solve contentious issues over a drink.[39] Reid came to the office late, slept for an hour every afternoon, left early and never took a file home.[40] He spent a significant amount of time away from Ottawa, visiting naval reserve divisions. As he enjoyed poker, liquor, hunting and fishing, these visits allowed him to pursue all four activities abundantly. Canada was under liquor rationing at the time, and Collins commented that "Reid would spill more than the authorized ration on any day."[41]

Fortunately for the navy, the "benign" Reid had strong personalities to whom he could delegate the business of rebuilding.[42] Rear-Admiral Harold Grant was Chief of [Naval] Administration Services (CNAS) — the navy's comptroller — and would be Reid's successor. Grant had a reputation as a warrior and was a man of both vision and energy who was ready to shoulder the responsibility of leading the navy. Commodore DeWolf, also a future CNS, continued as ACNS. Captain Horatio Nelson Lay was Director of Plans. DeWolf and Lay had made important contributions during the war towards establishing a separate identity for the RCN within the alliance structure.[43]

That the fleet was incapable of operations and the personnel structure in disarray belies the fact that many activities were lined up to position the RCN for its postwar development. Lay orchestrated the reorganization of the Naval Board, and regular meetings were reconvened by Reid under the chairmanship of the minister. He also inaugurated "senior officers' meetings," which became informal caucus meetings where the RCN flag-rank officers could address major issues facing the navy.[44] Some junior officers did perceive this as no more than a forum for the RCN's old guard to make decisions without benefit of staff advice.[45] The Naval Secretariat, introduced during the war, was made permanent under the direction of the Naval Secretary.[46] Also, the wartime Naval Information Organization was retained "to familiarize the public with the national importance, growth, and activities of the RCN in the postwar era."[47] In the personnel branch, work had begun to establish new branches and trades to meet emerging technical and operational challenges.[48] On the tri-service level, studies were underway to reconcile the rank and trade structures for non-commissioned personnel and to develop a new integrated pay scheme.[49]

On another level, developments were transpiring that would reorient the RCN from the RN to the USN and also redefine its role. In the new Military Co-operation Committee (MCC), a subcommittee of the PJBD, there was discussion of a new threat.[50] The Americans advanced the argument that the Soviet Union was the emerging maritime threat through its submarine and long-range bomber capability.[51] These MCC talks led negotiations between the Canadian and American governments that resulted in joint defence co-operation after the war.[52] The

Canadian naval staff shifted its vision from that of a fleet structured for a general-purpose operations role towards an anti-submarine warfare (ASW) specialization. The new role would significantly affect both fleet and personnel structure.

Concurrently, senior officers in the electrical, supply, communications and naval aviation branches were beginning to look towards the USN for answers to professional problems.[53] Communicators would be the first off the mark to shift over to USN communications and tactical procedures, task group organization, and USN equipment in ships.[54] On the administrative level, the automatic promulgation of Admiralty General Messages (AGMs) was curtailed.[55] These activities demonstrate the sort of bifurcation emerging through competing influences that produced what might be called cultural confusion.

The Royal Navy's influence remained important. Both the executive and engineering branches continued to rely exclusively on the RN for their technical training and senior staff courses. The senior executive was particularly inclined to follow the RN's lead in personnel policy matters, uniforms and routines, but here there were inconsistencies.[56] The RN introduced welfare committees and other progressive initiatives to improve morale, but some of these were deemed too progressive by the RCN.[57] The RCN retained many RN routines appropriate for men inducted from British society for compulsory national service, but which were inappropriate in an all-volunteer service recruited from modern postwar Canada. Moreover, while the Naval Board fought to obtain better pay and accommodation to improve morale, they took some no-cost decisions that were the source of major dissatisfaction. For example, a decision with far-reaching ramifications was to remove "Canada" badges from the naval uniform.[58] As a result of the tumult caused by demobilization, underfunding and a whole spectrum of influences, the RCN was being challenged to reinvent itself.

Reid was little more than a spectator to these developments. He was angered by inadequate funding and he vented his frustration to the press, stating, "The United States Navy plans a postwar personnel of 500,000 men. We have 10,000. Our population is one-twelfth that of the United States. You can figure out for yourself the arithmetic."[59] Mackenzie King was incensed, and he directed Abbott to reprimand Reid.[60] Reid's situation was worsened because a staff error had underestimated personnel requirementsl, and 12,000 were actually required.[61] And he was unlikely to receive a sympathetic hearing after his public outburst. Meanwhile, the government's new plans anticipated more cost reductions, the reorganization of service headquarters and a new Minister of National Defence. On 12 December 1946, Brooke Claxton took on the ministry, with instructions from Mackenzie King that he was to reassert government control, integrate common activities of the services, and achieve "the utmost economy consistent with security."[62] With respect to the navy, the prime minister stated, "We should have a purely coastal defence."[63]

Abbott moved to Finance, and his budget-slashing reflected Mackenzie King's decision to promote his program of social legislation at the expense of defence.[64] This set the precedent that would govern strategic development in Canada during the postwar period. The government would fund social and other politically attractive programs, after which defence might receive consideration. From the budget allocated to the department, it would be determined how much defence could be bought, and the funds would be divided among the three services. National defence strategy was determined not by alliance commitments but by what the government in power felt it could afford after social programs (which won elections in Canada) had been funded. Dan Middlemiss summed it up as "what politics has proposed, economics has disposed."[65]

Claxton brought energy and direction to the office and a determination to "shake up" the department.[66] He established strategic objectives designed to reorient priorities to protect Canadian sovereignty and to co-operate with the Americans in the defence of North America.[67] The navy's role would be coastal defence and escort work against submarines.[68] In a war outside of Canada, the navy would be employed in escort operations as in the Second World War. For the RCN, strategy was to be reordered from an imperial to a North American orientation, and ASW was to replace the task-force concept. Also, North America would become the primary source for material acquisition, and co-ordination with United States forces became the priority. Claxton's direction shifted the balance in favour of the pro-American lobby in the RCN. In Collins's view, the navy's reorientation was complete by the early 1950s.[69]

While there was to be a major shift in strategy, Claxton's major initiatives were to reduce costs and integrate National Defence Headquarters (NDHQ) and the three services as far as possible. The navy was immediately affected by a reduction in ceiling to 7,500 personnel and fuel restrictions that further handicapped an already labouring training program. There was no money to build new accommodations or to improve service conditions. Claxton's shake-up of headquarters directly impacted Reid's staff. "Babbling Brooke," as the minister was named by the naval staff,[70] decided to move himself and the heads of services into the navy's "A" Building. Claxton recorded that he arrived at NSHQ on Monday morning, to be greeted by Reid, and that he advised the CNS that he was setting up office there. Reid gave him a warm welcome "in joining the Navy."[71] Space was found that Claxton said could be made satisfactory by moving a few "partitions." He recalled, "the navy brass fainted at the use of such a land lubberly [sic] word as partition. When they recovered they rose saluting in their quaint little way saying 'Bulkheads, sir, bulkheads.'"[72] Claxton noted, "[T]he Navy ... was glad to have me join them in their building; but little did they know what a viper they were giving welcome to."[73] Claxton soon concluded that the senior naval officers "were not overly in tune with Canadian national feeling," and he made it his personal mission to Canadianize the RCN.[74] He was, however, impressed with what he saw of the navy's efficiency during his first tour of the fleet and the "shockingly bad" accommodations and messing arrangements.[75]

Vice-Admiral Reid was assailed by this hurricane of change and hamstrung by lack of funding. The prevailing circumstances — particularly in the fleet, where morale was rock bottom — gave little encouragement. There was an incident in HMCS *Nootka* on the east coast in May 1947 and another in HMCS *Ontario* in August. On 1 September 1947, Reid retired. Little has been written about his tenure as CNS, and what has been written tends to trivialize his efforts and accomplishments.[76] Certainly, some criticism is deserved. Reid was brought into a job he didn't want, during a very difficult time for the navy. His challenge was to oversee a navy in transition from war to peace. The dominant themes of the period are underfunding and instability. He was asked to make bricks without straw. In his favour, Reid championed the plight of the sailors and spoke out publicly against government penury that contributed to unsatisfactory service conditions.[77] At the level of the naval staff and in the branches there was a lot of productive activity. Many good ideas about the future were germinating, fostering a feeling of optimism. Of Reid's tenure as CNS, Rear-Admiral John Charles observed, "you could say the period from 1946 to 1947, as far as the operational side of the navy is concerned, was rather gaunt. However, there was a hell of a lot going on about how to make it a better navy."[78]

Vice-Admiral Harold Taylor Wood Grant took command of the RCN on 1 September 1947, when it was at its lowest ebb. Grant was born in Halifax in 1899, the youngest of six children. His father, MacCallum Grant, a descendant of United Empire Loyalists, owned a thriving shipping business and was a powerful force in the Halifax business community and society.[79] Young Harold was brought up in the conservative, Scotch-Methodist tradition of loyalty, hard work and self-reliance.[80] The call to the sea came naturally. Armdale, the family home, built originally for Sir Charles Tupper, overlooked the Northwest Arm that was the Grant brothers' playground. His elder brother, John, joined the first term of cadets at the new RNCC in 1911.[81] Harold Grant followed with the fourth term in 1914, the same year that his father was appointed lieutenant-governor of Nova Scotia.[82]

Small and frail as a boy, Harold was often ill as a cadet, but he was bright, quick-witted and determined. His term mates described him as "perhaps the finest example of what grit and will can do."[83] Grant was a born fighter, and the descriptors "character" and "determination" feature frequently in performance reports.[84] He passed out of the RNCC with a first-class certificate in 1917, and he continued his training as a midshipman in RN big ships until the end of the First World War. He saw no action.

Grant's career between the wars followed the standard RCN model. He specialized as a navigator and attended the RN staff course. He served in battleships and in the movements section of the Commander-in-Chief (C-in-C) Atlantic Fleet.[85] He also served in staff positions at Naval Service Headquarters as Director of Plans, and later the Naval Reserves. Superior performance won him accelerated performance to commander by 1935.[86]

Prematurely grey and with a commanding presence, he built a reputation as a solid professional officer and gentleman of modesty, but with a wonderful sense of humour. He handled both officers and men easily and was very popular socially. In 1932, Grant married Christian Mitchell, ten years his junior and from another old Halifax family. "Christie" Grant, his "old girl," became a universal favourite in naval circles.[87] She called Harold her "mischief maker" because he enjoyed fun, a good party and could be counted on to lead the "run ashore."[88] He once received the "Displeasure of the Department," reprimanded for a skylark ashore.[89] The incident Grant referred to as "the Chester Hanging" merely added to his growing reputation.[90] Grant's assertiveness could be overbearing and once earned him a rebuke from then CNS Percy Nelles, who thought his rapid promotion might have gone to his head.[91] Nevertheless, Nelles gave him command of *Skeena* in 1938. He was appointed ashore as the chief of staff to Captain Reid, COAC, shortly after war was declared.

Grant served with exceptional distinction during the war and emerged as one of Canada's most decorated naval officers.[92] He was promoted to captain in 1940, and assumed the critical position of director of naval personnel at NSHQ. He supervised the initial rapid wartime expansion, but in 1942 he strongly recommended that growth be checked in order to consolidate training. He was overruled owing to the critical need for escorts.[93] He was Captain (D) in St. John's, Newfoundland, for barely six months when, in March 1943, he was appointed to command the old RN cruiser HMS *Diomede*. Three months later he was reappointed to command HMS *Enterprise*, another vintage cruiser. On 28 December 1943, *Enterprise*, with HMS *Glasgow* — although heavily outgunned — engaged a force of eleven German destroyers, sinking three and damaging others.[94] Grant was awarded an immediate Distinguished Service Order (DSO) and the victory made banner headlines in Britain. This is the stuff of which legends are made.

Enterprise led the assault force to Utah Beach on D-Day and conducted bombardment operations. Grant was mentioned-in-dispatches. He was in action again on 25 June 1944 in a bombardment of Cherbourg, where *Enterprise* engaged enemy shore batteries at close range in support of the U.S. Army. In the intense exchange of fire he was wounded. For this action, Grant was awarded the American Bronze Star medal. Common in all citations is mention of Grant's "exemplary leadership and aggressive determination."[95] In early 1945, he commissioned and assumed command of the cruiser HMCS *Ontario* for the RCN and took the ship to the Pacific. Too late to see action, *Ontario* helped re-establish British civil control in Hong Kong. His final wartime distinction was an award of the Companion of the Order of the British Empire (CBE). Grant inspired all who served under his command, British or Canadian.[96] In the eyes of officers such as Harry DeWolf and Ken Dyer, he was a hero, but his illustrious war record remains little known to Canadians.[97]

Grant became the pivotal figure in forging the postwar navy. He was promoted to rear-admiral in February 1946 to be Chief of [Naval] Administration Services and Supply (CNAS) at NSHQ. He was Reid's deputy, but he was the real power on the Naval Board and influence on policy during the interim force. Like his cohort, he had ingrained ideas resulting from his pre-war RN training and orientation.[98] When Grant succeeded Reid, he brought renewed energy, confidence and a presence to the office of CNS. Rear-Admiral R.W. Timbrell recalls Grant as "a gentleman, considerate, a cheerful presence with soft manner of speaking and understanding of junior officers."[99] More importantly, Grant brought strong leadership, decisiveness and a sense of direction.[100]

Grant faced the Herculean challenge of rebuilding the navy. He told the National Defence College that "the size of the Fleet including ships in reserve is hopelessly inadequate to meet the most modest commitment of the naval role."[101] The active fleet was reduced to a skeleton force of eight partially manned ships in commission. Only the carrier HMCS *Warrior* retained a full peacetime complement. Plans for the balanced fleet had been scrapped.[102] The authorized complement was 7,500, but the number on strength in 1947 was actually 6,814, and wastage was outstripping gains.[103] Morale was low and plummeting. The government was reticent on the issue of increased pay and other improvements to conditions of service.[104] In this pre–Cold War intermission, Claxton's new strategic policy relegated the navy to an ASW training role. Moreover, the RCN lacked a clear mission in the defence of North America. An increasing concern for Grant was the impact of the government's integration policies on the traditional organization and structure of the navy. The navy itself was pursuing a rather ill-defined general-purpose training program owing to the instability caused by personnel restrictions, a burgeoning training load and uncertainty in funding.

Achieving improvements in conditions of service and the welfare of sailors and their families became Grant's first priorities as CNS. He commissioned two studies to identify problems. The first, entitled "The Morale of the Navy," provided a blueprint for a progressive personnel policy.[105] The study indicates that there was a substantial understanding that new conditions existed in the navy as well as in Canadian society, and that the one must replicate the other as far as the service could allow. There is also an admission that the navy had got into bad habits during the war which were having a telling effect on discipline and morale.

The study's recommendations aimed at improving training, morale and conditions of service. They addressed such major complaints as inadequate pay and accommodations, but also pointed to inadequate wartime training of junior officers and senior rates that resulted in poor leadership and an ineffectual divisional system. Demonstrating a radical shift in thinking, the document suggested that the USN provided the model for the postwar RCN. Grant formally submitted the navy's morale concerns with his recommendations to the minister.[106] These required increased government funding that would not be forthcoming. The consequence was continued undermanning of ships and instability, low morale and unrest. Action to implement recommendations was either in train or planned when a series of "incidents" occurred onboard RCN ships in 1949.

A second study identified professional problems related to training and advancement for the non-commissioned ranks, problems that stemmed mainly from the new integration policies that were prejudicial to sailors. Grant believed Claxton's initiative to integrate and restructure the trades of the three services on an industrial model disadvantaged the navy and was driving men out. Moreover, he also opposed the minister's plan for an integrated tri-service college system to train officers because it would not meet the navy's requirements, either professionally or numerically. Personnel issues set the stage for a confrontational relationship between the CNS and the minister. Claxton was of the opinion that the navy's hierarchy was out of step with Canadian society. Grant was uncompromising, fighting aggressively for the navy to retain its traditional structure and system of professional development. The Mainguy inquiry would conclude that there was wrongheadedness on both sides. Harold Grant confided after his retirement that failure to seek compromise on certain issues with Claxton had proved unproductive for the RCN, and if he had to do it again he would proceed differently.[107]

It is evident that by the beginning of 1948 Grant had checked the drift that characterized Reid's tenure and was forging ahead on a broad front. He proclaimed that the RCN would adopt the ASW role and directed that plans be drawn up for a new anti-submarine destroyer escort to be built in Canada and designed to meet North American technical and USN habitability standards.[108] Grant also authorized the adoption of USN tactical doctrine and signals publications. Respecting conditions of service, ships were to implement welfare committees that would allow free discussion by the lower deck on issues pertaining to morale and welfare onboard.

Grant was progressive in accepting staff recommendations to adapt the organization of both NSHQ and branch functional structures to the new administrative and technical environment that was developing. The Naval Board began to meet weekly and took on a more businesslike atmosphere. Grant approved the establishment of the Naval Secretariat Branch responsible for administration. The Naval Board also pursued the goal of devolving more responsibilities to the commands. This included the principle of establishing a separate command to administer the naval divisions.[109] Grant also approved the creation of three branches to develop and consolidate the skills and emerging technology needed by the postwar navy. The torpedo/anti-submarine (TAS), electrical and ordnance branches were the result. A complete departure from traditional structure was the creation of a supply branch on the USN model, in conjunction with a decision to adopt the USN system for supply and material management.[110] Adopting the USN model would achieve greater efficiency, a North American orientation and a superior uniformed personnel structure.[111] Grant was persuaded, Rear-Admiral Charles Dillon recalled, on the strength of the benefits for the RCN.[112]

Personnel problems remained acute and therefore gripped Grant's attention. His personal preference was that the RCN should rebuild from scratch, but the die was cast when he became CNS.[113] The navy was actually five times larger than before the war, and the majority of personnel were wartime volunteers whose training had been indifferent; they lacked any depth of experience. Moreover, as Harry DeWolf observed, the best hostilities-only personnel had gone back to civilian life, and many who transferred to the regular force were mediocre.[114] Wastage exceeded gains, and there were not enough personnel available to man the minimum number of ships needed to execute basic training requirements. The navy needed more personnel just to create a nucleus for expansion in an emergency. Grant made persistent representation and won a concession in October 1948 to allow the RCN to recruit to a ceiling of 9,047 personnel.[115] As a direct result, the navy had sufficient recruits in the pipeline to respond immediately when the Korean War broke out in June 1950.[116]

Concurrently, the government announced the St. Laurent–class program to build seven anti-submarine escort vessels.[117] This favourable decision was influenced as much by the Berlin blockade as by Grant's persuasive efforts.[118] The blockade inaugurated the Cold War and led directly to the establishment of the North Atlantic Treaty Organization (NATO). To meet projected expansion, the RCN reopened HMCS *Cornwallis* in 1949 as its new entry-recruit training centre, and commissioned HMCS *Shearwater* as its operational and training base for naval aviation.

The initiatives taken by Vice-Admiral Grant to improve conditions of service and morale either lacked government financial support or could not be implemented swiftly enough to quell growing unrest in the fleet. The incident that occurred onboard HMCS *Ontario* in 1947 was a precursor. It was essentially a work stoppage by men following, in Michael Whitby's words, "an Empire tradition extending back centuries."[119] However, it had been mishandled; an unfortunate precedent was set when the executive officer, who was the object of the men's complaints, was removed, and when the perpetrators, who were quietly drafted to other ships to create more mischief, were not punished. The *Ontario* incident provided the model in 1949, when incidents of mass insubordination occurred in succession within a month onboard *Athabaskan*, *Crescent* and the carrier *Magnificent*.[120]

This series of incidents caught the navy completely by surprise and sent shock waves through NSHQ and the government. The *Crescent* incident was reported in a Vancouver paper, so political intervention was inevitable. Grant had previously warned Claxton of the possibility of paid agents operating in the fleet, and now fear of subversive activity gained a purchase.[121] Claxton appointed a commission of inquiry to flush this out and determine the circumstances surrounding the mass insubordination. The CNS wanted an internal inquiry, but Claxton believed that it must be public. Upon Grant's insistence, Rear-Admiral Rollo Mainguy became the president of a three-man commission. Claxton selected two civilian commissioners, Leonard Brockington and Louis Audette, both personal acquaintances and lawyers with ties to the Liberal party. Audette tried unsuccessfully to persuade Claxton that the commission should be composed entirely of civilians.[122] Audette, a former RCNVR officer, had his own agenda and became the self-appointed champion of rights for the lower deck and critic of the navy hierarchy. He exhibited a strong personal animus toward Grant, and the favour was returned.

The Mainguy inquiry was a seminal experience for the RCN. Of import here is Grant's role in it. His testimony examined the full spectrum of naval issues.[123] He opened by stating, "I think that this is probably one of the best things that could have happened to the navy and it is probably just as well it happened now."[124] He remarked that the action taken after the incident in *Ontario* was a mistake and he accepted responsibility for his part in it. What emerges from a fair and balanced reading of Grant's testimony is a profile of a knowledgeable and highly professional naval chief who was exceptionally well informed of all the navy's problems and deeply concerned for the future and welfare of the RCN. Moreover, Grant had plans either in place or underway to correct deficiencies and to improve the men's welfare and conditions of service. We also see a CNS who was very conservative, reactionary, hard-nosed, vocal and strongly opposed to initiatives that he believed were against the navy's best interests. However, due largely to Audette's construct, an uncomplimentary and inaccurate portrayal of Grant persists. Less rigorous historians have focused narrowly upon Grant's angry response to Audette's intentionally provocative line of questioning.[125] As a consequence of biased interpretations, Grant's powerful leadership and immense contribution to the development of the postwar RCN have received neither the attention nor the credit they deserve.

The findings and recommendations of the Mainguy Report were farreaching. As stated, many issues had previously been identified by the RCN, and remedial action was either in train or planned and awaiting funding.

Grant took no issue with any recommendations to improve leadership training, conditions of service or welfare. These, in the main, reinforced such existing initiatives as welfare committees and revitalization of the divisional system. Harry DeWolf stated in his testimony that the regulations were in place and needed only to be followed.[126] The RCN was not broken and did not need fixing, only adjustments. However, Grant was adamant that naval recruits should be purged of the liberal excesses of Canadian society and taught loyalty and obedience. Accordingly, the intense recruit training and indoctrination period at *Cornwallis* was extended to twenty-one weeks. On issues such as "Canada" badges and symbols of Canadian identity, Grant demurred until directed by Claxton. Grant reinstated the symbols, then never looked back.

Rear-Admiral A.H.G. Storrs observed, "The Mainguy Report was good and the result excellent. It turned out to be beneficially cathartic. It exposed a lot and got it out of our systems and really gave us a clear identity."[127] Alec Douglas remarked it became a kind of *Magna Carta* signifying a break from RN influence.[128] The men of the lower deck clearly benefited from the exercise and for this both Rollo Mainguy and Louis Audette deserve much credit. Significantly, the report gave the navy no leverage in obtaining increased funding for improvements in conditions of service. This materialized only with the crisis created by the invasion of South Korea. Claxton seemed more interested in the optics of adopting Canadian symbols that satisfied his nationalist inclinations than correcting the root personnel problems caused by underfunding.

During October 1949, at the same time the Mainguy Report was released, Vice-Admiral Grant was engaged in a campaign that would decide the future composition of the fleet. At issue was the necessity of naval aviation to the RCN. Despite its cost, Grant had become convinced of the need for it and argued it was fundamental to the RCN fulfilling its role of protecting convoys against threats from both enemy submarines and aircraft.[129] He embarked on a public-relations campaign to muster support for naval aviation. Fortuitously, it was preceded by the Soviet's first atomic bomb test. He then consolidated the position of the carrier by committing the RCN's existing fleet to NATO's ASW force.[130] Grant also advised the North Atlantic Regional Planning Group that Canada wished to concentrate on the "organization, control and protection of convoys."[131] This would prove to be a critical initiative, not only to consolidate the position of naval aviation but also in determining the role, composition and disposition of the Canadian fleet and personnel requirements until the end of the Cold War.[132]

The issue over the future of naval aviation came to a head in March 1950 in the Chiefs of Staff Committee (CSC), when Air Marshall Wilf Curtis, Chief of the Air Staff, openly opposed Grant on naval aviation.[133] Curtis, whom Grant thought of as a used-car salesman, had the "Goering syndrome" and wanted to control everything that flew.[134] Grant forced the chairman of the CSC, General Charles Foulkes, to submit the issue to Claxton and won his case.[135] Thereafter, naval aviation was accepted by the government as having a key role to play in "the immediate defence of Canada" and "anti-submarine warfare."[136] The RCN went on to build its NATO contribution around a carrier and new St. Laurent–class destroyer escorts.

The decision on the concept of design and construction of the St. Laurent class was one of Grant's crowning achievements to advance the RCN's operational capability, habitability and technology. Rear-Admiral Charles opined that it was Admiral Grant's "stroke of genius" to borrow Captain Roland Baker from the RN for the project.[137] The St. Laurents and variants would add immeasurably to the growing national identity of the RCN. The profile of the new anti-submarine escorts, the "Cadillacs," was uniquely Canadian and became the RCN's hallmark in NATO. The concept of habitability was derived from the USN and based on experiments in HMCS *Sioux* initiated by Grant. The electrical system was designed to USN Bureau of Ships specifications and American radars, communications systems and Gunar fire control were to be installed. The Y-100 system was the standard propulsion system being installed in RN frigates. The new St. Laurent class required significant changes in the navy's personnel structure as well as training to operate and maintain its advanced ship's systems.

On the strategic plane, Vice-Admiral Grant anticipated that naval forces would be needed to meet contingencies in the unstable postwar world. In 1948, Grant told the National Defence College that the navy in peacetime must be prepared for international "police duties" and be "available at immediate notice to visit the scene of tension or disorder without deviating noticeably from normal routine."[138] Grant pressed hard to establish a degree of operational preparedness and efficiency in the fleet. Operational training of fully manned destroyers began in 1950, and this would prove decisive. The RCN was able to dispatch three destroyers to Korea on 5 July 1950, within two weeks of the war breaking out.[139] It was months before the other two services could respond.

The "sickly season," in which parsimony was the norm, ended — at least temporarily — for the RCN on 25 June 1950, when the Korean conflict erupted.[140] The Korean commitment marked the beginning of period of rapid expansion for the RCN similar to that experienced during the Second World War. A personnel ceiling of 13,440 was authorized. Grant proposed a fleet strength of twenty-six operational ships to be attained by 1953.[141] He also requested authorization to build all seven St. Laurents concurrently and pressed to increase Canada's shipbuilding capacity.[142] NATO was estimated to be short some 260 ASW vessels. When its military representatives met in Washington in October 1950, Grant committed the RCN to providing "as many A/S escorts as possible."[143] At this juncture, the RCN's commitment to NATO became virtually open-ended. In May 1951, an additional seven Restigouche-class escorts, a slight variation on the St. Laurents, were approved. Within a year, the naval staff was planning for a ceiling of 21,000 to be reached by 1954.

Vice-Admiral Harold Grant was the key transitional figure whose hard-driving Nova Scotian Presbyterian character could be misconstrued as that of a hidebound British traditionalist. He was determined and inflexible on points of principle and fought to retain those things he believed to be essential to the continuing existence of the RCN. To his naval colleagues, he was a hero whose wartime exploits set the standard of professional excellence for RCN officers to emulate. He provided strong, effective leadership with humour during the often-chaotic times the navy experienced during the late 1940s. His drive to succeed was contagious and became the RCN's sustaining strength. This "can-do" spirit was one of those things that the Mainguy report referred to as being "overwhelmingly right" with the navy. "Can-do" would become synonymous with the RCN within NATO. The RCN weathered the storm of the incidents and fiscal restraint under Grant and was immediately ready to deploy to Korea. The RCN did not emerge with a new identity in spite of Harold Grant. "Canada" badges were mere symbols. A new identity rooted in professionalism and closer association with the USN was already emerging across the spectrum of naval activity, and most of its necessary components were being put in place before the incidents. The Mainguy Report merely accelerated the process.

HMCS *St. Laurent* was launched on 30 November 1951, and Grant retired as CNS the following day. The launching of "Sally" was the physical and material expression of the new RCN. This was a key component of Grant's broad strategic plan to establish the postwar ASW specialization of the RCN and part of his great legacy to the navy. The RCN continued to develop its new identity and expand on the course that Grant laid out. His successors as CNS through 1964 — Mainguy, DeWolf and Rayner — followed it with no appreciable deviation. Harry DeWolf called Harold Grant "a unique Canadian" and "the best CNS we ever had."[144] To these accolades should be added "Father of the Postwar Royal Canadian Navy."

NOTES

1   Lund, *The Rise and Fall of the RCN, 1945–1964*, chapter 1. [Complete references for commonly cited secondary sources are included in the bibliography.]

2   Pullen, "The Royal Canadian Navy between the Wars," 67.

3   Commander H.S. Rayner to CNS, 22 June 1945, "The Continuing Royal Canadian Navy," Library and Archives Canada, (LAC), RG 24 (acc 83-84/167), box 610, NS 1818-3, vol. 1.

4   Meaning "to smell or suspect a plot." Dean King, *A Sea of Words: A Lexicon and Companion to the Complete Seafaring Tales of Patrick O'Brian*, (New York, 1995), 407.

5   Douglas, *Conflict and Innovation in the Royal Canadian Navy, 1939–1945*, 211–12.

6   Pickerskill and Forster, *The Mackenzie King Record* (3), 368.

7   Colonel R.L. Raymont, "The Evolution of the Structure of the Department of National Defence, 1945–1968," 1. Directorate of History and Heritage (DHH), 73/1223.

8   House of Commons, *Debates*, 1945, vol. 2, 1368.

9   King diary quoted in Pickerskill and Forster, *The Mackenzie King Record* (4), 6.

10   Donald Munton and Donald Page, "The Operations of the Post-War Hostilities Planning Group in Canada, 1943–1945," paper presented to the 55th Annual Meeting of the Canadian Historical Association, Laval University, 2 June 1976, 76/188, DHH), 50–51.

11   Directorate of Plans and Intelligence, "Royal Canadian Navy — Future Planning to 1956," 4 November 1946, LAC, RG 24 (acc 83-84/167), box 620, file NS-11818, vol. 1.

12   *Ibid.*

13   Shawn Cafferky, "The Organization of War: A History of the Directorate of Plans Division, 1939–1945," 143, DHH, 2000/5.

14   DND, Report of the Department of National Defence for the Fiscal year Ending March 31, 1946, 16.

15   Tucker, *Naval Service of Canada* (II), 269.

16   Between 27 June 1945 and 22 February 1946.

17   Vice-Admiral H.G. DeWolf, interview by the author, 1 November 1994.

18   DeWolf interview.

19   The origin of the nickname "Rastus" is not known but was in general use during the 1930s. See Lay, *Memoirs of a Mariner*, 85.

20   S.E. Morrison, "8 Midshipmen 1912," *Sea Breezes*, December 1915, I:2, 7. See also Vice-Admiral H.E. Reid personnel file, DHH, biog R.

21   Brock, "Commander E.A.E. Nixon and the Royal Naval College of Canada, 1910–22," 42–43.

22   "Band of brothers" was the term, derived from William Shakespeare, that Nelson used for the close-knit group of naval officers who served under his command and has persisted as a descriptor for the fraternity of British tradition naval officers.

23   Brooke Claxton, "Autobiography," LAC, MG32B5, Claxton Papers, vol. 221, 869.

24   Rear-Admiral H.F. Pullen Papers, RNCC File, Seamanship Notebook, Public Archives of Nova Scotia.

25   Commander Peter Chance, Eulogy to Rear-Admiral Patrick Budge, 9 January 1998, St. Mary's Anglican Church, Victoria, British Columbia.

26   Morrison, "8 Midshipmen 1912," 2.

27   Reid file, DHH. See especially Statement of Service and Naval Historian's notes.

28   HMCS *Patriot* 192325, HMS *Sepoy* 192930, HMCS *Skeena* 193637, HMCS *Fraser* 193738.

29   Lay, *Memoirs of a Mariner*, 85–86.

30   W.G.D. Lund, *Command Relationships in the North West Atlantic 1939–45: The Royal Canadian Navy's Perspective* (M.A. thesis, Queen's University, 1972), 11–14.

31   Captain E.S. Brand, interview by the author, 19 May 1972. Brand served in Ottawa on exchange from the RN before and during the war as Director of Naval Intelligence. He transferred to the RCN during the war. Holland was lost when HMS *Hood* was sunk by the *Bismarck*.

32   Nelles's S206 on Reid, November 1943, Reid file, DHH.

33   Lieutenant-General Maurice Pope, *Soldiers and Politicians: The Memoirs of Lt. General Maurice Pope* (Toronto: 1962), 163–64.

34   *Ibid.*

35   Vice-Admiral D.A. Collins interview by the author, 4 October 1994. Collins was Reid's secretary during his tenure as CNS.

36   Vice-Admiral D.A. Collins interview by Lieutenant-Commander. W. Glover, Victoria, BC, 4 February 1992, Collins File, DHH, 17. Reid had served at NSHQ as VCNS during 1941–42.

37   *Ibid.*, 17.

38   *Ibid.*, 19.

39   *Ibid.*, 20.

40   *Ibid.*, 19.

41   *Ibid.*, 49.

42   Collins interview by Hal Lawrence, 28 January 1986, DHH, biog C, 36.

43   See Lund, "The Royal Canadian Navy's Quest for Autonomy in the North West Atlantic," passim.

44   Minutes First Senior Officers' Meeting, 15 April 1946, LAC, RG 24 (acc 83-84/167), box 143, NSS 1279-118, vol. 1. Present were CNS (Reid), CNAS (Grant), ACNS (DeWolf), CNP (Miles), COPC (Brodeur), COAC (Taylor), and NMCS (Agnew).

45 Rear-Admiral A.E. Storrs interview by the author, 20 June 1995.

46 Naval Board minutes, 29 May 1946. Storrs interview. The Naval Secretary was of captain rank. It was planned that ex–naval secretariat officers would be recruited to fill the civilian positions.

47 Naval Staff minutes, 25 February 1946.

48 *Ibid.*, 4 February 1946.

49 Minutes, First Senior Officers' Meeting, LAC, RG 24 (acc 83-84/167), box 143, NSS 1279-118, vol. l.

50 "Post-War Canadian Navy. Notes prepared for joint Canada–U.S. discussions," 15 April 1946, LAC, RG 24 (acc 83-84/167), box 455, NSS 1650-26, vol. 1. This unsigned document was prepared for the first meeting, probably by Storrs, and shows the general-purpose carrier task group inclination of RCN fleet structure. Lay mentions the first Military Co-operation Committee meeting in his memoirs.

51 Storrs interview. The USN only recently had reached this conclusion; it was reorienting its strategy from fleet engagement to containment of the Soviet threat with its impressive long-range submarine and bomber capability. See Robert E. Fisher, "The U.S. Navy's Search for a Strategy, 1945-1947," *Naval War College Review*, vol. XLVIII, no. 3. (Summer 1995), 73–86. See also Henry and Curtis, "Report of Proceedings at Washington, D.C., 20–23 May 1946," 23 May 1946, with enclosures, printed in Donald M. Page, ed., *Documents on Canadian External Relations*, vol. 12: 1946 (Ottawa: Queen's Printer, 1977), 1615–27.

52 "PJBD Recommendation 35, A Joint Appreciation on Defence," LAC, Claxton Papers, vol. 222, file 7.

53 Collins interview by the author.

54 Rear-Admiral J.A. Charles interview by the author, 14 June 1995.

55 Naval Staff minutes, 12 August 1946. The Naval Secretary had recently initiated a campaign to adopt the USN Supply Branch model and career structure for the RCN suggesting waning of RN influence in the group. Rear-Admiral C. J. Dillon interview by the author, 6 October 1994.

56 Minutes Second Senior Officers' Meeting, 16–18 October 1946, LAC, RG 24 (acc 83-84/167), Box 143, NSS 1279-118, vol.1.

57 *Ibid.*

58   Naval Board minutes 167-3, 22 February 1946. The wearing of "Canada" badges had been "optional in Canada" to this time. The naval officers attending were Rear-Admiral Grant (CNA&S) and Commodores DeWolf (ACNS) and Miles (CNP). Grant, being senior, would set the agenda. The issue of officers obtaining pre-war uniform items such as frock coats was deferred until after the period of the Interim Force. Naval Board minutes, 22 February 1946.

59   "Reid Warns Our Navy Too Small," Ottawa *Morning Journal*, 7 November 1946, quoted in Eayrs, *In Defence of Canada* (3), 57.

60   *Ibid.*

61   ACNS to CNS, 13 November 1946, LAC, RG 24 (acc 83-84/167), box 455, NSS 1650-26, vol. 1.

62   Pickersgill and Forster, *The Mackenzie King Record* (3), 394.

63   *Ibid.*

64   *Ibid.*, 6.

65   Dan W. Middlemiss, "Economic Considerations in the Development of the Canadian Navy since 1945," 278.

66   Claxton, "Autobiography," 842.

67   Claxton to Mackenzie King, 17 February 1946 quoted in Captain P.C. Paterson, *The Defence Administration of Brooke Claxton: 1946 to 1954* (M.A. thesis, The Royal Military College of Canada, 1975), appendix 4, 126–29.

68   *Ibid.*, 127.

69   Collins interview by the author.

70   Captain Brant "Pop" Fotheringham, interview by the author, 13 June 2001.

71   Claxton, "Autobiography," 837–38.

72   *Ibid.*, 842. Claxton was being theatrical for the benefit of posterity. The navy did not salute in buildings, "under cover." He also had difficulty adjusting to the language of sailors, who customarily spoke in the symbolic language of the environment in which they fought. Officers and ratings of every navy in the world learned to call walls or partitions "bulkheads" from their first day in the service.

73   Claxton, "Autobiography," 842. Retrospectively, Claxton was probably referring to his policy of "Canadianization" that particularly affected the RCN.

74 *Ibid.*, 869.

75 *Ibid.*, 891

76 Eayrs, *In Defence of Canada* (3), 57.

77 When Claxton became minister he advised his Chiefs of Staff that only the minister could make public remarks or speeches on policy. They voluntarily showed him the texts of their speeches. Claxton, "Autobiography," 898. This was probably as a result of the Reid public criticism of policy that embarrassed the government.

78 Charles interview by the author.

79 Grant Family Genealogical Table, by Mrs. Sigrid Grant. MacCallum Grant descended from Captain John Grant of the Black Watch Regiment, who came to Nova Scotia from New York in 1783 and settled at "Loyalist Hill," near Kemptville.

80 DeWolf interview.

81 John Grant left the RCN in 1921 due to poor eyesight. He was re-enrolled in 1939 to train RCNVR officers and later became the first Commandant of the Royal Canadian Naval College (RCNC) Royal Roads. He retired when the war ended in the rank of captain and was awarded a CBE.

82 R.E. Bidwell, "Eight Cadets, 1914," *Sea Breezes*, I:4, December 1917, 6.

83 *Ibid.*

84 LAC, NPRC, Vice-Admiral Harold Grant personnel file, S206 Performance Evaluation Reports.

85 *Ibid.*, Certificate of Service.

86 *Ibid.*, S206 Performance Evaluation Reports by Jones (9 February 1931) and Murray (24 November 1932).

87 L.C. Audette, interview by the author, 2 November 1994. Audette was one of Grant's strongest critics, although he had nothing but praise and admiration for Mrs Grant.

88 Mrs Christian Grant, interview by the author, tape recording, 5 April 2002.

89 Grant was leading a lively party of naval officers on "a run ashore" in Chester at the time. A senior officer was dispatched from NSHQ to investigate after the secretary phoned her boss complaining of the antics of some drunken naval officers. Lay, *Memoirs of a*

Mariner, 56, records the incident with some inaccuracies. The investigating officer was Commander Beard, not Brodeur.

90 Colonel J.C. McLanahan to Commander C.T. Beard, 22 September 1930, Grant papers in possession of author. Grant wrote "The Chester Hanging" on the file containing information pertaining to the investigation.

91 Grant personnel file, S206 Performance Evaluation Report by Nelles (10 June 1936).

92 The other celebrated hero was Vice-Admiral Harry DeWolf, who won the DSC in addition to the CBE and DSO (see chapter 8). Grant was considered by DeWolf and others to be in a class by himself. DeWolf interview.

93 Milner, *North Atlantic Run*, 124.

94 HMS *Enterprise*, Report of Proceedings, 29 December 1943, DHH, 81/520 Enterprise 8000 File; C-in-C Plymouth's Report on Operation Stonewall, 17 February 1944, "Narrative of Important Operations," DHH, NSC 1870-7 vol. 2; M.J. Whitley, *Destroyer!: German Destroyers in World War II* (London, 1983), 192–99.

95 Grant personnel file, Bronze Star Citation.

96 Chaplain P.H. Husband, RN to Mrs. Grant, 13 April 1967, Grant correspondence in possession of the author; Commodore F.D. Elcock, interview by the author, 2 May 2001. Husband was Grant's chaplain in *Enterprise* and Elcock was his supply officer in *Ontario*.

97 DeWolf interview; Vice-Admiral K.L. Dyer, interview by the author, 3 November 1994.

98 Storrs interview.

99 Rear-Admiral R.W. Timbrell interview by the author, 2 May 2000. Timbrell was Staff Officer (TAS) at NSHQ for two years during Grant's tenure as CNS.

100 DeWolf interview; Dyer interview.

101 Vice-Admiral H.T.W. Grant, "Future Strategic Role of Naval Forces," Lecture to the National Defence College, 15 February 1948, Grant personnel file, DHH, Biog G.

102 J.F.K. Kealy, "The Development of the Canadian Navy, 1945–67," DHH, SGR II 223, 3.

103 Press release, 7 November 1951, DHH, 4000-100/14.

104 Bercuson, *True Patriot*, 177.

105 VCNS to CNS, "The Morale of the Navy," 29 September 1947, LAC, RG 24 (acc 83-84/167), box 1596, NSS 4490-1, pt. 1. Houghton called the study a "collation" of issues. The staff papers used as sources are contained in the file.

106 CNS to the Minister, 8 October 1947, LAC, RG 24 (acc 83-84/167), box 1596, NSS 4490-1, pt. 1.

107 Vice-Admiral D.S. Boyle interview by the author, 1 February 2000.

108 Minutes Fourth Senior Officers' Meeting, 26-27 November 1947, RG 24 (acc 83-84/167), box 143, NSS 1279-118, vol. 1.

109 Naval Board minutes, 8 September 1948.

110 *Ibid.*, 15 February 1949 and 1 June 1948.

111 *Ibid.*, 15 February 1949. The basis for the decision was a study of the RCN system conducted by Commander (SC) M. A. Peel, USN Supply Corps.

112 Dillon interview.

113 Grant evidence, Audette Papers, LAC, MG 31, E 18, vol. 4, file 14.

114 DeWolf interview.

115 PC 84/4994 amending PC 3/3144 of 6 August 1947 and PC 122/5111 of 12 December 1947 to allow the RCN to recruit 1399 officers and 7648 men: total of 9047.

116 Elcock interview.

117 For background on the St. Laurent program and decision, see Knox, *An Engineer's Outline of RCN History: Part II*, 317–33, and Davis, *The St. Laurent Decision: Genesis of a Canadian Fleet*, 209–32.

118 Naval Board minutes, 21 June 1948. When the blockade began Claxton directed that all three services look at emergency planning and to propose implementation procedures.

119 Whitby, *Matelots, Martinets, and Mutineers*, 99–102.

120 The incidents occurred on 26 February in *Athabaskan* at Manzanillo, 15 March in *Crescent* at Nanking, and 20 March in *Magnificent* in the Caribbean. See the Mainguy Report, 6–25, for a full description of the incidents and facts and causes relating to them. Also, Louis Audette's, "Board of Investigation…Brief of the Evidence" in the Audette Papers, LAC, MG31E18, vol. 1, file 5. The brief is Audette's independent submission. The other civilian

commissioner, Leonard Brockington, drafted the final report drawing heavily on Audette's brief.

121 CNS to the Minister, 8 October 1947, LAC, RG 24 (acc 83-84/167), box 1596, NSS 4490-1, pt. 1.

122 Audette interview.

123 Grant evidence, Audette Papers, LAC, MG31E18, vol. 4, file 14, 3462-3512.

124 *Ibid.*, vol. 4, file 14, 3462.

125 Audette, "The Lower Deck and the Mainguy Report of 1949," 247; Audette interview.

126 DeWolf evidence, Audette Papers, LAC, MG31E18, vol. 4, file 12.

127 Storrs interview.

128 W.A.B. Douglas, *The Canadian Encyclopedia*, (Edmonton, 1988), 117.

129 Vice-Admiral Grant, Speech to the Defence Services Institute of London Ontario, 14 October 1949, Grant file, DHH. Grant was influenced by Admiral Halsey, the USN carrier admiral. His decision was later reinforced when he visited Korea and General MacArthur told him, "The success of the Inchon landing was due to naval gunfire and carrier-borne aviation, which provided 100 per cent of the support." Naval Board minutes, 25 October 1950.

130 Sokolsky, *Canada and the Cold War at Sea, 1945–68*, 213–14. The RCN Force Requirements for protecting sea lines of communication built around the carrier and naval aviation were developed under ministerial direction and passed by the Naval Board in September 1948. Naval Board minutes 256-1 and 259-5. The RCN supported the choice of an American for Supreme Commander Atlantic (SACLANT) against the RN's bid to hold the position and their nominee, Admiral Louis Mountbatten. This indicated the extent that the RCN had moved into the USN sphere of influence.

131 Sokolsky, "The U.S., Canada and the Cold War in the North Atlantic: The Early Years," paper presented to the Canadian Political Science Association, May 1981, 30–31.

132 Davis to Douglas, 21 March 1984, enclosure "The DDE Decision Process-Involvement of Cdr/Capt AHG Storrs," Storrs personnel file, DHH, biog S.

133   Colonel R.L. Raymont, "Development of Canadian Defence Policy," 83–84.

134   Elcock interview.

135   Authors of popular histories on Canadian naval aviation have generally portrayed the role of Grant inaccurately. The truth is that without the tenacity and support of Grant, the carrier and naval aviation would have gone in 1950. See, for example, Soward, *Hands to Flying Stations* (1), 139–40, 173–74.

136   Department of National Defence, *Canada's Defence Programme, 1951–52*, (Ottawa: King's Printer, 1951), 7.

137   Charles interview. Tony Storrs is of the opinion that Baker designed the St. Laurent class by himself.

138   Vice-Admiral Grant, "Future Strategic Role of Naval Forces," Lecture to the National Defence College, 15 February 1948, DHH, Grant file. Grant's strategic thought reflected the emerging nature of the Cold War and was entirely consistent with Canada's foreign policy. Incidentally, Grant wrote all his many speeches and lectures.

139   CANAVHED to CANFLAGPAC 2030Z/30 June 50, DHH, 81/520, 1650-239/187 Operations Korea.

140   Tony German used "sickly season" as the title of his chapter on the period of fiscal restraint and personnel problems in *The Sea Is at Our Gates*. He takes literary licence with a naval toast that actually refers to opportunities for promotion.

141   The initial target was twenty-six ships, consisting of one carrier, two cruisers, one A/S escort, nine destroyers, five frigates, seven minesweepers and one icebreaker. This was increased in the final submission to Claxton by one destroyer and one frigate.

142   CNS to MND, "Accelerated Defence Programme, Accelerated Shipbuilding Programme," 31 July 1950, LAC, MG32B5, Claxton Papers, vol. 94, Folder Accelerated Defence Programme.

143   DeWolf interview. DeWolf had become VCNS and accompanied Grant to this meeting.

144   *Ibid.*

Vice-Admiral E. Rollo Mainguy

CHAPTER SEVEN

Vice-Admiral E. Rollo Mainguy: Sailors' Admiral

Wilfred G.D. Lund

Few names in Canadian naval history are as well known as that of Vice-Admiral Rollo Mainguy. Thanks to the report that bears his name, which is considered the "Magna Carta"[1] that released the Royal Canadian Navy (RCN) from subordination to the Royal Navy (RN) and its oppressive Nelsonian traditionalism, he is remembered as the champion of the sailor. It is said that in the absence of rigorous scholarship, myth abounds; there probably has been no Canadian naval officer who more faithfully represents the character and disposition of Nelson than Rollo Mainguy. Mainguy was a true "sailor's admiral," happiest in ships at sea, where he was an outstanding captain. He was larger than life, charismatic, loved and admired by those who served with him. And Mainguy, like Nelson, abhorred the bureaucracy ashore and the challenges of higher administration. It is doubtful that Horatio Nelson would have ascended to preside over the Admiralty. Rollo Mainguy, on the other hand, had no choice. He was predestined to be the Chief of the Naval Staff, probably to his deep regret.

Vice-Admiral E. Rollo Mainguy was appointed Canada's sixth Chief of the Naval Staff on 1 December 1951. His father, Daniel Wishart Mainguy, was a Guernsey islander and son of a parson[2] who emigrated to Canada at the age of twenty-one and took up farming in the Cowichan Valley on Vancouver Island.[3] Rollo was born in Victoria in 1901 and was raised on his family's farm at Chemainus. His father died when Rollo was five. He was schooled at Skrimshire's, a British-model private school at Quamichan Lake, the predecessor of Shawnigan Lake School. Mr. Skrimshire recalled that the young Mainguy was "a typical country boy, fond of sports and games."[4] At age fourteen, Mainguy was enrolled in the class of 1915 of the Royal Naval College of Canada (RNCC). The youngest in his class, and "Mangy"[5] to his term mates, he was "an excellent student" who excelled in seamanship, sailing and sports.[6] In the Halifax explosion of 6 December 1917, Mainguy was badly cut in the face by flying glass.[7] He rebounded from his wounds and graduated with a "first," having established a reputation as "a reliable cadet captain and [who] deserves well of the College."[8] Like his contemporaries, he was strongly imbued with the ethics propounded by Commander A.E.A. Nixon. His son, Daniel, later also a vice-admiral, reported that the elder Mainguy applied methods learned at RNCC to his role as a parent. He started a conduct sheet on Dan at age four.[9] He also required his children to ask for things to be passed at the dinner table by means of semaphore or Morse code.

Prior to the Second World War, Mainguy's career progression followed the normal RCN pattern. He became a signals specialist and established a reputation as "a sailor's sailor" who was recognized professionally as a well-connected "streamer." An imposing figure, he was described as "an affable giant with tattooed forearms, a friendly grin, a cool and decisive brain, a Canadian accent, and a secret hobby of needlepoint."[10] Handsome and full of natural charm, he was a popular social lion in the close and affluent circles in which RCN officers moved. He was also one of the hardest "runners" in a navy that excelled between the wars in "working hard and playing hard."[11] He was promoted to commander in 1936 and assumed his first command, HMCS *Vancouver*, followed by an appointment at Naval Service Headquarters (NSHQ) as Director of Naval Reserves.

His marriage in 1927 to Maraquita Nichol, daughter of the Honourable Walther Nichol, a former lieutenant-governor of British Columbia and founder of the Vancouver *Daily Province*, was termed "the wedding of the season."[12] The product of a privileged life, the imperious and "strong-minded" Quita Mainguy rose through the ranks with her husband and exercised command in naval society.[13] This alliance allowed Mainguy to live well, enabling him to acquire a country estate, Heavitree, not far from his family's farm on Vancouver Island, and to found a herd of Ayrshire cattle.

Rollo Mainguy had a very good war. He was at the RN Staff College in Greenwich when it broke out. War was his business, and he sent his family back to their farm and rejoined them when it was over.[14] He immediately took command of HMS *Kempenfelt*, which was transferred to the RCN as HMCS *Assiniboine*. The destroyer was not "winterized," so when she returned to Halifax, Mainguy was ordered to the Caribbean, where *Assiniboine* joined the RN force blockading German merchant ships.[15] On 8 March 1940, *Assiniboine* teamed with HMS *Dunedin* to capture the *Hannover*. The operation to save the burning *Hannover* as a prize was described by the Commander-in-Chief (C-in-C) of the Americas and West Indies station as a "feat of seamanship of which both officers and men can be justly proud."[16] *Hannover* later sailed as *Empire Audacity*. The prize money the RCN received went to establish the postwar RCN Benevolent Trust Fund.

Assiniboine returned to Canada for refit, and Mainguy was given command of HMCS *Ottawa* in April. *Ottawa* joined the Clyde Escort Group 10, operating from Greenock, Scotland, in August 1940. Rear-Admiral John Charles served with him in EG-10, remarking he was a "sharp and intelligent" captain.[17] Mainguy was in the thick of the fight against the U-boats concentrating in the Western Approaches. On 6 November 1940, *Ottawa*, with HMS *Harvester*, was ordered to the assistance of a merchant ship, *Melrose Abbey*, 500 miles southwest of Ireland. The destroyers arrived to find *Melrose Abbey* under fire from a surfaced U-boat. *Ottawa* got off five rounds before the U-boat dived. The destroyers gained asdic (sonar) contact and conducted nine attacks. Separate underwater explosions were heard, and at sunrise a large patch of oil was visible on the surface. *Ottawa* and *Harvester* claimed a kill, but it was not awarded by the U-boat Assessment Committee. Postwar reassessment awarded the kill in 1982, so that, forty-two years after the fact, Rollo Mainguy received credit for the RCN's first anti-submarine success of the Battle of the Atlantic.[18] Mainguy commanded *Ottawa* until she was transferred to the newly formed

Newfoundland Escort Force (NEF) at St. John's in June 1941. He was award-ed the OBE "for gallantry and distinguished service before the enemy" as senior officer of convoy escort groups.

Mainguy was promoted to captain in July 1941 and appointed briefly as Captain (D) Halifax before joining Commodore Murray as his Captain (D) in Newfoundland. This promotion, ahead of his senior Wallace Creery, almost assured his succession to the office of CNS should he survive the war.[19] Murray specifically asked for Mainguy to support him in the Herculean challenge of establishing the NEF.[20] Mainguy con-sidered himself "lucky to be chosen for the job."[21] While Captain (D) Newfoundland from 1941 until 1942, he established the Seagoing Officers Club — better known as the Crow's Nest — and "Donovans" rest camp for men. He became identified as a champion for better con-ditions of service that contributed to the growing Mainguy legend.

Conversely, there was the poor operational performance of the Canadian escorts, the "C" Groups, for which Mainguy was responsible to Murray for training and readiness. The problem was systemic, more the result of too-rapid expansion and overcommitment of the RCN than the fault of Murray's staff. However, Mainguy was responsible for sub-mitting reports and assessments to Western Approaches command for the operations of the NEF escort, and these lacked precision and detail.[22] RN criticism of poor staff work in the NEF's rendering of operational reports, and specifically of Mainguy's analyses, was warranted. The RN staff commented on one occasion that "neither FONF [nor] Captain (D) [Mainguy] have the remotest idea what is expected of them."[23] These were early days, and Mainguy and the RCN were learning ASW on the job, but too slowly in the RN's opinion. But the miracle of the fledgling NEF was that the Canadian escorts kept going at all, and Mainguy's contri-bution to their morale was enormous. The United States awarded him the Legion of Merit, in the rank of Officer, for his service with the NEF.

Mainguy's successor as Captain (D) Newfoundland in September 1942 was Captain Harold Grant. They switched appointments, with Mainguy taking over as Chief of Naval Personnel at Naval Service Headquarters (NSHQ) in Ottawa. The RCN was expanding too quickly, and the provision of trained personnel fell dramatically short of ship production. The burden of personnel "production" fell on the Chief of

Naval Personnel, and here, crisis management was the order of the day. Mainguy was obviously unhappy to be out of the action; however, he did his best to keep up the spirits of his overworked staff in "the depressing atmosphere of the Navy building." He admonished them that, "In all things, *ships must come first.*"[24] If something wasn't beneficial to the fleet or didn't promote fighting effectiveness, the staff was to figure out what would be effective, and that was to be the only reason for their existence. Mainguy endured NSHQ for nearly two years through the period when the RCN began to correct its personnel deficiencies.

Mainguy got back into the war in September 1944 when he took command of Canada's first modern cruiser, HMCS *Uganda*, transferred from the RN. The RCN arranged to take over two cruisers as part of its contribution to the war in the Pacific. The RCN intended to fight alongside the RN and USN as a partner and not a subordinate. The aim was "to ensure as far as possible 'Canadian identity' in the Pacific theatre is retained, so that any due battle honours may fall to the Canadian nation."[25] Mainguy was a "progressive" who wore "Canada" badges, and he ordered three green maple leaves painted on *Uganda's* aft funnel. *Uganda* joined the British Pacific Fleet (BPF) in March 1945 and was soon in action.[26]

In the cruiser, Mainguy was a popular captain who paced his bridge barefoot and stripped to the waist. He conducted "town hall meetings," a kind of open forum for the ship's company and a precursor to the postwar welfare committees. The success of *Uganda's* deployment with the BPF was mixed. As Bill Rawling has commented, the ship was still developing towards its full potential when it was prematurely withdrawn from operations. "*Uganda's* bombardment and anti-aircraft operations in the Pacific demonstrated that Canadians had much to learn about running larger ships."[27]

The circumstances of *Uganda* withdrawing from operations are probably as unique as they are infamous. The ship's company voted their ship out of the war. Prime Minister Mackenzie King decreed that all service in the Pacific would be voluntary. The policy was inane because everyone in the navy was either permanent force or had volunteered to serve for "the duration of hostilities." In the case of *Uganda*, Mainguy remarked, "We were already fighting the Japanese" when the message arrived from Ottawa.[28] A vote was held onboard in May to determine whether the ship would maintain the status quo and remain in active combat or return to Canada. Mainguy did his best to influence the outcome, labelling anybody who refused to as a quitter and saying, "I wouldn't want to be in his shoes for anything."[29] But 66 per cent voted to return home.

Admiral Sir Bruce Fraser, C-in-C BPF, was incredulous over the policy of the Canadian government. He signalled both the Admiralty and NSHQ, "That HMCS Uganda should have apparently sailed for Pacific without knowledge of the conditions of service, the form of announcement and with many rumours preceding it, have placed the C.O. and all onboard in a difficult position. It will have caused a fine ship to be withdrawn from line for other than operational reasons. It will cause me difficulty in forming the Fleet into 2 self-contained Task Groups which I had promised the Americans could be done."[30] As a consequence, Uganda remained with the BPF for over two months, until 27 July 1945. Several Canadians, mostly naval aviators, remained in the BPF after Uganda's departure. One of them, Lieutenant Robert Hampton Gray, RCNVR, sunk a Japanese destroyer on 9 August 1945 and was posthumously awarded the RCN's only Victoria Cross of the war. Atomic bombs abruptly ended the war, and Uganda never had the opportunity to redeem herself. Mainguy later commented, "It was probably the worst period I've gone through."[31] The Uganda affair left its mark on the RCN.[32] Certainly, enough to provoke Vice-Admiral Harold Grant's comment: "I think Canada makes a lot of damn noise in the world without doing anything about it."[33]

Mainguy retained command of Uganda until July 1946, when he was promoted to commodore and then acting rear-admiral as Commanding Officer Pacific Coast (COPC). He was forty-five years old and had served his last appointment at sea. He settled rather uncomfortably into flag appointments on his way to CNS. The navy had contracted to a non-operational state, and ships' programs were controlled by NSHQ. He saw his role as selling the RCN, and as flag officer there was little else for him to do. The RCN was easing back mentally into the prewar status quo, and taking Mainguy with it. He said of his new duties: "As shore jobs go, I suppose it's as good as they come. It is nice to be home for a while. But I definitely hope to get in some more sea-time before I am through." When asked if the postwar RCN was becoming "stuffy and 'super-pusser' with the emphasis on robot-like discipline,

Oxford accents and white handkerchiefs up the coat-sleeve, Mainguy staunchly denied it."[34]

However, in August 1947, HMCS *Ontario* — in his Pacific command — had an incident of mass insubordination onboard (RCN "speak" for a mutiny). The inquiry Mainguy chaired found that the executive officer in *Ontario,* Commander J.V. Brock, fitted that profile precisely. Brock was an ex-RCNVR officer with a fine war record, but he had spent most of it with the RN, where he acquired bad British habits that reinforced his natural arrogance.[35] His commanding officer, Captain J.C. Hibbard, told the Mainguy inquiry that the ship's company, "to a man could not tolerate my Commander."[36] Mainguy took the decision to transfer Brock quickly and quietly out of the ship, replacing him without an investigation.[37] Mainguy was so secretive as not to tell Brock's replacement, Commander P.D. Budge — whom he personally nominated — the truth why Brock was leaving or that there had been an incident.[38] It is not clear to what extent Mainguy may have discussed this course of action with Vice-Admiral Reid, the outgoing CNS, or Grant, his relief. The incident was dismissed. This was not out of the norm. The RCN had a history of incidents, a traditional method of airing complaints.[39] Incidents were handled unofficially and never reported. Hibbard said later that the men in *Ontario* were engaged in "collective bargaining."[40] There was no disciplinary action and ring leaders involved were drafted to other ships, sowing dragons' teeth for the next round of incidents.

The Naval Board certainly had identified and understood the basic causes of low morale and was endeavouring to correct them.[41] The RCN continued to struggle to man enough ships to carry out training. Consequently, advancement was slow and career prospects poor. A pay raise in 1947 brought some relief to personnel, but there was no money to improve accommodation or conditions of service. The families of young officers and junior ranks suffered particularly. Worse, the divisional system was in disarray, owing to instability — particularly of officers in the ships — and because divisional training for officers and senior rates had ceased during the war. However, the hierarchy did not appreciate that the morale problem included a strong desire for national identity. This became apparent only through the Mainguy inquiry.

Mainguy was confirmed in the rank of rear-admiral in 1947 and appointed to Halifax as Flag Officer Atlantic Coast (FOAC) in October 1948. The circumstances there were much the same as in Victoria, except the city and the weather were much less hospitable to the navy. Mainguy took measures to improve relations between the city and the navy that had been badly damaged by the riots in 1945. But Haligonians have long memories. Nor had the image of the navy been improved by the public misconduct of sailors — which included snatching purses from elderly ladies — that received wide coverage in the hostile local press.[42]

The sailors' behaviour ashore reflected problems in the ships — there had been an incident in HMCS *Nootka* in May 1947.[43] However, Mainguy's predecessor, Rear-Admiral Cuthbert Taylor, had dismissed the notion of a morale problem, stating that the ship's company's "greatest moan is homesickness."[44] Commander A.H.G. Storrs took command of *Nootka* in August 1948 and recalled that the ship was "simmering" and that there was a general air of discontent in all the fleet.[45] Incidents occurred in three ships: *Athabaskan*, *Crescent* and *Magnificent*. These sent shock waves through NSHQ and the government. The *Crescent* incident was reported in a Vancouver paper. There was a fear that subversive activity had gained a purchase in the navy, and politicians demanded answers. The inquiry called by the minister of National Defence, Brooke Claxton, would flush this out and also force the RCN to bare its soul.

At the insistence of Vice-Admiral Grant, the CNS, Claxton appointed Rear-Admiral Mainguy to chair the inquiry. There were two civilian commissioners, Louis Audette and Leonard Brockington. Audette opposed Mainguy's appointment; he thought it should be an all-civilian commission. Audette had his own agenda. Mainguy's appointment became a bone of contention between Grant and Audette that developed into open verbal warfare with Mainguy caught in the middle. However, Audette credited Mainguy with being "a superb chairman in that he drew them [the young sailors] out" when they testified.[46] Claxton directed, "no one except the members of the inquiry should know what evidence any man gave," and the sessions were held in camera.[47] Mainguy managed relations with the media superbly and held press conferences after every session. Audette ignored Claxton's orders and, years later, released the testimony.

Audette maintained that Mainguy was "bone lazy," and had little input in the proceedings and none in the production of the final report.[48] Most of the questions were asked by either Audette or Brockington. They also authored the report with the assistance of Commander P.R. Hurcomb, judge advocate of the fleet. Mainguy did nothing to curb Audette's aggressive interrogation of senior officers or his efforts to establish grounds for disciplinary charges against Commander D.W. Piers, who was the executive officer in *Magnificent*. However, Mainguy obviously had a moderating influence on the content of the report because Audette's more extreme views were not included. Audette submitted "additional observations" in a letter to Claxton that condemned the navy's system of officer education and professional development, later claiming that it produced senior officers that were "imbeciles."[49] He also advocated having "dry" ships. Mainguy must have blanched at that suggestion.

The final report achieved a reasonable balance. "We were asked to find out what was wrong with the navy," it stated. "If, therefore we stressed what is wrong, it should not be forgotten that a great deal also is overwhelmingly right."[50] Real mutinies are about adjustments in power. The incidents in the RCN in 1949 were mainly about conditions of service and symbols. It concluded, "We have also sought to interpret the wishes of a great majority of men stressing the need to 'Canadianize' our navy."[51] Significantly, the commission relied heavily on USN printed sources for information and guidance on personnel administration and leadership.[52] These reflected the norms of North American society — a style of officer–man relationships that Mainguy embraced. The RCN was already inclining itself towards the USN model. That Mainguy did not author the report is probably immaterial, and the myth will survive. He is inseparably identified with the cathartic exercise that Storrs and others saw as giving the RCN its own identity.[53]

Other than the inquiry, Mainguy's tenure as FOAC was not terribly significant. The buildup for NATO on the east coast was interrupted when the Korean War broke out in June 1950. The west coast became the priority, and the RCN's primary and all-consuming task was to maintain the three destroyers assigned to the United Nations. Mainguy bided his time in Halifax until he was inevitably summoned to Ottawa. He relieved Grant as CNS on 1 December 1951. Senior naval officers privately held fears that

Mainguy was not up for the job.[54] A close observer commented, "It always seemed that Admiral Mainguy had other concerns which seemed to interfere with his interest in what was going on in the service itself which made that period a very difficult one to deal with."[55] Mainguy's disinterest would decisively influence his effectiveness as CNS.

When Vice-Admiral Rollo Mainguy took command of the RCN, its fortunes were rising on a near-vertical trajectory. The Cold War and Korea had created an environment for rapid expansion. The Department of National Defence budget was 50 per cent of the national total, and the navy's share was 14.7 percent for the fiscal year 1952–53.[56] In accordance with Grant's program, fourteen St. Laurent–class escorts were approved and the navy was heading for a ceiling of 21,000 personnel. Negotiations were underway with the RN to acquire the unfinished light carrier HMS *Powerful* and complete her to modern standards as HMCS *Bonaventure*. Twenty-one Second World War River-class frigates were being modernized as the Prestonian class. Morale in the fleet was good. Claxton, in a display of radical optimism, projected a 100-ship navy by 1954 and 20,000 personnel by March 1955.[57] It could not have been a better time to be CNS, as opportunities abounded for the navy.

Moreover, the powers of the CNS had been expanded considerably by the new National Defence Act of 1950 that gave individual Chiefs of Staff statutory existence.[58] This consolidated the power of the Chief of the Naval Staff and spelled out his terms of reference, being "charged with the control and administration" of the navy "under the direction of the minister." Claxton was attacked in the press for elevating the military chiefs to pedestals of independent authority, but he believed that this move was necessary to maintain unity of command.[59] The act also set down the four functional branches supporting the CNS — the Naval Staff, the Naval Technical Services Branch, the Naval Personnel Branch and the Comptroller — along with their terms of reference. The composition of the Naval Board was also delineated. Integration was achieved through corresponding parallel and identical functional structures in the other two services to facilitate co-ordination through a tri-service committee system.

The opportunities and power that Mainguy enjoyed were more than balanced by many challenges. The RCN's priority was to close the capabilities gap that had been created by Canada's naval commitment to NATO. Equally critical was the need to recruit and train sufficient manpower to match the expanded inventory of ships and new construction. The RCN was extended to the limit maintaining the three destroyers in Korea and three fully manned destroyers in reserve. Claxton's integration policy not only demanded an alignment of the headquarters structures of the three services; the objective, under Treasury Board pressure, was to achieve symmetry between the three services so as facilitate the oversight of administration and fiscal management.

This was the "brave new world" of postwar government, and Mainguy and NSHQ faced a real challenge given the uneven quality of its constituent parts. Mainguy had not served at headquarters since 1944 and was unfamiliar with the new environment. Moreover, Claxton wrote, "He [Mainguy] made no bones about his dislike of desk work and, indeed, of pretty nearly everything to do with his job [as CNS]."[60] Also, the RCN never believed in staff training. Admirals and senior officers of the executive branch believed that the only qualification necessary to do any job in the navy was to hold an "Upper Deck Watch Keeping Certificate"; indeed, they prided themselves on this fact.[61] There were a few naturally gifted staff officers — such as DeWolf, Lay and Storrs — but they were not the norm. The RCN's standard procedure was to muddle through.

Mainguy's style stood in definite contrast to Grant's strong control of the staff and agenda at NSHQ. He decided to hold part of his first senior officers' meeting at the exclusive Seignory Club in Ottawa. He told the meeting that his rationale was, "If we could get everybody away from work, we could really get down to it and have plenty of home truths; which will undoubtedly spring up at the Seignory Club."[62] This was a variation on his successful town hall meeting model. Also, he made public relations a priority. He instructed his senior officers, "One thing I think we should all try to do wherever possible, and that is the propaganda of selling the navy wherever we may be."[63] He encouraged them never to turn down an invitation to speak and to tell Canadians that merely providing a navy was not enough: they had a stake in maintaining sea lines of communications.

Mainguy set the example, carrying this message to the public in his speaking engagements. His presentations, however, lacked the professional content and substance that had marked Grant's. There was a touch of the romantic in Mainguy, who was more comfortable speaking in generalities and appealing to chivalrous sentiments. He took the "I am a simple sailor" approach that enabled him to avoid complex issues and explanations. Illustrative is his address, "The True Glory," delivered at the convocation of the University of Saskatchewan in May 1952. The speech was a recruiting pitch to graduates with references to duty and Lord Nelson and an appeal to support the navy.[64] He began, "I shall certainly have nothing erudite to say, but assume that you are aware that sailors are not expected to be erudite." In contrast, the leadership of the USN was at that time publicly promoting nuclear propulsion, which would revolutionize naval warfare. John Harbron, a naval critic, suggested that "the postwar admirals during this difficult decade [1945–55], in the face of the swiftly moving events both in their own world and the wider international arena, represented a retarded point-of-view about change and function in the fleet."[65] Harbron, unlike James Eayrs, was unaware of Grant's grasp of contemporary naval strategy, but the evidence suggests that Mainguy gave the impression of an admiral sailing backwards into the future.[66]

The Korea commitment was the overriding factor that influenced naval strategic policy, ship availability and training. It fostered an ongoing debate that did not subside until the commitment was terminated in 1954. Various alternatives to the three-destroyer commitment were put forward, including sending the carrier *Magnificent*.[67] Captain Storrs, Director of Naval Plans and Operations (DNPO), opposed this and advanced the argument that Korea was really a sideshow. He recommended instead that the commitment be adjusted in order to fulfill the RCN's primary commitment to NATO in the Atlantic.[68] The VCNS, Rear-Admiral DeWolf, agreed in part, but stated he did not "consider a reduction in the Korean commitment [sic] should be recommended until all else has failed to meet the situation."[69] DeWolf understood what the government reaction would be. He also knew of Mainguy's reluctance to bring hard issues to the Minister's attention. Fortunately for the navy, DeWolf remained as VCNS during the first year of Mainguy's tenure, and it is apparent he was taking the hard decisions.

Storrs' recommendation did result in Mainguy ordering a redistribution of the fleet in November 1952, whereby two-thirds of the ships were to be stationed on the east coast and one-third on the west coast.[70] Sufficient ships became available on the east coast by September 1953 to form the First Canadian Escort Group (1st CEG — two destroyers and two frigates) around the carrier. The new distribution had immediate ramifications for the Home Port System in which men were assigned permanently to either Halifax or Esquimalt — that split was half and half. As approximately two-thirds of the navy's new recruits were from eastern Canada, the personnel staff thought the balance would correct itself over time. It did not.

Captain Storrs defined the commitments and the requirements problem and brought some badly needed discipline to the process. The debate over the Korea commitment underscores the deficiency in staff skills that handicapped the navy when it came to understanding complex problems and then solving them, particularly during this critical period.[71] There was no lack of dedication to problem-solving by naval staffers; quite the contrary: as Claxton's integration scheme worked its way through headquarters like yeast through dough, tri-service committees proliferated. Most staff naval officers spent their normal working days attending meetings, not starting their own work until 1600.[72] But in the broader context, the navy's overcommitment syndrome originates at this juncture, in the naval staff's impulse to respond "Ready Aye Ready" to any new operational commitment, regardless of whether or not it could be met.

The challenges in meeting the personnel requirements associated with rapid expansion were as daunting for Mainguy as they would be for his successors. For his part, Mainguy largely ignored the issue and left it for his staff to deal with. It is sufficient to say that the development and execution of personnel policy in the postwar RCN was an abject failure and represented muddling through at its worst.[73] Mismanagement eventually resulted in the collapse of manning on the east coast in 1963 and again in 1964. Given the abysmal state of readiness, linked directly to a shortage of trained personnel, under the Landymore Report the cyclic system was introduced in 1964, shifting the fleet's priority from operations to training.

Claxton's rosy optimism regarding personnel goals was misguided, mainly because he had no advice from his CNS to the contrary. The RCN was living hand to mouth just to maintain the Korea operation, and it narrowly averted manning "chaos" on the west coast through astute rescheduling. The Chief of Naval Personnel, Commodore J.C. Hibbard, believed that the greatest problem facing his branch was "how to meet commitments and yet maintain a steady and healthy growth."[74] Hibbard was the first to admit that the navy was overcommitted and was trying to do more than it was capable of doing efficiently. He had consulted his opposite number in the RN and found that the Admiralty had needed to tell the government to slow down on expansion. The Canadian government was asking the RCN to do far more in comparison to the RN, and without the advantage of Britain's compulsory national service. The RN was expanding merely 20 per cent while RCN expansion was in the order of 300 per cent.

Hibbard's major concern was that, short of mobilization, the navy could not maintain the current rate of expansion without lowering minimum standards of training. He feared that "the Service will suffer a blow from which it will be difficult to recover."[75] Mainguy did not respond to Hibbard's warning, nor did he take up the issue with Claxton. The CNS simply encouraged his senior staff "not to be downhearted, or if one is, for heaven's sake don't say so, not to everybody in sight anyway and don't exaggerate."[76] Mainguy set an example of procrastinating and hoping for the best.

The navy made extraordinary efforts to recruit and train the needed personnel. In the officer category, the navy was about 33 per cent short, with the majority in bridge watch-keeping officers.[77] The men's situation was even more critical, and remained so, with the greatest deficiency being in the technical trades. Engineers could expect to spend no less than eighty per cent of their career in seagoing billets. This was a huge demotivator for junior men, and the wastage rate was high. Moreover, there were not enough ships available to allow for substantive training, so advancement was slow. The navy had to recruit two men for every one required.

Cornwallis, the new entry training base, operated at 140 per cent capacity, but recruiting quotas were seldom met owing to competition from the civilian sector. HMCS *D'Iberville* was opened to attract and train francophone recruits, and the Women's Royal Canadian Naval Service (WRCNS, pronounced "wrens") was reinstated to free men for sea duty.

Superimposed on this was the requirement to restructure the rank and branch and trade structures to meet Claxton's integration policy. Moreover, the St. Laurent–class destroyer escorts were introducing a whole new generation of technology that required new skills and qualifications. The personnel production lagged, but fortunately this was matched by slippage in the new construction schedule. This merely postponed the crunch, however. It may be argued that navies have historically had personnel shortages and it is the natural state: like the poor, they will always be with us. The highly technical postwar Canadian navy required a well-educated and trained permanent work force. At issue here is the degree to which Mainguy engaged the problem.

It is apparent that the strong leadership Grant had provided was no longer present. The government's strategic direction was clear: the RCN would become an ASW–oriented navy, a model that Grant developed. However, the issue of the RCN not being a "balanced fleet" was raised by ACNS (Air) Commodore Keighly-Peach, the RN staff officer on loan to direct naval aviation.[78] He did not support what DeWolf referred to as "the NATO principle of balanced collective forces," wherein all countries shared resources that they were capable of providing[79] (in Canada's case, an anti-submarine capability) and the "have" members shared with "have nots." Some RCN flag officers also had trouble with the concept and had to be schooled in it by DeWolf. But DeWolf was now in Washington, and Keighly-Peach was free to press the issue in different staff forums. Mainguy, meanwhile, seemed to vacillate. The minutes of one meeting he chaired recorded, "It was agreed that limited thinking in respect to the role of the RCN is a dangerous thing, and that we should not be concentrating on A/S Warfare only." Direction was given "to soft-pedal" publicity of the RCN as an "A/S Warfare navy."[80]

Mainguy's style was to give his staff officers their head. However, there was some residual "big ship" navy sentiment, and the focus on ASW had created an identity crisis for some officers.[81] Subsequently, Captain D.G. King — the DNPO and the officer primarily responsible for planning the new ASW navy — wrote to the VCNS, "[I]t would be deplorable from the national point of view, if the RCN ever became officially an anti-submarine navy only."[82] This was in response to a proposal by CNP to pay off the cruisers. The issue resurfaced when the disposal of the cruiser *Quebec* came up the following year. This indecision raises the question of the extent to which Mainguy was firmly directing the policy-development process and providing leadership with respect to maintaining the strategic aim. The evidence suggests that was he was not.

The Korean War ended in July 1953. Stalin was dead, the Cold War seemed to be warming up and the Liberals seized the opportunity to retrench on military spending. For the armed forces, the halcyon days of commanding nearly 50 per cent of the national budget vanished as quickly as they had appeared. Claxton no longer spoke of a 100-ship navy, and the 1954–55 estimates included a 10 per cent cut in the defence budget.[83] Finances began to drive military strategy. Claxton introduced the Estimate Review Committee and the service chiefs were directed to tighten up on their financial management. The chiefs were called before this so-called "screaming committee" to justify expenditures.[84] SACLANT force goals would be directly affected by the reductions, and C.M. Drury, the deputy minister, bore down on Mainguy to provide more detailed justification for the navy's requirements. Commodore Nelson Lay came up with plans to create the Policy and Project Coordination Committee (PPCC). The PPCC was to be a working committee of the Naval Board to ensure adequate coordination and consideration of policy proposals, both before they reached the Naval Board and after approval.[85]

Brooke Claxton retired in June 1954 and was replaced by Ralph Campney, a no-nonsense administrator with good knowledge of the defence portfolio. The strategic climate was changing. NATO was adopting the "New Look" strategy and plan, entitled MC-48, that shifted dependence to nuclear deterrence and downgraded the importance of conventional forces. New Look and MC-48 introduced new factors and imperatives that affected every area of naval planning at a time when the RCN was extremely hard-pressed to meet its original NATO commitments. Strategy was now governed by a "forces-in-being" concept because a surprise enemy nuclear strike would cripple mobilization efforts. The war would have to be fought with forces existing on D-Day, and this rendered mobilization plans and reserve forces redundant. "Seaward defence" described the concept of defending Canada and North America against aircraft carrying nuclear weapons and against missile-firing submarines.[86] The RCN's current plans were based on the parameter of

21,000 personnel, temporarily capped at 20,000. Commitments to SACLANT and North American defence under the Canada–U.S. Regional Planning Group (CUSRPG) were 91 ships and two squadrons of aircraft.[87] The 21,000 ceiling meant that the RCN could actually man only 58 warships, including the fourteen St. Laurents under construction, to SACLANT minimum peacetime standards. A trained reserve force was needed to bring them up to wartime strength. Unless the government was prepared to raise the navy's manpower ceiling significantly, further expansion to meet agreed commitments would be impossible. The ramifications of any new strategic requirements were unknown.

The naval staff turned their attention to the task of developing a seaward defence plan while achieving the necessary reductions. The Korean commitment had ended. The naval staff noted that, "in the past few years our ship's movements have often been dictated by sheer expediency" and "since World War II, the Fleet, necessarily, had existed on a hand-to-mouth basis."[88] The navy was to begin a concentration on the east coast that would result in the formation of the 1st Canadian Carrier Support Squadron consisting of *Magnificent* and four destroyers in 1955.[89] The Seaward Defence Committee produced a program featuring a rapid response capability that included helicopters, helicopter carriers and a notional hydrofoil craft to respond to submarine detections from a projected chain of Canadian LOFAR (Low Frequency Acoustic Ranging) stations.[90] Concurrently, a complementary personnel plan was developed to reflect total commitments as result of the new strategy.[91]

The result showed that the staff was beginning to work well together under Rear-Admiral Lay, the new VCNS, with strong support from Commodore D.L. Raymond (ACNS Plans) and Commodore H.S. Rayner who did the personnel study. Mainguy's input in the planning exercise is not apparent. When the Seaward Defence Plan was brought to the Naval Board, Raymond was strongly supported by Lay in arguing that the Vancouver-class frigates, planned to replace the Prestonians, were unfit for the LOFAR support role because of limitations in speed, armament and electronic installations. Raymond recommended cancelling the program and building seven more St. Laurents that had the minimum capability for the task. Mainguy initially was swayed by Rear-Admiral J.G. Knowlton, Chief of Naval Technical Services, who argued there was a continuing requirement for that class, and for which plans had been drawn and some machinery ordered.[92] When Lay subsequently pressed Mainguy to review the decision, the CNS deferred to the indisputable logic in the original argument. He reversed his decision and the Vancouver program was scrapped.[93] In addition to being indecisive, Mainguy appears to have had difficulty assimilating complex briefings.

It soon became apparent that Mainguy had been performing unsatisfactorily in areas other than directing the RCN's strategic planning process. Producing the 1956–57 estimates proved to be a profound challenge for the naval staff after the government reduced the navy's preliminary estimates by about 25 per cent. Chief amongst the fallout from this difficult budgetary exercise was the replacement of Mainguy as CNS. His early retirement on 16 January 1956, to be relieved by Rear-Admiral DeWolf, was announced by Campney on 20 September 1955.[94]

Mainguy had expected to stay on until May 1956, which would have been his normal retirement date.[95] The first indication that Vice-Admiral DeWolf in Washington received of the change took the form of an unexpected telephone call from Campney, who advised him that he would relieve Mainguy early[96] — Mainguy was being fired. The issue that precipitated Mainguy's dismissal was an error in the navy's estimates submission. It appears that Mainguy had failed to act on Campney's personal direction (arising out of the previous submission) that the navy must absorb costs for additional personnel expenditures from other programs and not ask for a funding increase. The CNS did not pass the minister's direction on to the staff, and the error was repeated in the subsequent submission, which Mainguy failed to review.[97]

It is doubtful that Campney acted impulsively, but that this was the last straw in a pattern of performance that failed to meet his expectations. Mainguy was notorious for his administrative laxity and his predisposition to delegate everything without supervising.

Of this development, Claxton concluded, "He [Mainguy] was happy to be relieved."[98] The problem for the navy was that Mainguy, who had not been particularly effective in fighting the RCN's battles, was now a lame duck. It would be left for Rear-Admiral Lay to defend the RCN's commitment strategy to NATO, and particularly the naval aviation program, when the revised estimates were taken before the Estimate Review

Committee in November 1955. The RCN emerged from these interrogations with the futures of its NATO commitment and of naval aviation in jeopardy. Intervention by a powerful advocate could have made a difference. The one bright spot at the end, and possibly the highlight, of Vice-Admiral Mainguy's tenure as CNS was the commissioning of HMCS *St. Laurent* on 29 October 1955. "Sally" was a tangible symbol of the new national identity of the RCN.

When Vice-Admiral Rollo Mainguy was relieved by Vice-Admiral Harry DeWolf as CNS, he left an uncertain legacy. He had been neither a strong nor effective champion for the RCN where it really counted, at the committee tables in Ottawa. The navy's policies on how it determined its commitments to NATO and naval aviation were in question at the highest level. Mainguy's succession to the highest administrative appointment in the RCN had been predetermined by the ironclad rules of seniority. As in the tradition of primogeniture for selecting a king, it was simply his turn. It was not a question of competence or desire. How well was he equipped to be CNS? When asked to compare Mainguy with Grant, DeWolf, who was vice-chief to both, rendered this opinion: "Grant was a leader who told us where to go and what to do. Mainguy relied completely on his staff. If his staff said 'do this,' he would. I don't think Mainguy had any ideas of his own. He was a hell of a nice guy [but] as a leader, as a man of ideas for the navy, I don't believe he had any."[99]

The evidence supports the view that, as in the Mainguy Report, it was his associates who had the ideas and originated the policy initiatives. It might be argued in the case of Mainguy's time as CNS that this was the staff's job. However, it is apparent — as demonstrated by the lingering "big ship navy" debate in the face of declared government policy on ASW, the persistent personnel crisis, and inattention to strategic and fiscal matters — that both leadership and direction from the CNS were lacking. Good senior staff officers, like Storrs, Lay, Raymond and Rayner, could keep the RCN going, but strong leadership, energy and vision were required from the CNS for the navy to be administered efficiently and to achieve maximum effectiveness. The evidence leads to the conclusion that Mainguy failed to provide that leadership and performed ineffectively as CNS. He was a great "sailor's admiral," but was not an "admiral's admiral," and he was out of his depth as CNS.

The fault, however, should not be found so much with Rollo Mainguy as with the system that had elevated him to a position for which he had no vocation. Like the unwilling "Rastus" Reid, Mainguy was obliged to take the job without wanting it. As a consequence, there was drift and vacillation in the administration of the RCN during a critical four-year period in its postwar development.

NOTES

1   W.A.B. Douglas, *The Canadian Encyclopedia*, (Edmonton: Hurtig, 1988), 117.

2   Vice-Admiral D.N. Mainguy, interview by the author, 18 April 2001. Vice-Admiral Mainguy opined that the Mainguys were smugglers up to the end of the Napoleonic Wars, when the RN could turn its attention to suppressing that pursuit.

3   Clyde Gilmour, the Vancouver *Daily Province*, a biographical sketch reprinted in the Cowichan *Leader*, 6 February 1947, 9.

4   *Ibid*. Mr. Skrimshire's school consisted of one room in which he taught twenty-five to thirty boys of all grades up to senior high.

5   *Ibid*.

6   P.W. Brock, "Four Cadets, 1915," *Sea Breezes*, II:1, June 1919, 5.

7   R.E. Bidwell, "Epilogue" *Sea Breezes*, I:4, December 1917, 47.

8   P.W. Brock, "Four Cadets, 1915."

9   D.N. Mainguy interview.

10   The Cowichan *Leader*, 6 February 1947, 9 & 12. Needlepoint embroidery was a favourite hobby of officers of Mainguy's era.

11   Rear-Admiral J.A. Charles, interviews by the author, 14 June 1995 and 7 June 2001.

12   Cowichan *Leader*, 6 February 1947, 9.

13   See Lay, *Memoirs of a Mariner*, 72–73 [complete references for commonly cited secondary sources are included in the bibliography]. Lay obviously has his dates wrong, but the portrayal of Maraquita Mainguy (née: Nichol) was confirmed by Vice-Admiral K.L. Dyer, interview by the author, 3 November 1994, Ottawa. Rear-Admiral Storrs related an account of Mrs. Mainguy publicly ordering his wife

to perform baby-sitting duties at a social function. The function was in Mrs. Storrs's home and she refused. Storrs was commanding officer of HMCS *Shearwater* at the time. Rear-Admiral A.E. Storrs, interview by the author, 20 June 1995.

14 D.N. Mainguy interview.

15 CNS to C-in-C AWI, 23 November 1939, Directorate of History and Heritage (DHH), 81/520 8700-353/2.

16 D.N.Inf Monthly Historical Paper, 18 June 1952, DHH, 81/520/8000 Assiniboine (I) file.

17 Charles interviews.

18 McKee and Darlington, *The Canadian Naval Chronicle*, chapter 5. The RN Historical Branch reassessed the claim, based on Italian naval records.

19 Creery had lost *Fraser* in collision with HMS *Calcutta* during the war, and although he was not officially censured, in the opinion of Captain Brand it hindered Creery's promotion to captain. Captain E.S. Brand, interview by the author, 17 May 1972. A year senior to Mainguy as a commander, Creery was promoted to captain in 1942. He subsequently served as VCNS under Mainguy.

20 Diaries, Rear-Admiral L.W. Murray Papers, Libraries and Archives Canada (LAC), MG30E207. NSHQ originally proposed Mainguy to command the NEF, but the RN insisted on Murray.

21 Vice-Admiral E.R. Mainguy, interview by Jean Donald Gow, August 1973, Qualicum Beach, B.C. Copy of interview and original letters from Mainguy in possession of the author.

22 Milner, *North Atlantic Run*, 116, 120, 151, 164.

23 SO(A/S) minute, 20 October 1942, C-in-C WA to Admiralty, 29 November 1942; and DCOS (Operations) minute, 20 October 1942, Public Record Office (PRO), ADM 237/90 quoted in Milner, *North Atlantic Run*, 165.

24 Captain E.R. Mainguy, CNP Memo to staff, 28 December 1942, DHH, Mainguy personnel file, Biog M.

25 SO Plans to DOP, memo, 24 June 1944, LAC, RG24, vol. 8150, NSS 1655-2, quoted in Rawling, "A Lonely Ambassador," 45. Rawling noted that Mainguy had virtually no "big-ship" experience and *Uganda* had a long way to go to achieve a modicum of operational

effectiveness when she departed the war.

26 "History of HMCS *Quebec*," Naval Historical Section, November 1958. DHH, 81/520/8000, Uganda-Quebec file.

27 Rawling, "A Lonely Ambassador," 60.

28 E.R. Mainguy interview by Gow.

29 Ron Armstrong, "The ship that left the war," *Times-Colonist Islander Magazine*, 13 August 1995, 1.

30 C-in-C BPF to Admiralty, NSHQ 0201Z/27 May 1945, DHH, 81/520/8000, Uganda-Quebec.

31 E.R. Mainguy, interview by Gow.

32 Rear-Admiral W.M. Landymore, interview by the author, 7 July 1997, Halifax, N.S. Landymore was the assistant gunnery officer in *Uganda* with the BPF and said he never again spoke to permanent-force officers who voted against the status quo.

33 Grant Evidence, Audette Papers, LAC, MG31E18, vol. 4, file 14, 3496. Grant followed Mainguy into the Pacific in HMCS *Ontario*. Eighty-five per cent of *Ontario*'s ship's company voted to fight the Japanese.

34 Cowichan *Leader*, 6 February 1947, 11–12.

35 Rear-Admiral P.D. Budge, interview by the author, 15 June 1995.

36 Captain J.C. Hibbard evidence, Audette Papers, LAC, MG31E18, vol. 2, file 8.

37 Mainguy Report, 37.

38 Budge interview. Hibbard did not even tell Budge that there had been an incident when he reported onboard. He had to find out from one of the chaplains.

39 Whitby, *Matelots, Martinets, and Mutineers*, 99–102. See also Lieutenant-Commander David Groos to Louis Audette, 15 April 1949, Audette Papers, LAC, MG31E18, vol. 1, file 3. Groos was the commanding officer of HMCS *Crescent* when she had her incident in 1949 and explains how the system worked in the RCN.

40 Hibbard evidence, Audette Papers, LAC, MG31E18, vol. 2, file 8.

41 COPC to the Naval Secretary (NSec), 21 January 1947, LAC, RG 24 (acc 83-84/167), box 1596, NSS 4490-1, pt. 1. Mainguy was forwarding an extensive report entitled "Morale in the Canadian Navy" conducted by the commanding officer HMCS *Naden* (Esquimalt naval Barracks) into conditions in the command.

The beginning. Armed with two 6-inch, six 4.7-inch, and four 12-pound guns, the 3,600-ton HMCS *Rainbow* was the first warship commissioned into the RCN.

The Rivers. With the King and Queen of Thailand embarked, this unique shot from September 1931 shows the River-class destroyer HMCS *Skeena* flying the Siamese ensign.

The workhorse. Showing the wear and tear of operations, the corvette HMCS *Oakville* won much acclaim for the destruction of *U-94* in the summer of 1942.

The traditional navy. Marking the end of a distinguished career, which included tours in the Second World War and the Korean conflict, the Tribal-class destroyer HMCS *Huron* requires balloons to keep her paying-off pennant aloft.

The big-ship navy. HMCS *Ontario* conducting trials off the coast of Ireland. Too late for the war in the Pacific, *Ontario* operated on the west coast until she was paid off in 1958.

DND

The Cadillacs. HMCS *St. Laurent* and her sisters had many distinctive features that made them uniquely Canadian, and they became the pride of the postwar navy.

DND

The Golden Age. HMCS *Bonaventure*, the centrepiece of the RCN's 1960s ASW fleet, is about to be overflown by a flight of Trackers and Sea Kings, with the support ship HMCS *Provider* alongside.

The vanguard of Canada's modern navy. The Canadian Patrol Frigate HMCS *Toronto*, like the eleven other vessels of this class, performs a litany of tasks ranging from fishery patrols off Canada's coasts to blue-water work such as Persian Gulf operations in support of the war against terrorism.

42 RCN Press Release, 10 November 1948, DHH, 73/1066.

43 Rear-Admiral D.L. Hanington, interview by the author, 22 January 1998. Hanington was serving in *Nootka* at the time.

44 COAC to NSec, 30 January 1948, LAC, RG 24 (acc 83-84/167), box 1596, NSS 4490-1, pt. 1.

45 Storrs interview.

46 Louis Audette, interview by the author, 2 November 1994.

47 MND to Members of the Board of Inquiry, Memo, undated, Audette Papers, vol. 3, file 3.

48 Audette, interview by the author.

49 Audette to Claxton, 13 October 1949, Audette Papers, LAC, MG31E18, vol. 1, file 3; Audette, interview by the author.

50 Mainguy Report, 4.

51 *Ibid.*, 73.

52 See "Board of Investigation Brief on the Evidence," Audette Papers, LAC, MG31E18, vol. 1, file 5.

53 Storrs, interview.

54 Commodore F.D. Elcock, interview by the author (addendum), 2 May 2001. Elcock was Mainguy's personal secretary as CNS. He reported receiving a "posse" of five retired senior officers. "Their purpose was to indicate measures that should be taken to ensure that the new CNS did not sell the RCN down the drain [sic]."

55 Elcock interview (addendum).

56 Department of National Defence, *Canada's Defence Programme 1952–53*, (Ottawa: Queen's Printer, 1952), 25.

57 MND address, Minutes Ninth Senior Officers' Meeting, 17 and 23 March, 1952. LAC, RG 24 (acc 83-84/167), box 143, NSS 1279-118.

58 House of Commons, *Special Committee on Bill No. 133, An Act Respecting National Defence* (Ottawa: King's Printer, 1950). Section 19 pertains to the Chiefs of Staff.

59 Claxton Papers, LAC, MG32B5, "Autobiography," vol. 221, file 4.

60 *Ibid.*, vol. 222, file 9.

61 Rear-Admiral Storrs, interview by Hal Lawrence, 31 July 1985. DHH, Storrs personnel file, Biog S.

62 Minutes Ninth Senior Officers' Meeting, 17 and 23 March 1952, NAC, RG 24 (acc 83-84/167), box 143, NSS 1279-118, vol. 3.

63 *Ibid.*

64 Mainguy, "The True Glory," an address at the University of Saskatchewan, 9 May 1952, DHH, Mainguy personnel file, Biog M.

65 Harbron, "The Uncertain Heritage," 19. Harbron, who served in the RCNVR during the war, was motivated in his criticism through Mainguy's failure to support a current affairs instructional program that was being promoted to DND by the Canadian Institute of International Affairs of which Harbron was a director.

66 Eayrs, *In Defence of Canada* (3), 58.

67 FOAC, "Appreciation of the Employment of H.M.C. Ships in the Atlantic Command," 29 February 1952, LAC, RG 24 (acc 83-84/167), box 1392, NSS 4100-1, vol. 6. This had been proposed in 1951 by Captain D.W. Piers, DNPO in 1951, and rejected at the staff level.

68 DNPO to VCNS, 29 May 1952, LAC, RG 24 (acc 83-84/167), box 455, NSS 1650-26, vol. 6.

69 VCNS minute, 12 June 1952, on DNPO to VCNS, 29 May 1952, LAC, RG 24 (acc 83-84/167), box 455, NSS 1650-26, vol. 6.

70 CNS Information Book to MND, dated 18 November 1952, quoted in DNPO to ACNS(W), CNP, VCNS, memo, 8 March 1954, LAC, RG 24 (acc 83-84/167), box 1392, NSS 4100-1, vol. 5.

71 Rear-Admiral Lay commented frequently on the deplorable state of staff work at NSHQ through lack of training.

72 Rear-Admiral R.J. Pickford, interview by the author, 1 November 1994, Ottawa.

73 Lund, "The Rise and Fall of the RCN."

74 CNP address, Minutes Ninth Senior Officers' Meeting, 17 and 23 March 1952, LAC, RG 24 (acc 83-84/167), box 143, NSS 1279-118, vol. 4.

75 *Ibid.*

76 CNS address, Minutes Ninth Senior Officers' Meeting, 17 and 23 March, 1952.

77 Naval Board minutes, 14 January 1953.

78 ACNS (Air) address, Tenth Senior Officers' Meeting, 6 and 8 May 1953, LAC, RG 24 (acc 83-84/167), box 143, NSS 1279-118, vol. 4.

79 VCNS minutes on FOPC to NSec, 21 January 1952, LAC, RG 24 (acc 83-84/167), box 455, NSS 1650-26, vol. 5. There was an important mutual aid element in these early days of NATO.

80 Minutes Tenth Senior Officers' Meeting, 6 & 8 May 1953. LAC, RG 24 (acc 83-84/167), box 143, NSS 1279-118.

81 See Hennessy, "Fleet Replacement and the Crisis of Identity," 131–153.

82 DNPO (King) to VCNS (Creery), 10 June 1953, LAC, RG 24 (acc 83-84/167), box 455, NSS 1650-26, vol. 8.

83 DM to CNS, 26 March 1954, LAC, RG 24 (acc 83-84/167), box 1392, NSS 4100-1, vol. 6.

84 Colonel R.L. Raymont, "The Formulation of Canadian Defence Policy, 1945–1964," 187, DHH, 79/17.

85 Naval Board minutes, 17 June 1954.

86 *Ibid.*, 29 December 1954. The Naval Board was aware of the developing threat and the shift in strategic thinking towards developing plans to defend North America. An important anti-air component was evident, as well as the need for ships and aircraft with sufficient speed, endurance and command-and-control capabilities to react effectively to the new threat, particularly that anticipated from submarines surfacing to fire missiles.

87 DNPO to CNS, memo, 24 February 1955, LAC, RG 24 (acc 83-84/167), box 1392, NSS 4100-1, vol. 6. The breakdown to SACLANT was as follows: 1 light fleet carrier; 18 destroyer escorts (DDEs); 24 frigates; 1 squadron A/S aircraft; 1 squadron fighter aircraft; 1 flight AEW (air early warning) aircraft; and to CUSRPG: 34 coastal escorts; 14 minesweepers.

88 DTSD to VCNS, 21 October 1954, LAC, RG 24 (acc 83-84/167), box 455, NSS 1650-26, vol. 12.

89 FOAC to NSec, 1 October 1954, LAC, RG 24 (acc 83-84/167), box 455, NSS 1650-26, vol. 12.

90 A LOFAR station had been established at Shelburne, Nova Scotia, in conjunction with the USN, which was building a chain around North America.

91 Commodore H.S. Rayner, "Report By The Ad Hoc Committee On RCN Commitments," DHH, 81/520/1440-5, XXI.

92 Knowlton's purely parochial argument was that his staff had done all the design work and the machinery plants for the first five of class ordered.

93 Naval Board minutes, 1 June 1955. When essentially the same information pertaining to cancellation of the Vancouver class was

presented at a separate meeting, Mainguy was convinced and again reversed his decision.

94 Armed Forces News Release, 393/55, 20 September 1955, Mainguy personnel file, DHH, Biog M.

95 Rear-Admiral Bidwell to DeWolf, 6 September 1955, DeWolf Papers, LAC, MG30E509, vol. 1. Bidwell wrote "Rollo told me he would probably be leaving next May." Mainguy would have expected to retire at age fifty-five in May 1956.

96 DeWolf interview. DeWolf related that Campney originally told Mainguy to contact DeWolf to find out how long it would take him to disengage from his Washington duties. DeWolf told Mainguy seventy-two hours, but that he expected to relieve him in May. Mainguy reported to Campney that DeWolf would be up in May and the minister responded that he didn't get the point. DeWolf was to relieve him early. Then Campney called DeWolf and advised him of the earlier relief.

97 DeWolf interview. DeWolf stated, "Campney fired Mainguy, in fact." Mainguy provided DeWolf with the details during their turnover briefing.

98 Claxton, "Autobiography." LAC, MG32B5, vol. 222, file 9.

99 DeWolf interview.

CHAPTER EIGHT

Vice-Admiral Harry G. DeWolf: Pragmatic Navalist

Michael Whitby

Vice-Admiral Harry DeWolf at his desk. The model is of the nuclear submarine USS *Skipjack*, which the RCN wanted to acquire but could not afford.

Harry DeWolf[1] had one of the most challenging watches of any Chief of the Naval Staff (CNS) in our navy's peacetime history. That statement may seem improbable; the years 1956 to 1960, after all, formed the rump of what has often been trumpeted as the "Golden Age" of the Royal Canadian Navy (RCN). It is not hard to appreciate that sentiment. In the forty-three months that DeWolf was CNS, twenty-one new or significantly modernized ships were commissioned — including the modern, angled-deck aircraft carrier HMCS *Bonaventure* and thirteen new destroyer escorts derived from the successful St. Laurent–class. Such totals were unprecedented in the navy's peacetime history. And that was not all. The navy also took delivery of 100 CS2F Trackers, a state-of-the-art carrier-borne ASW patrol aircraft; sent its first jet-powered, Sidewinder-armed, all-weather fighters to sea; and won approval for a submarine force, operational support ships and a maritime helicopter. The RCN was also positioned at the sharp end of the naval technology curve, developing such innovative systems as variable depth sonar (VDS), the Digital Automatic Tracking and Remoting system (DATAR), tactical data trainers and the destroy-er-helicopter marriage. The navy was making a positive contribution to NATO, and its voice was respected in allied councils. Morale was good — how could it not be?

But the seascape upon which Canadian naval planning rested was restless. There was a strong undercurrent of change in the mid-to-late 1950s that threatened to rip away the pilings supporting traditional naval concepts. Nuclear propulsion, supersonic attack aircraft, guided-missile technology, and cruise-missile submarines all appeared in work-able form during that period, turning naval thinking on its head. Within the RCN, significant personnel management problems have been revealed by Wilf Lund's research. And, despite the new additions to the fleet, many of the navy's ships were still of Second World War design or vintage.[2] Most importantly, money was scarce, and successive govern-ments drew the purse strings even tighter. Indeed, naval disbursements plummeted a staggering 38 per cent during DeWolf's tenure as CNS (see Table I).[3] Scarce financial resources are a constant of Canadian naval history; less common was the combination of dramatically dwindling resources at a time of such profound change in naval weaponry and platform technology. It was that combination that made DeWolf's watch exceedingly difficult.

DeWolf responded well to the challenge. While his presence at the helm during the arrival of the new equipment and the other trappings of the Golden Age was, to a degree, serendipitous — as VCNS in the early 1950s he had been a key decision-maker behind the equipment acquisi-tions — he did have to confront the complex and often contentious issues cited above. He succeeded by maintaining a practical strategic outlook, by proceeding cautiously with force generation, by streamlin-ing management practices and by maintaining a firm grip on the helm. In short, he supplied effective leadership and realistic vision at the pre-cise moment they were needed.

TABLE I: DECLINE IN NAVAL EXPENDITURE, 1956–1961[4]

Fiscal Year Ending 31 March	DND expenditure ($000s)	RCN Expenditure ($000s)	Percentage Decline
1956	1,750,112	340,800	
1957	1,759,426	326,700	4.2%
1958	1,668,463	295,000	9.8%
1959	1,424,741	273,000	7.5%
1960	1,516,572	255,800	6.4%
1961	1,517,531	245,500	4.1%

Overall decline from 1956–1961: 38%

Of all the officers who rose to become CNS, Harry DeWolf was arguably the best prepared. Notwithstanding the legendary status he achieved as a result of his service at sea, he also had considerable experience in handling complex policy matters at the service, national and alliance levels. The Second World War especially brought DeWolf the "fortune of opportunity," and he made the most of it. After graduating from the Royal Navy College of Canada in 1921, his career initially followed the standard pattern, but from the mid-1930s he held a series of appointments that thrust him into important, and at times critical, moments of decision-making and policy development. DeWolf excelled at these jobs, earning a reputation as an outstanding staff officer with shrewd judgment, a diplomatic manner and immense common sense. Space precludes mentioning all these experiences, but certain of them stand out.[5] As a junior staff officer at NSHQ between 1935 and 1937, DeWolf played a key role in administering the procurement of the four River-class destroyers from Great Britain. That work impressed the CNS, Commodore Percy Nelles, who later pulled him out of the RN staff college at Greenwich for seven weeks to serve as his aide-de-camp during the 1937 Coronation of George VI and the associated Imperial Conference. That duty often entailed looking after Mrs. Nelles — which, by all accounts, could have been a career-breaker in itself — but DeWolf was also a fly on the wall at discussions concerning international diplomacy and naval strategy, a process he found fascinating. After finishing at Greenwich, he received an introduction to the "sharp end" of naval planning as Staff Officer (Operations) for the 1st Cruiser Squadron in the British Mediterranean Fleet. The appointment came at the peak of the Spanish Civil War, and DeWolf helped to plan blockade operations off the embattled country and was even ashore in Valencia, making contingency plans for the evacuation of British nationals, when it was bombed. In his evaluation of DeWolf's performance, Vice-Admiral C.E. Kennedy Purvis, RN (CS 1), commended his ability and character and recommended him for accelerated promotion.

Such praise was common in DeWolf's evaluations, but promotion was slow in the small interwar RCN. C.P. Nixon, a young watch keeper under DeWolf in the destroyer *St. Laurent*, remembers him arriving on the bridge on 26 June 1940, his thirty-eighth birthday, and accepting congratulations by grumbling, "Too damned young for the last war and too damned old for this one!"[6] He had reason to think that: he was a somewhat long-in-the-tooth lieutenant-commander whose prospects did not look great, at least not to him. Four days later, everything changed. The 1 July promotion list revealed that he had made commander, and his chief benefactor, Rear-Admiral G.C. Jones, then Commanding Officer Atlantic Coast (COAC), immediately whisked him to Halifax.[7] Opportunity now came fast and furious. As Staff Officer (Operations) and later Chief Staff Officer in Halifax, DeWolf was deeply involved in planning convoy escort operations in the northwest Atlantic. It was a critical time in the RCN's history, when it never had enough resources to fit mushrooming demands and those burdens fell heavily on the few naval professionals who knew what they were about. Jones was flattering in his evaluation of DeWolf, noting that he was performing the duties of a Chief of Staff in the rank of captain.

In May 1942, DeWolf moved to NSHQ as Director of Plans and Secretary to the Chiefs of Staff Committee (CSC), arguably the most influential appointments of his career. Whereas in Halifax he had been embroiled in the day-to-day running of the war from an operational command perspective, he was now occupied with strategic planning at service, national and alliance levels. Besides attending all CSC meetings, he maintained regular contact with the influential secretary to the cabinet, Arnold Heeney, and with the heads of the Canadian military missions overseas; he also occasionally briefed the prime minister and Cabinet War Committee on naval issues. His signal accomplishment came during the negotiations surrounding the creation of the Canadian Northwest Atlantic Command. Besides providing shrewd counsel in NSHQ, he twice took the lead in presenting the Canadian position at sensitive, high-level discussions in Washington. DeWolf not only had a firm grasp of the issues at hand, but his naval superiors were confident that he could present the RCN's point of view logically and forthrightly, without offending American and British allies.[8]

Later staff and flag appointments increased that experience. As Assistant Chief of the Naval Staff (ACNS) in 1945–46, DeWolf virtually ran the day-to-day affairs of the navy. The CNS, Vice-Admiral Jones, spent much of his time in Halifax — and, according to DeWolf, even when Jones was in Ottawa, he so abhorred attending meetings that he usually dispatched his trusted ACNS instead. It is worth mentioning one decision DeWolf took at this time, as it underscored his practical approach to naval planning. The RCN had agreed to take over two light fleet carriers and eight Crescent-class fleet destroyers from the RN, but with the war won in September 1945, steps were taken to cancel some of the ships as the constricted peacetime navy would not have the personnel to man them. In a memorandum to the CNS, the Director of Plans, Captain H.S. Rayner, recommended giving up the commitment to man the second carrier, taking the first two Crescents but manning a third only "if circumstances permit."[9] DeWolf disagreed, telling Rayner that the third Crescent should be cancelled outright: "Does it matter if we only have 11 destroyers instead of 18, if 3 or 4 must be in reserve?" Regarding the second carrier, DeWolf grasped the political component of the decision, instructing Rayner, "I think we must plan to man the 2nd Carrier—whatever the delay."[10] He understood instinctively that if the requirement for a second carrier was taken off the books, it would be difficult, if not impossible, to resurrect it in the more cautious peacetime environment. DeWolf's steady performance as ACNS impressed politicians as well as his naval superiors, and upon Jones's sudden death in February 1946 he was one of four candidates considered as his replacement.[11]

In 1948, DeWolf became Flag Officer Pacific Command (FOPC), where he passed two relatively tranquil years until the Korean War burst forth in the final weeks of his appointment. He guided the preparations for the immediate deployment of the first destroyers to the Far East. From 1950 to 1952, DeWolf served as VCNS under his friend and mentor Harold Grant.[12] Although the two had similar philosophies, their tenures as CNS were vastly different; the naval budget had almost tripled during Grant's time, while it fell by more than that during DeWolf's. Nonetheless, as VCNS, DeWolf worked closely with Grant and was involved in critical issues, including defining the RCN's role in NATO, planning expansion activities, and guiding the development of the new St. Laurent–class destroyer escorts. From late 1952 until he became CNS in January 1956, DeWolf served as chairman of the Canadian Joint Mission in Washington, where, among many duties, he represented Canada on the influential NATO Standing Group. He forged useful contacts with key American officers[13] and formed working-level relations with naval representatives of other NATO countries, who used DeWolf as a conduit between themselves and the Americans. He travelled widely on inspection tours, and in 1955 attended an atomic test where he witnessed first-hand the massive destructive capability of nuclear weapons.

If DeWolf's vast experience in the policy and strategic-planning arenas taught him how to cope with the issues he would encounter as CNS, his reputation as Canada's pre-eminent fighting sailor earned him the respect and loyalty of the navy he would lead. Known as a brilliant navigator and ship handler from the time he was a junior officer, DeWolf's experiences in the destroyers *St. Laurent* and *Haida* during the Second World War lifted him to legendary status within the navy and earned him the moniker "Hard Over Harry." As captain of *St. Laurent* in European waters during the dark days of the summer of 1940, he ordered the first shots ever fired in anger by a Canadian warship while covering the evacuation of British forces from France, and weeks later he led the well-publicized *Arandora Star* rescue, in which 857 survivors were plucked from the North Atlantic after the ship had been torpedoed. As captain of *Haida* from 1943–44 he became Canada's most illustrious naval hero, sinking or forcing aground three enemy destroyers, participating in the destruction of a U-boat, shooting up coastal convoys, and courageously stopping close off an enemy coast to rescue survivors of his stricken flotilla mate, HMCS *Athabaskan*.[14] DeWolf's performance received official and public acclaim, and although he was not Canada's Nelson by temperament or personality, he was by reputation.[15]

DeWolf's personality also contributed to his reputation. He was by nature quiet and reserved; C.P. Nixon recalled that he "was not given to making inspiring speeches or pep talks to his men; in fact he did not need to because his professional skill was always so apparent that it earned them his automatic respect."[16] Peter Chance, who also served under DeWolf in *St. Laurent*, described him as "curt in his manner, always fair, didn't laugh much, he smiled and had short chuckles."[17] DeWolf was also renowned for his short fuse, and he did not suffer fools gladly. An incident in *Haida* illustrates that well. In a tribute written after DeWolf's death, Lieutenant Ray Phillips recalls that he was dutifully plotting contacts as officer of the watch one night in early 1944 while the destroyer was steaming down the Irish Sea: "About 0200 Commander DeWolf arrived on the bridge and said 'Where are we?' to which I proudly replied, 'We were there [pointing to the chart] about a minute ago.' Wrong! The captain said, 'Phillips, when I want a history lesson, I'll ask for one,' then looked at the chart, took a couple of quick bearings, and left the bridge without comment."[18]

DeWolf's countenance did not improve with age. Commodore James Plomer dubbed him "Admiral Bang" for his abrupt style,[19] and subordinates who ventured into the CNS's office before 1000 in the morning would usually next be seen scurrying from the flats, brow-beaten and in complete disarray. When queried on this by the author, an impish admiral admitted to often being in a sour mood in the mornings due to the mountain of files that confronted him each day.

It is easy to gain the impression of a distant, ill-tempered officer, but that was not the man. He had a wonderful sense of humour, but rather than being marked by loud guffaws, it was expressed by a quiet chuckle and sparkling eyes. He enjoyed the company of friends, particularly over a game of golf, fishing or poker, would do anything for a former ship-mate, and was exceedingly loyal to his friends.[20] He was a natural com-petitor, but none of his compatriots doubted that his rise to the top was due to anything but skill, honesty and hard work.

DeWolf's reputation and experience gave him the confidence of the service. That, in combination with his reserved personality, may account for the independent approach he took in running the navy. As just one example, unlike his predecessors and successor, he did not convene any formal senior officers' conferences during his time as CNS. Rear-Admiral Robert Timbrell remembers DeWolf instructing members of the Naval Board that he alone would make, and be responsible for, board decisions.[21] There were many talented thinkers in naval staff positions during his tenure as CNS who produced some remarkable, wide-ranging studies, and it is evident from his statements in Naval Board and Chiefs of Staff Committee meetings, as well as from his own memoranda, that he had a firm grasp of the many issues that crossed his desk. Moreover, although he may not have been all that approachable as CNS, he was not isolated from his advisors and often called upon them for technical advice.[22] He simply wanted the last word, and events bear out that when he was CNS, it was very much Harry DeWolf's navy.

Over the past few years there has been much debate about whether senior officers should be warriors or managers. If DeWolf's example is to be followed, they can, and must, be both. With Vice-Admiral Mainguy leaving early over fiscal mismanagement, it made sense for DeWolf to focus on that part of the ship when he became CNS. But no matter what the fate of his predecessor, it was in his philosophy and experience to concentrate on what is now referred to as resource management. It may seem odd, given DeWolf's reputation as Canada's most renowned naval warrior, but perhaps his greatest legacy as CNS was the steps he took to tighten up and professionalize fiscal management within the navy.

The key move in this process involved the establishment of a naval comptroller. The genesis of this position can be traced to the navy's Committee on the Control of Manpower and Money, which, as a result of pressure on all three services to tighten up, was charged with recommending the most suitable organization for the RCN to screen financial requirements and administer naval appropriations.[23] The committee found inefficiencies that they thought could best be improved by establishing a comptroller-type organization. With several examples to follow, including the RCAF and the army, they settled on the USN model as the most appropriate because its comptroller acted only in an advisory role, in contrast to other models such as the RCAF's, where the office exercised considerable control. The RCN thought that would diminish the responsibility of the VCNS organization, and instead recommended that the naval comptroller should "be responsible to the Chief of Naval Staff for advising all Members of Naval Board, but not be a Board member."[24]

It is unclear how DeWolf came by his business acumen — probably through his family, who ran T.A.S. DeWolf and Sons, a private shipping firm in Halifax — but he had firm ideas about how things should work, and they reflected his practical, common-sense philosophy. When the committee's report was tabled before the Naval Board, DeWolf disagreed with the premise that the naval comptroller should have only an advisory role, and cited an obvious inconsistency in the proposed organizational structure that everyone else had overlooked. According to the minutes, "CNS pointed out that the Comptroller was shown as acting in an *advisory* capacity whereas his three Directors were designated *control* over manpower, materiel and money respectively. CNS considered this principal [*sic*] to be wrong. He drew a comparison with the position held and responsibility exercised by a Comptroller in industrial organizations."[25]

Despite his usual autocratic style when running board meetings, in this case he did not force a revision of the terms of reference for the comptroller position. Instead, after "lengthy discussion" he said he was not still "fully convinced," but noted that the DND Rank Structure Committee still had to approve the new organization.[26] As he probably suspected it would, that committee shared his thinking. At the Naval Board meeting on 2 May 1956, it was confirmed that the naval comptroller would be "a member of the Naval Board responsible to the CNS for an effective co-ordinated control over manpower and money." DeWolf told his officers that the comptroller "would be in a position to exercise a policing authority. If in the event a certain programme or project appeared as though it were going to exceed its authorized expenditure, the Comptroller would be in a position to hold up an expenditure or commitment." Treasury Board had advised him, he continued, that such an organization "should follow the pattern of the business administration in most large companies where the

Comptroller did control all financial aspects once company policy and budgets were set."[27]

This gave the naval comptroller considerable power and responsibility, which is what DeWolf wanted and what the fiscal environment demanded. The officer DeWolf selected for the position, Commodore (S [Supply]) R.A. Wright, proved a perfect fit. A former supply officer-in-chief, Wright had a reputation for integrity and for putting the good of the navy ahead of all else. Importantly, he had taken advanced courses in business administration and was known to be a severe critic of naval administration, feelings he apparently expressed freely and bluntly. As comptroller, he wielded his power most effectively. It is beyond the scope of this piece to detail his activities, but a few examples demonstrate how he not only tightened up financial accounting but also introduced budget forecasting as a planning tool. At a meeting on 10 July 1957, he tabled an analysis of the 1957–58 estimates broken down on a functional basis, providing a forecast of expenditure trends up to 1962.[28] A year later, on 30 October 1958, he introduced an agenda item in the estimates by illustrating "general trends over the past few years in relation of the National Defence Budget to the Gross National Product, the Financial Position of the Navy, Naval Expenditures by Cost Category, and Distribution of the Defence Dollar by Requirement."[29] Finally, in January 1959, when considering ways of gouging some $14 million out of the 1959–60 estimates, members of the board had for reference a graph prepared by Wright's section that illustrated how, since 1952, the estimates had been divided between personnel costs, other operating costs and new programs, and provided a forecast ahead to 1962–63. It is evident from the minutes that this analysis enabled them to calculate the funds that would be available for future programs.[30] Although such practices are routine today, they were unique to Naval Board in that period.

Wright served as comptroller until March 1962. He set a high standard for those who followed, and wielded the power associated with his new position with skill and imagination. He can probably be credited for introducing modern management thinking into the RCN, and he certainly injected it into high-level decision-making. That this approach was accepted by a generation of senior officers with a reputation for being hidebound was due not just to Wright's obvious talent; other members of the Naval Board knew he had the complete support of the CNS, and that he was doing what DeWolf wanted done.

Placing the RCN on a firm course in terms of fiscal management was only one of a number of urgent priorities that DeWolf faced as CNS. Fleet composition and ship replacement were others. When we consider the history of the Canadian navy, it is an understatement to observe that its leaders have traditionally had immense difficulty in persuading politicians to accept their justification for forces. Indeed, except during times of national mobilization or when there was a clear threat on the horizon, it has been a difficult row to hoe indeed. In the navy's early history, leaders often depended upon outside influences to make their case to government. There is no better example than during the 1943 Quebec Conference, when Vice-Admiral Nelles went behind the back of Prime Minister Mackenzie King to convince the Admiralty to have Winston Churchill, rather than Canada's own naval staff, propose cruisers for the RCN.[31]

NATO commitments and SACLANT force goals filled much the same role during the 1950s. Indeed, these numbers became almost sacrosanct, a practice Doug Bland calls "the strategy of commitments."[32] The naval staff would present a number formulated by SACLANT — as in 1958 when, under MC-48, one CVL and twenty-nine escorts were to be made available by D+30[33] — and say that is what they had been asked to commit. The numbers did reflect a certain strategic reality, but they were also a handy tool to persuade politicians of the navy's requirements. Sometimes, it even appears that these recommendations sometimes originated with Canadian officers appointed to SACLANT. Under DeWolf, these force goals played a different role; rather than the goal to be attained, they became the bottom line. Quite simply, as resources got tighter, platforms that he considered extraneous to the navy's SACLANT ASW commitment could go. This was not without controversy, and, as discussion over the fates of the cruiser *Quebec* and the carrier *Magnificent* demonstrate, in taking that course DeWolf sometimes had to overcome opposition from officers who remained wedded to the principal of a balanced fleet, or at least the RCN notion of it.

Quebec was the first to go. Two days after becoming CNS, DeWolf recommended to Minister of National Defence Ralph Campney that the cruiser should be paid off in April 1956. Only a month earlier, in the face of naval advice to the contrary, the minister had ordered Vice-Admiral Mainguy to keep the cruiser in commission, but now Campney approved DeWolf's recommendation.[34] The timing and manner in which the decision was made are telling. Not only did they indicate that DeWolf held some sway over the minister, but he made the move — his first as CNS — unilaterally, sending a clear message that he was in control and that there would be firm direction from the top. Three days later, when he chaired his first Naval Board meeting, he explained, "There is no requirement for *Quebec* other than for training purposes and she has reached the point where it has become questionable whether her training value justifies the cost of maintenance." He then ordered a study to investigate whether the cruiser should be kept in reserve or declared surplus. Ultimately, the latter choice was made, and the navy's other cruiser, HMCS *Ontario*, later suffered a similar fate.[35] At the same meeting he directed that discussions be launched with the Admiralty for the return of the carrier *Magnificent* to the RN.[36] With *Bonaventure* due to join the fleet in January 1957, "Maggie" was no longer required.

This latter directive caused angst among officers with visions of retaining *Magnificent*, and they fought hard to save her. Indeed, the debate to retain or acquire a second carrier was one of the most contentious DeWolf faced. When a staff committee reappraising naval war plans presented its conception of the fleet to Naval Board on 18 April 1956, it included both *Bonaventure* and *Magnificent*, with the latter in the guise of a helicopter carrier. Despite the fact that, as ACNS ten years earlier, he had left room for a second carrier, he would now have none of it, pointing out that "it was unrealistic to include *Magnificent*, as the requirement for a helicopter carrier had yet to be established and [government] support for this addition to the Fleet was remote." This response should have been predictable. In February, DeWolf had both dismissed the idea of a helicopter carrier for the fleet ("no authority exists to provide such a ship") and the helicopter squadron that would operate from it ("no authority exists to form a squadron of 12 helicopters as an ASW squadron").[37] In May, Maggie's supporters tried again when the Warfare Study Group included her as a helicopter carrier. DeWolf commented that the helicopter's ASW capability had yet to be proved, and after listening to what is described as "discussion at length," he concluded that "no case had yet been presented to justify the RCN operating a second carrier within our present [budgetary] limitations."[38] That marked the end of Maggie, but not the notion of a second carrier.

Stuart Soward's study of Canadian naval aviation suggests that DeWolf was less supportive of naval aviation than he should have been. One vehicle used is the fate of the report of the Ad Hoc Committee of Naval Aviation, which was struck in the summer of 1956 to analyze RCN air strength in relation to the RCAF's. Among other measures, the report recommended that the navy should have two operational carriers to bolster the fleet's air-defence capability through the use of all-weather fighters with aerial early warning (AEW) support. *Bonaventure* could serve as a specialized ASW carrier, while the second, larger carrier could carry out more of a general-purpose role, flying off ASW and AEW CS2F Trackers, ASW helicopters and all-weather F2H-3 Banshee fighters. It was an ambitious plan, and the group was clearly pointing to an Essex-class for the second carrier, which they went so far as to name HMCS *Vancouver* in their presentation.[39] Soward's account explains how the report went through the Policy and Projects Co-ordinating Committee (PPCC)[40] screening process, but got no further. "It was Commodore Storrs' belief that the report was no doubt taken to CNS Vice-Admiral DeWolf by [VCNS] Rear-Admiral Lay, where it was probably summarily rejected and died right then and there. Storrs is certain the report never appeared on a Naval Board agenda."[41]

In fact it did. The Naval Board minutes show that it was discussed in detail, and rather than "summarily rejecting" the report, DeWolf in fact congratulated the committee on its work.[42] Storrs may have been correct in the sense that, although the concept of a second carrier made it to Naval Board, it did not get serious consideration. That should not surprise. The ad hoc committee had been established as a result of pressure from the Chiefs of Staff Committee for the navy to justify a total strength of more than 100 aircraft to support the twenty-four that went to sea in the carrier. The navy made its case well and had its position accepted by the CSC, albeit grudgingly. But DeWolf realized that, in the fiscal climate of the day, it would be foolhardy to seriously consider a second, larger carrier that would require more aircraft, aircrew, sailors and infrastructure.[43] Although DeWolf recognized the critical role of naval aviation — he had co-authored with Nelson Lay the original wartime study that recommended a Canadian naval air service — he thought it expensive and that something closer to the bare minimum would have to suffice; an Essex-class carrier was far from that. Moreover, these discussions were held in December 1956; within months, the helicopter-destroyer marriage would prove viable, forever torpedoing the idea of a second carrier.

As hard as they were for an officer who, with many others, had striven for years to build a balanced fleet centred around "big ships" like carriers and cruisers, the decisions over which ships to cut were relatively straightforward compared with the complex machinations required to gain approval for the various ship-replacement programs DeWolf tried to get through. The one he was proudest of — indeed, which he considered his greatest achievement as CNS — was the six-ship Mackenzie-class program, approved by the Cabinet Defence Committee in April 1958.[44] For DeWolf, the strength of the program lay in the fact that it kept Canadian shipyards busy and reduced costs by closely following the proven Restigouche design.[45] Unfortunately, the ships barely fulfilled operational requirements. The navy initially investigated a design that was larger than the Restigouches and would have more effective weaponry, including Tartar guided-missile systems for air defence as well as improved sonar systems. Conceptualization and design work had fallen behind, however, and had that design been selected there would be a delay in the shipbuilding program. DeWolf therefore approved a design with clear limitations. As a result of this compromise, only the final two ships of this program — *Nipigon* and *Annapolis* — were fitted with helicopter decks and VDS, and could be considered state-of-the-art ASW platforms upon completion.

Two other ship-replacement programs, neither of which received approval, provide other insights into DeWolf's vision for the navy, demonstrating how he stayed inside the box of fiscal reality. The first was the escort-replacement program discussed in late 1958 and early

1959. The threat of submarine-launched cruise missiles and nuclear propulsion had altered the maritime defence environment; especially alarming was intelligence that the Soviets would put the two together. In a 1958 speech, DeWolf summed up the threat succinctly: "war today — we can compete. But the nuclear s/m is quite another matter. Being a sailor I believe the nuclear submarine, with the IRBM [intermediate-range ballistic missile], is a superior weapon, and will have greater influence in peace or war, than the ICBM [intercontinental ballistic missile]."[46]

DeWolf's statement reflects deep concern about the RCN's ability to handle such a threat. Staff studies indicated that ASW capability could be improved by modernizing existing ships with a combination of the new long-range, hull-mounted SQS-503 sonar, SQS-504 variable depth sonar, and ship-borne helicopters.[47] Due to the age of most destroyer hulls, however, as well as the impossibility of mounting VDS in the Prestonian-class frigates, such improvements could not be made uniformly throughout the fleet. With war-built destroyers such as the Tribals nearing the end of their life expectancy, and with only the Mackenzies on the way, new oceangoing escorts were required if the RCN was to be capable of handling foreseeable operational requirements on the North Atlantic. The Golden Age may have been shiny, but the plating was thin indeed.

On 24 September 1958, the Naval Board directed the preparation of new ship designs.[48] The staff requirements bypassed PPCC screening and were to be completed by 1 January 1959, which would indicate that DeWolf wanted to move quickly so that the navy would have a design ready to follow the final two Mackenzies, "so as not to fall behind on the 2 a year replacement programme."[49] Initially, staff directorates focused on three types of ship: a general-purpose destroyer, a destroyer escort and an ASW frigate.[50] The main difference between the frigates and destroyers was that the latter had superior air-defence capability and possessed greater general-purpose capability, but all three were equipped with ASW helicopters as well as the latest models of hull-mounted and variable-depth sonar. Interestingly, staff dubbed the $30 million ASW frigate "the austerity A/S vessel,"[51] presumably on the assumption that it represented the cheapest option. At some point in December 1959, however, DeWolf inserted an option for an even less expensive frigate, which could be constructed for $19.7 million. It had the same weaponry and sensor suite as the "austerity" ship, but was shorter at 330 feet overall (versus 390), had less displacement at 2,310 tons (versus 3,650), and was slower at 21 knots, versus 26 (see Table II). Thus, on 28 January 1959, the ACNS(W), Commodore Jeffry Brock, laid four options before the Naval Board: an ASW frigate, an ASW fast frigate, an ASW destroyer escort and a general-purpose destroyer. In keeping with his practical bent, DeWolf led the board to a decision for the ASW frigate.

Table II: COMPARISON OF SHIPS' CHARACTERISTICS[52]

	ASW Frigate	ASW Fast Frigate	ASW Destroyer Escort	General-Purpose Destroyer
Primary Task	(a) to detect, locate and destroy enemy submarines, singly or with other vessels, aircraft and in support of other detection systems	(a) to detect, locate and destroy enemy submarines, singly or with other vessels, aircraft and in support of other detection systems	(a) to provide defence against submarines and air attack launched from the sea, singly or with other vessels, aircraft and in support of other detection systems	(a) to provide defence against submarine, surface and air attack launched from the sea, singly or with other vessels, aircraft and in support of other detection systems
	(b) to provide very limited protection to own ship against air attack	(b) to provide very limited protection to own ship against air attack	(b) to provide limited protection to own ship against air attack and to contribute in some measure to the air defence of the fleet	(b) to provide limited protection to own ship against air attack and to contribute in some measure to the air defence of the fleet
Secondary Task	(a) to operate as part as an A/S group, and convoy escort	(a) to operate as part as an A/S carrier group, and convoy escort	(a) to operate as part as an A/S carrier group, and convoy escort	(a) to operate as part as an A/S carrier group, and convoy escort
	(b) informative control of fixed-wing A/S aircraft	(b) informative control of fixed-wing A/S aircraft	(b) Direct aircraft	(b) Direct aircraft

	ASW Frigate	ASW Fast Frigate	ASW Destroyer Escort	General-Purpose Destroyer
Secondary Task			(c) Air Defence Control Ship	(c) Air Defence Control Ship
			(d) Detect and defeat guided missiles	(d) Detect and defeat guided missiles
			(e) Seaward extension to the air defence of Canada	(e) Support ship in combined/joint operations
				(f) Destroy enemy vessels
				(g) Seaward extension to the air defence of Canada
Armament	(a) 3 A/S helicopters	(a) 3 A/S helicopters	(a) 2 A/S helicopters	(a) 2 A/S helicopters
	(b) 2 NC torpedo throwers with 12 Mk 44 torpedoes	(b) 2 NC torpedo throwers with 12 Mk 44 torpedoes	(b) 2 NC torpedo throwers with 12 Mk 44 torpedoes	(b) 2 NC torpedo throwers with 12 Mk 44 torpedoes
	(c) 2 Torpedo tubes with 6 wire-guided torpedoes	(c) 2 Torpedo tubes with 6 wire-guided torpedoes	(c) 2 Torpedo tubes with 8 wire-guided torpedoes	(c) 2 Torpedo tubes with 8 wire-guided torpedoes
	(d) 1 A/S Mortar Mk 10 with 60 projectiles	(d) 1 A/S Mortar Mk 10 with 60 projectiles	(d) 1 A/S Mortar Mk 10 with 60 projectiles	(d) No A/S Mortar fitted
	(e) 1 Green Light quad mtg. with 36 missiles	(e) 1 Green Light quad mtg. with 36 missiles	(e) 1 Tartar mtg. with 42 missiles	(e) 1 Tartar mtg. with 42 missiles
				(f) 1 5/54
Cost (For vessels to be provided for in fiscal 1960–61)	$19,750,000	$30,800,000	$47,750,000	$55,000,000

DeWolf's rationale reflected his understanding of the realities both of operations on the North Atlantic and in the corridors of power in Ottawa. Speed was the big factor in determining the cost of oceangoing warships. "By accepting a reduction in speed," the board minutes argue, "more weaponry could be carried and greater endurance obtained within the same cost. Surface ships capable of, say, 30 knots can rarely keep up that speed in North Atlantic conditions in any event. The differential in speed is not so important when a helicopter is carried." In terms of threats: "It seems likely that in future the submarine is going to have the advantage of speed over the surface ship. Having recognized this factor it is doubtful whether a difference of five knots speed would justify the additional construction cost." Finally, the 21-knot ships would fit into the performance of the current fleet: "The slower of the two proposed Frigates would still have sufficient speed for employment, under normal conditions, in escorting duties with the Carrier."[53]

The ASW frigate could do the job expected of it, albeit with little margin. DeWolf, however, was willing to sacrifice capability in order to get the ship-replacement program approved. Recall that he considered the Mackenzie program — which maintained the momentum of the RCN ship-replacement program and kept Canadian shipyards busy — to be his greatest accomplishment as CNS. In that instance, he had been willing to forgo capability to get that program through. He was following the same strategy by selecting the relatively inexpensive ASW frigate over other, more capable, designs.

Brock's role in this process still is unclear, but it is of interest to note that, while he failed to gain approval from DeWolf for the general-purpose destroyer, he later won approval from his successor, Vice-Admiral H.S. Rayner, for the general-purpose frigate (GPF) that was only slightly less capable. "The GPF never struck the right note with me," DeWolf asserted later in life. "If we built a good ASW ship, she would be capable of doing what the government wanted the RCN to do; we didn't need the GPF for that."[54] That expresses, in a nutshell, his philosophy of naval pragmatism: this is the navy's precisely defined role, and here is what is needed to carry it out. Some would argue that by making such a choice, DeWolf was rejecting the "balanced-fleet" concept. What he actually envisioned and worked towards was a "balanced ASW fleet," which would fulfill the navy's role as defined by Canadian defence policy. DeWolf freely admitted that, while officers like Brock, Plomer, his old friend Nelson Lay, and others formulated ambitious plans for the navy, he proceeded cautiously because he believed that support for a large, expensive navy simply did not exist within either the government or the public that elected it.

Working within a tight budget requires a deft balancing act, and by choosing the cheaper ASW frigate, DeWolf left flexibility for other projects. The RCN Medium-Range Plan for the period 1960–1965, submitted three months after the frigate decision in March 1959, projected a fleet for 1966 that included eight ASW frigates. Strength in other types remained relatively consistent — except for submarines. Whereas the 1960 force would comprise one USN and three RN submarines, all on loan, the 1966 force increased that by one USN boat, but also included two Canadian nuclear submarines.[55] Not only would the RCN have its own submarine service, but also, for planning purposes, it was to be nuclear-powered.

The nuclear submarine program of the late 1950s is a complex tale, with many gaps in the historiography. DeWolf's role is one such gap — in fact, his name seldom appears in published literature on the subject, which emphasizes the role of the technical branch and such officers as Commodore B.R. Spencer, the RCN's engineer-in-chief, and Captain S. Mathwin Davis. To be sure, they were significant actors, especially Spencer, but since DeWolf kept firm control over most issues, it seems critical to understand his role in the most expensive and potentially most revolutionary project under consideration on his watch. Although he has usually been portrayed as some sort of Gloomy Gus who greeted the navy's report on nuclear submarines with reluctance and disdain,[56] his interest and involvement was far greater, and far more objective. He realized that, given their enormous cost, it would be extremely difficult to gain government support for nuclear submarines, but he thought it vital that the navy have its own submarine service for ASW training, and he recognized the capability of submarines, both nuclear and conventional, as anti-submarine platforms.

The navy's first formal interest in nuclear power appears to have come in late 1949 when, after a visit to the reactor at Chalk River, Ontario, Commander (E) Geoff Phillips recommended that the navy launch a feasibility study into that form of propulsion. It seems to have gone nowhere. In August 1954, however, the month before the world's first nuclear-propelled attack submarine (SSN) was commissioned, the Naval Board launched engineering studies for a fast escort with a steam-turbine plant with gas-turbine boost and for "the practical application of nuclear fuel in warship propulsion plants."[57] The matter rattled around the naval technical community until the summer of 1956, and the outspoken naval constructor-in-chief, Captain Rolly Baker, perhaps best expressed their opinion. Baker said that to match the 35-knot sub-merged speed of nuclear submarines — or even fast conventional boats based on the *Albacore* design — would require a 4,000-ton, 600-foot surface ship. "It is clear, however, that if *Albacore*-type submarines are to be Nuclear propelled, the only possible Naval counter measures, whether surface or submarine, must also employ Nuclear power. Therefore the RCN as an anti-submarine force must go Nuclear or *go*."[58]

DeWolf shared Baker's prediction. In October 1958, he told the Ottawa *Citizen* that the Skipjack-class SSN under construction in the U.S., which was essentially a nuclear-powered Albacore, "will be one of the best anti-submarine ships in sight." He emphasized, however, that "considerable study has to be completed before any decision is reached whether Canada actually will secure a nuclear-powered submarine." By underscoring that, he was following the strictures set out by the Naval Board in 1954, which cautioned that long-range engineering studies were a prerequisite for any new propulsion systems. It was a strategy that DeWolf adhered to closely; if the navy was going to acquire nuclear sub-marines, the groundwork had first to be laid. Moreover, if he could not get SSNs for the navy right off — and by that time he was working with-in an overall naval planning window starting in 1964 — DeWolf seemed determined to lay the groundwork for their acquisition in the future. From the start, he saw three inhibiting factors: a lack of nuclear expert-ise within the navy; whether Canadian industry could actually build nuclear propulsion systems; and, of course, the extremely high cost.

To foster the development of expertise within the service, he sup-ported the program to send engineering officers on nuclear power courses at the Massachusetts Institute of Technology (MIT) or to train at the RN's nuclear-engineering establishment at Harwell.[61] Thus, engi-neers like Commander (E) R.S. Stephens and Lieutenant-Commander

(L) C.R. Nixon learned the basics of nuclear propulsion, as well as how the RN and USN proposed to harness it for use in warships. It is a measure of DeWolf's interest in the welfare of his personnel that, when it was later brought to his attention that these two officers might suffer in the promotion "sweepstakes" because they had not registered the requisite sea time as a result of their nuclear studies, he wrote the head of personnel: "I agree with the importance of this project and that the officers selected should not suffer any career disadvantage. How can I assure this — e.g., after my own time [as CNS] is up?"[62]

Establishing whether or not Canadian industry had the expertise and capability to manufacture nuclear power plants was the main focus of DeWolf's attention. He worked closely with senior officials at Atomic Energy of Canada Limited (AECL), the Defence Research Board (DRB), in the shipbuilding industry and elsewhere. Beyond trying to establish Canadian industrial capability, he appears to have been seeking to build a broad base of support for an SSN program that had its foundation in industry, which would make it more politically attractive. The RCAF had played that game masterfully with the Avro Arrow, and would play it again for other aircraft.

Rather than a naval priority, DeWolf also wanted to establish nuclear submarines — or at the very least, nuclear propulsion — as a national priority, and he went public to build support. Although he normally kept a low profile, in this instance he mounted a national media campaign, albeit with mixed results. He must have winced at the May 1958 front-page headline in the Victoria *Times-Colonist*: "Hunting, Killing, Nation's Role: Canada-Made, A[tomic]-Powered Submarines to Form RCN's Major Fighting Force." Worse still was the statement, also above the fold, that proclaimed "the first nuclear sub will join the Canadian fleet in about two years or a little more."[63]

Similar reports appeared sporadically in Canadian papers throughout 1958, and they would have caused alarm in the two other services fighting for their own major projects — in the RCAF's case the Avro Arrow, and in the army's the Bobcat fighting vehicle. In an effort to win them over, DeWolf was cautious in his discussions about SSNs within the Chiefs of Staff Committee. Also, when he went to sea in U.S.S. *Seawolf* on a fact-finding trip in December 1957, he invited scientists from DRB, as well as senior officers from the other two services, to come along.[64] *Seawolf*'s performance impressed DeWolf. In a letter to the chairman of Canada Steamship Lines, he wrote, "On Friday 13 December, I was at sea in U.S.S. *Seawolf*, the second nuclear powered submarine. I was greatly impressed with the apparent simplicity of the operation and with what they were able to tell us about future types and costs. Any relaxation of the U.S. Government of the atomic security legislation would be of immediate interest to the RCN. There is no question in my mind that the sooner Canadian industry gets into the nuclear propulsion field the better for all concerned, and anything the navy can do to hasten the day, will have my support."[65]

Establishing industrial potential was clearly uppermost in DeWolf's mind, and he took great care to make sure the navy understood that that was the main purpose of any initial studies. Commodore B.R. Spencer, was a key figure in the early investigation into nuclear propulsion — to the point that he established a small working group that met monthly over lunch. However, when Spencer began discussing specific staff requirements for a Canadian design, DeWolf yanked the leash tight. "I hope there is no misunderstanding about this 'study,'" he cautioned. "I have no thought of starting the development in Canada of a nuclear steam plant. Our entry into this field will depend upon whether or not the USN will pass on their designs and knowledge. Our study is to determine whether or not Canadian Industry could take on the work — given U.S. plans and specs!" The exclamation mark and the tone undoubtedly rattled Spencer, and he responded "Noted. CNS's views are well appreciated and his wishes in this respect will be carried out."[66]

The study DeWolf referred to was being conducted by the Nuclear Submarine Survey Team, and it represented the culmination of DeWolf's strategy. Representatives from DRB, DDP (the Department of Defence Production) and AECL played key roles, emblematic of the industrial-naval consensus that DeWolf tried to put together, and two of the members, Commander Stephens and Lieutenant-Commander Nixon, had built up nuclear experience with the RN and USN respectively. The report, when submitted in June 1959, was comprehensive — not only examining the most suitable boat for the RCN, but also looking into the financial, industrial and infrastructure implications of such a program.

There were gaps, to be sure, especially in terms of understanding personnel requirements, but the report presented a fairly realistic blueprint for the process of acquiring or building SSNs for the Canadian navy.[67]

Realistic, perhaps, but distinctly unaffordable in the Canadian context. At about $55 million per Skipjack if bought direct from American shipyards, and about $65 million each if built in a Canadian shipyard, the price tag was simply too high.[68] When it became apparent that conventional boats such as the USN's Barbel class could be effective ASW platforms at far less cost, DeWolf pursued that course. By doing so he was following the same strategy as when he selected ASW frigates over more expensive designs. "In the present economy," he told shipbuilders in 1958, "there is, of course, the conflict between the need for numbers and the need for quality."[69] Like the frigates, conventional submarines would provide adequate ASW quality in better numbers.

Formulating programs within the navy was one thing; getting them approved by the Chiefs of Staff Committee was something else entirely. The CSC's role was to advise the minister and the Cabinet Defence Committee on defence policy, to prepare strategic appreciations and military plans, and to co-ordinate the efforts of the three services. DeWolf was familiar with the environment from his service as secretary to the committee during the Second World War. Much had changed since then, mainly due to General Charles Foulkes, who served as chairman from 1951 to 1960. Opinions of Foulkes vary; many of his army colleagues detested him, but historians have generally been kinder. Jack Granatstein describes him as a "shrewd and political" officer who became "Canada's most powerful military mandarin and the creator of the post-war Canadian armed forces," while Sean Maloney considers him a man of vision whose career serves as a primer on how to be an effective Chief of Defence Staff (CDS).[70]

Foulkes understood politics and politicians, and the committee minutes are full of references to what the government might or might not approve. Colonel R.L. Raymont, who worked closely with Foulkes for a number of years, described his approach as "the art of the possible." That coincides with DeWolf's philosophy, which indicates that, besides the fact that both were quiet men who enjoyed the peaceful pursuit of fishing, they also shared a professional outlook in that they appreciated the limits of defence in the Canadian context. It is of interest, therefore, to see how the naval programs brought forward by DeWolf survived the shrewd political scrutiny of Foulkes. Of course, the other service chiefs also had a say in the process, as did Air Vice-Marshal Frank Miller (RCAF, retired), the deputy minister for most of DeWolf's time, but the minutes of the CSC make it clear that Foulkes was chairman in more than just name.

DeWolf's indoctrination came quickly. When the development of a new naval tactical trainer was discussed at his second CSC meeting, DeWolf had to endure a lecture from Foulkes on the elements of good naval training. Introducing the item, DeWolf explained that "the primary function of the trainer was to exercise force commanders and staffs, operations personnel and aircrews in anti-submarine warfare and it could be readily adopted to simulate any foreseeable maritime warfare situations likely to confront the RCN and RCAF.... While it was not suggested that the Trainer would take the place of exercises at sea, it would add very considerably to the value obtained in such exercises." Foulkes countered that he was not convinced that the trainer "was an essential requirement for training of naval personnel in peacetime. It was his belief that the environment where a man was required to fight — in the case of the Navy, a ship — was the best training area."[71] Miller expressed dissatisfaction with the structure of the proposal, and eventually, despite the support of the Chief of the Air Staff (CAS) and the chairman of the Defence Research Board (DRB), DeWolf lost the fight, and the navy was directed to consider trainers already developed by the British.[72]

The push to "go allied" confronted DeWolf again when the navy's Digital Automatic Tracking and Remoting system (DATAR) went before the committee. What follows is a long and complicated story, but it indicates both the difficulty of gaining support for such programs and the strategies DeWolf utilized to try to win that battle. DATAR was a truly cutting-edge plotting system designed to handle the increasingly complex tracking problems associated with modern naval warfare. The projected cost of the project was immense — $80 million, or the price of 1.25 nuclear submarines — and the navy and DRB initially wanted $650,000 as seed money to conduct preliminary reliability studies. Foulkes opposed DATAR from the moment it first came before the CSC in July 1956, questioning Canada's unilateral development of the system for small ships. In view of the high cost, he believed the government "would feel that Canada could afford to await the outcome of either United States or United Kingdom development in this field."[73]

Foulkes refused to budge when the issue came up a second time in October 1956, despite the fact that both the CAS and the chairman of the DRB declared the system essential for the RCN. He also went against the arguments that the RN and USN were developing an air defence and not an ASW plotting system, and that after they had finished their project it would take at least another three years to modify the system for Canadian use. DeWolf was strangely quiet at that meeting, but was tasked to approach the USN about developing DATAR as a joint system.[74] Nine months later, he informed the CSC that the RCN and DRB had reduced requirements for the system, tailoring it specifically for Canadian needs. When pressed again by Foulkes on American and British approaches, the CNS replied that they would only get around to small-ship development after they had fitted their carrier task forces, thus causing an unacceptable delay. This time, Foulkes's response appeared a bit more hopeful, and DeWolf and DRB agreed to review the program with an eye towards spreading out costs over a longer period.[75]

The DATAR debate came to a head at the end of 1958, almost two years after it was first brought forward for consideration. To this point, DeWolf had used different strategies, letting others lead the discussions and offering to streamline the system. At a meeting on 13 August 1958, he announced that he had slashed the study program by more than a third, to $450,000; but, opening the door to working with allies, he emphasized that only through such an investigation could it be determined whether a Canadian-developed or modified British or American system would be best. The deputy minister and the chairman remained unconvinced. Miller suggested that the government would not believe that $450,000 was not substantially part of a development program, while Foulkes pushed again for a joint approach. This was more than DeWolf could bear, and for perhaps for the only time, the CSC minutes reveal a degree of testiness on his part: "The Chief of the Naval Staff expressed doubt that either the USN or the RN would be interested in joining in a study designed to point the best way to meet a Canadian requirement." DeWolf indicated that those navies were developing a system designed for large carrier and striking forces, and that "its capabilities would be more comprehensive than the RCN was likely to need and its complexity and cost correspondingly large.

"He was of the opinion," the minutes continued, "that in order to avoid further delay in provision of equipment to meet the vital need to speed up data processing, the Canadian study should be initiated at this time with the expectation that this study would reveal whether the RCN requirement could best be met by procurement from the UK or U.S.A. or by Canadian development." Despite his passionate appeal, the CNS was directed to propose a joint study on a cost-sharing basis with the RN and USN. DeWolf was an accomplished golfer, and after work he often stopped at a driving range to relieve his frustrations. That day he probably pounded his drives long and hard.[76]

DeWolf enjoyed an effective working relationship with both the American Chief of Naval Operations, Admiral Arleigh Burke, and the British First Sea Lord, Admiral Lord Louis Mountbatten, and it appears that he used them to help grease the ways for the final confrontation over DATAR. On 3 December 1958 he informed the CSC that the RN and USN "definitely desired a CANUKUS [Canada–United Kingdom–United States] meeting in mid-1959 to work out a common operational requirement for a tactical data processing system for ASW ships." But before that, "both the USN and RN consider that the RCN should determine its own view independently and assess its own capacity to collaborate on the system." And, in a broadside levelled at Miller's remarks at the previous meeting, he emphasized that the required $450,000 was to investigate means to meet a requirement as opposed to actual development of a system. Finally, Foulkes agreed to put the proposal before the minister.[77] Sadly, DATAR went no further, and the Canadian ideas went south of the border, incorporated into the USN's Naval Tactical Data System (NTDS). It was to be years before Canadian warships had a system equivalent to the one that showed so much promise in the 1950s.

This was typical of the battles DeWolf had to wage within the CSC. He admitted to disappointment in his early days as CNS, when what he considered to be a well-conceived, well-defined, affordable ship-replacement program for four Repeat Restigouche–class DDEs a year was summarily cut in half by the CSC.[78] He also had some tough exchanges with Foulkes, Miller and the CAS over naval aviation.[79] But he won some victories. He gained approval for the support-ship program that ultimately bore fruit with HMCS *Provider*, *Preserver* and *Protecteur*, despite continued questioning from Foulkes as to why the RCN did not use commercial tankers or adopt an RN or USN design.[80] DeWolf also argued successfully for the acquisition of Sidewinder air-to-air missiles, despite opposition from the CAS,[81] and at the end of his appointment he gained agreement over the establishment of a Canadian submarine service. Overall, however, the navy and its programs were a relatively minor concern when defence was considered as a whole, and it is obvious throughout the late 1950s that the RCAF's role in continental air defence was king.

For the most part, DeWolf remained silent during discussions related to the other services, especially during the first couple of years. He would speak out, however, when he thought resources were being allocated unwisely or outside the general areas of NATO and continental defence. In the final CSC debate over the controversial Avro Arrow, for example, he pointed out that Canada would be laying out $5 billion for an aircraft that would not be ready for another five years, and which would then be ineffective against the ICBM threat on the horizon.[82] In January 1959, he questioned the RCAF's acquisition of specialized search-and-rescue aircraft when the government had stipulated in 1946 that those services must be provided from existing forces.[83] In the end, one can conclude that in the CSC as well as the navy, DeWolf maintained a consistent approach to defence policy.

In 1960, speculation mounted as to who might replace Foulkes when his tenure as chairman of the Chiefs of Staff came to an end. Charles Lynch, a plugged-in, widely read political columnist, postulated that DeWolf had the "inside track" by reason of seniority and in the event that "the government wishes to set a precedent that the chairman rotate among the three services." But he noted that, at fifty-six, DeWolf was only a year younger then Foulkes. Lynch outlined other factors against him. One was "getting the man best-fitted for a job that calls increasingly for dealing with top officers in the U.S. and other NATO countries," a statement that overlooked DeWolf's considerable experience in doing precisely that as CNS and as chairman of the joint mission in Washington. Lynch also observed that the navy, "while perhaps the best equipped of the armed services, is the smallest from the point of view of manpower and expenditure." Lynch then presented a case as to why Frank Miller, the current Deputy Minister, was best qualified for the job.[84] When all was said and done, Miller replaced Foulkes and re-entered the air force to become chairman of the CCS and later the first CDS.

Although DeWolf would have appreciated an accurate, objective discussion of his qualifications, it is doubtful whether he was interested in succeeding Foulkes. He was worn out after four and a half years at the helm, and uncomfortable with the defence policy and general practices of the Diefenbaker Government — he complained that John Diefenbaker only met once with the CSC, and on that occasion lectured them on loyalty. "Hard Over Harry" was ready to go alongside.

Did he leave the navy in better shape then he had found it as CNS? Undoubtedly. His pragmatic navalism helped keep the service on track at a time of extreme fiscal pressure and dynamic change. He may not have chosen the course that others wanted to follow — or would indeed follow subsequently — but it was the prudent one for the time.

NOTES

1 Despite being Canada's most famous naval officer, his name is also probably the most misspelled, appearing often as *de Wolfe*, *de Wolf* or *Dewolfe*. Also, although he is often sometimes referred to as Henry, *Harry* appeared on his birth certificate and was his actual given name.

2 Lund, "The Rise and Fall of the RCN." [Complete references for commonly cited secondary sources are included in the bibliography.]

3 Report of the Ad Hoc Committee on Defence Policy, August 1963, app 10, Directorate of History and Heritage (DHH), 99/31 box 5, II-3.

4 Figures derived from Middlemas, "Economic Considerations in the Development of the Canadian Navy Since 1945."

5   The author, who is preparing a biography of Vice-Admiral DeWolf, had the pleasure of many conversations with the admiral. Much of the career information and opinion-related material is from those interviews and from the DeWolf Papers at the Library and Archives Canada (LAC). Other papers on his career have also come into the author's possession from various sources. Thanks also go to Jim DeWolf, the admiral's son, for both information and support.

6   Captain C.P. Nixon to author, 29 March 2001.

7   Jones's endorsement was probably critical to his promotion. It is interesting to note, given the attention paid to the feud between G.C. Jones and Leonard Murray over seniority, and the negative light in which Jones is usually cast, that in half-yearly recommendations for promotion in April 1940, Jones refused to give either DeWolf or Nelson Lay an edge and bracketed them equally. Citing his long familiarity with both officers, Jones noted: "I will pay these officers the high tribute of believing that neither would wish to be promoted at the expense of the other. In my judgment, both are equally deserving and any preference might have a disturbing influence on the morale of the flotilla." Jones to Naval Secretary, 23 April 1940. (DeWolf papers in authors' possession.) It seems Jones wished to avoid a repeat of the poisonous situation between himself and Murray. In 1944, DeWolf was later promoted to captain ahead of Lay, and told the author that their friendship was never as close.

8   Rear-Admiral Victor Brodeur and Captain Horatio Nelson Lay, both then senior to DeWolf, and involved in the discussions, had reputations for being overly aggressive during negotiations with allies.

9   Director Plans to CNS, 6 September 1945. LAC, RG 24 (acc 83-84/167), Box 455, 1650-20 pt 1.

10 *Ibid.*, ACNS minute, ud.

11 The minister of National Defence, John Abbott, discussed four candidates with Prime Minister Mackenzie King: DeWolf, Harold Grant, Nelson Lay and "Rastus" Reid, but noted that the navy might prefer Reid. King said he would be agreeable to whatever choice he made. Mackenzie King diary, 21 February 1946.

12 Harold Grant's wife, Christian Mitchell, had been an especially close, childhood friend of DeWolf's. Mrs. C. Grant to author.

13 For example, DeWolf had direct access to Captain George Anderson, USN, Special Assistant to the Chairman, Joint Chiefs of Staff.

14 For a full account of *Haida*'s brilliant success see Gough, *HMCS Haida: Battle Ensign Flying*.

15 Upon learning that the author was writing DeWolf's biography, Commodore Bruce Oland, scion of the famous Nova Scotia brewing family, exhorted, "You don't tell me how to make beer and I won't tell you how to write history, but you must say that Harry DeWolf was Canada's Nelson!"

16 Captain C.P. Nixon to author, 12 March 2001.

17 Chance, *Before It's Too Late*, 57.

18 Raymond Phillips, "An Admirable Admiral … Some Reflections," *Starshell*, Vol VII, No 13, (Winter 2000/2001), 16.

19 Vice Admiral R. Hennessy, interview by Wilf Lund, 20 April 2002, Ottawa, 33.

20 As one example, DeWolf met with Louis Audette late in life to discuss the latter's continual criticism of Harold Grant. According to DeWolf, Audette admitted that he consistently derided Grant because he perceived him as being anti-francophone.

21 Rear-Admiral R.W.Timbrell to author, 20 December 1999.

22 See for example, endnotes 79 and 80 below.

23 "RCN Rank Structure for 1956–57," 16 March 1956, app P, "Report of the Committee on the Control of Manpower and Money," 17 February 1957, 1. DHH, 73/1223, series 1, file 661. The ACNS (W), Commodore K.L. Dyer, chaired the committee. The other members were Commodore D.L. Raymond and Captains G.A. Woollcombe, H.G. Burchell and D.D. McClure.

24 "Report of the Committee on the Control of Manpower and Money," 17 February 1957, 13.

25 Naval Board minutes, 22 February 1956, DHH, 81/520/1000-100/2. Author's emphasis.

26 *Ibid.* The deputy minister chaired the Rank Structure Committee, and its members included the Chairman CSC, the service chiefs and a representative from Treasury Board.

27 *Ibid.*, 2 May 1956.

28 *Ibid.*, 10 July 1957.

29 *Ibid.*, 30 October 1958.

30 *Ibid.*, 14 and 16 January 1959.

31 DeWolf was Director of Plans at that time and may have been involved in the decision to use that strategy.

32 Bland, *Chiefs of Defence*, 13–14.

33 See for example Director of Naval Plans and Operations, "Some Factors Pertinent to the MC-48 War Concept," 14 February 1956, LAC, RG 24 (acc 83-84/167), box 457, file 1650-26, vol. 15.

34 CNS to MND, 18 January 1956, LAC, RG 24 (acc 83-84/167), box 455, vol. 16.

35 For the discussion over *Québec*'s future see DNPO, "Disposition of HMCS *Quebec*," 30 January 1956, LAC, RG 24 (acc 83-84/167), box 457, file 1650-26, vol. 15. Among the options considered were refitting her for use as an operational cruiser, using her as a training ship to replace *Ontario* while in refit, and conversion to a helicopter carrier. All were considered too expensive and the report recommended that she be declared surplus to requirements.

36 Naval Board minutes, 19 January 1956.

37 *Ibid.*, 8 February 1956.

38 *Ibid.*, 23 May 1956.

39 The Naval Board minutes for 14 December 1956 include the discussion over the Ad Hoc Report. Included at back is a photograph of a display board, which lays out the air strength of *Bonaventure* (14 CS2F, 8 HSS, and one H04S) and the proposed HMCS *Vancouver* (28 CS2F, 12 F2H3, 8 HSS and one H04S). LAC, RG 24 (acc 83-84/167), box 141, 1279-65-1.

40 The PPCC was established in 1954 to screen policy recommendations before they reached Naval Board and the CNS. The committee was chaired by the VCNS.

41 Soward, *Hands to Flying Stations (II)*, 61–62.

42 Naval Board minutes, 14 December 1956.

43 According to the Ad Hoc Study on Naval Aviation, a second carrier of the size of the Essex class would require an increase in strength of 34 pilots, 23 Observer Mates and 32 aircraft.

44 Minutes of the Cabinet Defence Committee, 28 April 1958. LAC, RG 2, vol. 2750, file D2-58.

45 DeWolf was especially sensitive to the needs of shipyards. Rear-Admiral Mike Martin, who served as staff officer to the Naval Board when DeWolf was CNS, remembers that DeWolf maintained a close relationship with shipbuilders, meeting regularly with their representatives.

46 DeWolf speaking notes, 1958. DHH, 99/31 Box 4, 1B-6. The remarks were likely prepared for the First Sea Lord's visit to Canada.

47 ASNS (A&W) memo, 12 January 1959, LAC, RG 24 (acc 83-83/167), Box 4029, NSS 8885-12.

48 Naval Board minutes, 24 September 1958. The Board's goal was not to make any specific recommendation, but "it was hoped agreement in principle could be reached as to broad areas of policy within which detailed planning could proceed."

49 Ibid., 24 September 1958; and Chairman, Ship Staff Requirement Panel, "New Surface A/S Ship" [n.d., but between 25 September and 15 October 1958], LAC, RG 24 (acc 83-83/167), box 4029, NSS 8885-12.

50 The general-purpose destroyer has escaped notice by historians or been confused with the later general-purpose frigate. It was modelled on the USN's Charles F. Adams–class destroyer then coming into service. See Norman Friedman, *U.S. Destroyers: An Illustrated Design History* (Annapolis: Naval Institute Press, 1982), 308–11.

51 A/CNTS (Ships), "A/S Frigates Estimates," 26 November 1958; and Chairman, Ship Staff Requirement Panel, "Draft Staff Requirements Austerity A/S Vessel," 5 November 1958, LAC, RG 24 (acc 83-83/167), box 4029, NSS 8885-12.

52 Naval Board minutes, 28 January 1959.

53 Ibid., 28 January 1959. DHH, 81/520. This would only apply to a CVL like *Bonaventure*; if the RCN had acquired an Essex-class CVS, the only ships capable of keeping pace at its full 33 knots would be the Second World War destroyers, but their fuel consumption would have been too high to make that a realistic proposition.

54 DeWolf to author, 20 August 2000.

55 ACNS (Plans), "RCN Requirements Plans (Medium Range) for Period 1960–1965," 5 March 1959. DHH, 125.089 (D3).

56 See especially various accounts by S. Mathwin Davis, whose recollections of the nuclear submarine program have dominated historiography on the subject.

57 Naval Board minutes, 25 August 1954.

58 DeWolf papers in author's possession. Ironically, Baker, who was on loan to the RCN, soon returned to the RN to run their nuclear submarine–building program.

59 Ottawa *Citizen*, 29 October 1958.

60 Naval Board minutes, 25 August 1954.

61 C.R. Nixon to author, 2001.

62 DeWolf papers in author's possession. Vice-Admiral Bob Stephens was unaware that DeWolf had protected his career in this way, but it was typical of the quiet way that DeWolf went about his work.

63 Victoria *Times Colonist*, May 1958.

64 so CDS, "Visit to New London, Connecticut — 12–13 December 1957," DHH, NHS 6901-50 Nuclear Propulsion. The AOC Maritime Air Command, Air Commodore M. Costello, represented the RCAF, while Brigadier J. Allard, GOC Eastern Quebec command, represented the Army.

65 DeWolf papers in author's possession.

66 DeWolf papers in author's possession.

67 "The Report of the Nuclear Submarine Survey Team," June 1959, DHH, 75/147. The NSST was dissolved on 11 August 1959, but to keep abreast of advances, and presumably to keep the navy's oar in the nuclear water, a Nuclear Submarine Project Group under Commander Stephens was established in the technical services branch. SECTEMP Memo, "Nuclear Submarine Survey Team," 13 August 1959. DHH, NHS 6901-50 Nuclear Propulsion.

68 NSST, "The Report of the Nuclear Submarine Survey Team," 1.

69 DeWolf speaking notes, 1958, DHH, 99/31 box 4, 1B-6.

70 Granatstein, *The Generals*, 178; Maloney, "General Charles Foulkes," 219–32.

71 Minutes of the Chiefs of Staff Committee, 21 February 1956. DHH, 73/1223.

72 CSC minutes, 22 February 1957.

73 *Ibid.*, 12 July 1956.

74 *Ibid.*, 10 October 1956.

75 *Ibid.*, 6 June 1957.

76 *Ibid.*, 13 August 1958.

77 *Ibid.*, 3 December 1958.

78 *Ibid.*, 12 April 1956. At a Naval Board meeting on 9 September 1956 the CNS admitted "disappointment to some degree."

79 *Ibid.*, 10 October 1957.

80 *Ibid.*, 4–7 June 1956 and 10 June 1958.

81 DeWolf told the author that, during the deliberations over Sidewinder, the CAS, Air Vice-Marshal Campbell, tried to warn him off the weapon system, telling him that the heat-seeking Sidewinders would not work effectively because they could be distracted from their target by the heat of the sun. DeWolf telephoned Captain V.J. Wilgress, Director of Naval Aviation, who refuted the argument. The RCN's two fighter squadrons went on to use the system with tremendous success. Author interview with Captain V.J. Wilgress, RCN (ret'd) 27 February 2001.

82 CSC Minutes, 15 July 1958. According to Captain Wilgress, senior navy staff officers were concerned that the Arrow would eat up the defence budget for years to come. DeWolf asked him to find reasons he could introduce to the CSC as to why the Arrow should not be built. Author interview with Wilgress.

83 *Ibid.*, 22 January 1959.

84 Charles Lynch, "Civilian May be Successor to Foulkes," Vancouver *Province*, 23 January 1960.

CHAPTER NINE

Vice-Admiral Herbert S. Rayner: The Last Chief of the Canadian Naval Staff

Peter Haydon

Rear-Admiral Herbert Rayner as Flag Officer
Pacific Coast in the late 1950s

On the morning of 22 July 1960, Rear-Admiral Herbert Sharples Rayner met with the members of the Naval Board for a comprehensive briefing on the state of the Royal Canadian Navy (RCN). Presided over by the retiring Chief of the Naval Staff (CNS), Vice-Admiral H.G. DeWolf, the session lasted a scant two hours, but it covered just about every aspect of naval management: from shipbuilding programs, to helicopters, to ammunition, to manpower, to uniforms — all the things that Rayner would have to oversee during his tenure as the head of Canada's small but efficient navy.[1]

As the incoming CNS, Rayner had achieved the pinnacle of a naval career. Theoretically, the cumulative experience of thirty-two years in the navy prepared him for the weighty responsibility he would carry, but as it turned out, no seagoing or staff experience — in war or in peace — could have helped him deal with the succession of crises and near-crises he would face in overseeing the affairs of the RCN during the politically charged and often tumultuous years of the early 1960s.

So, who was this man and why did he face such difficulties?

Rayner entered the RCN as a cadet in September 1928, at the age of seventeen. Like all young Canadians joining the navy as officers at that time, once he passed the civil-service exam he was sent to the Royal Navy (RN) for training at sea and ashore.[2] After three years at sea aboard the battleships *Revenge* and *Warspite* as a midshipman, followed by the usual round of sub-lieutenant's courses, his formal training was complete, and he returned to Canada in July 1933 to serve aboard the destroyer *Champlain*, his first Canadian service since joining the RCN five years earlier. But after only eighteen months in Canada, Rayner was back in the bosom of the RN onboard the battleships *Rodney* and *Nelson*, and then ashore in HMS *Vernon* for specialist training in torpedo and anti-submarine warfare.

It may seem strange that an RCN officer should spend so little time in his own navy, but that was the way Canadian naval officers, including all the previous CNSs, were trained and socialized in those days. Not surprisingly, and perhaps necessarily, the youthful RCN had a distinct RN culture — not to the point that the officer corps considered themselves "displaced Englishmen," as some would believe, but they were certainly marked by their exclusively British naval upbringing. This "Britishness" would be misinterpreted in the 1960s as being an obstacle to progress in "Canadianizing" the military.

By August 1937, Rayner was back in Halifax as the first lieutenant of the destroyer *Skeena*, and from July 1940 was the commanding officer of HMCS *St. Laurent*, one of the "C"-class destroyers acquired for the RCN in the modest rearmament of the late 1930s. While in command of *St. Laurent*, he was awarded a Distinguished Service Cross (DSC) in December 1940 for "courage and enterprise in action against enemy submarines" in the Western Approaches. That *St. Laurent* went to war alongside the RN was not remarkable. With the outbreak of war, all Canadian destroyers were quickly integrated into the RN concept of operations. This was one of the ironies of Canadian naval planning: despite the efforts of William Lyon Mackenzie King during the interwar years to protect the young Canadian navy from the "evil clutches" of imperial defence, the onset of war quickly drew the RCN into the imperial fold. There was really no alternative; Canada did not have its own plans for the war, and the naval leadership had always envisaged the small RCN fleet as working as part of the RN in a crisis. This concept of integration into a larger fleet became the strategy under which the RCN would participate in the Cold War.

Rayner came ashore in February 1942 as Staff Officer (Operations) to the Commanding Officer Atlantic Coast (COAC) at Halifax, staying until May 1943, when he went back to the war at sea as the commanding officer of the new Tribal-class destroyer *Huron*, which, predictably, was duly integrated into the RN's Home Fleet and then the 10th Destroyer Flotilla in Plymouth Command. During this period Rayner was twice mentioned-in-despatches, and in 1944 received a Bar to his DSC as a result of an action in the western English Channel against four German destroyers trying to break through to attack the Allied invasion fleet off Normandy. He left *Huron* and the war at sea in September 1944, when he was appointed to Naval Service Headquarters (NSHQ) as Director of Plans. (It was to be the first of several tours in Ottawa.) In this job he was the architect of the controversial paper "The Continuing Royal Canadian Navy," which laid out options for the structure of the postwar RCN.[3]

He escaped the bureaucracy in December 1945 to go back to sea in command of the brand-new Tribal-class destroyer *Nootka* and also as Captain (D) at Halifax. Eighteen months later, in June 1947, he was sent to command the naval air section at RCAF Station Dartmouth. Rayner's career was moving along rapidly as he gained experience, and he was clearly headed for flag rank. However, the postwar navy was an unsettled and not particularly happy organization, lacking political support as it struggled to remain operationally relevant and re-establish itself as a credible anti-submarine force during the early days of the Cold War.

During those years, Rayner, like most of the "old guard" of the pre-war RCN officer corps, survived and moved from position to position. He was duly promoted to commodore in July 1951, at the height of the rearmament program triggered by the Korean War and the general deterioration of East-West relations, upon becoming Co-ordinator of the Joint Staff of the Chiefs of Staff Committee (CSC) in Ottawa. Two years in command of the carrier HMCS *Magnificent*, from March 1953 to February 1955 — which included participation in the near-disastrous Exercise Mariner, when fog endangered scores of allied naval aircraft — capped his seagoing career. After two and a half years back at NSHQ, mainly as chief of naval personnel, Rayner went west as the Flag Officer Pacific Coast (FOPC), where he stayed from August 1957 until July 1960, when he was appointed CNS.

Rayner's career path to CNS was not greatly different from those of his predecessors, all of whom had been trained in the RN, commanded RCN ships, and served in various capacities on the naval and joint staffs. The only significant difference was that Rayner was the first CNS not to have graduated from the Royal Naval College of Canada. Nevertheless, he was a member of the small RCN elite and had been groomed for high command. That DeWolf had picked him as his replacement as CNS should not have been a surprise to anyone, and this choice was almost certainly endorsed by the outgoing minister of National Defence, retired Major-General George Pearkes, who had worked closely with Rayner during the British Columbia centenary.

With his broad experience base and extensive formal naval training at the hands of the RN, Rayner should not have found the responsibilities of CNS either daunting or difficult, but in his case the job became enormously complex, and his loyalties and integrity were put under great strain in the process. Why did this happen?

To answer this question we need to look at Rayner himself a little more closely. The image that persists is one of an efficient but somewhat distant man of great personal integrity. Another, fairly popular, image of a wooden officer with a Bible under one arm and a telescope under the other is unfair and shows little real understanding of the man or his values. The navy was his life, and he resolutely upheld the principles upon which he had been raised. In many ways, Rayner was typical of his generation of senior Canadian naval officers: traditionalist and outwardly rather British, enormously competent professionally, but somewhat naïve politically.

In terms of filling the shoes of his immediate predecessor, Harry DeWolf, he may have been at a disadvantage. DeWolf was an adept politician, able to relate easily to his political superior, the minister of National Defence, and to understand the many political nuances that came into play in the development and implementation of defence and naval policy. These skills did not come as easily to Rayner. It might even be fair to categorize Rayner's attitude towards politicians, and perhaps equally to army generals, as one of inherent distrust. After all, they had not been raised under the code of naval discipline and were, therefore, suspect. So, upon taking up his new job in August 1960, Rayner was faced with the need to confront the "political beast" in managing his beloved navy. Unfortunately, he would not fare well, but in some ways the deck was stacked against him.

One of the long-standing naval problems in Canada is that no national consensus exists on the structure, or the purpose, of the navy. In some respects, the Canadian navy exists at the minister's pleasure. Even though the prime minister and Cabinet are involved in the decision-making process, they are greatly influenced by what the minister presents to them, and they invariably turn to him — rather than the service chiefs — for military advice. To be effective, the service chiefs have to accept, and learn to work within, the prevailing political environment.

The title Chief of the Naval Staff is somewhat misleading because the office had acquired far wider responsibilities over the years. By 1960, the incumbent had become akin to the United States Navy's (USN) Chief of Naval Operations in the broadest sense and was directly responsible to the minister of National Defence for the efficient running of the RCN. The navy was essentially a fiefdom over which the CNS reigned, but within limits set by the minister. In part, these limits were controlled by the Chairman of the Chiefs of Staff Committee (CCSC), who co-ordinated the programs and activities of the three services in their passage through the departmental and government bureaucracies for final political approval, but he had no operational function in the running of the Canadian forces. Although the CNS had the right of direct access to the minister — defence ministers did not attend Naval Board meetings — it was a right that had to be exercised with care in non-operational matters, lest the delicate departmental balance be disturbed in a way that might be counterproductive. It was not an ideal system, and it would shortly be changed to provide a better chain of command, at least from a political perspective. One of the hallmarks of Canadian defence policy is that operational considerations are invariably subordinated to political and bureaucratic requirements, as Rayner was to learn the hard way during the opening phases of Paul Hellyer's turbulent reign as minister.

When Rayner took over the watch in August 1960, a new concept for the operation of NSHQ was introduced whereby naval headquarters would be primarily concerned with policy and organized functionally, leaving the commands largely responsible for the routine running of the fleet. In theory, decentralization put the oversight of the naval staff in the hands of the Vice-Chief of the Naval Staff (VCNS) and the other members of the Naval Board, thereby allowing the CNS greater freedom to travel and focus on relationships with the other chiefs of staff and the minister.[4]

Unfortunately, what made infinite sense in theory would fail in practice. The complexity of the issues that faced the Naval Board and Naval Staff in the first four years of the 1960s would demand that the CNS become deeply involved not only in programs, but also in some operational activities. Criticism of the RCN's command structure during the 1962 Cuban Missile Crisis became a catalyst for political change at the end of Rayner's tenure.

Rayner's term as CNS would be dominated by three issues. The first was the need for new ships to replace the obsolete and obsolescent Second World War destroyers and frigates, and the related problem of meeting the NATO naval force goals — invariably referred to as the SACLANT force goals — with the concurrent requirement to modernize the fleet in an era when technology was forcing change in virtually all aspects of operations. The second issue was the never-ending personnel problems, especially the difficulty in balancing recruiting with attrition, and the related constraints imposed on new commitments and new construction. Third was the RCN's long-standing quest to acquire adequate submarine training services, which evolved, of necessity, into a requirement that the navy acquire and operate its own submarines in both training and anti-submarine roles.

Some will claim that the 1962 Cuban Missile Crisis was also a test of Rayner's effectiveness as CNS, but when examined in the light of all the facts, especially under the delegated concept of command, the value of the crisis as a case study in naval management is limited.[5]

Until the fall of John Diefenbaker's Conservative government to Lester Pearson's Liberals in April 1963, the navy enjoyed considerable freedom in managing its program, albeit within a politically established budget that was always too small. However, the political necessity of imposing fiscal constraints did not alter the government's support in principle for the naval program, and thus the need for a modern Canadian navy. The arrival in April 1963 of the reform-minded Paul Hellyer as the new minister changed the way the naval program was managed. In place of the essentially collegial approach to the naval policy process, a distinctly confrontational approach became the hallmark of the new administration. For many reasons, which will be explained later, the navy did not fare well at Hellyer's hand. The question that has to be asked is, Did Rayner fail as CNS, or was the decline of naval fortunes inevitable? This can only be answered by looking at the course of the naval program during his tenure.

The Canadian forces managed the capital program, through which new equipment was acquired and existing items modernized, under a rolling five-year plan that looked at force requirements ten years ahead but budgeted on the basis of the next five years. The annual appropriation process also served as the political checks and balances. Rayner's initial briefing from the naval staff on 22 July provided an overview of the RCN program that showed that ship-replacement programs were approved only for the six Repeat Restigouche–class escorts,[6] at the rate of two ships a year to replace the oldest of the wartime destroyers and frigates beginning at the end of 1962. The next phase of the program to replace the remaining twenty-three obsolete ships was being worked upon cautiously with a view to a further ASW escort program. However, nothing had been done about replacing the RCN's only aircraft carrier, *Bonaventure.* More importantly, nothing was being done to replace the F2H-3 Banshee fighters that were due to be phased out in 1962–63, leaving the RCN's ASW carrier group without effective air defence.

Political pressures, as well as those brought to bear by the other services, left the navy in a financial and strategic bind. In some respects, the navy could not afford to spend about a third of its declining budget on the naval aviation capability, yet that capability formed the operational heart of the RCN, and thus the service could not afford to be without it. On a brighter note, the seven St. Laurent–class destroyers were being converted to helicopter-capable ASW escorts with the new variable depth sonar. The plan was to use the Kaman CHSK helicopter, but this was to change when it was discovered that the Kaman was already obsolescent.[7] Fortunately, there was time to re-examine the helicopter issue.

A new fleet support tanker, eventually named *Provider*, was under construction and would enter service in late 1962. Planning was progressing, albeit slowly, to acquire submarines for the RCN. The USN had agreed to lend the *Burrfish* to Canada as a way of meeting the need for a training submarine on the west coast. East coast requirements were met under the agreement with the RN whereby two British "A"-class submarines were provided with an offset of two and one-half submarine crews of RCN personnel loaned to the RN. But the RN's ability to continue the agreement was coming to and end, and so steps were being taken to acquire submarines for the RCN — but in the face of considerable political skepticism, as we shall see.

The rationale for maintaining a fleet of that size, and a not-inconsiderable infrastructure, was primarily to meet commitments to the NATO contingency planning process of one carrier and twenty-nine escorts, with a secondary commitment for fourteen escorts on the west coast for continental defence under the Canada–U.S. joint defence structure. The east coast fleet, other than for mine countermeasures and port defence, was integrated into the NATO framework and also dual-tasked into the bilateral continental defence structure.[8] There was also a growing belief that the RCN should be able to support a United Nations (UN) police action, but in 1960 the nature of that task had not been defined.

By 1960, financing the naval program was becoming increasingly difficult, and in some ways it might seem that the navy was reaching the point where it had overcommitted itself by embracing a well-intentioned but unrealistic philosophy. Over the years, a succession of RCN admirals believed that, provided that sufficient ships existed, the RCN would be able to meet whatever tasks the government required it to undertake. The problem with that approach was that as the ships became more technologically complex, they were increasingly expensive to build and maintain. Rayner's already constrained budget was not large enough to meet all the future requirements; something would have to change.

The other key dimension of the RCN program, and the one that in many respects governed the overall program, was manning. One of the means the government used to impose limits on the services was by dictating manpower ceilings. This meant that the RCN was constantly fine-tuning its personnel numbers to keep ships fully manned, while also ensuring that the officers and men received the necessary training. The personnel balance, if it could be called that, was always fragile and susceptible to fluctuations in retention and recruiting cycles. Because attrition could not be managed as easily as recruiting, fleet morale was a constant concern. As a result, the navy needed to keep as many trained people as possible. When Rayner took over, the RCN had 20,608 uniformed people on the payroll. Of these, 2,577 were officers, 17,495 were noncommissioned men and women, and there were about 600 cadets and apprentices under training. Almost half of the people were at sea in ships, submarines and air squadrons, which created a good sea-to-shore ratio and allowed ample time for shore training while ensuring that people did not spend unrealistically long periods at sea without a break, but there was very little flexibility. The retention rate, meanwhile, was not good; the navy lost just under sixty per cent of men at the end of their first engagement. Recruiting, fortunately, was better — there was a waiting list — but the training pipeline limited the number who could be enrolled at any one time. Morale was said to be "good," although some serious problems existed, especially the availability of affordable housing on the east coast, but personnel staff were optimistic that the various problems could be managed. This would prove to be false optimism, though, as the personnel situation deteriorated.

On the surface, the RCN seemed to be in pretty good shape, but some very major problems lurked in the background. As Rayner would discover in his first year as CNS, the naval program was like a house built on sand; without a solid foundation, it could quickly become unstable. Throughout his tenure as CNS, Rayner's primary concern was to correct those deficiencies, but he had to do so in an increasingly adversarial environment. In this he failed; he could not rebuild the naval program on a firm foundation. But the blame cannot be laid entirely at his feet; other factors came into play.

The naval program was never a static entity; it was always under internal and external review and, increasingly, being modified to draw in new technologies and operational concepts. In September 1960, the navy's requirement for both training and ASW submarines went forward to Cabinet with the recommendation that "six *Barbel* type submarines be built in Canada at the rate of two a year commencing in 1961," but Cabinet dithered and asked for more information. Specifically, it sought confirmation that SACLANT would accept six conventional submarines as replacements for six overage anti-submarine escorts, and that the Barbel class was the best foreign-built option.[9] This modest program was a far cry from the earlier idea of obtaining a fleet of nuclear submarines (SSNs), and it seemed that any notion of Canada operating its own submarines crossed some political threshold that moved the government away from its military comfort zone. Although DeWolf has been accused of conservatism in his direction of the naval program, it would seem that he understood this concept of political "comfort zones" for military capabilities. Rayner, or at least his staff, did not have the same sense of political caution.

The second major change came as a result of a new fleet air-defence study that, in January 1961, led the Naval Board to conclude that *Bonaventure* would remain as an ASW carrier, but without integral air defence. Carrier operations would have to be either geographically restricted or conducted within the air-defence umbrella of another navy. The board also decided that a dedicated air-defence ship was out of the question. DeWolf would have endorsed this decision because it did not move the fleet away from its ASW focus, which he saw as the navy's only raison d'être. However, when discussing the NATO force goals with the CSC later that month — specifically the increases in submarines and air-defence ships proposed by SACLANT — Rayner suggested that it might be possible to combine ASW and air-defence capabilities in the next generation of Canadian destroyers. This, as it turned out, was the genesis of the ill-fated general-purpose (GP) frigate program. While the other chiefs expressed some concern over the apparent expansion of the RCN's roles, the need for the fleet to remain operationally effective was never in doubt militarily, although the politicians might have endorsed a lesser naval capability if it cost less.

As the 1961 edition of the naval program took shape, Rayner submitted his requirements for a new shipbuilding program, including picking up on the postponed submarine decision from the previous September. The essence of the new shipbuilding proposal was that, to maintain the NATO and Canada–U.S. force assignments of forty-three vessels, a new shipbuilding program should start without delay so that the obsolete ships — Tribals and other war-vintage destroyers and frigates — could be replaced. He therefore proposed that Canada build nine submarines and eight GP frigates over the next six years.[10] This, he explained, would go a long way towards meeting Canada's part in the collective mission of defeating the Soviet naval threat against North America. At that time, defence policy required that the RCN be prepared to undertake a fairly wide range of tasks, including protecting the sea lines of communication, defending shipping and ports against attack from the sea, locating and destroying enemy submarines, contributing to the early warning of attack on North America, and conducting operations at sea in support of national, NATO, UN or other commitments the government might make.[11] That, however, was the extent of political direction. Developing the force structure to do all these things was essentially left to the navy with the belief that, by meeting the NATO and Canada–U.S. force goals, sufficient forces would be available for other situations short of war.

While the shipbuilding program was under political review, Rayner commissioned a new staff study to "define the purpose of the Navy and make recommendations concerning the role, tasks, and composition of the fleet required to meet the Navy's responsibilities in the future in the most effective and economical manner."[12] This was to be a detailed examination of the likely nature of naval forces and weapons systems over the next twenty-five years. One of the main reasons for initiating the study was "the rapidly accelerating pace of technological and scientific development in the fields of weapons systems and fighting equipments [that] will continue to impose considerable and increasing strain upon RCN resources." Unfortunately, what Rayner sought was not forthcoming. The study's director, Rear-Admiral Jeffry Brock, who was about to become Rayner's VCNS, produced a fleet concept for the next ten-year planning period that was beyond the capability of the naval budget or Canadian industry to produce.[13] Brock simply did not understand, or take into consideration, the politics and economics of naval policy. Also, he missed some of the significant advances that naval technology would make in the next twenty years, which prevented him from fulfilling the mandate of providing a useful long-term assessment of future Canadian naval requirements.

To many, the greatest failing Report of the Ad Hoc Committee on Naval Objectives — better known as the Brock Report — was its omission of a coherent personnel policy to "man" the new fleet. The RCN's personnel problems were, and would remain, a governing factor in new programs, and to exclude them from a major study of this nature was a grave mistake. Nevertheless, some of his proposals were echoed in subsequent planning documents, even though the Brock Report never received wide distribution outside the naval staff. The lack of a sound long-term vision would be felt during the Hellyer reforms when they started in 1963.

The 1961 version of the shipbuilding program was as politically troublesome as its predecessors, and thus remained stalled. Again, submarines were the stumbling block. After many informal discussions, the logjam began to shift in November, when the minister sent a memo to the Cabinet Defence Committee recommending that Canada should either procure six Barbel-class submarines or purchase three Oberon-class submarines from Britain as Phase I of a larger submarine program. For political reasons, this recommendation was later narrowed to the purchase of the three Oberons.[14] In addition to political reluctance to commit to a major submarine building program, one of the problems was an intervention by the Vice Chief of the Defence Research Board (DRB) stating that "the proposal to build six *Barbel*s in Canada has in it, to my mind, all the seeds that could lead by 1970 to another situation in which DND [the Department of National Defence] becomes accused of the expensive provision of obsolete equipment."[15] The record is incomplete, but it seems Rayner did not ensure that he had sufficient support to push the program through. If it was as important as the navy claimed — and it was given top priority in the naval program — one would have expected the naval staff and CNS to ensure that it had widespread backing within the department, including DRB.

On 11 April 1962, the minister informed the House of Commons that the government would proceed with the acquisition of three Oberon-class submarines from Britain and would build eight general-purpose frigates. The navy was happy, the media skeptical, and NATO concerned that Canada's ASW capability was beginning to slip. After a series of fairly acrimonious discussions, it was established that Canada would not accept SACLANT's new force goals calling for additional submarines and frigates.[16] This decision was the beginning of the process whereby the RCN's long-standing and unwavering support for SACLANT's force goals was put under siege.

To some, this was an overdue correction. In fact, the previous Chairman of the Chiefs of Staff, General Charles Foulkes, was suspicious of the way the navy held the SACLANT force goals as sacrosanct, and on one occasion suggested that, since the navy had essentially created the SACLANT force proposals itself, the navy could quite easily reduce them.[17] This was in fact true, and a weak link in the navy's planning process that would be attacked vigorously within the year.

Undaunted by political opposition, Brock commissioned yet another staff study to re-examine the RCN's needs for submarines. When the committee reported two months later, the recommendation was for a program to build six Thresher-class SSNs in Canada, with the aim of having the first one in service about 1968.[18] The plan was wildly ambitious and little more than a regurgitation of all the SSN arguments that had made and rejected before. As DeWolf had ruled, such a concept was simply beyond the RCN's financial means. The personnel staff would have added that an SSN program was beyond the manpower capacity of the RCN and could only have been introduced at the expense of destroyers and frigates. Wisely, the report was kept within the naval staff.

The RCN was tested by the October 1962 Cuban Missile Crisis, and gave a good account of itself operationally. Politically, it was a highly confused and controversial incident in which Prime Minister John Diefenbaker's personal dislike of U.S. President John Kennedy almost prevented the necessary military preparations from being taken. Throughout the crisis, Rayner stayed out of the actual direction of operations at sea — other than in areas where he had specific responsibility, such as recalling *Bonaventure* and the 1st Escort Squadron from Britain. His efforts were directed, correctly, towards ensuring that the minister was kept fully aware of events at sea. By doing this — and only this — Rayner allowed Rear-Admiral Ken Dyer, Flag Officer Atlantic Coast, to run the operation, as the new concept of decentralization required.[19] Although purists have howled in outrage that Rayner, Dyer (as FOAC) and the minister (Douglas Harkness) broke the rules for civil control of the military, they did what had to be done to prevent a possible disaster as a result of Diefenbaker's idiosyncrasies and indecisiveness.[20]

Although the Chairman of the Chiefs of Staff, Air Vice-Marshal Frank Miller, accompanied Rayner to some of the meetings with Harkness, he was largely excluded from naval operations decision-making, and correctly so under the prevailing concepts of command and control, despite his own desire to exercise greater control over all aspects of Canadian military activity. As Opposition defence critic, Paul Hellyer was concerned that the navy had overstepped its authority in sailing the fleet and engaging in ASW operations on the northern flank of the USN's quarantine of Cuba without Diefenbaker's authority. Hellyer used the crisis as one of the reasons for instigating tighter control over military operations and for creating the new position of Chief of the Defence Staff. Ironically, while the RCN's response to the Cuban Missile Crisis brought much praise from Washington and Norfolk, it was viewed with concern in Ottawa. Unfortunately, it would appear that in doing what was morally right, the navy created powerful political enemies. But the worst was yet to come: 1963, to borrow a well-worn term, was to be the navy's *anno horribilis.*

In April 1963, the Liberal party led by Lester B. Pearson defeated John Diefenbaker's Tories in the federal election. As the new minister of National Defence, Paul Hellyer wasted no time in challenging the traditional course of Canadian defence policy. Pearson already had committed his government to a defence review under a parliamentary committee headed by Maurice Sauvé. Hellyer saw his task to be the direction of a parallel internal review and to produce a new defence white paper. He set about this task with a zeal unmatched in recent history. His intent was to have things done differently — very differently.

This chapter is not about Paul Hellyer or unification; it is about Herbert Rayner and naval policy. However, in the very difficult period from April 1963 until the end of July 1964, when Rayner took early retirement, Hellyer and his quest to rationalize and unify the Canadian military were dominant factors that cannot be overlooked in telling the narrower naval story. It is necessary, therefore, to pause and look at Hellyer himself and his aims.

From the onset of his ministry, Hellyer intended to institute structural reform of the Canadian forces. In this, he wanted to pick up where Brooke Claxton had left off, seeing the Diefenbaker years as some sort of interregnum. However, he was constrained by Lester Pearson's views expressed at a meeting of the Liberal Association in Scarborough on 12 January 1963, calling for a complete re-examination of the basis of Canadian defence policy. Pearson stated then that any future Liberal government would "look at defence policy emphasizing maximum mobility for the forces to be able to intervene wherever and whenever required for United Nations, NATO or Canadian territorial operations; and that the three armed services should be fully integrated for maximum efficiency and economy both in operations and administration."[21] In carrying out his mandate to reform the military, Hellyer made it quite clear on more than one occasion that he considered the Tory defence policy to be out of control. Not only was the equipment procurement program ill considered and lacking a clear policy foundation, but the concept of civil — or political — control of the military had been seriously usurped during the Cuban Missile Crisis. These problems, he believed, had to be corrected without delay. As he explained in his biography, *Damn the Torpedoes*, "each service was preparing for a different kind of war."[22] His plan, about which he made no secret, was to bring the three services together.

Irrespective of whether one agrees with Hellyer's analysis, his perception of these systemic faults became the driving force behind his reforms. His determination to reassert complete political control over the military is evident in the way he directed the initial policy and program reviews and later established himself as the authoritarian chairman of the reconstituted Defence Council. To some, these actions represented an abuse of ministerial power and a significant break from the unwritten but well-understood concepts of civil-military relations in Canada, whereby the military leadership acknowledged the need for political control, while the politicians acknowledged that they must heed military advice on military issues.[23] The point has been made frequently that the integration/unification process was as much about civil control of the military as it was about achieving greater efficiency. It was also intensely political, because Hellyer saw military reform as the issue to increase his stature within the Liberal party. As he stated in his book: "The real battle, however, was much more important.... It is the issue of who is going to set military policy — the military or the government. They had been unfettered so long they just can't get used to the idea of taking direction."[24] Hellyer's ambition and his insensitivity to military concerns, seen by some as iconoclastic, made for innumerable confrontations throughout the reform process.

In hindsight, it is easy to criticize Hellyer's lack of true understanding of military issues and his complete disrespect for military tradition, and see them as warning signs that should have been heeded. Even if they had been recognized as such, however, it would not have made much difference. Hellyer was intent on reform, and he tried to emulate the American Secretary of Defense, Robert McNamara, who ruthlessly but effectively applied business practices to military management.[25] Seeing the Canadian military as a recalcitrant spendthrift, Hellyer imposed a series of initial demands on the defence program, which, interestingly, he established without the benefit of any formal analysis or prior consultation. However, he almost certainly had ample advice from his "insiders." The initial arbitrary controls were: a ten per cent cut in personnel, a freeze on all capital programs, and a comprehensive review of roles and capabilities. These made a recipe for confrontation, especially for Rayner where the naval program was concerned.

By the time Hellyer became Minister of National Defence in the spring of 1963, Rayner had made several significant changes to the naval program. A number of new factors, including the growth of the Soviet submarine fleet, the increasing ability of Soviet long-range naval aviation to operate in NATO areas, the major increase in SACLANT force goals, and the advances in naval technology — especially in ASW — forced Rayner to abandon DeWolf's more cautious plan. The rationale for change, simply, was that new capabilities had to be integrated into the program to prevent the RCN from falling even further behind on the capability curve. A meeting of the Naval Board in May 1963 established procurement priorities as:

- the General Purpose Frigate program, which was essential if the navy was to retain a general purpose capability and continue with a ship replacement program that met NATO force goals;
- the modernization of the Restigouche and Mackenzie classes;
- the delivery of twenty-four CHSS-2 helicopters by the end of 1964–65; and
- the construction of modern submarines in Canada.[26]

Unfortunately, this concept was completely divorced from reality. The RCN did not have the people to make those changes, and getting approval for the necessary increase was highly unlikely in the prevailing political climate. In other words, the naval program was very vulnerable.

It took a while before Hellyer was in a position to begin his assault on the service programs. Among his early actions were reviews of major capital programs, including the GP frigate, by a small group of senior officers under the leadership of Dr. R.J. Sutherland, the director of operational research. The paper on the GP frigate explained, in simple terms, that if the RCN needed some form of tactical air defence, the guided missile–equipped frigate proposal made eminent sense. Even though the report did not give Hellyer any reason to cancel the program, he would cancel it arbitrarily. As he explained later:

> To avoid being taken captive I not only held firm but cancelled the general-purpose frigates that Gordon Churchill, my immediate predecessor, had ordered during the election campaign. I suspected that the hastily awarded contracts were more closely related to the ability of the Tory Party to raise campaign funds from the shipyards than they were with defence requirements.[27]

Hellyer's internal defence policy review was conducted by an ad hoc committee of senior military officers and civilians, again under Sutherland's leadership. His mandate was to look at alternative defence policies, and he did as he had been asked by producing a highly innovative report, which he presented at the end of September 1963.[28] Despite the fact that Sutherland's new study travelled through previously uncharted waters, it did not provide Hellyer with the option that alone would solve all the problems he saw in the defence structure. To do so was asking the impossible, especially as some of the minister's perceptions of disorganization and lack of cohesion were functions of his own lack of knowledge and, in some ways, his naïveté. Significantly, the report stated that creating a defence policy uniquely Canadian in character was an impossibility; Canada's policies would always have to reflect not only the proximity of the United States but also the very nature of the international system and Canada's traditional commitment to maintaining order in that system. As Sutherland pointed out so rightly, defence policy had always been a function of political choices but could not be crafted in isolation, especially without direct reference to foreign policy. Nevertheless, the report offered new policy options, all but one of which was dependent in one way or another upon sealift, and this, Sutherland pointed out, was an area where capability improvements could be made relatively cheaply. According to his account of the process, Hellyer was not very impressed with the report, referring to it as "pretty bland stuff" — even though by his own admission he later used much of it in writing the 1964 Defence White Paper.[29]

Hellyer's actual assault on the naval program began in July with a memo from the deputy minister (DM) establishing the individual service budgets for 1963–64. The RCN's budget was to be pegged at $282 million for each of the next three years and would then increase by three per cent for the following two years, a far cry from the $307 million Rayner originally sought for 1963–64. Rayner quickly went back to the DM, pointing out that financial cuts of that magnitude would have a "damaging effect on the capability of the RCN to discharge its responsibilities now and in the future." His main point was that unless a shipbuilding program was started very soon, the navy would not be able to honour its NATO and CANUS commitments. As he explained, the Second World War destroyers and frigates needed replacing and were becoming increasingly expensive to maintain. This did not change anything, and a revised naval program was demanded. Writing to the minister a few days later, Rayner again summarized the implications of reducing the budget so severely and concluded:

Financial restrictions of the order of magnitude considered in this paper would seriously reduce the effectiveness of the Fleet and the activities which support it. Indeed they would have a most damaging effect on the capability of the Navy to discharge its current responsibilities and to keep up-to-date in future years.[30]

Rayner also pointed out that unless the navy's personnel strength was increased, there would be no option but to pay off some of the older ships and thus reduce the number of escorts available for NATO. Hellyer was unimpressed and eventually replied with another tersely phrased memo stating that the RCN's budget for 1963–64 would be $270 million, which ended the discussion. Rayner had no option but to return to the drawing board yet again and try to find a naval force structure that met the minister's somewhat fuzzy vision. The one factor in his favour was the arrival that summer of Rear-Admiral Ken Dyer as the new VCNS — replacing Brock, who went to Halifax — and a further confrontation with Hellyer.

Dyer's influence on the naval staff was immediate and one saw a distinct improvement in tone of correspondence and in the care with which staff work was produced. To make the navy's case with Hellyer, Rayner needed a new degree of consistency and steadiness in the final, and probably most difficult, year of his tenure.

In the midst of Rayner's skirmish with Hellyer over the naval program, and at the same time that the Sauvé Committee was being extensively briefed on the navy's long-term needs, Commodore James Plomer launched a potentially damaging assault on the Canadian naval establishment. In a wide-ranging, highly critical article published by *Maclean's* magazine on 7 September 1963, the recently retired Plomer systematically attacked the RCN's management system, its equipment, its ability to conduct operations at sea and it personnel policies.[31] Although Plomer's assertions were later repudiated and publicly shown to be self-serving, his onslaught did produce some fallout — especially in his criticism of the GP frigate program. He later testified before the Sauvé Committee and was able to stir up considerable skepticism over the navy's plans, which had been presented a few days before. Fortunately, Rayner was given an opportunity to rebut Plomer's biased views, but the suspicions lingered — especially with Hellyer, who was present at those sessions.[32]

What is particularly troubling about Plomer's article and his testimony, especially concerning his belief that a purge of the navy's senior ranks was needed to restore equilibrium to the organization, is that Hellyer adopted precisely that strategy. Just as troubling, despite what Rayner was to say much later, was the fact that Plomer's rant against the navy, and the GP frigate program in particular, damaged the navy's political credibility, making it much easier for Hellyer to cancel the program and deal with the naval leadership in a particularly heavy-handed manner.

Yet another ad hoc working group was formed that September — the second within the navy in almost as many years — to look into the "size and shape of the navy over the next five to ten years." The study was based on a series of strategic assumptions drawn from Sutherland's study, including the continuing need for a naval contribution to the mobile force concept by providing sealift, support and protection for army formations up to brigade-group size. The working group also had the benefit of some sound forward thinking done by the Naval Operational Research Group, including a modularization concept that would be recognized today as the Task Group Concept.[33] Working under newly imposed budget ceilings, the working group came up with a new force structure based on the primacy of the NATO and continental ASW missions, but with the flexibility to meet the mobile force sealift and support requirements. The proposed force structure was centred around three task groups — two on the east coast and one on the west. The plan did not survive politically; like the preceding Brock Report, it was far too ambitious and was not in lock-step with Hellyer's plans, however difficult these were to divine. The CNS and the naval staff were wallowing; they could not come up with a politically acceptable force plan.

Hellyer went to Cabinet in September with the proposal that the GP frigate program be cancelled and that Canada buy three Oberon-class submarines from Britain. His memo to Cabinet was blunt in stating that, although the cancellation of the frigate would leave the RCN without an air-defence capability, the economic realities dictated that despite SACLANT's repeated requests for that capability, it would not be acquired. Cabinet approved the changes.

If 1963 was the navy's *anno horribilis*, 1964 was to be the most confusing year as force models and service structures were reviewed at all levels in an effort to find ways of meeting the minister's ill-defined concepts while remaining within the severely constrained budget. Some things became obvious — one of which was that the minister did not hold the naval force assignments to SACLANT sacrosanct. Not surprisingly, the majority view was that what the navy had created, the navy could change. And so it was that the older ships were paid off and a few put in reserve, with NATO commitments reduced accordingly. In terms of manpower, this was necessary because the navy simply could not meet all its commitments and accommodate the personnel cuts also demanded by the minister.

Although the requirement for a major shipbuilding program was acknowledged even by the deputy minister, the consensus within the Chiefs of Staff Committee was that it was not about to happen. The best solution for the navy was to concentrate on the planned modernization of the St. Laurent– and Restigouche-class destroyers and plan for a small class of flotilla leaders with a limited air-defence capability. Another point made frequently by naval officers and members of the army and air force alike was that the navy's future might well lie in the helicopter-destroyer team. Although this may have been a quiet signal of the beginning of the end of the Canadian aircraft-carrier experience, there was great reluctance to abandon a capability so deeply treasured by the navy and revered as the centrepiece of the modern RCN.

Hellyer presented his white paper to Parliament on 26 March 1964. Rather than the result of many long hours of consultation and staff work, as most such documents usually are, the paper was very much the product of the minister's own hand.[34] This should not have been unexpected. From the beginning, Hellyer had made it clear that *he* would be in control of the reform process. He had also made it clear that he would determine the nature of the reforms. In this, he stated publicly on a number of occasions that "he saw a relationship between the economics, policy, and organization of defence," all of which he intended to address, and that the 1964 white paper would launch the reform process.[35] The problem was that little consultation had taken place within the department over the direction of the new policy. In fact, Hellyer chose to ignore much of the limited military and expert advice given to him. Nevertheless, while his initiatives to reduce personnel costs and generally rein in expenditures made sense as a way of making more cash available for major capital programs, his method of enforcing those cuts was heavy-handed.[36] What bothered a number of people was that Hellyer began dictating changes long before Parliament had approved the white paper, or even his policy changes.

Despite Hellyer's enthusiasm for change, the white paper was largely a status-quo policy. Some promises of change were offered, but not nearly to the extent of the innovative thinking in Sutherland's report. It did, however, contain the necessary marker for future deep reform in the shape of unification. In discussing the reorganization of the command structure, the paper stated, "This will be the first step toward a single unified defence force for Canada," but no amplification was provided.[37] Despite Hellyer's many reassurances prior to the publication of the white paper that any move towards unification would be gradual, the actual changes would take place quickly amidst widespread controversy. What the white paper did not spell out was that Hellyer's reforms had three distinct objectives:

- integration of the national command structure and the re-establishment of civil control;
- rationalization of defence policy to provide a more "Canadian" approach; and
- total unification of the three services into an organization with a single defence mission.

Even though Hellyer had already cut the individual services' programs, military capabilities were not to be changed significantly by the white paper. Provision was made for greater mobility and for a larger UN support role, but without specifying how these would be done. As far as the navy was concerned, the retention of the ASW role and the promise — albeit guarded — of studies to determine the most effective ASW systems meant there was little need for immediate concern other than over a new shipbuilding program and the possible loss of identity through unification at a later date.

Hellyer had given the three service chiefs an opportunity to discuss the general provisions of the white paper. Rayner, in particular, expressed concern over both the concept of unification and the process by which the command structure was to be integrated. In each case, Rayner believed that service identity and control of service policy (doctrine) and equipment procurement were in jeopardy, while the risk was being run of losing operational effectiveness. He therefore advocated caution and gradual implementation of change. Even though Rayner was a strong supporter of reorganization at the command and national-headquarters levels, his concerns over unification put him at odds with the minister. These differences soon became irreconcilable, and Rayner eventually chose to take early retirement rather than continue to fight.[38]

Exhausted, discouraged and unwell, Rayner left the navy in July 1964. Curiously, he chose to go quietly rather than make one final stand against the Hellyer reforms. Others might have taken the opportunity to depart with a final fanfare and a closing condemnation in the press. Rayner did not. His staff had noted with concern a gradual decline in his health and stamina for some time. The months of intense battle with Hellyer over the naval program and unification had taken their toll. Perhaps the fight had gone out of him; we do not know what his thoughts were at the time. The prospect of pointlessly rapid change to a unified force, with the almost certain loss of traditional service uniforms and identity, had discouraged him enormously. To the end, Rayner lived in hope — perhaps naïvely — that the minister would eventually see the folly of his ways and heed sound military advice.

On 1 August 1964, the new Canadian Forces Headquarters (CFHQ) organization came into force. The Naval Board and its Naval Staff were replaced by an integrated staff structure based on functional rather than service lines. Dyer was promoted to vice-admiral and became chief of personnel with the companion title of senior naval advisor. It would be up to him to maintain the navy's ability to address naval problems and issues. It was not an easy task, and was one made more complex by the fact that many of his colleagues and subordinates looked to him for help and advice in dealing with the impending unification of the services.

The naval program was in tatters and would need attention very soon if anything was to survive.

The next phase of the confrontation between the navy and Paul Hellyer would be bloody. It seems apt that, in his memoirs, Hellyer summed up his attitude towards the senior service in saying, "The Navy was going to need a lot of modernizing to make it contemporary, and that wasn't going to be easy." Hellyer had essentially determined that naval tradition was expendable, as were those who upheld it in the face of his reforms. Herbert Rayner had lost the first round of "The Navy versus Mr. Hellyer," not because of his intransigence over the need for new ships or over the need to retain a unique naval identity, but simply because he did not believe in Hellyer's ill-founded concept of a uniquely Canadian military identity and stood firm on his principles. But in standing tall he became living testimony of the stark reality of Canadian defence policy: political requirements always prevail. Nothing in his training and experience could have prepared him for the political situation he had to face in 1963 and 1964. Others would attempt to stand up to Hellyer, and they, too, would lose, but that is another story.

NOTES

1   Special Meeting of the Naval Board, 22 July 1960, DHH, 81/520/1000-100/2.

2   Between 1910 and 1922, cadets entering the RCN received their initial two years' training at the Royal Naval College of Canada. When the college was closed as a part of the postwar disarmament program, cadets were sent directly to the RN for training (for instance: Dyer, Finch-Noyes, Hennessy, Leir, Murdoch, Rayner, Stirling, and Welland). From 1932 to 1941, some naval cadets received their initial military education at the Royal Military College of Canada (for instance: the Caldwell brothers, Charles, Hayes, Landymore, O'Brien, and Piers). Also, several RCN officers joined through merchant navy training establishments such as HMS *Conway* (e.g., Boyle, Medland and Timbrell). The Second World War saw the entry of officers into

the RCN from the Reserve Force and from HMCS *Royal Roads* once it opened as a "naval" college in 1942.

3 This memo, "The Continuing Royal Canadian Navy," was apparently written in July 1945 and provided three options for the postwar naval force structure. Not surprisingly, the politicians opted for the smallest as the basis for the "interim force" of 10,000 naval personnel. The memo can be found in Library and Archives Canada (LAC), RG 24, vol. 8186, NS 1818-9.

4 Naval Board minutes, 27 July 1960.

5 Haydon, *Cuban Missile Crisis Reconsidered.* [Complete references for commonly cited secondary sources are included in the bibliography.]

6 These were the four Mackenzie-class DDEs and the two Annapolis-class DDHs. See the Memo to Cabinet Defence Committee, "RCN Ship Replacement Programme," 20 January 1960, Directorate of History and Heritage (DHH), 73/1223, file 380.

7 This concern was raised by the Treasury Board in June 1960 when approving the funding for the conversion of the St. Laurent–class escorts. DHH, 73/1223, 403.

8 This dual tasking was a source of confusion for many politicians, defence bureaucrats and members of the other services (except the RCAF maritime aviation people). The concept of operations was that the NATO commitment would not be called upon until the declaration of a "general" or "reinforced" alert. Until then, Canadian maritime forces would work with their USN counterparts in ASW and air defence tasks associated with continental security. This was how the naval response to the Cuban Missile Crisis was managed in Canada.

9 Record of Decision for the 132nd meeting of the Cabinet Defence Committee on 14 September, 1960. DHH, 73/1223, (404).

10 "Naval Shipbuilding Policy," 8 May 1961, which was reviewed by the Chiefs of Staff Committee at their 692nd meeting on 18 May 1961 and endorsed for early action by the minister. NSS: 8000-35 (CNS) "Naval Shipbuilding Policy," DHH, 73/1223 (404).

11 "RCN Future Requirements Planning Guide for the Period 1962–72," 25 January 1961, DHH, (Naval Plans) 124.019 (D1).

12 Naval Board minutes, "Ad Hoc Committee on Naval Objectives," 5 April 1961.

13 There are some who say this was a make-work project for the industrious Brock. This is very likely. Brock and Rayner were opposites: where Rayner was essentially cautious, Brock was somewhat cavalier in his approach to management. As future events and staff activities would prove, the Rayner-Brock team did not work particularly well; Brock was not really a team player unless he was captain of the team. From discussions with those who were there, and by reading between the lines of correspondence and minutes, one gets the sense of fairly widespread friction throughout the naval staff during Brock's tenure as VCNS.

14 See MND Memo to Cabinet, 7 February 1962, "Naval Ship Replacement Programme," DHH, 73/1223, (404).

15 Vice-Chairman DRB to Chairman DRB, "Naval Ship Replacement Programme," 25 January 1962, DRBTS 170-80/P44 (VC/DRB), DHH, 73/1223, (404).

16 The end-of-1966 NATO force goal for the RCN consisted of: one carrier; thirty-four DDG/DDE/DDs, of which twenty-nine would be Category A and five Category B or C; and nine submarines, of which six could be Category A and three in Category B and C. To meet the full force goal, the naval staff estimated that the RCN would require two additional surface ships and two submarines by the end of 1963, two additional submarines by the end of 1964 and a further three surface ships and five submarines by the end of 1966, all on the east coast. The new fleet structure would require an increase in the personnel ceiling from 22,469 officers and men to 26,209, and an additional 400 dockyard civilians also would be needed. Naval Board minutes, 2 April 1962.

17 See Memo from VCNS to CNS, (undated by almost certainly of 16 November 1955) "Final Screening Committee," in which he states, "General Foulkes mentioned that the RCN contribution to NATO had not been based on particular plan, but rather on the actual number of ships which were currently available, i.e., 42 Ocean Escorts. If replacements for these ships were going to be larger and more expensive vessels he could see no reason why the allocation to SACLANT should not be reduced numerically." LAC, RG24 (acc 83-84/167), box 456, 1650-26.

18 "Report of the 1962 Submarine Committee," July 1962, DHH, 75/149. Some saw this study as an attempt by Brock to vindicate his own 1961 study, which had fallen into disfavour.

19 See Haydon, *The Cuban Missile Crisis Reconsidered*.

20 See, for instance, David A. Welch, "Review of Haydon, *The 1962 Cuban Missile Crisis: Canadian Involvement Reconsidered*," *Journal of Conflict Studies*, 25(1) Spring 1995, 149–53.

21 Cited in R.L. Raymont, *Report on Integration and Unification 1964–1968*, DHH, 79/12, vol. 2.

22 Hellyer, *Damn the Torpedoes*, 33.

23 This complex issue is discussed at length by Professor Rod Byers, "Reorganization of the Canadian Armed Forces: Parliamentary, Military and Interest Group Perceptions," especially chapter VI.

24 Hellyer, *Damn the Torpedoes*, 45.

25 The difference was that McNamara had extensive corporate experience and Hellyer did not. Hellyer's belief in a "business" approach comes out in many places in *Damn the Torpedoes* — e.g., ix, 11, 85, 113, 158 and 223.

26 Naval Board minutes, 21 May 1963.

27 Hellyer, *Damn the Torpedoes*, 33.

28 Much of the underlying strategic rationale of this study reflected Sutherland's earlier, and masterful, analysis of Canada's strategic situation, "Canada's Long Term Strategic Situation," published in the summer of 1962 in the *International Journal*.

29 Hellyer, *Damn the Torpedoes*, 34.

30 CNS to Minister, "Summary of the Revised Naval Programme 1963 to 1966," NSTS 2200-5, 25 July 1963, DHH, 121.089 (D1).

31 James Plomer, "The Gold-Braid Mind Is Destroying Our Navy," *Maclean's*, 7 September 1963, 22–23 and 44–50.

32 Rayner presented the naval program in considerable detail to the Sauvé Committee on 8 October 1963, answering questions well and generally leaving members confident that the navy knew what it was doing. Plomer testified before the committee on 10 October 1963, essentially expanding on his *Maclean's* article but leaving many members with new concerns over the general state of the navy contrary to Rayner's briefing. Rayner was allowed a rebuttal of Plomer's

testimony on 15 October 1963 and was able to show that he was essentially angry at the navy for not promoting him to Rear-Admiral and determined to lash out in revenge. House of Commons, Special Committee on Defence, Minutes of Proceedings and Evidence of the Special Committee on Defence, Nos. 11, October, 8, 1963.

33 The RCN had studied the sealift requirements for UN "police operations" in mid-1961 on the basis of using the carrier, *Bonaventure*, as the primary support ship. It also was assumed that RCN forces would be largely independent for self-defence and logistic support.

34 Hellyer, *Damn the Torpedoes*, 46–47.

35 Knonenburg, *All Together Now*, 20.

36 *Ibid.*, 22–23.

37 Honourable Paul Hellyer and Honourable Lucien Cardin, *White Paper on Defence*, (Ottawa: March 1964), 19.

38 Hellyer, *Damn the Torpedoes*, 86.

DND 88-235

Rear-Admiral William Landymore

CHAPTER TEN

Rear-Admiral William M. Landymore: The Silent Service Speaks Out

Robert H. Caldwell

*"If I didn't speak out, who would?... It was necessary to alert
the people of Canada to a perilous state of affairs in defence matters."*[1]

As most readers know, the story of the Royal Canadian Navy (RCN) and unification is a controversial one. There are a number of different interpretations of these pivotal events, and Rear-Admiral William Landymore's perspective is just one. Paul Hellyer, the minister of National Defence in those days, has his own story to tell, of course, as do the many officers who remained in the navy and served into the 1970s and '80s. This examination of Landymore's experience during unification will shed some light on the circumstances surrounding the actions that he took, so that perhaps we can better understand the reasons for his actions, and his legacy to the navy.

Between 1963 and 1967, Hellyer singlemindedly pursued a policy of integrating and unifying the armed forces, the essence of this policy being to create a single service constituted from the RCN, the Canadian Army, and the Royal Canadian Air Force (RCAF). Rear-Admiral Landymore conducted a spirited campaign against this legislation. After

Hellyer had dismissed him from the RCN in 1966, Landymore made his concerns public and eventually became the inspiration for English-Canadian opposition to unification and the destruction of the RCN's identity as a national naval service.

William Moss Landymore was born in Brantford, Ontario, on 31 July 1916.[2] He attended high school there, and in 1934 he enrolled as Gentleman Cadet Number 2399 at the Royal Military College of Canada in Kingston. Having chosen a career in the RCN, upon graduation in 1936 he was sent to HMCS *Stadacona* for basic training. He joined RCN Special Entry Group Number 40 for training on RN cruisers: *Frobisher* in 1936–37, *Emerald* in 1937–38 and *Glasgow* in 1938. His term mates included Robert Welland, Ralph Hennessy and Bob Murdoch, all of whom were promoted to flag rank.[3]

The special entry method of training was, according to one source, "the RCN as it used to be… If any training scheme defined quality, this was it…. Collectively they created a sense of naval and even social identity, which in turn promoted a deep sense of loyalty in what some might call the finest years of the RCN."[4] In March 1939, while training in the UK, Bill Landymore was promoted to sub-lieutenant. He was twenty-three.

In September 1939, Britain and Canada declared war on Germany. On 6 March 1940, Sub-Lieutenant Landymore joined HMCS *Fraser* as the torpedo and communications officer. *Fraser* was a River-class destroyer, and she served in the North Atlantic and the Caribbean until the fall of France in June 1940, where she participated in the evacuation of the British Expeditionary Force. A few days afterwards, *Fraser* was sunk after colliding with the British cruiser *Calcutta* in the Gironde River estuary. Landymore was between the wheelhouse and the bridge when the collision occurred, and he was thrown, along with the bridge structure, onto *Calcutta*'s forecastle. Sixty-six lives were lost.[5]

The RN provided *Margaree* to replace the lost destroyer, and Landymore and many of *Fraser*'s crew were drafted to her. He joined as the navigator in early September, and experienced the London Blitz when *Margaree* was narrowly missed by a German bomb while alongside. A little over a month later, on her first convoy, *Margaree* was sunk when she collided with the merchant ship *Port Fairy* in the North Atlantic. Landymore was one of the last officers to abandon the ship. The captain and 141 officers and men, many of whom had survived the sinking of the *Fraser*, were lost.[6] Landymore had experienced what few Canadian naval officers would in the Second World War: two sinkings in a four-month period. He returned to Canada, this time to the west coast, where he undertook general duties ashore for over a year.

In the spring of 1942, Landymore returned to England to attend the Long Gunnery Course at HMS *Excellent* on Whale Island off Portsmouth. At "Whaley" he learned to take a fast decision and stand by it. Now prepared to work at sea as a Lieutenant (G), he joined the RN cruiser *Belfast* as the assistant gunnery officer. Soon afterwards, he was sent to an RN work-up team based at the Home Fleet's main base at Scapa Flow, where he trained the gunnery departments of modern radar-equipped destroyers.[7] Here he would again encounter many of his RCN friends while training the Canadian Tribals *Huron* and *Haida*, commissioned in July and August 1943.

In June 1944, Landymore joined the Canadian cruiser *Uganda*, which was working up for operations in the Pacific. He was promoted to acting lieutenant commander in March 1945. For his work as a gunner aboard *Uganda*, Landymore received a mention-in-despatches on the New Year's Honours List of 1946. He was thirty years of age.

After the war, Landymore worked in Naval Service Headquarters, then attended the RN Staff College Greenwich and the Joint Services Staff College in 1948–49. He was promoted to commander in 1950, and in September 1951 was appointed an acting captain and commanding officer of the destroyer HMCS *Iroquois*. He worked up *Iroquois* for her first Korean tour in 1952, and he remained with her for a second tour in 1953. Landymore fought under the appointment Canadian Commander Destroyers, Far East and saw much action on both tours. He received a second MID in June 1953, and upon completing his double tour was awarded the Order of the British Empire.

In January 1958, a year after she was commissioned, he was appointed captain of the light carrier HMCS *Bonaventure*, the flagship of the east coast fleet. Landymore conceived the idea of sustained operations, or "sustops" — keeping aircraft airborne around the clock. If the carrier and its aircrew could not do that, he thought, the viability of naval aviation could be threatened. This bold policy caused some tension between the admiral and his embarked flying squadrons. Stuart Soward, author of the two-volume history *Hands to Flying Stations*, described the admiral as "a determined, ambitious, self-admittedly stubborn and 'gung-ho' type of officer who was resolved to see the flying program and operational schedule proceed as planned."[8]

Upon leaving *Bonaventure* on 1 September 1959, he was promoted to commodore and appointed chief of staff to Flag Officer Atlantic Coast (FOAC). His first task ashore was as parade commander for the presentation of colours to the RCN by the Queen in Halifax in September 1959. This Royal visit was the last of the old-fashioned visits to Canada, but the first to be fully televised. For the forty-three-year-old Landymore, his place in the ceremony must have reinforced the close relationship between Britain and the RCN that he had known for over twenty years.

Landymore was promoted to rear-admiral and appointed Flag Officer Pacific Coast (FOPC) on 1 November 1962. He apparently had heard of Paul Hellyer earlier in the year, when the future minister recommended in a speech that the RCN should have a transport role.[9] The minister visited him in the spring of 1964 following the publication of his White Paper on Defence.[10] At this first meeting Landymore remembered that the minister

> explained the integration policy of the White Paper, and told us he intended to press on with integration, but in the matter of unification there was no intention to force it down anyone's throat, that he expected it would evolve naturally as a result of a desire within the service to unify. I had personal reservations about the unification concept but his statement that it would be allowed to evolve naturally ... put my fears to rest....[11]

Following his visit, Hellyer quickly introduced Bill C-90, amending the National Defence Act and permitting the creation of an integrated Canadian Forces Headquarters (CFHQ). On 1 August 1964, Hellyer's sweeping reforms replaced the three service chiefs and their headquarters' staffs with a Chief of Defence Staff (CDS) and, in theory, a common staff. Then, immediately following the loss of the Chief of Naval Staff (CNS) with his Naval Board and Naval Staff, came a second blow. On 5 August, Hellyer fired Rear-Admiral Jeffry V. Brock, Flag Officer Atlantic Coast (FOAC). Vice-Admiral K.L. Dyer was appointed chief of personnel and also "principal naval advisor," a secondary duty in CFHQ. On 16 November, Admiral Landymore took command of the east coast fleet from Brock. He was now the de facto head of the navy.

Rear-Admiral Landymore's career was informed and shaped in the close relationship that he had known between Britain, the RN, and the Canadian naval experience in the Second World War and Korea. It was the war and the values of "men of action" that mattered to his generation, and not the more abstract views engendered by, for example, a university experience. His war was somewhat worse than others': he saw dozens of shipmates die under the White Ensign in *Fraser* and *Margaree*, and he learned firsthand about the importance of tradition to a fighting sailor's life and death. These lessons were acquired pragmatically, and after the war the precepts did not have to be recalled, for they had become part of him.

What was Landymore like? Vice-Admiral R.L. Hennessy always maintained that in 1966 Landymore was "our best admiral," who was "one of the only two political-military brains that we had."[12] His opinion appears to be shared by many. Like everyone, Landymore probably had enemies, but if so, there is no direct evidence. Indeed, just the opposite is the case. He was popular, admired by all ranks, and is remembered as being a forthright, four-square, hands-on commander and staff officer, who was not pretentious and who could pass the time of day amongst ratings. He was concerned with the well-being of his men and women. In August 1966, a petty officer told Mrs. R.E.S. Bidwell, wife of Rear-Admiral Roger Bidwell, that:

> The firing of Admiral Landymore was a real shock to me — when he became F.O.A.C. he went around to every ship and establishment on the Atlantic Coast and talked to the men and answered their questions. Of

course we all thought, "Here is an admiral who is interested in our welfare" and were very impressed — I'd sailed under him in *Bonaventure* so had a high opinion of his ability as a naval officer…[13]

In Paul Hellyer's personal papers there is a character sketch of Landymore written by a member of Hellyer's staff in 1963 or early 1964. Perhaps, for our purposes, this is the best summary of what he was like. It reads: "Bright. Imaginative. Driver. Not too much humour. Can be tough. Not universally liked but good in the Navy. Doubtful integrator."[14]

We must leave the admiral for a moment and describe the military and political circumstances that were present during his commands from 1962 to 1966. While Landymore was making a steady rise to high command, the military, political, cultural and social conditions around him were changing rapidly.[15] In Britain and the United States, the RN, United States Navy (USN) and United States Marine Corps (USMC) responded to defence reforms in their own way.[16] In Canada, military issues like the Avro Arrow, Bomarc missiles, disarmament and nuclear weapons received much public attention in the late 1950s and early 1960s. With the exception of their deployment in the Cuban Missile Crisis, the RCN was not a player in these controversial questions of defence policy, and the navy remained quietly isolated on either coast, seemingly impervious to the ebb and flow of Canadian politics, which had become part of national security in an age of change.

The impetus for military transformation came from many sources, but two of the most important were the drive for government reorganization and the new international strategic environment. Canada had grown dramatically after the Second World War, and as Canadians made more demands on their government, so too did the federal public service. The three armed services were not immune to this trend. The government's response was to look for ways to rationalize and to provide clearer, achievable mandates, goals and objectives, to deliver services more efficiently and to administer departments more effectively. The result was the Royal Commission on Government Organization, headed by J. Grant Glassco. The need to question defence policy, study roles, centralize staffs and administration, all in order to reduce costs, underlay the Glassco Commission's recommendations, made in 1963, to integrate the armed forces.[17]

General Charles Foulkes, who had been chairman of the Chiefs of Staff Committee (CSC) through the 1950s, had laid the groundwork for Glassco. In 1961 he pointed out that the Canadian armed services were poorly organized because their staff system resembled

> the UK system "in miniature" with all the staff and services to look after forces many times the size of the Canadian military effort. [Moreover] … the Chiefs of Staff are heads of their respective services with strong loyalty to their service … [this] creates difficulties in taking decisions … which may not be advantageous to the individual service.[18]

To solve these problems he called for a fresh, efficient and economical approach to meet the ever-changing requirements arising from Canada's role "in the collective defence of the West."[19] His conclusion was that Canada required "a single service with one Chief of Staff, a combined administration and a series of task forces to replace the service field forces."[20]

Foulkes's call for reorganization was made even more urgent by the changing strategic environment. Canada's postwar foreign and defence policies had been based on support to international institutions such as NATO, the UN, the Commonwealth and North American Air Defence Command (NORAD).[21] By 1959, Soviet developments in nuclear weaponry and rocketry forecast a strategic revolution. The Warsaw Pact had apparently caught up to the west in deterrent power based on nuclear-armed inter-continental ballistic missiles (ICBMs).[22] The NATO policy of massive retaliation and trip-wire nuclear defence was now redundant. Deterrence and "flexible response" replaced it. Western nations reconsidered their options in favour of a policy that "ranged over the whole strategic scale — conventional forces to fight brush-fire wars; preparation for limited wars; finite deterrence by attacks against Soviet cities;

and insistence upon the necessity for a "counter-force" or "infinite deterrence" to destroy Soviet missile bases."[23]

An era of muddled strategic direction in the U.S. and NATO had begun.

The critical problem that faced defence ministers and the armed services was how to structure forces to meet the uncertain requirements of the age. Foulkes demanded a new paradigm that would replace threat-based defence economics.[24] Clearly, Canada could not continue to fund the vastly changing requirements in the face of rapidly evolving technology and weaponry. Defence commitments and capabilities had to be carefully thought through. While the CSC knew what was needed to meet the many roles, there were too many hard choices, given the resources available. The threat was no longer clear, and neither were the missions. Not surprisingly, veteran diplomats and scholars like John Holmes, as well as politicians on both sides of the House of Commons, began to challenge Canada's role as a middle power and suggest new foreign and defence policy options.[25]

The dilemma was not without a maritime dimension. Again, we can turn to Foulkes, who concluded:

> The Canadian effort to support the deterrent in the North Atlantic … is the largest and most expensive of all the defence undertakings…. There is an urgent need for a complete scientific and operational reassessment of this question and a strenuous effort made to work out with our NATO partners a single and comprehensive solution to ensure that more adequate results are attained commensurate with the effort being expended in this maritime field.[26]

Foulkes, and most officials in the government, knew that from the late 1940s onwards, NATO depended on command of the sea, and especially the Atlantic. The RCN commitment of warships to NATO had been the basis of Canadian postwar naval policy.[27] As one analyst has pointed out, in the 1950s "the naval tasks of national-sovereignty protection, continental defence of North America and NATO were nearly indistinguishable." The RCN's postwar ambitions had become integrated "into

NATO strategy with an ease not present in other areas of defence activity."[28] The Cold War threat was clearly defined, and the result was "the new principle of specialization of missions."[29]

Although a certain level of security was derived from specialization and the perceived twinning of national and NATO tasks, the RCN nevertheless enjoyed little operational stability during the 1950s. Sea-launched ballistic missiles increased the threat to North America, while at the same time NATO approved the strategic concept MC-14/2 (Revised) in 1957. NATO's minimum force study, MC-70, was based upon this strategic concept. It stated that

> it will be essential to have a timely projection of Allied sea-borne nuclear offensive power against enemy naval ... targets; and also to engage the enemy as soon as and as far forward as possible; so as to reduce to the minimum the number of his units which can penetrate to the broader reaches of the Atlantic and threaten the vital Allied sea lines of communication.[30]

These NATO policies sustained the sense of uncertainty for the RCN. On the one hand, preparations had to be made for nuclear naval war in the eastern Atlantic (EASTLANT), while on the other there was an increasing need to conduct anti-submarine warfare in WESTLANT. As if this did not provide enough instability, a completely new American and NATO concept loomed on the horizon in the early-1960s Kennedy era: "flexible response."

The Berlin Crisis of August–September 1961 caused a brief military expansion, and the U.S. and Britain responded by creating new, rapid-deployment forces at the divisional level. In Canada, "the horizon for naval planning broadened immediately,"[31] and the three services began to study concepts for rapidly deployable, air-portable forces that could be used either on the flanks of NATO, in limited war or in policing operations. In his survey of naval requirements Rear-Admiral Jeffry Brock, VCNS, pointed out in 1961 that "for limited war, intervention or policing action, the basic maritime requirement is for general purpose, versatile forces which can co-operate with the other services ... a capability is needed for escorting and transporting army units to almost any area in the world where trouble might develop and support them."[32]

In November 1963 in Ottawa, the tri-service Mobile Force Planning Group provided an interim report, and the service chiefs were not enthusiastic about the notion of a dedicated, air-transportable force. The CNS was particularly quick to point out the conflict with his SACLANT wartime roles. Vice-Admiral H.S. Rayner considered "that the impact of such a mobile force must be examined in relation to Canada's commitment to SACLANT. In some instances, although by no means all, it was possible that one type of ship might meet the requirements of both roles. However he questioned the validity of such a concept, as it was likely that both commitments might arise at the same time."[33]

Clearly, the RCN was not in support of the minister's new concept because it threatened relations within SACLANT's command.

In early 1964, the government's response to the Glassco Commission, as well as the diverse military requirements raised by "flexible response," was expressed in Hellyer's dramatic White Paper on Defence. This policy provided the official push for multipurpose forces. At the same time, fundamental attitudes towards NATO commitments began to change. For several years, Hellyer demanded publicly that Canada "take a hard look at the alliance":

> The [NATO] ... status quo will not prevail and this must be accepted.... NATO is becoming top-heavy with headquarters and bureaucratic machinery.... The balance of power within NATO had changed since 1949. Now a restored Europe was more powerful ... [nevertheless] Canada considers NATO a vital part of its foreign policy. It was needed to keep stability in Europe. But Canada would be looking at how it could be made more effective.[34]

The white paper acknowledged that Canada would maintain "a modern and well-equipped fleet of appropriate size... [to] continue in the anti-submarine role," and that "maritime forces will continue to have an important role in conjunction with the strategy of flexible response."[35] However, the white paper followed Foulkes's recommendation and directed that, "In order to get the maximum effectiveness for our investment in the anti-submarine force, we are conducting a major study to determine the best combination of weapons systems for this task. We have the active co-operation of our allies in this research."[36]

So there was to be further study, and major projects like new ship construction remained on hold.

For Paul Hellyer, the triumphs of 1964 were not repeated the following year. Relations were tense and uncertain in his new Canadian Forces Headquarters. The senior staff were resisting unification. Rumours abounded of unilateral decisions taken in Ottawa that were based neither on consensus nor cohesive policy. Hellyer remembered that

> delay created chaos.... Lack of co-operation in the personnel as in other departments really reflected the fact that many senior officers hoped that the whole thing would go away and wouldn't happen. The impasse in personnel was the principal reason why unification was proceeded with at once ... the climate they created left no choice.[37]

The result was a sense of distrust, as well as uncertainty, throughout the armed forces over the meaning of unification.

Nevertheless, Hellyer pursued a policy of studies, administrative integration and tighter civilian and ministerial control in Ottawa, and he also stood behind the concept of a national mobile force. This force, in theory, catered to the need for high readiness to support limited war or policing operations, either on the flanks of NATO or into trouble spots made unstable due to continued decolonization by Western nations.[38] Maritime Command was formally authorized in January 1966, and Forces Mobile Command (FMC) replaced the organization of the Canadian Army on 1 April 1966, combining the resources of the army and the tactical elements of the RCAF.

In summary, when Landymore took command of the west coast fleet late in 1962, the new cults of rationality challenged the orthodoxies of traditional military thought. Novel terms like "the philosophy of management," "flexible response" and "air-portable" became de rigueur. Ministers, commanders and staffs required sophisticated and flexible thinking to carve out specific service needs to meet these innovative and often abstruse operational and administrative demands.

Notions about commitments to NATO also were changing. Services' arguments for funding to match inviolate NATO commitments were becoming irrelevant. Moreover, NATO nations increasingly foresaw the need for dual-purpose forces that would prepare to engage the Soviet Union in general war, but which also could be used in lighter versions on the flanks of NATO, in limited war, or in peacekeeping. The latter tasks sidelined naval involvement, and limited war forced navies to consider maritime transport and possibly amphibious forces. Thus, for the RCN there was a potential conflict of roles. The well-known tension between SACLANT tasks in the eastern Atlantic and defence-of-Canada tasks in WESTLANT, which was not new, was complicated by possible tasks in support of rapid deployments — for example, NATO's new emphasis on operations requiring light, mobile forces.

Increasingly, Landymore and the RCN faced many vital questions. What did unification mean? What roles would the RCN be given as the smallest element of a single service? How would the RCN participate in low-intensity conflict? What was the future of the RCN as a balanced fleet in an Atlantic coalition? There were few forthright answers available. As we have seen, studies were called for, and uncertainty surrounded the RCN, the admiral, and political and military officials in Canada as well as Britain and the United States. By 1964 Landymore, his senior officers and his navy, faced profoundly uncertain circumstances, ripe with potential for rumour, misunderstanding and misperception.

After he was dismissed in July 1966, Rear-Admiral Landymore explained the reasons for his actions during the previous year in a new brief for the Standing Committee on National Defence. As a document, the brief is a story in itself. It was translated into French, and that text was copied on the back of each page — a rarity at the time. He combined this brief with two other papers, and he widely distributed this set to members of Parliament and government officials during the fall and winter of 1966–67, to be used as background documents to the next session of the Standing Committee.[39] This brief will be used to present Landymore's side of the deteriorating relationship with Hellyer during 1965–66. It is a story, from Landymore's point of view, of the alienation of the RCN from participation in the evolution of defence policy in a volatile age of uncertainty.

Landymore took over Maritime Command from the recently fired Rear-Admiral Jeffry Brock in November 1964, and shortly after was summoned to Ottawa. He described the visit as "the only [tri-service] Commander's Conference to be called during my twenty months in command on the east coast."[40] He recalled that the minister told his officers that they were to "go along" with integration and unification — or else, as he put it, "put their letters on his desk." He clearly remembered advising the minister "that unification would destroy the spirit of the navy, and that, unless he would provide the details of the unification programme and the time span over which it was to be achieved, I could not support the policy." According to Landymore, this "frank and honest disclosure … relieved me of any necessity to resign. If there was to be a move to discuss the matter further or to call an end to my service it was the Minister's move, not mine."[41]

In June 1965, CFHQ announced that a new single-service walking-out dress and a common rank structure would be in place by July 1967. Landymore recalled that this caused "a most serious setback in morale." It was like being struck by "a bombshell," and the "officers and men were deeply distressed by it." Landymore claimed that he was "personally so concerned about its effects that I ordered an informal poll to be carried out."[42] He wrote the CDS, Air Chief Marshal Frank Miller, on 21 June and advised him that:

> I cannot overemphasize the adverse result which will occur if the present course toward unification is continued. This being so, the choice seems either to live with a service which will have no heart for its work for years to come, or to pursue integration with all its benefits

leaving the matter of identity intact. I most strongly urge the second alternative. It is requested the Defence Council be made aware of the foregoing observations.[43]

He received no written answer to this letter.

The action that Landymore then took has been, ever since, the subject of mess-deck and wardroom legend. He called a meeting of all the officers in his command in "the rank of Commodore, Captain and Commander." At the end of the session he "asked them to stand to signify agreement with the following [five] points .... all but one stood." The five points were:

[1] That they wished me to represent their viewpoint.

[2] That they wouldn't feel they couldn't speak openly and frankly about their views on unification in the service and outside ... this would be the state of affairs until the law was changed in Parliament ... it was quite proper to talk about it but that I encouraged them to do so.

[3] That they should not consider a loss of identity for the navy inevitable and so become apathetic about it.

[4] ...this is most important — that they wouldn't ask to be retired because they couldn't accept the theory of unification ... I pledged that if their viewpoint was ignored that it would be I alone who would take appropriate action in protest.

[5] That for the information of people outside the room the purpose of our meeting was to discuss morale.[44]

Following that meeting, which he judged highly successful, he held meetings for all his naval officers in the rank of lieutenant-commander. He now was convinced of two things: "there was absolutely no support for full unification amongst naval officers in my Command, and ... it was therefore my responsibility firmly and consistently to represent their point of view."[45] Rightly or wrongly, Landymore believed that he had the full support of all his senior officers. He advised Dyer of his actions, and pleaded with him "to put the case to the Chief of Defence Staff and the Minister, to encourage the pursuit of progress in integration, to abandon the attempt to force the single service concept down the throats of unwilling recipients and to restore the lost confidence of officers and men by standing up for individual service identity."[46] Again, he received no written reply.

In December 1965, the RCN, in Landymore's opinion, received a further alienating jab from the minister's office. He recalled that "a member of the Minister's personal staff" had "generated" an article warning of the possibility of the three armed services becoming "Royal Canadian Marines." Landymore, and his command, were disturbed by this suggestion. In his opinion it "caused more bitterness and resentment than anything that had happened previously."[47]

Landymore again wrote the CDS, as he had done in June. He ended his letter of 29 December with an alarming statement of conditions in the RCN:

> I expect you have heard my views often enough to find them boring. If this is the case, and if my protestations have become meaningless, and if the ill-considered press releases continue, there won't be a chance for effective leadership here to be exercised by anyone. In any event, as you can appreciate from the tone of the letter, my task of providing effective command is becoming increasingly difficult and may prove to be impossible.[48]

No evidence has survived of the action taken by either the CDS or Dyer over these alarming reports from Landymore. He was not visited by either Hellyer or the CDS during his twenty months in command.[49] Moreover, they took no action over the meetings Landymore held with his officers, meetings that Hellyer had been advised of by an anonymous RCN senior officer.

While the early months of 1966 were uneventful, on 14 April 1966, Landymore believed that more evidence had surfaced to indicate that the minister's office was intentionally provoking the RCN. This blow was delivered by an article in *The Globe and Mail* about re-engagement rates in the three armed services. The worst rates, it reported, were in the navy. Further, the article linked the low rates to upper- and lower-deck relations in the navy. The source quoted was the special assistant to the minister, Group-Captain William Lee, RCAF (retired), who claimed that an important factor was

> the generally acknowledged difference in officer/man relationships in the Navy. Defence officials say that naval officers still retain to some extent an above decks, below decks mentality where personnel are concerned. They've got to realize that this is now a highly technical service…. Sailors don't just scrub decks and set the sail now, they're skilled men and the old attitudes of officers just don't fit. We're trying to change that.[50]

Instead of rising to the bait, Landymore remembered that he reacted carefully and did not give the minister's staff the chance to pursue the issue. In his opinion, "an influential person on the Minister's personal staff had publicly criticized the whole officer corps of the navy." He concluded his description of this incident by commenting that "[w]hile this matter is not related to unification it illustrates that the Minister has no regard whatsoever for the state of morale in the navy."[51]

The final stage in Landymore's declining relations with Ottawa began on 22 June 1966, when he was preparing to brief Parliament's Standing Committee on National Defence. He presented two briefs to the minister — "one unclassified, one secret" — to inform the committee about the state of the RCN. His original brief included a remark about a serious personnel situation on the east coast. This observation was toned down by Hellyer's staff, and the "personnel section was virtually rewritten."[52] Neither script, however, connected poor morale with unification, or indeed even mentioned the term. However, during questions following the presentation, the linkage *was* made. Landymore testified to the committee that "morale is bad — that there is a great deal of unrest amongst officers and senior men, that I didn't agree with unification, that there was reluctance in the navy to accept unification, that identity is most important as far as servicemen are concerned, and that sailors dislike khaki uniforms."[53]

Landymore met with Hellyer twice after the briefing.[54] At a second meeting, the minister gave the admiral "his views on a number of matters including some points on unification." Landymore remembered that he "warned the Minister the present course toward full unification was simply not being accepted by the Navy and that if he forced a loss of identity on the Navy it would lead to disaster."[55] On 4 July, the minister announced the new senior appointments for CFHQ to take effect just a week later. The list included the retirement of Vice-Admiral K.L. Dyer and the double promotion of Commodore R.L. Hennessy to Vice-Admiral.[56]

The next meeting between Hellyer and Landymore took place a week later, on 12 July.[57] The minister asked the admiral to resign. Landymore refused. The minister advised that he "would be compulsorily retired."[58] Landymore remembered this period in mid-July as "days charged with a great deal of emotion." He recalled that in rapid succession, two lieutenant-generals, one vice-admiral, three rear-admirals and himself "were either to be retired 'by mutual agreement,' for reasons of dissatisfaction or, as it was, in my case, simply … fired."[59]

That same afternoon, still in Ottawa, Landymore passed along the results of his meeting with Hellyer to three key people: Air Chief-Marshal Frank Miller, the CDS; Vice-Admiral Dyer; and Captain David Groos, RCN (retired), a Liberal member of Parliament representing a riding in Victoria, British Columbia — and the new chairman of the Standing Committee on National Defence.[60] Groos arranged a meeting between Prime Minister Lester B. Pearson and Landymore on the evening of 13 July. According to Landymore, the prime minister told him "he fully supported the Minister's policy on integration but that he didn't know to what depth he intended to carry on unification." He added that "he had visited the Ship's Company of HMCS *Saskatchewan*, on the West Coast, and had promised them [that] the government would not interfere with naval traditions."[61]

The following day, 14 July, Landymore returned to Halifax. He recalled that he received "local and long distance calls from the press asking if rumours of… [his] retirement were true." He referred all of them to Ottawa, saying, "I had no comment until any official announcement was made." The next morning, Landymore was called by a "highly respected member of the Halifax press, Mr. Jack Brayley."[62] Brayley was a senior Canadian Press journalist with a reputation for getting to the bottom of a story.[63] He told Landymore that his "retirement had been announced, that the wires were full of the story, and that great harm would be done to the Navy if... [the admiral] didn't answer the questions of the press." Brayley was right. *The Globe and Mail* managed to cobble together a surprisingly accurate picture of what had happened in Ottawa over the previous three days.[64]

Landymore then took his next fateful decision, which was probably one of the most important of his life. He agreed to speak to the press, and told Brayley that he would be at home "that afternoon and would answer questions for anyone who was interested." Because of what Brayley had told him, Landymore insisted that he "was not responsible directly or indirectly ... for leaking the news to the press."[65] The story was front-page news across Canada, under headlines such as "Revolt Against Hellyer: Defiant Halifax Rear-Admiral Sacked,"[66] "Revolt of the Admirals — Only the Beginning,"[67] "Hellyer stakes his job against ousted admiral," and "The admirals can't scuttle unification policy."[68]

Landymore justified speaking out publicly because "[b]y appointment, I was the next senior naval officer to Admiral Dyer." For one with a high sense of duty, the question was obvious: if he didn't speak out, then who would? He believed that "it was necessary to alert the people of Canada to a perilous state of affairs in defence matters."[69] Moreover, he was certain that he had no other choice because he had spent many months "attempting, unsuccessfully, to indicate through official channels, available to me, the seriousness of the situation in my Command directly related to the matter of unification."[70]

By late July, Landymore's name was a household word in Canada. The issue caught and held the attention of thousands of Canadians through to December. Open warfare was conducted between opponents of unification and the government. Critics of unification inside and outside the government seemed to be galvanized by the catalytic effect of Landymore's firing. Hundreds of letters and telegrams were sent to the prime minister, the minister and members of Parliament. The debate on Bill C-243, the unification bill, became a highly sensational and contentious issue. The three main adversaries against unification were the Progressive Conservative party, the Tri-Service Identities Organization

(TRIO) and a diverse group of retired officers from all three services. Veterans, friends and families of the RCN, the WRCNS, reserves and naval associations participated in each of these groups. Although the RCN had few political connections, they had powerful connections in the English-language media.[71] Thus, "the navy," as represented by its associations and many retired senior officers, which had been prior to 1966 the smallest, quietest and least politically controversial of the three services, contributed disproportionately to the campaign against the minister and his policy of unification.[72]

Throughout the autumn, Landymore continued to do his part, working from his farm outside Halifax. He was kept informed, and he worked on the new brief for the Standing Committee. As we have seen, it represented a synthesis of all his concerns, including emphasis on future roles for the RCN. In the brief, Landymore raised, for the first time, a second argument against unification. He warned of the limited prospects for a national navy in a unified single service that would be oriented towards a single role — operating with the Mobile Force preparing for multipurpose rapid deployment operations. His argument turned on the fact that, given the many studies conducted by the minister, unification itself had not been studied. Had it been, he argued, "it would have been obvious that the basic premise, and only justification, for a single force, on which the proponents for full unification could hang their argument was that the armed forces had only *one* role."[73] Landymore saw a threatening linkage between disarmament arguments, unification, a single service, and therefore a tri-service force with a single role and the resulting loss of purely naval roles in NATO.

While Landymore was aware that Hellyer had emphasized anti-submarine warfare in SACLANT in the white paper, he considered the possibility of unification superceding the NATO commitment by adding support to Mobile Command. He believed Hellyer had created a situation where a hard choice had to be made about these roles and, therefore, about the future of the RCN. Here he expressed the wide limits of RCN uncertainty in 1966:

> I think there grew up an idea that the policing role *was* the only role, and if that was the case why not have a

single force, a highly mobile force which could go anywhere quickly to deal with policing situations? This
idea was expanded with the argument, that if the police
force was properly equipped with modern weapons it
would, in fact be a mobile army capable of dealing with
policing situations and able also to meet army commitments in an emergency. Along with this there grew up
the idea that because of inter-continental ballistic missiles and nuclear weapons war was unthinkable. War of
all sorts was unthinkable, and always has been, but it
hasn't prevented us becoming involved in war, nor can
a defence of Canada be based on a gamble that we cannot become involved in war.[74]

Landymore went on to argue that there was a "distinct and separate
role" for the RCN. It was required to be

a highly specialized and professional ... [navy] that is distinct and separate from the mobile force and police force
concept.... [T]his role is a continuing one, and ... it is so
vastly different and far removed from the predictable
tasks for the Mobile Force that to lump all three services
into a single force makes no military sense whatsoever.[75]

He concluded by reminding the reader that:

The Chiefs of Staff in Britain, in the United States, in all
of NATO to my certain knowledge, share my concern
over the situation at sea, and have no doubts whatsoever as to the distinctly separate role of the navies ...
there can be no merit in causing a complete upheaval
of the navy to remold it into a single force ... having
two completely separate reasons for its existence.[76]

In summary, Landymore presented two broad arguments against unification. Each addressed a separate threat. The first, as we have seen, was

the well-known argument about the risks of incorporation into a single service, with a common uniform, leading to the loss of naval traditions and lowered morale. This argument, while perhaps persuasive on the surface, is difficult to substantiate with hard evidence. Ultimately, it was based on Landymore's highly subjective analysis of the future. Moreover, it was not likely to help his cause since it only reinforced some Canadians' perception that the service was hidebound to tradition and out of step with the changing realities of the Cold War in the mid-1960s.[77]

Landymore's second argument over the conflict of roles and diminished credibility from the RN and USN, while important, was not, in this author's opinion, very effective. Although his instincts and principles were sound, his case did not reflect any of the higher-level thinking available at the time. By the fall of 1966, there was no shortage of studies, books and unclassified writings on the future of Canadian foreign and defence policy linked to economics. Nevertheless, to be fair, these publications did not offer a blueprint for a Canadian maritime security policy and for a navy that could participate in national as well as alliance roles. Neither, however, did Landymore.

It is easy, in hindsight, to criticize Rear-Admiral Landymore for overreacting to a threat that did not exist, or for being out of step with rapidly changing times. There have been many claims and counterclaims made about his actions, their origins and their impact. But to Landymore and many of his friends in the three services, the threats to the RCN during those days were very real. They knew that, in the age of flexible response, many critics saw Canada's navy as unnecessary, or as part of the Mobile Force subordinate to Mobile Command in peacekeeping and wartime, as well as retaining an effective ASW capability. The white paper clearly directed the first priority to be the "direct protection of Canada."[78] Landymore and his supporters, increasingly alienated by the policy-makers in DND, saw great risks for a navy relegated to providing territorial defence, or sealift and possible amphibious support to the army and air force. For those reasons, as well as for emotional reasons over the loss of naval uniforms and ranks, Landymore was convinced that the RCN was threatened, and he knew this view was shared by thousands of serving and retired officers, men and Wrens who saw their wartime identities threatened by opportunistic landsmen, politicians, soldiers and airmen.

Although Landymore believed that he was fully supported, there is strong evidence to suggest that he failed to persuade the entire navy that change was unnecessary. In September 1966, for example, the executive director of the Nova Scotia Liberal Association had reported to Hellyer's special assistant, William Lee, that

> I've been beaten and battered by Chiefs and Lieutenant-Commanders during the past few hectic weeks but ... I am convinced that any criticism or disagreement with the programme "as we know it" is confined to a certain small element with the [RCN] based here. The rank and file, in other words the majority, aren't as incensed or overly concerned as our local newspaper would lead readers to believe.[79]

A few months later, in December, "a navy wife," who claimed "to have had the opportunity to hear views on unification, expressed by the 'lower deck,'" advised Hellyer that

> objection in the lower ranks is almost negligible.... Able Seamen, Leading Seamen and Petty Officers second class, by a large majority, favour the proposed idea of unification, and are very much satisfied with integration. The R.C.N. has been in a slump for quite some time: morale has been low. Finally, someone proposes to do something about it, and the men await the change with eager anticipation. The idea of a new uniform is particularly appealing. Despite the traditions behind the present uniform, the men who wear it are not impressed. Theirs is a responsible position in society, and they want a uniform befitting the dignity of this position. A forty-year old petty-officer, second class, looks and feels ridiculous in the "little

boys uniform" he is … compelled to wear. He doesn't want to look "cute."[80]

About the same time the "navy wife" wrote the minister, a serving RCN lieutenant wrote Hellyer a personal letter describing the strong support for unification that existed on his recent staff course.

> The ninety-three students, staff, and guests had finished their farewell mess dinner and had retired to the bar where, lo, the president of TRIO appeared on deck … the consensus amongst the students was that he thought that … relaxed and uninhibited, [they] would be in a mood to express derogatory opinions about unification … the students turned out to be very … uninhibited all right — but very unified and especially against the president of TRIO. People seemed to be queuing up to have a go at him … we had indeed fought our first unified action … [one student said] "that SOB wouldn't have found six guys in the school to support him." It was a damn fine experience, and a number of us thought it a pity that you weren't there to share it.[81]

Clearly, the younger officers, as well as their ratings, seemed to sense something that their seniors did not. For example, despite Landymore's dire warnings, the RCN did not collapse under the impact of single-service administration, nor did Mobile Command become the single operational authority for tri-service operations after 1968, nor did limited war and policing tasks detract from Canadian naval relations with the RN and USN. Moreover, there is no evidence that unification caused morale to decline, that it increased the rate of attrition or that recruiting dropped. The navy, like the other two services, learned to accept being part of a single service, with a single identity. Although considerable bitterness existed amongst senior officers and ratings, the armed forces apparently voted strongly Liberal in the federal elections of 1968 and 1972.[82]

* * *

What is Rear-Admiral Landymore's legacy to the navy? Opinions may vary, but his difficulty was a universal one, not strictly a product of the war or the 1960s. He was struggling to express the three-way relationship between national interests, collective security and the need for a balanced and respected fleet. Within a few years, analysts would find the key to this dilemma by linking the purpose of the navy to sovereignty, particularly of the north, and stressing the unique Canadian three-ocean requirement. In 1966, however, these subtle notions were not widely understood.

Landymore felt that he had to aggressively apprise politicians and the public of Canada — who had no experience with either a large peacetime national navy nor a national maritime security policy — that the RCN was a first-class national institution *because* it had a distinct identity and *because* it was highly respected by the allied navies for the way it had responded to the changing roles in SACLANT. In a sense he was not championing the cause of a distinct national navy, but instead the cause of a distinct navy in an RN and USN coalition.

Nevertheless, one can hear an echo of Landymore's plea for systematic study in the 1967 CFHQ Maritime System Study, and later in ORAE publications on a maritime security policy for Canada.[83] For that reason, it is possible to conclude his legacy to the Canadian navy is this: his experience reminds us how easy it is to forget that the central question he faced is a constant one — how does Canada structure small forces in alliances whose policies we do not always agree with? Landymore may have misjudged the outcome, but he did not misjudge the need to think things through. His fight against the single force with a single mission predates the present debate on how a small Canadian defence budget can maintain a general-purpose combat capability. His response to the questions that were caused by the circumstances in the 1960s was new — and lasting.

NOTES

1 "A Brief By Rear-Admiral Landymore OBE, CD, RCN, Prepared for the Standing Committee on National Defence," Directorate of History and Heritage (DHH), 87/146, 7. The origin and use of this document are explained in endnote 39. I have included long quotes from the document in order that Admiral Landymore may speak for himself. Hereafter cited as "Brief."

2 The biographical details in the rest of this part, unless otherwise specified, are drawn from the DHH Landymore Biog File. This file contains various DND press release and information sheets on Landymore as well as the extensive interview notes made by Hal Lawrence during 1986.

3 R.P. Welland interview by Hal Lawrence, 4, 25 May 1983, DHH, Welland Biog File.

4 Laurie Farrington, "Of Such People Are Legends Made — RCN Special Entries," *Soundings*, November 1995, 27–95, 24–25. From 1922 to 1942, RCN officers were trained by the RN as "special entries." There were a total of eight RCN special entries in Number 40. I am indebted to Captain Gordon Armstrong, RCN (retired), for this reference.

5 German, *The Sea Is at Our Gates*, 79; Milner, *Canada's Navy: The First Century*, 84. [Complete references for commonly cited secondary sources are included in the bibliography.]

6 Milner, *Canada's Navy*, 87.

7 A brief description of Scapa Flow gunnery training is in Richard Baker, *Dry Ginger: The Biography of Admiral of the Fleet Sir Michael Le Fanu* (London: W.H. Allen, 1977), 51–58.

8 Soward, *Hands to Flying Stations*, 137. See also J. Allan Snowie, *The Bonnie: HMCS Bonaventure*, 91–116.

9 David Burke claimed that the first entry in Landymore's press clipping scrapbook was the account in the Victoria *Daily Colonist*, 13 May 1962, of Hellyer's speech recommending a transport role for the RCN. Burke, David, "Hellyer and Landymore," 24. Burke was an officer in the United States Air Force in Ottawa in the 1960s. See endnote 37.

10 In early 1964, as FOPC, Landymore was given the task of heading a study on personnel problems in the navy. Then-Commodore

R. Hennessy was Deputy Chief of Naval Personnel (DCNP) and a member of the Landymore study team. He remembered that: "We were still deliberating in Bill's office on the west coast... [when] Hellyer's '64 White Paper came out. So we dropped what we were doing to comment on the thing.... Bill wasn't having any of it. He was totally opposed and said he was going to fight it tooth and nail." Vice-Admiral R.L. Hennessy interview by Wilf Lund, 20 April 2001, 39. Interview held by DHH Naval History Team.

11 Brief, 5. The visit was 11 April 1964. Landymore's flag lieutenant remembered that the admiral and his staff instantly disliked Mr. Hellyer and especially his special assistant, Mr. William M. Lee, a recently retired RCAF group captain who had specialized as an information officer during the previous decade. The feeling apparently was mutual. The admiral and his flag lieutenant travelled east on the same RCAF aircraft that the minister and his entourage used to return to Ottawa. During the trip, neither group spoke to the other. Interview with flag lieutenant and author, January 2002, Ottawa. Interview notes held by author.

12 Hennessy interview with Hal Lawrence, 11 April 1985, DHH Hennesy Biog File, 34, 39. The other "brain" was Rear-Admiral Jeffry Brock. Hennessy defined his term to mean an "appreciation of the linkage between the political side and the military side, global strategy, etc...," 39.

13 Mrs. R.E.S. Bidwell to Mr. Paul Hellyer, 2 September 1966, Hellyer Papers, Library and Archives Canada (LAC), MG33 B32, vol. 80, 80-1.

14 Hellyer File, "Department of National Defence," Hellyer's personal papers, Toronto. I am indebted to Mr. Hellyer for allowing me access to these private papers.

15 Beyond the scope of this survey of the late 1950s and early 1960s, but still important, was the Canadian "identity crisis," as well as the serious economic recession that began in 1958. Granatstein, "When Push Came to Shove," 86–88.

16 The period was a dark one for the RN. The large fleet-carrier project was cancelled in February 1966 and the First Sea Lord resigned in protest. The USN and USMC had an easier time. The election in 1960 of

John F. Kennedy, a wartime naval officer, "opened up new opportunities for the Corps... [JFK believed in] the wisdom of a 'flexible response' strategy that offered more military alternatives than nuclear war.... [The White House and Pentagon] were impressed by the Corps' Limited War capability." Allan R. Millett, *Semper Fidelis: The History of the United States Marine Corps* (New York: Macmillan, 1980), 545.

17 *The Royal Commission on Government Organization*, 5 Volumes, Ottawa, January 1963. Also see Bland, *The Administration of Defence Policy in Canada*, 6–12, and Chapter III, "The Glassco Commission and Issues in Defence Administration," 25–32. Bland inferred that there was a link between U.S. Defence Secretary McNamara's "reforms" and changes in Canadian defence policy. See also *White Paper on Defence, 1964*, 17–20.

18 General Charles Foulkes, "The Case for One Service," July 1961, Hellyer Papers, LAC, MG32B33, vol. 82, 82-8, 1 and 13.

19 *Ibid.*, 14.

20 *Ibid.*, 23.

21 Holmes, *The Shaping of Peace*, 377: "...the health and strength of institutions was consistently the prior claim on Canadian policymakers throughout [the 1950s]."

22 See Friedman, *Fifty Year War*, chapters 21 and 22, for the political uses made of the "missile gap" in 1959–1961.

23 Richard A. Preston, *Canada in World Affairs* (Toronto: Oxford University Press, 1965), 42–43.

24 Foulkes, "The Case for One Service," 11–13.

25 John Holmes, "Canada and the United States in World Politics," *Foreign Affairs*, XL (July 1961), 105–117, and "Canada in Search of its Role," *Foreign Affairs*, XLI (July 1963), 659–72; Sutherland, "Canada's Long Term Strategic Situation"; Peyton V. Lyon, *The Policy Question* (Toronto: McClelland and Stewart, 1963); Eayrs, *Northern Approaches*.

26 Foulkes, "The Case for One Service," 18–19.

27 SACLANT was formed 10 April 1952. Polmar, *Chronology of the Cold War at Sea*, 35.

28 Sokolsky, *A Question of Balance*, 8. Sokolsky drew the second quote from Cuthbertson, *Canadian Military Independence in the Age of the*

Superpowers, 127. See also Milner, "A Canadian Perspective on Canadian and American Naval Relations Since 1945," 153.

29 *White Paper on Defence, 1964*, 9. The white paper reviewed the history of Canadian defence policy and programs, and expanded on the point of specialization: "With comparatively minor exceptions, Canada's defence programs now were specific in nature and made sense only in relation to the total capabilities of the entire group of NATO nations and to the Alliance objective of creating balanced collective forces," 9.

30 Pedlow, NATO *Strategy Documents*, 308. I am indebted to Dr. Isabel Campbell of the postwar naval team at DHH for advising me on NATO matters in this period.

31 Hennessy, "Fleet Replacement," 376.

32 *The Report of the Ad Hoc Committee on Naval Objectives*, July 1961, known as the "Brock Report," DHH, 81/481. It was formulated as the basis for naval policy in the 1960s. It was approved by the Conservative government in 1961, but not the Liberals after April 1963.

33 Chiefs of Staff minutes, 21 November 1963, LAC, RG 24 (acc 83-64/215), box 22, S-1200-M4. About a month earlier the minister had cancelled the general-purpose frigate (GPF) program.

34 "NATO changes are inevitable, Hellyer says," Toronto *Globe and Mail*, 2 March 1966.

35 *White Paper on Defence, 1963*, 23.

36 *Ibid.*, 14–15.

37 Hellyer to Lieutenant-Colonel David P. Burke, USAF, June 1978 (draft letter), Hellyer Papers, LAC, MG32B33, vol. 82, file 82-1, 7.

38 The term "Mobile Force" was used in the White Paper on Defence, 1964, 22. The force was to consist of two brigades stationed in Canada, to "be available for use where and when required."

39 The two other papers were: "The Navy's Place in Unification," which he had written in February 1966, and his script for his presentation, titled, "Brief for the Standing Committee on National Defence Concerning Unification of the Armed Forces," dated February 1967. Landymore sent a set of the papers to the Directorate of History and Heritage in December 1984. These documents were made available to the public in 1987 as DHH, 87/146.

40 Brief, 7

41 *Ibid.*, 5.

42 *Ibid.*, 7.

43 *Ibid.*, 8.

44 *Ibid.*, 9–10.

45 *Ibid.*, 10.

46 *Ibid.*

47 *Ibid.*, 11.

48 *Ibid.*

49 *Ibid.*

50 *Ibid.*, 12–13.

51 *Ibid.*, 13.

52 *Ibid.*, 15.

53 Minutes of Proceedings and Evidence No. 12, Standing Committee on National Defence, 23 June 1966, Ottawa, 1966. See the following pages: "there is a great reluctance [to accept unification] on the part of the navy" (334); "the morale is bad…" (350); on the need "to clarify the definition of unification" and related problems (350–3).

54 Brief, 15–16.

55 *Ibid.*, 16.

56 "Commodore Hennessy Surprised by Sudden Entrance Into Spotlight," Halifax *Mail-Star*, 11 July 1966.

57 The delay was probably due to the fact that the House of Commons Emergency Session was to end 14 July, and Hellyer probably did not want to fire Landymore and face a sitting House if other resignations followed.

58 Brief, 1.

59 *Ibid.*, 3. It should be noted that several of these senior officers were retiring on age; see Vice-Admiral R.L. Hennessy interview by Hal Lawrence, 9 April 1985, DHH, Hennessy Biog File, 42. Apparently, it was during this sad time that the minister's office coined the term "admirals' revolt." The term possibly was derived from two earlier "revolts": first was the USN admiral's "revolt" in 1949 over strategic policy; see Jeffry G. Barlow, "The Revolt of the Admirals Reconsidered," in William B. Cogar (ed.), *New Interpretations in Naval History* (Annapolis, Md.: Naval Institute Press, 1989), and

George Baer, *One Hundred Years of Sea Power: The U.S. Navy, 1890-1990* (Stanford, Calif.: Stanford University Press, 1994), 309–13. Second was the use of the term "generals' revolt" more than twenty years earlier to describe senior Canadian army officers' actions during the Second Conscription Crisis in November 1944.

60 Brief, 17.

61 *Ibid.*, 17.

62 *Ibid.*, 18.

63 Garry Myers, Mrs. Tinker McKay and (her husband) Mr. McKay, interviews by R.H. Caldwell, March 2002. Mr. Myers was a freelance news photographer in Halifax; Mrs. McKay is Rear-Admiral Pullen's daughter and friend of the admiral's late wife, Mrs. Judy Landymore; Mr. McKay is a retired CBC Halifax producer. Biographical information on Brayley is held at the Public Archives of Nova Scotia.

64 "4 Admirals reported leaving in Defence Feud," *The Globe and Mail*, 15 July 1966.

65 Brief, 18.

66 *Ottawa Citizen*, 15 July 1966.

67 Halifax *Chronicle Herald*, 16 July 1966.

65 *Toronto Star*, 16 July 1966.

69 Brief, 3.

70 *Ibid.*, 4.

71 The best account of the opposition to unification from the government's perspective is J.L. Granatstein, "Unification: The Politics of the Armed Forces," 218–42. Granatstein had access to the Hellyer papers. A useful thesis is Simkoff, "The Opposition… to Bill C-243, The Canadian Forces Reorganization Act."

72 The principal naval associations that developed position papers were the Naval Officers' Association of Canada (NOAC) and the Navy League of Canada.

73 Brief, 20. The emphasis is Landymore's.

74 *Ibid.* The emphasis is Landymore's.

75 *Ibid.*

76 *Ibid.*, 20–21.

77 James Jackson, "Mr. Hellyer and the Officers," *Saturday Night*, April

1967, 23–25. Jackson referred to these officers as "ancient militarists," 25.

78 *White Paper on Defence, 1964*, 24.

79 Letter W. Brian Myers, to W.M. Lee, 29 August 1966, Hellyer Papers, LAC, MG32B33, vol 80, 80-9. Pearson and Hellyer knew that there was high support for unification; for example, Pearson replied to Rear-Admiral H.N. Lay, RCN (retired), 24 November 1966, and advised him that "I am far from convinced, however, that 'an overwhelming majority,' as you state in your letter, opposes the Government's policy." Pearson Papers, LAC, MG26N4, vol. 37, 100.82, "Policy."

80 Letter to Hellyer, 7 December 1966, Hellyer Papers, LAC, MG32B33, vol. 79, 79-5.

81 Letter from RCN Lieutenant (name withheld) to Hellyer, 17 December 1966, Hellyer Papers, LAC, MG32B33, vol. 81, 81-4.

82 Author's discussions with the Hon. Paul T. Hellyer, March 2002.

83 Milner drew attention to the 1967 Maritime System Study in his "Canadian Perspective on Canadian and American Naval Relations Since 1945," 164–65. The leader in the early articulation of a national maritime security policy was Dr. George Lindsay, a scientist with ORAE, and later head of that institution. For example see his "Canadian Maritime Strategy: Should the Emphasis Be Changed?," August 1969, DHH, 87/253-II-20.9. See also J.W. Cox (also at ORAE), "The Requirements for Maritime Forces," 19 November 1968, DHH, 87/253-18, 14.

Part II:
Commanders of
Maritime Command

CHAPTER ELEVEN

Vice-Admiral Harold A. Porter, 1970–71

Vice-Admiral Harold A. Porter

I took up my appointment as Commander of Maritime Command on 6 July 1970. It is interesting to note that my appointment message gave my rank as MGen(S) — that is, Major-General–Sea. The reason for this, in part, was that the early version of the personnel branch computer was too full to accept naval rank titles! But at that time, the use of naval rank titles also was a subject of controversy and a morale factor among all ranks in the navy. I will deal with that issue in more detail later in my recollections.

The appointment as MARCOM was my sixth successive appointment to jobs almost exclusively dealing with naval matters at senior levels. In succession, I had been naval assistant to the Chief of the Naval Staff (CNS), captain of the *Bonaventure* with CANCOMFLT (the Commander of the Canadian Fleet) embarked, Director General Maritime Forces at NDHQ, then CANCOMFLT myself, followed by Commander Maritime Forces Pacific (MARPAC), and finally Maritime Commander (MARCOM), all from 1962 to 1971.

During this nine-year period there were four areas of main concern to me. First, the Cold War was an era when Canada, as a member of the NATO bastion defending against the Soviet Union, saw our potential adversary —

especially the Soviet Navy — making great strides to become a major maritime power, thereby threatening the west. Second, the turmoil in Ottawa during the period I was Director General Maritime Forces (DGMF) in the late 1960s, when Canadian Forces Headquarters (CFHQ) was struggling to become unified at the same time that budget restrictions and personnel reductions were being made. Third, was it to be *integration*, or both *integration* and *unification*? — an era, again, of general turmoil in the personnel area, with the requirement to push the personnel of the navy, army and air force into a unified force with all its implications; in particular, to be outfitted in a green uniform made no sense for the navy, as it destroyed all links with the uniforms of the worlds' other navies. Finally, when it came to be both integration *and* unification, the resulting confusion and plummet in morale, as to when naval officers, men and women should use unified rank titles or traditional rank titles.

I will deal with each of these in turn.

The Cold War

To begin, it is appropriate to record the operational resources that Maritime Command had in July 1970:

- twenty destroyers, nine of which were DDHs (helicopter-carrying destroyers), thirteen deployed on the Atlantic coast and seven on the Pacific;
- three Oberon-class submarines based in Halifax, and an ex-USN submarine in Esquimalt;
- thirty-two Argus maritime patrol aircraft in four air squadrons, three of which were in Atlantic Canada at Greenwood and Summerside, and one in Comox;
- thirty-three Tracker patrol aircraft, most of which were at Shearwater, with seven based at Comox;
- Sea King helicopters, all of which were based at Shearwater;
- three operational support ships, of which *Provider* was based on the west coast, *Protecteur* in Halifax, and *Preserver* to be commissioned in 1970;

- six minesweepers in Esquimalt, used mainly for training purposes; and,
- there was also a diving tender and a deep submersible, and other types of aircraft, including those specifically used for search and rescue.

The personnel in the command totalled 15,441 in uniform and 5,355 civilians.

In 1970 it became obvious that the Soviet Union was developing a maritime strategy aimed at world supremacy, not only with naval power, but also with its merchant marine and fishing fleets. Earlier in 1970, the Soviets carried out, for the first time, simultaneous naval exercises in the oceans of the Northern Hemisphere with a force of 250 ships, plus submarines and aircraft. They could not have amassed such an operation as recently as ten years earlier.

The Soviet Union's submarine fleet consisted of about 350 conventional and nuclear submarines spread across three types: ballistic-missile boats, cruise-missile boats and attack boats. The submarine fleet was changing continually, with a reduction of conventional boats offset by a rapid increase in nuclear-powered vessels of all types. For a number of years, Soviet submarines (both conventional and increasingly the nuclear) had been carrying out patrols off both the Atlantic and Pacific coastlines of North America. Under the CANUS Defence of North America Agreement, the coasts were divided into Canadian and American areas of responsibilities, with very close co-operation between the two navies in the areas of both operations and intelligence.

Initial detection of the submarines was usually by SOSUS in the Atlantic and sometimes by HF/DF on both coasts. In some cases, it was assumed that the submarines were engaged in oceanographic research and general intelligence-gathering, but more often it seemed they were seeking to find out whether we could detect them and track them, and to determine the methods we were using to do so. Anyway, it was a cat-and-mouse game played most often by maritime patrol aircraft with SOSUS guidance and then using sonobuoys to detect and seek to track the submarine for a number of days. Whenever possible, ships also took part in the game, taking over the contact with their active sonars to track the submarine.

When it seemed likely that the contact would cross the border of the CANUS areas of responsibility, there was a takeover procedure, one that became very effective. This procedure also applied to Soviet intelligence-gathering ships, as one particular episode demonstrates. A Russian ship spent several weeks off the west coast of the United States. At one point, the ship came north and appeared about to enter Canadian-controlled territory. A destroyer was sent to take over surveillance from a USN destroyer. At this point, the Russian turned and went directly out into the Pacific, and after a day or so turned south again, where surveillance was resumed by the USN. This particular manoeuvre was probably to test the co-ordination of CANUS defences. In an emergency, high alert, or for planned exercises, NATO assumed control on the east coast and the CANUS Agreement came into effect on the west coast. The areas of responsibility, the U.S. and Canadian naval authorities, and communications channels remained the same. The only things that did change were the titles of the individuals involved.

To turn to the Soviet merchant marine, by 1970 the number of ships had increased to the point where they had gone from having few ships to having the seventh-largest merchant fleet in the world. We did not see many of these in Canadian waters; however, after my retirement and during several visits and tours in the Mediterranean, many of the merchant ships one encountered flew the Soviet flag and had the hammer and sickle on their funnels. From talking to Western ship owners, it was evident they were aggressive competitors.

In addition to merchant ships, the Soviet Union also produced "spy ships" of all sorts and sizes, from trawlers to small ocean liners. One of these latter ships visited Halifax in 1971. From the impressive array of all sorts and types of aerials on its masts, some covered with canvas, it was evident that the ship could be — and probably was — engaged in monitoring electronic signals emanating from Halifax and vicinity, including transatlantic telephone traffic. It was arranged that some of the crew were invited to be entertained by our sailors. There is no doubt they were men of the Soviet Navy. The Soviet fishing fleet comprised sometimes as many as 300 to 400 vessels fishing in east coast waters and about 100 on the west coast. While the majority harvested large quantities of Canada's fish for processing on accompanying factory ships, there were some that were not fishing at all, but were instead conducting oceanographic research or intercepting electronic signals.

Other things occurred during my watch as maritime commander that need to be mentioned. At that time, the maritime commander was responsible for aid to the civil power for the four Atlantic provinces. As a result, I called on and established a relationship with all four Atlantic premiers, the most notable of whom was Premier Joey Smallwood of Newfoundland. He was a little late in receiving me because he was having a cabinet meeting in the room next to his office. He came out when he could and almost immediately took me into the room where his ministers were assembled, shooed away the minister sitting on his right and sat me down next to him and introduced me to his entire cabinet, then took me with him to the cabinet dining room for lunch with his ministers. Throughout it all, he was in great form, full of humour and a great host.

In July 1970, the experimental hydrofoil HMCS *Bras d'Or* was well into her initial trials. These were proceeding very well, to the extent that she had probably established a world record for warships by attaining a speed of 63 knots. However, she had no fighting equipment onboard yet and so had not been tested operationally. In early 1971 I was attending a Defence Council meeting in Ottawa, during the course of which the minister, the Honourable Donald MacDonald, noted out of the blue that Maritime Command's two top priority systems for new equipment were new maritime patrol aircraft and hydrofoils. He went on to say that there were not enough new-equipment funds available for both of these projects and asked me which one I supported as the first priority. Such a question was totally unanticipated. After several moments of reflection, I replied that the new maritime patrol aircraft was my first priority for new equipment and went on to say that the hydrofoil project still had several years of testing to go before it would be ready for production.

It was also a time when considerable attention was being given to becoming familiar with Canada's Arctic. Maritime Command carried out Arctic surveillance patrols by aircraft on a fairly regular basis, and also deployed ships as far north and west as practicable during periods when the ice was retreating. Tasking requested by other government departments included such things as reporting on caribou herds and snow geese populations.

One sad note, especially because of my association with her, was the moment in 1971 when the *Bonaventure* was towed out of Halifax going to the breaker's yard. With reference to reports that either all or parts of Bonnie made it into other navies, having had a good tour of her before she left, I can tell you that the only parts of her that may still be "in use" by other navies still operating ships of the same class are some items of machinery and equipment such as the steam catapult, the deck wire mechanism, and the mirror landing system. I can truthfully say that if any of her *can* come back to Canada, it would be as razor blades or Toyota cars!

One matter I found particularly vexing as head of the navy was that I did not have enough knowledge of what was going on in NDHQ that might affect the navy, including the daily morning meetings of the Chief of Defence Staff's advisory council. Granted, there were senior naval officers on staffs in NDHQ, but they were in "unified" positions that tended to occupy their whole attention. This situation consolidated, in my mind, the requirement for the "Service Chiefs" to be moved to Ottawa. In any event, to ameliorate this disparity of information, Maritime Command's Director of Plans spent a good deal of his time in the corridors of NDHQ to give me as much information as he could ferret out.

To conclude this section on Maritime Command during my short fourteen months as the commander, it is appropriate to comment on the state of the command and the morale of its people. The ships and air squadrons were busy with day-to-day surveillance operations, particularly of Soviet submarines and ships engaged on duties other than normal commerce. This was recognized as an important and worthwhile duty in protection of Canadian sovereignty and CANUS defence. In addition, NATO exercises gave participating crews an opportunity to hone their ASW skills and show their merit as being as good as — if not better than — the ships, aircraft and submarines of our allies, through friendly but keen competition.

But unification and all it encompassed, together with budget and personnel reductions, were having a negative effect on the morale of all ranks. Added to this was the uncertainty about the future brought on by personnel reductions and the perception of a slowdown in promotion opportunities as a result. All this resulted in the morale of the personnel in training establishments ashore and others in administrative positions and shore-based units being just "satisfactory." On the other hand, the morale of people in operational units with duties they enjoyed and which they found to be worthwhile was always "good," especially in units where they were well led.

The equipment in the ships, air squadrons and submarines, in the main, gave good results. In most cases, when equipment was getting old and on the verge of becoming obsolete, there were good prospects of replacement, such as in the case of the Argus aircraft. In addition, the navy was going to have the addition of four DDH-280 Tribal-class destroyers due to be commissioned starting in 1972.

THE TURMOIL IN OTTAWA

When I took up my appointment as Director General Maritime Forces (DGMF) in 1966, it was the fifth time I had served in headquarters in a naval position. The unification of the headquarters was underway and the new organization was being developed. My position and staff had just been created. Confusion was rampant. It was an era when the budget was being pared down, and less than ten per cent of it was allocated to new equipment. Fortunately, the navy had two major programs underway: two operational support ships were due for delivery (one in 1969 and the other in 1970), and the four DDH-280s would be delivered starting in 1972.

One of DGMF's first tasks was to prepare a "maritime systems" study for the CDS, who "directed the study group to consider the requirement of flexibility, at the same time appreciating the importance of maintaining watch on pre-positioned submarines in the seaward approaches." This directive made me immediately aware of the major task ahead: to acquaint this newly organized general staff with the Canadian navy and the duties it was engaged in for the maritime defence of our country.

Later, I was directed to appear before the Standing Parliamentary Committee on National Defence to present the navy's requirements for the 1970s and 1980s. There was little background material that could be located in NDHQ. The best to be found was a well-reasoned report, commissioned by the maritime commander with the help of the Defence Research Establishment Atlantic (DREA) and completed about a year before, which enunciated a fleet program for that period. This was used as the basis for the presentation. It seemed to be well received by the committee. Admiral Landymore, then retired, was present as an observer; he was surprised but well pleased, as it was more or less his report, although I had not attributed it to him.

Integration, or Both Integration and Unification?

This was a hot topic when Paul Hellyer was testing the waters in NDHQ in 1963 and 1964. It was debated at great length up and down the corridors of the buildings occupied by the "three services." Simply stated, integration was taken to mean the creation of an organization with a CDS at the head, with three "service chiefs" reporting to him, while he in turn reported to a single Minister of National Defence — somewhat similar to the arrangement already in effect in Britain and the United States.

When I left Ottawa in 1965 to take command of the *Bonaventure*, this seemed to be accepted as the main hope, although there were growing rumblings of the concept of unification. That meant the disbandment of the three services, and the creation of a single service, uniform and set of rank titles for all, with a single chief of personnel administering all personnel in the existing three services. This change became a reality in 1966, when the Minister tabled Bill C-243 (An Act to Amend the National Defence Act) in the House of Commons.

The Effect of Unification

The immediate effect of unification, when it was announced, was very negative. Many serving sailors, soldiers and airmen just did not understand its rationale. Talk of resignation was rampant, and many followed through. The decision to decrease the total number of personnel in the single service caused great concern, especially among the younger officers and men, who felt uncertain about their future prospects.

The thought of losing their naval uniforms and replacing them with a green "bus driver's" uniform, totally different from that of any other navy in the world, was considered to be deplorable. This unhappiness was increased by unfortunate glitches in the supply of uniforms. However, in due course the uniform was issued, but worn by sailors with little enthusiasm.

Another matter affecting morale in Canada's navy was the uncertainty about when naval officers, men and women should use unified rank titles or traditional naval rank titles. Unfortunately, Bill C-243 established a set of single-service rank titles in which the officers' and most of the men and women's ranks would be those currently used by the army. However, when the act was under debate in Parliament, the article on rank titles was amended to give the governor-in-council some latitude in the use of previous service rank titles. In one of the last debates, *Hansard* records the then Minister of National Defence, the Honourable Leo Cadieux, stating that "members of the naval element would continue to use naval rank titles until such time as other navies adopted a unified force with unified rank titles."

In due course, Canadian Forces Administration Order (CFAO) 3-2 was drafted and promulgated as Canadian Forces General (CANFORGEN) Message 234 on 30 January 1968 and distributed to all ranks of the Canadian Forces. This CFAO permitted individuals some latitude in that they could elect to use, and be referred to by, their previous service rank titles, an amendment in no way reflecting the minister's statement above. On the other hand, it was much against the wishes of the senior officers at NDHQ directly responsible, particularly the chief of personnel, who effectively blocked the issuance of the CFAO. Although the CANFORGEN was in effect for some time, it was never cancelled but allowed to lapse "as sufficiently promulgated." A policy vacuum existed on the use of naval rank titles.

I raised this matter at a meeting of the CDS Advisory Committee in February 1972. At that meeting the consensus (the lone dissenter was the chief of personnel, Lieutenant-General Jacques Dextraze) was that all personnel in the naval operations branch, and all officers promoted therefrom, should use naval rank titles while on duty wherever they were serving. This policy was taken under advisement by the CDS, General Sharp, and eventually accepted by him. General Sharp informed me that he had sent the necessary documents to the minister, then the Honourable Edgar

Benson, who had agreed with the policy but would defer his approval until after the federal election on 30 October. But then General Sharp retired and the minister, defeated at the polls, also retired.

When General Sharp retired, Prime Minister Trudeau, on the advice of the deputy minister and others, appointed General Dextraze as CDS. At a luncheon in the senior NDHQ Officers' Mess in early 1973, General Dextraze announced he was preparing a CFAO to establish rules for the use of naval rank titles. He inferred that the order would include provisions that naval rank titles would be authorized to be used only by officers, men and women serving in naval operations postings, and that in all other postings unified rank titles would be used. Having said that, he turned to me and said, "and Harry Porter will be addressed as lieutenant-general." To say the least, I was flabbergasted and upset; I didn't say anything but decided immediately that I would explore ways of having him change his mind, and his draft CFAO.

I sought the aid of senior serving naval officers, the Naval Officers' Association, the Navy League and other friends of the navy. Fortunately, one of them was a past president of the Navy League, a wartime naval officer who happened also to be a friend since boyhood of the then Minister of National Defence, the Honourable James Richardson.

Successive drafts of the CFAO, together with other memoranda and material, were sent to this friend, who in turn discussed the drafts and provided other supporting documents to the minister and discussed them with him. Minister Richardson then made up his mind and informed the CDS of changes he proposed. This process went on through 1973 and into the first two months of 1974. At one point, because the discussions with the CDS sometimes were quite heated, the minister decided that, when the CFAO was agreed to and published, it would be a ministerial and not a CDS administrative order. In due course, in March 1974 the CFAO was approved and issued, and naval officers, men and women were given the authority to use naval rank titles wherever they were serving.

In conclusion, in the period covered by this paper, the Canadian Forces went through the jaws of a powerful wringer, with three separate services going in and a single service coming out, with a single, green-coloured uniform, new badges and insignia, a single set of rank titles totally foreign to the navy and the loss of the title "Royal" from the

Canadian Navy and Canadian Air Force. This was difficult, and very painful, to experience.

However, optimism was always there, and to some extent has been rewarded. The clock that began to tick in 1966 has slowly come around, and is on its way back to twelve o'clock again. There has been a recognition that there are indeed three "services" — maritime, land and air. Each of these now has distinctive and (mostly) traditional-coloured uniforms. There is once again a Naval Board responsible for some naval matters. The heads of the three services are once again in the headquarters in Ottawa, assuming, it is hoped, their rightful place in the hierarchy of that establishment. Lastly, the Canadian Navy has the authority to use their traditional rank titles again. For one who considered resigning, it is rewarding to see this happening and to have been able to play a small part in it.

CHAPTER TWELVE

Rear-Admiral Robert W. Timbrell, 1971–73

Rear-Admiral Robert W. Timbrell

Since 1910 the Royal Canadian Navy has been subjected to many political decisions that have directly affected the size, the mission and the morale of our navy, and these decisions were, in the main, concluded without the benefit of any study to outline the gains and losses.

Before launching into some thoughts and factors affecting Maritime Command during my tenure as commander from 1971 through 1973, I intend to outline three background factors that took place in and out of Ottawa from 1965 to 1970, resulting in major changes to the three services.

First, there was the unification of the Canadian Forces, approved by the government and initiated by Minister of National Defence Paul Hellyer. Many of you will recall that this plan was neither well received nor popular with the navy or army, but that it had the full support of the air force. At that time, the navy and the army were prepared to support *integration* — a very different concept under which common support functions would be joined together in the interests of efficiency and cost savings. Examples of this would be the medical branch (including hospitals), the dental branch (which was already integrated and working well) and the supply branch (including food, fuel, transport, administrative and spares common to all services).

Second, from 1965 to 1967 I served at the unified Training Command Headquarters in Winnipeg, which had just been established to implement the first stages of unification. The scope of activity included training from first entry into the services through specialized courses, but not, as it was then known, "environmental training" — for the ship, ship knowledge and extra requirements such as damage control, and for the army, self-defence in the field. At that time, the favourite training expression emerging from the Defence minister's office was "a cook is a cook is a cook," meaning a trained cook would meet the requirements of all three services. How wrong this was — for the navy and the army, this was operationally unacceptable, and the fight continued. During this period at Training Command Headquarters, there were three "one-star" officers — one from each service, reporting to the commander, a "two-star." As expected, the one-star had many phone calls and other directives to and from their service commanders, where again it was clearly stated by the Maritime and Mobile Commands not to interfere with operational training — an example here being that the naval entries would report to *Stadacona* or *Naden* when their initial recruit training was completed, and the army recruits to Camp Borden for their service training.

As an aside, to this point I have given only very limited reaction to unification, but the negative reaction was much greater than the positive. Now, with the passage of time and patience, the wheel has returned to a point of integration and not unification, but the price was high and very uncomfortable. At the time, the atmosphere in Ottawa — at defence headquarters and elsewhere — was very acrimonious, resulting in many well-trained and experienced senior officers of the navy and army resigning — a great loss. Outside of Canada the support for unification came from the U.S. Secretary of Defence, Robert McNamara, who had many meetings with Paul Hellyer, whereas in the United Kingdom the message from the Chief of Defence Staff was exactly the opposite: "Do not touch it with a barge pole."

The third background factor, then, was that from 1967 to 1970 I was appointed to Ottawa as chief of plans at defence headquarters.

Shortly after my arrival, the government implemented a decision to freeze the defence budget to the 1965–1968 level for at least the next three years. With inflation factored in, the result was a major reduction in the size of Canada's armed forces. Implementing this de facto personnel reduction fell on my shoulders, and would require a downsizing from 120,000 to approximately 80,000 uniformed personnel. It was neither an easy nor a pleasant task. To add to this difficult duty, the prime minister decided on his own initiative to call for a further major reduction of the Canadian army and air force detachments stationed in Europe. You can well imagine the reaction from the three commands, together with SACEUR and SACLANT. This task required two years of travel and negotiations, with each commander offering reductions in the other commands, but not his own.

For the navy, this ultimately required the paying-off of our naval air. Having served at *Shearwater* and later in command of the *Bonaventure*, I found this a very difficult pill to swallow. Here, in our naval air arm we had a dedicated, loyal and efficient sector of our navy, one recognized by our fellow NATO partners as second to none in the field of ASW. To add to this loss was the decommissioning and sale of the *Bonaventure*. At this point in my discussions, I was surprised and dismayed when I did not receive any support from my fellow "dark blue" officers in headquarters. Of course, this action with respect to our naval air was strongly and vocally supported by the air force, even at Defence Council, where I planned to retain our naval air at the expense of a destroyer squadron. But Minister Hellyer said "No"; naval air and *Bonaventure* had to go. Needless to say, neither SACLANT nor SACEUR were happy with our force reductions.

Now to my actual time in command. For the period 1971–72 our relationship with Ottawa was, in the main, friendly, and the prevailing co-operative spirit was observed throughout the whole command. However, when it comes to the interpretation or understanding of a government's policy and/or its intentions, I have found it wise, whenever possible, to be prepared for a change, major or otherwise, to a previously approved policy by the current or new governments.

It was to this end that I wanted the CDS to be up-to-date on my recommendations for the Maritime Command Force requirements

to meet national and NATO requirements. The required force structure saw the need for one aircraft carrier, thirty-six destroyers, twelve
minesweepers, ten submarines, four operational support ships,
thirty-six long-range patrol aircraft, forty short-range patrol aircraft
and forty helicopters. Along with attendant support facilities, the
forces outlined had to be designed and equipped to meet the "next-
century" conditions. I emphasized, also, the need to pay attention to
our Arctic requirements, including the need for the submarines (of
conventional power) to be equipped with a small nuclear power
plant for charging the batteries to provide for a capability of under-
ice operations.

With the reductions to both personnel and ships, it was essential to
encourage and hopefully maintain a positive outlook with our remaining operational capabilities. To this end, the Maritime Command briefing team travelled across the country to give the message to Reserve
Divisions, service clubs and conventions (such as the mayors of
Canadian cities), all to spread the gospel and gain support. I, like previous Maritime Commanders, was determined to maintain, both in presence and spirit, a healthy and progressive reserve-division organization
across Canada in the major cities, and also to encourage and support the
Sea Cadet units, whose history and achievements for support of the navy
has always been outstanding.

In the field of research and development, one of our early losses was
the termination of the *Bras d'Or* hydrofoil program. As fate would have
it, this event occurred following a successful trial run to Bermuda, then
to Norfolk, returning to Halifax. My own observation is that in Canada
we often lack the confidence and determination to complete a program
for "Canadian benefits" — the other services have experienced similar
losses. However, we have had many successes, such as the variable-depth
sonar, the helicopter "Bear Trap" and the CCCS-280 command and control systems for the DDH-280 class destroyers. One very important project that is still underway, following many years of support, is the long-
range sonar now installed in our frigates.

The second year of my tenure, 1972–73, witnessed a complete
change in our relations with Ottawa — a turn of 180 degrees. The new
CDS had concluded that Maritime Command in the whole was not

taking a positive outlook towards unification; that we were not sup- porting the wearing of the green uniform, that we continually pushed for capital funds both for major and minor programs, and that we pre- vented our Naval Reserve Divisions from being moved in with army or air force reserve units. I am the first to agree that this attitude and action does not enhance the opportunity for advancement, but so be it.

We have been proud of our naval service and remain so, but to meet future commitments we need the political will for necessary funding and support.

CHAPTER THIRTEEN

Vice-Admiral J. Andrew Fulton, 1980–83

DND

Vice-Admiral J. Andrew Fulton

In this survey of my time as Maritime Commander, I shall start with a short review of the world situation as I saw it in the early 1980s, and discuss three major issues for the navy during that period. Succinctly put, these issues were: the need to replace a largely outdated fleet that would be marginally effective in a modern war — this was forcefully demonstrated in the Falklands War; the need to maintain the present fleet so that we could meet our commitments to NATO until new ships were commissioned; and lastly, our personnel.

The year 1980 was the twenty-eighth year of the Cold War. NATO was the predominant defence issue, and would remain so as long as the Cold War lasted. In the early years, peace was maintained by the mutually-assured-destruction strategy, but as time passed this was modified to a concept of "flexible response." Flexible response required an increase in conventional forces in an attempt to reduce the nuclear threshold. Plans were made to send large convoys from North America to reinforce Europe with troops and equipment, requiring Canadian naval participation in convoy protection and general anti-submarine warfare activities.

The Canadian Armed Forces were in their green uniforms and in the fifteenth year of unification. The process of managing this disparate force was still slowly taking shape, with all of us at the top trying to do our best for the forces under our command while keeping in tune with government policy. By 1980 we had reached the stage where we were spending between 25 and 26 per cent of the military budget on capital acquisitions. Both the land and air elements had purchased new equipment and, as the press used to say, "It was the navy's turn."

At this time I was reminded on a daily basis that the Cold War was not far from our shores. Virtually every day there were four Soviet nuclear-powered Yankee-class ballistic missile submarines (SSBN) operating off North America, three on the east coast (with one usually in the Canadian sector) and one on the west. Also there were several larger SSBNs operating in the Norwegian Sea. For many years, the Soviet Navy had been classified by NATO intelligence as a coastal defence force, but by 1982–83 this was no longer the case. In addition to the submarines, the Soviet Navy was building four large aircraft carriers, larger ballistic submarines of 30,000 tons displacement, and a new class of nuclear missile cruiser. The Soviets had a large number of nuclear attack submarines as well as aircraft and ships fitted with surface-to-surface and surface-to-air missiles.

In 1982, the Falklands War took place, clearly demonstrating the need for modern, well-equipped warships. In that war the Royal Navy (RN) lost four warships and a large cargo ship to air attacks by missiles and bombs. The Falklands War had not gone unnoticed by my friends in NATO, who knew the age and capabilities of Canada's ships and asked me when Canada would commence the new shipbuilding program announced in 1977.

The only new piece of equipment to arrive at Maritime Command during my watch was the CP-140 Aurora maritime patrol aircraft. Several months after the aircraft arrived in Greenwood, two Soviet SSBNs were detected by SOSUS in the Canadian sector. The new Auroras were dispatched to locate and track the submarines. This they did very well for about three days — in fact, their reconnaissance was so good that they discovered that each submarine had a USN submarine trailing it. These excellent results led me to believe that the equipment we were planning for our new frigates would be very good.

Dealing with the ship-replacement program, in December 1977 the government had approved $63 million to conduct a "definition stage" for the Canadian Patrol Frigate (CPF) project. A request for proposal was issued in August 1978, to which five companies responded. Of those five, two were selected in December 1980 as finalists to enter the contract definition phase, and contracts for that phase were signed in 1981. These two companies submitted their design proposals in October 1982, and then we had to wait for government evaluation and final Cabinet approval, scheduled for July 1983.

In order to maintain a "combat-capable fleet" until the arrival of the new ships, it was necessary to prolong the life of the existing destroyers. The program to accomplish that was known as the Destroyer Life Extension program, or DELEX, to be implemented in the 1981–1983 timeframe. The urgency of this program was demonstrated in 1981, when a routine boiler inspection of HMCS *Saguenay* revealed a deep crack in one of her superheaders. Cracks had been found in the superheaders before, but those were always shallow and reparable. This time it was different, and the superheader had to be replaced. I recall asking if this problem might be a result of age, and whether the other ships of that class were similarly affected. It turned out that all ships of the St. Laurent and Restigouche classes needed the same work. We required twenty superheaders, and only two were in stock. The net result was that ten ships, or fully half of the destroyer escorts, were alongside for varying lengths of time during the next eight months.

During this period when the destroyers were undergoing repairs, the east coast had six operational ships and the west coast four. The Standing Naval Force Atlantic and the officer training commitments were met, but other commitments were scaled down. In fact, the situation was not all bad — it allowed the navy to progress with badly needed shore training and to give leave. There was also a good deal of publicity about these needed repairs, and in a perverse sense it was useful publicity in that the public at large became aware of the state of the navy and of the very real requirement for new ships.

Shortly after I arrived in the command, I wrote to the CDS that I was constantly reminded of the critical state of our principal resource, namely our men. Consequently, the leadership, management and care of the people within my command were my primary concerns. The offi-cers were in good shape: the recommendations of the Maritime Officer Production Study had been fully implemented by 1980 and the fleet was very pleased with its young officers. One change I did make early in my tenure was to the method of selecting commanding officers. The prac-tice had been that the career manager drew up a slate of eighteen offi-cers to present to the Maritime Commander for approval and appoint-ments at the appropriate times. There were several things that I did not like about the first list presented to me, one of which was the age distri-bution. The recommended officers all seemed to be rather old to go on to senior rank. But of much greater importance, the list was prepared with no outside assistance in order that the career manager could be very selective about whom he presented for consideration. Also, he could be subject to all sorts of pressures from fellow officers and well-meaning senior officers. To get around the problem as I saw it, I insti-tuted a Commanding Officers Selection Board to be composed of a rear-admiral and three commodores. The selection board was to exam-ine all officers eligible for command and submit its list to the com-mander for final selection. I was extremely pleased with the lists that I received in 1981 and 1982. I believe that the army and air force now use this system for the selection of their commanding officers.

As for the men, the navy had serious manpower problems on the lower deck going back to at least 1974. The "hard sea trades" suffered from a myriad of difficulties, some of which were high attrition rates, shortages of junior technicians, top-heavy rank-to-rank ratios and high training costs. The Maritime Other Ranks Production Study (MORPS) was initiated in January 1977 to look into the problems and make rec-ommendations to correct them. The study was completed in June 1978, and a team was formed to plan and implement the eighty-six recom-mendations on service conditions and thirty recommendations on sea trade structures. One recommendation that should be mentioned was that the "user-maintainer concept" should be abandoned. MORPS was formally completed in June 1982.

In addition to the MORPS implementation, we conducted a Maritime Command Establishment Study. Simply put, this study showed that we needed more manpower to make the system work. Together, these studies told us what had to be done to make a better navy and to prepare the fleet in the best possible way for the new frigates.

But, of course, the study did not get us the men. Maritime Command started to take a direct interest in recruiting and how the recruiting numbers were calculated. A naval platoon was started at the Canadian Forces Recruit Schools at Cornwallis and St. Jean to initiate the young recruits into our unique environment. The shortage of marine technicians was acute, and new methods were needed to address the problem quickly. For the first time, the navy started training its new entry marine technicians at St. Lawrence College in Cornwall, Ontario. This reduced their training time by about 50 per cent.

It will be remembered that in the early 1980s inflation was in double digits, affecting the standard of living. This was especially noticeable in the military, as we were lagging behind the civilians both in the civil service and on "civvy" street. With my confreres in the air force and the army, I made it very clear to the CDS that this had to be corrected, otherwise we could expect a large exodus of officers and other ranks.

Unfortunately, in the 1970s and 1980s the armed forces emulated society at large in its increased use of illicit drugs. Shortly after I arrived in the command, the Assistant Judge Advocate General (AJAG) informed me that the navy had a drug problem. In this regard, Canada was no better or worse than her allies. But, simply put, we did not want our personnel using drugs aboard ships and aircraft — for obvious reasons. If the use of drugs got out of hand there would be serious disciplinary problems. As far as the AJAG was concerned, the military police were inadequately trained to handle this invasive new problem. I sent a general message to the fleet to the effect that there was a "no-tolerance" policy for the use of illicit drugs and those caught would be severely punished. I required each commanding officer to "clear lower decks" and inform the men of the policy. In order to apprehend the offenders and obtain convictions, we had to train our military police. This was done with the help of the RCMP, and the results were startling. We began to get convictions, and there was a decrease in the number of drug incidents on military property. When it became clear that I meant what I said, a most welcome trend occurred: drug users were being turned in to the military police by superiors, peers and acquaintances.

Women had served in the navy during the Second World War and were reintroduced in 1953, but had never served at sea. In 1977 a women's group vigorously petitioned the Department of National Defence that women be admitted to the "combat arms" of the navy. The fact that women were already serving in various capacities was not deemed relevant. The complaint was that *all* ranks and trades were not open to women.

To get an understanding of the problems facing women serving in HMC ships, a three-year trial was conducted in HMCS *Cormorant* from 1980–1983. In general, the report was favourable, but it did say that most of the women who participated in the trial would not want to make the navy a career. Personally, I was against women going to sea, as the Forces knew from experience that men and women serving in isolated posts "get together," later resulting in divorces and other problems. Canada repatriated the Constitution in 1982 and introduced the Charter of Rights and Freedoms. When I read the Charter I was impressed, but I knew that unless there were very compelling reasons other than sexual, women would serve in the combat arms. Needless to say, like many Canadians, I could not anticipate the ramifications for all of us, let alone the Armed Forces.

In July 1981 the government had signed the contract for the definition phase of the CPF program with two companies, Saint John Shipbuilding and Dry Dock Company of Saint John, New Brunswick, and SCAN Marine Incorporated of Longueuil, Quebec. These companies were to produce their design proposals for the construction of the new frigates.

Although everything appeared to be going well, I was concerned that there could be a delay in the actual awarding of the contract, and given the state of the fleet, delay was not something the navy could afford. I remembered from my time in the policy branch that the prime minister was the final arbiter on all large government projects. In February, I phoned the CDS, General Ramsey Withers, to suggest that Prime Minister Pierre Trudeau visit the fleet so that he could experience the navy firsthand and become more aware of our problems. While it was a bit risky, I thought it would be worthwhile, and Withers agreed. As well as talking to Withers, I was advised that if I *really* wanted the prime minister to visit the fleet I should invite his children as well. I did want him, so I sent an additional invitation for his children — and they all came. We spent an afternoon and overnight in HMCS *Iroquois*. While in *Iroquois* there was a 5-inch gun surface shoot, an air-defence exercise and a tour of the ship. There were no formal briefs for the prime minister, only an explanation of what was happening with each event, and, of course, he was free to ask as many questions of the ship's company as he wished.

The following morning we were to join the submarine HMCS *Okanagan*. I took the children with me. But the prime minister had seen photos of men joining a submarine by high wire from a helicopter, and that was the way he wanted to join *Okanagan*. So, he did. Once on board, *Okanagan* dove and Mr. Trudeau and children were shown around the boat. When that was finished the prime minister and I had about thirty minutes in the wardroom together. We discussed the state of the navy, the requirement for the frigates, the Falklands War and possible lessons learned, and nuclear submarines.

We arrived at Shearwater in midafternoon so that Mr Trudeau could get to a political meeting in Halifax that evening. I escorted him down the jetty to his car and thanked him for visiting the navy. Then he said to me, "The next time you are in Ottawa, come and see me." I was not sure if he was just being polite or if he really did want me to come. The command photographers had been busy recording every aspect of Trudeau's visit and had put the collection together in a very nice album. On the occasion of my next trip to Ottawa, I used the album as a reason to call for an appointment. Much to my surprise, Trudeau's secretary called back immediately and set a date. I saw the prime minister in his office, accompanied by the minister of national defence, and had about twenty minutes with them. When Trudeau ushered me to the door, he said, "Goodbye," and then, "Admiral, you will get your ships." Whether or not his visit made a difference to the final outcome I will never know, but I left his office feeling very satisfied. The contract was awarded one week before I retired in July 1983.

I have reflected since on the fact that the first general meeting for the senior staff that I attended at defence headquarters on the frigate program was chaired by the Vice-Chief of Defence Staff (Vice-Admiral R.H. Falls) in 1976. If all went well — and this was a very big *if* — the first ship was supposed to be in service by 1987–88. In other words, the gestation period for this ship would have been eleven to twelve years. In light of this length of time, and knowing the great need for replacement helicopters, it is interesting to recall that the last letter I signed as Maritime Commander was a letter to the CDS urging that the Forces proceed with great haste to select a new helicopter to replace the aging Sea Kings.

In conclusion, I believe that the officers and men of my era, who spent many long hours studying the navy's manpower problems and providing solutions, deserve our thanks and gratitude. In the officers' rank we have five vice-admirals on strength, a large number for such a small corps. I note in the *Matelot* naval personnel newsletter of July 2002 that an occupational analysis was recently carried out on the sea trades. I quote from the letter: "Despite the fact that most of the occupations had not been closely analyzed since MORPS (1982), the Occupational Analysis (OA) found that the fundamental taskings and jobs have not significantly changed and that the basic occupational structures were sound."

CHAPTER FOURTEEN

Vice-Admiral Charles M. Thomas, 1987–89

Vice-Admiral Charles M. Thomas

I must begin by noting that my story would be more accurate and complete if my immediate predecessor, Vice-Admiral Jim Wood, had also been able to share his. He was "first in column" in a collective process, and his contribution and leadership are historically important.

Let me explain and perhaps set the scene. Jim Wood, myself and my immediate successors were part of a continuum. We had a common agreed purpose and intent, and we understood and operated on a ten-year "time plus" timeframe. This had its beginnings when Vice-Admiral Dan Mainguy supervised the frigate specification and took the first six-ship "batch" and its documentation through the departmental approval process.

With that base, the rest of us decided we were going to pursue the niche that he had created: we were going to have a full-blown "replace-the-navy" capital-equipment program. We became convinced that, if we collectively addressed both the NDHQ and the governmental processes in a cohesive and continuous fashion, a "New Navy" could be built. We recognized that progress took longer than anyone's tenure in any position of leadership or influence, so continuity of effort and approach became a

e. Amongst the people critically involved were Commodore E. Ball Healy (in four ranks from captain to assistant deputy minister). The ... gisticians and senior finance officers were onboard, and together — often with tactical officer, engineer and logistician occupying the same physical office — we put together a force-development process. To create the larger tapestry against which individual programs made sense, we had a force development guide in circulation in the city when the other services did not. We learned the new and evolving approval processes within the Department of National Defence and government-wide. We left critical people in place so they would become known to and trusted by Treasury Board officials. We did the documentation and we won the debates.

There came to be a single song sheet for the navy's point of view and intent. It led to a "navy of the future," and it was, I think, Vice-Admiral Nigel Brodeur who first enunciated the order of the day for all to understand: "You are with us or you are out."

This united front was a prime factor in winning the battles within the bureaucracy in Ottawa. It should be understood that "battle" is not too strong a word. If the navy achieved a capital program, or programs, then somebody else did not. There were not sufficient monies in the capital account, and everything was getting old and becoming obsolete. Moreover, every penny spent by DND was money not available to other departments and agencies, so there were few friends in Ottawa. However, our unity of purpose and common song sheet also allowed for a single focus within the navy. We knew where we were going, and therefore, what we had to do to get ready.

Let me also briefly paint the larger picture that was in place when I took over from Vice-Admiral Wood. The 1987 Defence White Paper had been published. Its focus was west and north and maritime and Canadian. Consequently, when I arrived as MARCOM the new frigates were real, and "Batch Two" was coming. The DDH-280s were being updated, the nuclear submarines were still intended, and the torpedoes and towed-array sonars for the Ojibway-class boats were in contract. The coastal patrol vessels were in the last stages of approval and did arrive. The shore trainers, the logistic system updates, the new accommodation and messes for chiefs and petty officers and other ranks, and the like, were all approved and underway.

It came to pass therefore, and should be no surprise, that MARCOM was agreed on the first priority: we had to get our people ready for this wave of new ships and new technology. That meant academic upgrading in math and physics, follow-on revamped trade courses, and teaching of the system and of equipment-specific maintenance and operating skills. And with Jim Wood as MARCOM, it all was set in motion. I didn't have to invent a course; rather, I continued in the wake of my "next ahead," and the lead marks were clear.

There were some new things. We had agreed on their necessity and timing. The Naval Board was proving again to be a powerful tool. My job was to put them in play in their turn.

First amongst these involved getting the tactical officers, those who would command and fight the new ships, intellectually ready to fight the next war. It needs to be recognized that the aged ships with which we had been living served mainly to keep crews in being. Tactical reality and weapons that were lethal were mostly a matter of pretending. In fact, for ten years we emphasized damage control — a good thing and obviously necessary — replenishment at sea and man-overboard and flying stations, because that was what we could actually do.

Captain "Dusty" Miller was put in charge of the Canadian Forces Maritime Warfare School, and we started challenging squadron commanders, ships' captains and tactical officers to think their way through how we could use the new ships and their step function change, from grease pencils to distributed digital tactical machines. And our weapon fit now mattered. We were liable to be asked to do things that had been foreclosed for decades. A keen researcher might usefully examine the warfare school exercises to find that the range of tasks this navy has taken on in the last ten years were forecast, thought through and practised before the ships were delivered. The transition did work.

The staff process in the MARCOM headquarters is of interest. A highly organized chief of staff had priority-listed the "issues" and "problems." It was organized and effective, but if you were in the naval reserve and naval reserve items were priority number 26, then a certain level of discouragement was noticeable. I preferred to give twenty-six problems to twenty-six competent staff officers and let the hierarchy deal with the outcome. By way of example of this view, Captain (N) Tom Brown, the fleet school commander, added modems to Jim Wood's computer-based math and physics "learning laboratory." More than 50 per cent of the master seamen and below ranks had computers at home, and an hour or two in the den was not one more night away from wife and kids. Course results showed a useful difference.

The Halifax base commander and the chief of staff (materiel) encouraged me to become involved in the living conditions at Windsor Park, Shannon Park and the Maritime Apartments. Footage of the conditions in our married quarters was edited into a tape of a television documentary about Halifax slum landlords, and it convinced NDHQ and the deputy minister that we should not be the next exposé on a slow news day. Approval was obtained to renovate Shannon and Windsor Parks and to build a new recreation centre. We also started the process of getting out of the Maritime Apartment contract. My view was that if we could not do better for our people than that, we should not be in the housing business, no matter what the rent. Within the year, the public-education authorities told me of the positive differences evident in the attitudes of children from these complexes.

We made the Commander Maritime Forces Pacific, Rear-Admiral Bob George, the Deputy Commander in lieu of the Halifax-based chief of staff. It was a little less convenient, but Halifax-based naval staff who had a certain Atlantic and European bias found that, if the last in the chain of command to see their work before it went to the maritime commander was a "west coaster," then some greater balance was appropriate. It made us a Canadian, and not only an Atlantic, navy. Given the transition of the Soviet Union into Russia, the 1994 white paper and the change of the focus of problems we have come to be involved in, this was a useful initiative.

There was a problem in the submarine squadron. An underranked squadron commander and his small staff had been left to run the boats and deal with all the problems that the rest of the navy staff addressed for all the other ships. Captain (N) Dave Pollard's one-man review was precise, concise and useful. It led to the submarines becoming the responsibility of all of us. Upgrading the squadron commander brought an end to a condition of less-than-useful isolation.

There was an issue of ethics and morality flowing from an incident and court-martial in the submarine squadron. I became convinced that we had for too long assumed that our potential leaders came to us from the civil population having inculcated a comprehension of right and wrong at mother's knee, or church, or school. I did not consider this a valid assumption. If you want leadership to think and act in an ethical and moral manner, then you must teach — formally — ethics and morality. That process was initiated.

As Commander MARCOM I also spent a lot of time talking to our people. All the change was exciting, but it was also a little scary. "How do I fit in?" was a common concern. I spoke to sailors in the messes in each east coast ship two or three times in the first year. These were informal sessions where questions were answered until there were no more, and the rapport improved as concerns about the future diminished. The west coast ships' companies heard and saw me less often, but Rear-Admiral George was acting in my stead. After the budget leak, there was great angst, particularly amongst the submariners. I suspect the echoes continue today: "no news" is not "good news," and the absence of decisions about future capital investment and the next ships leads thinking men and women to begin the process of individually arranging a rational future.

In the first year of my term, the minister of the day released — nay, encouraged — the senior leadership to go out and talk to Canadians about their military. I probably averaged one night out of every four or five giving a speech somewhere in Canada. The reception from those audiences, as well as the press, was universally supportive. After the leaked budget, the cancellation of the nuclear submarine program and the change of minister, the tapestry became less certain and politically less supportive. The intent expressed by the government, when the nuclear program was cancelled, of providing an alternative program for the continued rebuilding of the navy remains unfulfilled to this day. Moreover, the process of building of a constituency for defence, which serving senior officers speak frankly in the public domain, has not been much tolerated and certainly not encouraged.

The consequences are obvious. There were not then, and have not been since, sufficient moneys in the defence budget to maintain — or to build for the future — meaningful combat-capable forces in the three environments. The examples and proof of this are legion, and perhaps a subject for another day. I would, however, remind you that the frigates — the "new navy" — are now more then ten years old and their half-life updates should be underway, as should be replacement programs for the DDH-280s and the Protecteur-class AORs. Any of these three future programs, so necessary to having a navy, would take a minimum of ten years to achieve anything useful, even if we had the money and the political will today. And neither money nor will is evident.

CHAPTER FIFTEEN

Vice-Admiral Robert E. George, 1989–91

Vice-Admiral Robert E. George

Speaking to those in Maritime Command in 1989, I suggested the upcoming year would be one of change, challenge and satisfaction. Looking back a year later, over a period of government financial problems, environmental concerns, drug wars and European changes, all of which brought increased pressure to reallocate defence spending to more popular causes, I jested that getting two out of three forecasts was not all that bad!

While Europe experienced rapid change throughout the late 1980s, Canada's navy saw a continuation of programs and trends that had been underway for several years — a carefully worked-out plan, keeping us on a steady course. I propose to present a series of snapshots of this period, relating to the navy's social change, public image, international presence and place in the agenda of the government of the day.

I use "social change" to refer to those changes in service life that were driven in many cases by legal challenges under the Charter of Rights and Freedoms introduced in 1982. Policies that had worked and been deemed acceptable in the past became major issues and, in some cases, the subject of litigation. For example, the exclusion of individuals of certain religions or ethnic backgrounds from military operations was not new, but it was judged unacceptable by our courts. One's age was no longer to be used in arriving at decisions concerning employment or promotion or severance of service. How often did we hear, "He is too old for promotion" in the past?

While I still subscribe to the belief that life at sea is extremely demanding and hence more suitable for the young and energetic, in the navy overall, promoting those older members as well as the younger benefited the service equally well. On the other hand, the removal of restrictions concerning medical impairment was more contentious. While the navy did not face cases like the army did, with a visually impaired soldier demanding to be trained as a parachutist, there was always a valid question about the maintenance of operational effectiveness without this restriction.

The removal of sexual barriers gained momentum with each passing day. Although I recall the Chief of Defence Staff (CDS) of the day pronouncing that he would not have the Canadian Forces become a platform for "social experimentation," the pressures against the barriers continued to mount until they were dismantled. September 1987 had seen the first mixed crews at sea in HMCS *Provider*; with the departure of HMCS *Protecteur* to the Persian Gulf War in August 1990, the first women were off to serve in combat. The familiar concerns of unit cohesion, operational effectiveness, privacy, and so on had been debated at length, but the fact remained that other navies already were successfully integrating women into their services, and this beckoned us forward. In retrospect, one might ask if change could have come faster? I, for one, believe it was done in a deliberate, adequately cautious manner, cognizant of the risks involved, for the stakes were high, and the consequences of failure damaging to the service and individuals. Today, amongst our allies, there are still many that are more restrictive than Canada's navy, but that should not surprise anyone, considering that there are some places in Europe where women's suffrage still does not exist!

The recognition of the need for Family Support Centres had been well established by the start of the Persian Gulf War. These proved to be most valuable. Without these facilities during the crisis in the Gulf, dealing with the many concerns of families and serving personnel would have been chaotic, and the burden on them all would have been significantly greater.

Perhaps the hardest policy change to accept at the time was the concept of switching ship's crews during the Persian Gulf War deployment. It challenged the age-old wisdom about the relationship between competence and preparedness on the one hand, and sailors' pride in their ship and familiarity with their equipment on the other. I recall telling the CDS, General John de Chastelain, during discussions on the idea, that it was as foreign to the navy as the idea of marching the Princess Patricia's Canadian Light Infantry into La Citadelle to relieve the Royal 22ème Régiment! However, the *Preserver* crew did march onboard *Protecteur* and, with good leadership and pride in service, and exceptional motivation, they excelled in their task.

Nor was it accepted that there was any serious support in the public, and hence the government, for any debate about defence. In late 1989 a poll was taken to determine the prominent issues on Canadians' minds. Pollution of our environment was number one on the list, and the drug problem number two. Defence ranked forty-ninth — just one place ahead of the Meech Lake accord!

As for the navy's image in the public eye, we continued to face challenges, for we had often been accused of being out of touch with the Canadian public. Certainly, it was not in our interest for Canadians to be unaware of what the navy was about. Even in Halifax and Victoria, there was frequently a lack of understanding about what went on behind the dockyard gates. Some saw the navy as being unwilling or unable to be more open.

Closely related to these public perceptions were the messages being carried by our media — or the *lack* of messages about the navy and the Canadian Forces in general. But that was going to change as steps were taken for us to "tell our story" more effectively. Recall that "media training" was finally being given the attention it deserved. Few officers had had the luxury of attending the media courses being conducted in the United Kingdom. From 1987 onward there had been a concerted effort to give officers training in front of microphones and cameras, and training in "how" to tell the navy's story. We had learned from the experiences of other navies, as we saw in the Falklands and in American military operations, how to work with the media.

By 1990 we were prepared to deal with the media as our naval contribution to the Gulf Crisis took shape. My policy at the time was that MARCOM would do its best to ensure that every Canadian, "from Quidi Vidi to Qualicum," knew what an important part Canada's maritime forces were playing in the crisis — that they were aware of the unbelievable preparations that were underway in those action-packed weeks before our forces sailed on 24 August, fourteen days after Prime Minister Brian Mulroney had announced that Canada would contribute to the multinational military effort in the Persian Gulf.

As an aside, I have to pay tribute to the staffs, dockyard workers, families, servicemen and women whose dedication, loyalty, ingenuity and resourcefulness made a superhuman effort to pull off — technically and operationally — an amazing feat. Could such a performance be repeated? I would like to think so, but it *was* a unique time. For once, it was not a case of the "can-do attitude leading to chaos," as one of my predecessors had described earlier situations. As well, it is worth remembering that we in the navy had done a superb job of describing the plight of the "rusted-out" navy — badly in need of new ships and helicopters — to Canadians, only to find ourselves in the corner and able to fight our way out.

An analysis by two University of Windsor professors, S. Hibbard and T. Keenleyside, on "The Press and the Persian Gulf War" concluded that the Canadian press did not play the type of "cheerleading" role that American studies suggest the U.S. media played in building up support for a war against Iraq. Instead, our navy's message did not justify why the Canadians were or should be in the Persian Gulf, but communicated the importance of the Canadian contribution to the operation. We were effective in getting our story told to Canadians, which demonstrates that the media skills gained by our team reaped enormous benefits in those days and, I suggest, in the years that followed.

Beyond the navy's control was the rapidly changing international scene: the continuously growing importance of the Pacific, the disintegration of the Soviet bloc and the increasing role of the United Nations. The move to balance our Atlantic and Pacific fleets was being realized in a most significant way. It is worth noting that the the Tribal-class destroyer *Huron* had been based in Esquimalt in 1987, at a time when two 280s were undergoing conversion — in other words, half of the Tribal capability had moved west. Notwithstanding the obstacles to effectively operating these ships and the Sea King helicopters out of a home port other than Halifax, it happened. It was made to work through the perseverance of those in dark- and light-blue uniforms, and our civilian work force.

The disintegration of the Soviet bloc relieved the situation in the Atlantic and made the shifting of Canadian maritime assets less problematic. There were other shifts as well. We saw a steady stream of Russian generals and admirals touring Canada. Those historic "meetings" between my predecessors in MARCOM and Soviet naval officers transiting through Gander on their way to Cuba were now being replaced by official visits to Halifax and Esquimalt. A constant theme amongst those I met was one of concern for the future of the Russian Navy in the face of enormous cutbacks. They looked in awe at our sparkling ships and facilities. On a trip with the CDS across Canada to Esquimalt, their Chief of the General Staff, General Mosiyev, told me that the new Admiral Stephens Engineering Facility must have been temporarily assembled for his visit; he looked in disbelief at *Provider* — then over a quarter of a century old, looking as good as she did on commissioning. These visits left me with the sense that, despite some of the difficulties our navy faced from time to time, our service had good reason to be proud of our facilities, ships and crews that so impressed our visitors.

The other international aspect that had a significant impact on our naval operations was the commencement of more aggressive actions by the United Nations, either by way of resolutions — giving some legitimacy to the actions by the "coalition forces" in the Persian Gulf War — or successive international actions, resulting in more and more involvement by Canada's forces, and maritime forces in particular.

Those in the CF Maritime Warfare Centre were already well aware of this shift as they deliberated the many contingency operations in which our navy could become involved. The emphasis on exercises was changing, but not at the expense of war-fighting skills, so that when the centre was assigned to carry out the risk assessment on the various operating areas in the Persian Gulf for our task group it was done professionally and convincingly. Their work was critical in my decision to agree to the task group's assignment for operations. More UN involvement would follow, and my conclusion, shared by many colleagues in Canada and abroad, was that the utility of maritime forces would continue to be demonstrated.

As far as the government's agenda for defence was concerned, deficit reduction and cost-cutting were the constant theme, and there was little if any public debate of the effect on the armed forces. For those who might be tempted to draw comparisons about the government of the day, I recall former Honorary Captain (N) Peter Newman observing that he had "failed to discover any fundamental difference between Liberal and Conservative governments except Liberals tended to fish from the sterns of rented rowboats, while the Tories preferred to cast their lures off docks, encouraging the fish to come to them."

The "Last Spike," or more appropriately the final nail in the coffin, always seemed to be drawing nearer, for the never-ending rounds of cost-cutting efforts continued. Lines were drawn in the sand, and were continually crossed. I used to recall Vice-Admiral Douglas Seaman Boyle's comment that Maritime Command's "can-do" attitude led to chaos. By the end of the 1980s, "doing more with less" had lost its credibility with the fleet, for the extra effort inevitably fell on the backs of the sailors. Doing less with less seemed more appropriate in these circumstances, but who wanted to do that at the expense of capability?

The "capability-commitment gap" referred to in the 1987 white paper was cause for sleepless nights for many. It was here that pressure was placed on staffs and fleet to come up with the answers. The watchword became to try something new rather than just do something better than we did before, while at the same time attempting to maintain "core" capability. Out of all these discussions and brainstorming sessions came the decision to build the business case for activities and a new approach to justifying why and how the navy, and the Canadian Forces, should do their business.

Of course there was resistance, especially if it meant reducing the number of bases, which some communities believed were there for their well-being. I recall that after the Associate Deputy Minister (Materiel) in NDHQ, Rear-Admiral Ed Healey, had been directed to close one of his many field units, was happy to report that, after three years of effort, growth in that unit had been restricted to one additional person-year!

This small collection of snapshots is indicative of the many challenges faced by our navy during the late 1980s and early 1990s. It was my perception at the time that, notwithstanding comments from our allies who had in some cases been less than candid about the ever-shrinking capability of Canada's military, there was a positive attitude amongst those in the navy towards change, that they could be proud of their accomplishments and that there was growing recognition by Canadians of what their navy was doing. All at a time when the fleet was being renewed.

CHAPTER SIXTEEN

Vice-Admiral John
R. Anderson, 1991–92

Admiral John R. Anderson

I, too, was part of the continuum of the naval effort to stay the course as we renewed that navy. During Chuck Thomas and Bob George's tenures I had run the nuclear submarine project, lost my job with the tabling of the April 1989 budget and reverted behind John Slade to again serve as the Chief of Maritime Doctrine and Operations. Thus, many of the issues my colleagues have raised had, in some way or an-other, also crossed my desk in Ottawa.

The backdrop for the change of command between Bob George and myself was, in a break with tradition, HMCS *Halifax* — still not officially commissioned, but the pride and joy of Maritime Command. *Halifax* was commissioned almost one year later, on 29 June 1992.

I mention *Halifax*'s status because her commissioning was the first of twelve such ceremonies, which for the first time in many years, if not ever, was held in the city for which the ship was named. Several years earlier, a decision had been taken to hold the commissioning ceremony in this fashion as another way of bringing the navy to the people. Some traditionalists had some problem with this approach, but I believe it was the right thing to do and I hope the practice will continue.

Early in my command, I suffered withdrawal symptoms. I had just spent the period from summer 1983 to summer 1991 serving in Ottawa (with ten months out to study French). Throughout that time, I had lived and breathed naval requirements, operations and doctrine at the high end. Submarines had been close to the surface of my mind through that entire period. I was close to the action and the hallway jungle drums. I was missing Ottawa — hard to believe, but true. That said, it did not take me long to stop missing the Ottawa scene and to enjoy the experiences of working from a waterfront office here in Halifax.

Let me refresh your memory to provide some background for some of my following comments. The federal budgets of 1989 and 1990 removed some $3.3 billion from defence over the subsequent five-year planning period. Remember that this time frame is immediately after the fall of the Berlin Wall and other rapid changes in central and eastern Europe. The so-called "peace dividend" was being cashed in. The Department of National Defence held three key meetings from the fall of 1989 through mid-1990 to develop a high-level approach to the new fiscal situation. One of the principles agreed to at the February 1990 meeting was to assume that there would be zero-per-cent growth in the department's reference levels. This was a dramatic change from earlier years of assuming, for planning purposes, a two-to-four-per-cent growth rate.

The outcome of these meetings and the decisions taken would affect the department's program for the next ten years. What was known as Critical Review 90 continued through the rest of 1990 and the first half of 1991. Because of the continuity of approach that Vice-Admiral Thomas has mentioned in his presentation, the navy entered this review from a position of strength. We had a good portion of the capital program. Our force-planning process was highly regarded and difficult to fault. You would not be surprised, then, to hear me say that anyone and everyone was targeting the naval plan, and in particular our capital program.

There was much relief when, on 17 September 1991 — just two months after I assumed command — the Minister of Defence of the day, the Honourable Marcel Masse, announced a new defence policy. That policy "promised" the navy twelve CPFs, up to four updated Tribal-class destroyers, up to twelve maritime coastal defence vessels, three of six submarines (three outside the planning period), and four to six fast corvettes. For maritime air, "up to" thirty-five new helicopters and twenty-one CP-140s were included. (The term "corvette" got everyone up in arms because no one knew what it meant. This label was introduced to serve as a "place-holder" for some planning money for a ship that fit, in terms of capability, between the destroyers/frigates and the coastal defence vessels.)

By the time of the 24 October 1991 Naval Board meeting, there were danger signs regarding the submarine program. The naval community was still not 100 per cent behind the program. There were worries about the affordability of the naval program and concerns that the submarine project would be a hard sell. The value of the Naval Board for airing in-house issues was again demonstrated as we were able to sort out differences of opinion and re-establish the common ground. I cannot overemphasize the importance of this forum for facilitating the frank exchange of information and debate amongst senior naval leaders.

Since I have already mentioned Marcel Masse, let me bring up the issue of the Naval Reserve and the Naval Presence in Quebec (NPIQ) project. My naval career began as a naval cadet under the Regular Officer Training Program serving in HMCS *Discovery* and attending the University of British Columbia. Four winter seasons of training in that establishment contributed to my developing a high regard for the serious full-time naval reservist. I admired, and still do, their dedication to two careers. I have always been impressed with the sacrifices they make each year in order to serve. We must continue to take pride in the achievements of Canada's Naval Reserve.

It should not surprise you, then, to know that coming to grips with Naval Reserve issues was one of my priorities during my time in command. There were many problems involving reserve training, particularly in light of the plans to introduce the Coastal Defence Vessel. The peak demands created by the summer flow of reservists were a continual frustration for many regular force members, and this did nothing to engender a positive reception for them on bases and in our ships. If we were to truly embrace the Total Force concept, that had to change. Naval reserve activity needed total visibility. We also had to bring more of the regular force to the reservist. My flag flew in a gate vessel on at least one occasion. The first Naval Board I chaired was held in NCSM *Montcalm* in October 1991. I believe it was the first Naval Board held in a reserve division, and may have been the first of the re-established boards held in Quebec.

The NPIQ project was continuing to receive lots of attention from Marcel Masse. He was pressing for a reserve unit on the south shore of the St. Lawrence River. We were all looking at how we might station some regular-force naval units in Quebec. Recall that we already had established a new reserve division in Trois-Rivieres, and within a month of taking command I attended the ground-breaking ceremony for the new reserve division in Chicoutimi. We were examining the options associated with establishing a fleet school and stationing some of the Coastal Defence Vessels in Quebec, as well as transferring French second-language training for junior naval officers to Quebec from St-Jean-sur-Richelieu. As you can imagine, keeping naval requirements and politics in line in a sensible and affordable way was a real challenge.

Many successes in advancing programs in our National Defence Headquarters are gained through exercising the "art of the possible." This is something I learned very early on from Chuck Thomas, who was my director-general when I started in the requirements business. After the nuclear submarine program was cancelled, we continued to push for a conventional submarine replacement with some priority. However, as CR-90 continued to develop, it was clear to me that the climate was not right to move this program through all of the approval hoops. With the support of senior naval leadership resulting from the fall 1991 Naval Board meeting, I took the decision that the navy must delay the submarine program again, and a two-year delay was agreed upon with the Vice-Chief of Defence Staff, Lieutenant-General Fred Sutherland.

The other big capital program that required continued attention was the helicopter-replacement program. Although managed and accounted for under the air force portion of the capital plan, it required much involvement on the part of us sailors to help our maritime air colleagues fight for its priority and to discipline the requirement. Its future was considered in the decision to delay the submarines.

Social issues also required attention. For the traditional Commander's Conference in January of 1992, I decided to take advantage of the tremendous brainpower gathered for this event and convene a multi-branch exercise. One of the issues that participants were assigned to consider was bilingualism and how the navy could better achieve elements of the Department and Canadian Forces Official Language Plan. Clearly, this was linked to the NPIQ issues mentioned earlier. Brainstorming has been used extensively to solve problems over the past ten to fifteen years and represents an evolution in the way military stakeholders were and are being included in the decision-making process.

This same inclusive process was used when I was asked to consider permitting Maritime Command personnel to travel to and from work in their work dress. The command chief, Chief Petty Officer Buster Brown, led a consultative process with his colleagues. This resulted in a fashion show one afternoon so that all of us could understand the variations of uniform that had crept into our sailors' lockers. It was a thorough staff process with input from many, and it resulted in a change to the dress policy, supported by the chief and petty officers of the command, who had been involved from the beginning in developing a recommendation on the way ahead.

The question of the navy's smoking policy was never far from my door. The command surgeon continued to challenge the navy's policy of selling cheap cigarettes in our ships, while at the same time the Canadian Forces were emphasizing a healthy lifestyle. The increasing sophistication of naval equipment required the elimination of cigarette ash from operational spaces in our ships and shore facilities. Federal regulations were also a factor. Our sailors were already dealing with the integration of women into our ships, the downsizing of the forces, the need for fluency in both official languages, and the steady operational tempo with a decreasing number of ships as the old were paid off and the new not yet introduced into service; I was therefore not prepared to introduce another "downer" by stopping the sale of duty-free cigarettes or banning smoking in ships altogether. My successor, Vice-Admiral Peter Cairns, dealt with the issue during his tenure as Commander MARCOM.

The funding reductions of the early 1990s had an impact on other issues that in themselves were small, but had the potential for much consternation outside the service — and a lot of unneeded publicity for the navy. The Nova Scotia Tattoo was one example where federal funding was gradually going to disappear. Demands for DND support for

HMCS *Sackville* and the preservation of other vessels that are significant to our naval history were often on the agenda. It took a concerted effort by the Naval Board members to ensure that DND money acquired military-effective programs. In the broader scheme of things, this does not seem important, but these "little" items often take an extraordinary amount of a commander's time since, if the fire is not extinguished quickly, one soon had a roaring blaze on one's hands.

My time in command was just three days over one year — I had expected to have two or three years in the job. Little did I know that I was destined to join the short-timers' list along with Vice-Admirals Harry Porter and "Jock" Allan. Because of the continuity that Chuck Thomas and Bob George have discussed, I did not feel that I was "just passing through." Rather, I was executing a continuum of program — granted, with variations brought about by differences in approach.

Commander Maritime Command was a busy job, which, among other things, entailed:

- travelling to Ottawa every month for Armed Forces Council and Defence Management Committee;
- extensive national travel to visit, inspect and represent the command;
- international travel to represent one's navy and develop international networks;
- exercising the duties required by the military justice system of the day;
- speaking to various audiences such as Rotary, the media, National Defence College, the Royal College of Defence Studies, our own Command and Staff College, to name a few;
- hosting official visits of the Chiefs of Defence of NATO, the Chiefs of Defence of Germany and Finland and the Chiefs of Naval Staff of the UK, Turkey, Sweden and Belgium
- participating in the meeting of the Canadian Armed Forces Council with the U.S. Joint Chiefs of Staff;
- responding to the many calls from the Chief of Staff to deal with command issues (and you all know that the easy ones never reached your desk);

- dealing with the many other events that placed demands on ones time and energy.

It was also the best naval job in my career. But the greatest honour and privilege was to have had the opportunity to command and lead the very fine men and women, military and civilian, who made up Maritime Command.

APPENDIX I

Canada's Naval Commanders, 1910–2005

1910–1920	Admiral Sir Charles Kingsmill	Director of the Naval Service
1921–1928	Commodore W. Hose	DNS
1928–1934	Rear-Admiral W. Hose	Chief of the Naval Staff
1934–1944	Vice-Admiral P.W. Nelles	CNS
1944–1946	Vice-Admiral G.C. Jones	CNS
1946–1947	Vice-Admiral H.E. Reid	CNS
1947–1951	Vice-Admiral H.T.W. Grant	CNS
1951–1956	Vice-Admiral E.R. Mainguy	CNS
1956–1960	Vice-Admiral H.G. DeWolf	CNS
1960–1964	Vice-Admiral H.S. Rayner	CNS

BETWEEN 1964 AND 1968, RESPONSIBILITY FOR COMMANDING MARITIME FORCES, AND IN PARTICULAR THE RCN, OVERLAPPED BETWEEN OTTAWA AND HALIFAX.

1964	Rear-Admiral J.V. Brock	Flag Officer, Atlantic Coast
1964–1966	Vice-Admiral K.L. Dyer	Principal Naval Advisor, CFHQ

1964–1966	Rear-Admiral W.M. Landymore	Flag Officer, Atlantic Coast
1966	Rear-Admiral W.M. Landymore	Commander, Maritime Command
1966–1968	Vice-Admiral R.L. Hennessy	Principal Naval Advisor, CFHQ
1966–1970	Vice-Admiral J.C. O'Brien	Commander, Maritime Command
1970–1971	Vice-Admiral H.A. Porter	Commander, MARCOM
1971–1973	Rear-Admiral R.W. Timbrell	Commander, MARCOM
1973–1977	Vice-Admiral D.S. Boyle	Commander, MARCOM
1977–1979	Vice-Admiral A.L. Collier	Commander, MARCOM
1979–1980	Vice-Admiral J. Allan	Commander, MARCOM
1980–1983	Vice-Admiral J.A. Fulton	Commander, MARCOM
1983–1987	Vice-Admiral J.C. Wood	Commander, MARCOM
1987–1989	Vice-Admiral C.M. Thomas	Commander, MARCOM
1989–1991	Vice-Admiral R.E. George	Commander, MARCOM
1991–1992	Vice-Admiral J.R. Anderson	Commander, MARCOM

1992–1994	Vice-Admiral P.W. Cairns	Commander, MARCOM
1994–1995	Vice-Admiral L.E. Murray	Commander, MARCOM
1995–1996	Vice-Admiral L.G. Mason	Commander, MARCOM
1996–1997	Vice-Admiral G.L. Garnett	Commander, MARCOM
1997	Vice-Admiral G.L. Garnett	Chief of the Maritime Staff
1997–2001	Vice-Admiral G.R. Maddison	CMS
2001–2004	Vice-Admiral R.D. Buck	CMS
2004–	Vice-Admiral M.B. MacLean	CMS

Naval Officers who served as Chairman, Chiefs of Staff Committee

| 1942–1944 | Vice-Admiral P.W. Nelles |

Naval Officers who served as Chief of the Defence Staff

| 1977–1980 | Admiral R.F. Falls |
| 1993 | Admiral J.R. Anderson |

APPENDIX II

Career Summaries of the Flag Officers Included in This Volume

ADMIRAL SIR CHARLES EDMUND KINGSMILL

Promotions

Entered training, HMS *Britannia* at Dartmouth (Devonshire) as Naval Cadet, 24 September 1869; appointed Midshipman, 20 June 1871; Sub-Lieutenant, 20 December 1875; Lieutenant, 5 September 1877; Lieutenant and Commander, 5 February 1890; Commander, 30 June 1891; Captain, 31 December 1898; Rear-Admiral, 12 May 1907; Vice-Admiral, 17 May 1913; Admiral, 3 April 1917.

Decorations, Campaign Stars and Medals

African General Service Medal with Bar (Somaliland 1902–1904); Egypt Medal (1884–1885); Bronze Star of the Egyptian Khedive; Grand Officer, Order of the Crown of Italy; Officer, Legion of Honour (France); Commander of the Order of St. Michael and St. George and Knighthood, 1918.

Courses and Qualifications

Sub-Lieutenant's Qualifying Course, Royal Naval College, Greenwich, England, September 1876–April 1877; Torpedo Specialist Course, Royal Naval College, Greenwich, England, 30 September 1879.

Ships and Appointments

Midshipman aboard HMS *Ariadne*, 20 June 1871; HMS *Topaz*, 9 October 1872; HMS *Bellerophon*, 21 July 1874; also served on HM Ships *Bullfinch, Druid, Aboukir* and *Dryads*; HMRY *Victoria and Albert*, 25 June 1877; HMS *Research*, 21 October 1878; HMS *Vernon* after Torpedo Specialist Course, September 1879; First Lieutenant, HMS *Arab*; Service in Sudan (1884) as Vice-Consul and British Agent at Zeyla; First Lieutenant, HMS *Cormorant*, 5 June 1885; assumed command upon Captain's death, 10 October–20 November 1889; Lieutenant and Commander (Commanding Officer) of HMS *Goldfinch*, 5 February 1890; Dockyard Reserve, HMS *Victory*, 12 November 1892; Executive Officer, HMS *Immortalite* (Channel Squadron), 6 October 1893; Commanding Officer, HMS *Blenheim*, 26 May 1894; Commanding Officer, HMS *Archer*, 27 August 1895; Commanding Officer, HMS *Mildura*, 10 September 1900; Commanding Officer, HMS *Scylla*, 24 November 1903; Commanding Officer, HMS *Majestic*, 9 January 1905; Commanding Officer, HMS *Dominion*, 14 March 1906; Commanding Officer, HMS *Repulse* and Division of Special Service Vessels, Davenport, 8 May 1907; Commander Canadian Marine Service, Department of Marine and Fisheries, 12 May 1908; placed on Retired List, 12 September 1908; Director of the Naval Service of Canada, 5 May 1910.

Honourably discharged from service on 31 December 1920.

REAR-ADMIRAL WALTER HOSE, CBE

Promotions

Entered the Royal Navy as Cadet, 7 January 1890; appointed Midshipman, 15 March 1892; Sub-Lieutenant, 15 September 1895; Lieutenant, 31 December 1897; Commander, 31 December 1908; Acting Captain (N), RCN, 1 January 1916; Captain (N), RCN, 19 March 1918; Commodore (First Class), 14 August 1923; Rear-Admiral, 30 June 1934.

Decorations, Campaign Stars and Medals

Awarded Commander of the Most Excellent Order of the British Empire (CBE), Military Division; China Medal (1900–1901); Sacred Treasure of

Japan, 3rd Class; 1914–15 Bronze Star; Victory Medal; British War Medal; Mention-in-Dispatches.

Courses and Qualifications

Seamanship 2nd Class certification; Pilotage 2nd Class certification; Torpedo qualification.

Ships and Appointments

HMS *Britannia*, 7 January 1890; HMS *Imperieuse*, January 1892; HMS *Centurion*, January 1894; HMS *Calypso*, May 1895; Sub-Lieutenant in Command of Torpedo Boat (TB) 44 for Naval Manoeuvres, August 1896; HMS *Skate*, October 1896; HMS *Polyphemus*, January 1897; HMS *Dragon*, June 1897; HMS *Bonaventure*, March 1898; Lieutenant in Command of HMS *Tweed*, China Station for Special Service on the West River, 15 October 1899; HMS *Bonaventure*, December 1899; HMS *Jupiter*, September 1901; HMS *Charybdis*, April 1902; Lieutenant in Command of HMS *Ringdove*, North Africa and West Indies Station, 14 April 1905; Lieutenant in Command of HMTBD *Kale*, Devonport Flotilla, 1 November 1905; Lieutenant in Command of HMS *Redbreast*, Persian Gulf, 19 January 1906; Lieutenant in Command of HMS *Jason*, Home Fleet, 15 August 1908; HMS *Cochrane*, February 1909; lent to RCN as Commander in Command, HMCS *Rainbow* and Commander-in-Charge of Esquimalt Dockyard, 24 June 1911; retired from Royal Navy and transferred to RCN, 1 January 1912; appointed Acting Captain, 1 January 1916; Commanding Officer, HMCS *Lansdowne* in Command of Sydney base and as Captain in Command of Patrols (temporarily), 14 August 1917; Commanding Officer HMCS *Seagull* (Patrol Depot) as Captain of Patrols, 1 May 1918; Superintendent HMC Dockyard, Halifax, 15 May 1919; Naval Assistant to the Minister of the Naval Service, 30 March 1920; Naval Assistant to the Minister of the Naval Service and Acting Director of the Naval Service of Canada, 1 July 1920; Director of the Naval Service, 1 January 1921; Naval Advisor to the Canadian Delegation at the 1923 Imperial Conference, November 1923; Naval Advisor to the Canadian Delegation at the 1926 Imperial Conference November 1926; Naval Advisor to the Canadian Delegation at the Three Power Naval Limitation Conference, Geneva, July 1927; Chief of the

Naval Staff of Canada, 7 March 1928; Naval Advisor to the Canadian Delegation at the London Naval Conference, January 1930.

Honourably discharged from service on 30 June 1934.

Admiral Percy Walker Nelles, CB

Promotions

Entered the RCN as Midshipman, 21 October 1910; promoted Acting Sub-Lieutenant, 14 January 1913; Lieutenant, 14 July 1914; Lieutenant-Commander, 14 July 1922; Commander, 1 December 1925; Acting Captain, RN, 23 August 1930; Captain, RCN, 1 January 1933; Commodore (First Class), 1 July 1934; Rear-Admiral, 1 August 1938; Vice-Admiral, 19 November 1941; promoted Admiral on Retired List, 7 January 1945.

Decorations, Campaign Stars and Medals

Awarded Companion, the Most Honourable Order of the Bath (CB); 1914–15 Bronze Star; Victory Medal; British War Medal; Commander, Legion of Merit; Defence Medal; War Medal 1939–45; Canadian Volunteer Service Medal (CVSM) with Clasp.

Courses and Qualifications

Staff Course, Royal Navy Staff College; PSC qualification; Royal Navy Senior Officer's Technical Course; Imperial War College.

Ships and Appointments

HMS *Dreadnought*, 14 December 1911; HMS *President*, 15 January 1913; HMS *Dryad*, 1 April 1913; HMS *Neptune*, Flagship, Home Fleet, 12 July 1913; HMS *Excellent*, 5 August 1913; HMS *Victory II*, 8 November 1913; HMS *Suffolk*, 25 February 1914; HMS *Antrim*, North America and West Indies Station, 26 August 1916; Flag Lieutenant to Admiral Sir Charles Kingsmill, April 1917; HMS *President*, 1 October 1920; District Intelligence Officer, 4 January 1921; HMS *Vivid*, 12 February 1923; HMS *Caledon*, 14 April 1923; Royal Navy Staff College, Greenwich, 16 September 1924; HMS *Victory*, 11 July 1925; HMS *Victory I*, 11 July 1925; HQ, 1 October 1925; Senior Naval Officer, Esquimalt, 1 December 1925; HMS *Victory*, 1 April 1929; on Staff, Operations Division of the Naval Staff, Admiralty, 1 July 1929; HMS *Pembroke*, 15 November 1929; Executive Officer, HMS *Dragon*, 18 March 1930; Commanding Officer, HMS *Dragon*, 23 August 1930; HMS *Victory I*, 1 March 1931; Commanding Officer, HMCS *Saguenay* and Commander (Destroyers) Eastern Division, 23 January 1932; Commanding Officer and Commander-in-Charge, Halifax, 7 June 1932; Imperial Defence College, 15 January 1933; Acting Director of the Naval Service and Acting Chief of the Naval Staff, 1 January 1934; Director of Naval Service and Chief of the Naval Staff, 1 July 1934; Senior Canadian Flag Officer Overseas, 15 January 1944.

Honourably discharged on 6 January 1945.

REAR-ADMIRAL LEONARD WARREN MURRAY, CB, CBE

Promotions

Entered the Royal Naval College of Canada as Cadet, 19 January 1911; Midshipman, 25 January 1913; Acting Sub-Lieutenant, 1 December 1915; Lieutenant, 1 January 1917; Lieutenant-Commander, 1 January 1925; Commander, 1 January 1929; Captain, 2 August 1938; Commodore, 1 June 1941; Rear-Admiral, 2 December 1941.

Decorations, Campaign Stars and Medals

Awarded Commander, Military Division of the Most Excellent Order of the British Empire (CBE); Companion, the Most Honourable Order of the Bath (CB); 1914–15 Star; 1914–15 Bronze Star; King's Silver Jubilee Medal (King George V); King George VI Coronation Medal 1937; Defence Medal (DM); Canadian Volunteer Service Medal (CVSM); with Clasp; War Medal (1945); Victory Medal; General Service Badge; Legion of Merit; *Cravate de Commandeur de la Légion d'Honneur (accompagnée de la Croix de Guerre avec Palme)*.

Courses and Qualifications

Watch-Keeping Certificate; Navigation and Pilotage Qualification; PSC Qualification; War Staff Course; Royal Navy Staff College; Imperial Defence College.

Ships and Appointments

HMS *Berwick*, 25 January 1913; HMCS *Margaret*, 15 April 1915; HMCS *Rainbow*, 2 October 1915; HMS *Leviathan*, 11 March 1916; Assistant Navigating Officer, HMS *Agincourt*, 24 March 1918; HMS *Hercules*, 1 April 1919; HMS *Calcutta*, 1 July 1919; Navigating Officer, HMS *Crescent*, 16 September 1919; HMS *Victory I*, 2 December 1919; HMS *Dryad*, 1 January 1920; HMS *Victory*, 17 July 1920; Navigating Officer, HMS *Vivid*/HMCS *Aurora*, 1 September 1920; Guelph Depot, 30 August 1922; HMS *Revenge*, 10 October 1922; Navigating Officer, HMS *Queen Elizabeth*, 15 May 1923; HMS *Dryad*, 12 May 1924; HMS *Victory*, 6 July 1924; HMS *Dryad*, 15 July 1924; Executive Officer, RCN Barracks (Halifax), 6 February 1925; HMS *Dryad*, 14 March 1927; Navigating Officer, HMS *Tiger*, 11 April 1927; HMS *President*, 4 October 1927; HMS *Victory*, 21 December 1928; Senior Naval Officer, Esquimalt, 23 January 1929; Naval Staff Officer, 26 June 1931; Commanding Officer, HMCS *Saguenay* and Commander (Destroyers) Eastern Division, 3 June 1932; Commander-in-Charge HMC Dockyard, 1 May 1934; HMS *President*, 6 June 1936; Executive Officer, HMS *Iron Duke*, 12 January 1937; Commandant, HMS *Victory*, 12 January 1938; HMS *President*, 18 January 1938; HMS *Victory*, 17 December 1938; Director of Naval Operations & Training, 16 January 1939; Deputy Chief of Naval Staff, 30 August 1939; Commanding Officer, HMCS *Assiniboine*, 24 October 1940; HMCS *Dominion*, 15 January 1941; Flag Officer Newfoundland Force, 10 June 1941; Commanding Officer Atlantic Coast, 18 September 1942; Commander-in-Chief Canadian North West Atlantic, 1 April 1943.

Honourably discharged from service on 15 March 1946.

Vice-Admiral George Clarence Jones, CB

Promotions

Enrolled in Royal Navy College of Canada as Cadet, 19 January 1911; Midshipman, 25 January 1913; Acting Sub-Lieutenant, 1 December 1915; Sub-Lieutenant, 1 December 1916; Acting Lieutenant, 1 January 1917; Lieutenant, 1 June 1917; Lieutenant-Commander, 1 January 1925; Commander, 1 January 1929; Captain, 1 August 1938; Commodore, 7 June 1940; Rear-Admiral, 1 December 1941; Vice-Admiral, 9 May 1944.

Decorations, Campaign Stars and Medals

Awarded the Companion of the Most Honourable Order of the Bath (CB), 2 June 1943; King's Silver Jubilee, 6 May 1935; 1914–15 Bronze Star, 14 July 1921; Victory and British War Medals, 25 April 1923; 1939–45 Star, 6 March 1944; Atlantic Star, 2 January 1946; Canadian Volunteer Service Medal (CVSM); Legion of Merit (Posthumous), 29 January 1946; Officer, *Croix de la Légion d'Honneur* (Posthumous), 29 August 1947.

Courses and Qualifications

Enrolled in the Royal Naval College of Canada, 19 January 1911; returned, 8 February 1914; returned, 12 February 1919; War Staff Course, 25 September 1923; PSC War Staff; Imperial Defence Course, 14 January 1929.

Ships and Appointments

HMS *Berwick*, 25 January 1913; HMS *Suffolk*, 15 September 1914; HMS *Cumberland*, 10 December 1915; HMS *Victory II*, 21 October 1916; HMS *Excellent*, 7 November 1916; HMS *Woolwich/Pelican*, 11 November 1916; HMS *Helca*, 1 September 1917; HMS *Woolwich/Vanquisher*, 22 October 1917; HMS *Wallington*, 1 June 1918; HMS *Leander*, 1 July 1918; HMS *Victory/Patrician*, 16 July 1920; HMS *Aurora/Patrician*, 1 November 1920; HMS *Vivid III*, 22 September 1923; HMS *President*, 25 September 1923; HMS *Resolution*, 4 September 1924; Naval Staff Officer, 15 June 1925; HMS *Victory*, 1 November 1927; HMS *Iron Duke* 15 November 1927; HMS *Benbow*, 12 May 1928; HMS *Victory*, 5 January 1929; HMS *President*, 14 January 1929; Commanding Officer, HMCS *Skeena*, 25 May 1932; Director Naval Operations and Training, 19 May 1936; Captain (Destroyers) and Commanding Officer, HMCS *Ottawa*, 17 November 1938; Captain (Destroyers) and Commanding Officer, HMCS *Assiniboine*, 3 April 1940; Commodore Commanding Halifax Force and Commanding Officer, HMCS *Assiniboine*, 7 June 1940; Commanding Officer Atlantic Coast, 28 September 1940; Vice-Chief of the Naval Staff, 9 October 1942; Chief of the Naval Staff, 15 January 1944; Commander-in-Chief Canadian North West Atlantic, 12 May 1945.

Discharged dead on 8 February 1946.

VICE-ADMIRAL HOWARD EMMERSON REID, CB, CD

Promotions

Entered the Royal Naval College of Canada as Cadet, 27 January 1912; appointed Midshipman, 13 February 1914; Acting Sub-Lieutenant, 1 December 1916; Acting Lieutenant, 4 April 1918; Lieutenant, 5 September 1918; Lieutenant-Commander, 5 June 1926; Commander, 1 January 1933; Captain, 30 August 1939; Commodore (First Class), 1 July 1941; Rear-Admiral, 1 December 1943; Vice-Admiral, 28 February 1946.

Decorations, Campaign Stars and Medals

Awarded Companion, the Most Honourable Order of the Bath (CB); Defence Medal; Granted two Hurt Certificates; 1914–15 Bronze Star; Victory Medal; British Medal; Canadian Volunteer Service Medal (CVSM) with Clasp; Legion of Merit; Commander, *Croix de la Légion d'Honneur*; Canadian Forces Decoration (CD) with 3rd Clasp; King's Silver Jubilee Medal and King George VI Coronation Medal 1937.

Courses and Qualifications

Received the following qualifications for command of Torpedo Boat Destroyers: Navigation and Pilotage, Torpedo and Signals and Wireless Telegraphy (W/T); awarded PSC qualification.

Ships and Appointments

HMS *Berwick*, 13 February 1914; HMCS *Niobe*, 2 January 1916; HMCS *Rainbow*, 1 March 1916; HMCS *Niobe*, 17 December 1916; HMS *Victory II*, 25 January 1917; HMS *Vivid II*, 5 March 1917; HMS *Apollo-Attack*, 1 September 1917; HMS *Blenheim*, 1 December 1917; HMS *Blake*, 1 January 1918; HMS *Greenwich-Viscount*, 1 March 1919; HMS *Niobe*, 7 June 1919; HMS *Tatania*, 8 September 1919; HMS *Victory*, 18 November 1922; HMCS *Patriot*, 24 August 1923; HQ- 1 November 1925; HMS *Victory*, 13 October 1928; HMS *Vernon*, 31 October 1928; HMS *Tamar II*, 2 February 1929; HMS *Victory*, 3 January 1931; HMS *President*, 13 January 1931; HMS *Victory*, 19 December 1931; HMS *Warspite*, 1 January 1932; HMS *Valiant*, 14 May 1932; HMS *Warspite*, 8 July 1932; HMS *Victory*, 17 August 1932; Director, Naval Operations and Training, 21 May 1934; Commanding Officer, HMCS

Skeena, 8 January 1936; HMCS *Fraser*, 28 March 1937; Commander-in-Charge HMC Dockyard, Halifax, 1 October 1938; Captain-in-Charge, HM Establishments and Commanding Officer Atlantic Coast, 2 September 1939; Deputy Chief of the Naval Staff, 15 October 1940; HMCS *Avalon*, Commodore Commanding Newfoundland Force, 23 October 1942; Naval Member, Canadian Joint Staff (Washington), 1 December 1943; Chief of the Naval Staff, 28 February 1946.

Honourably discharged from service on 26 March 1948.

Vice-Admiral Harold Taylor Wood Grant, DSO, CBE, CD

Promotions

Entered the Royal Naval College of Canada as a Cadet on 3 August 1914; Midshipman, 2 February 1917; Acting Sub-Lieutenant, 2 December 1918; Sub-Lieutenant, 1 May 1919; Lieutenant, 2 December 1920; Lieutenant-Commander, 2 November 1928; Commander, 1 August 1935; Captain, 1 July 1940; Commodore, 1 January 1946; Rear-Admiral, 28 February 1946; Vice-Admiral, 1 September 1947.

Decorations, Campaign Stars and Medals

Awarded the Naval General Service Medal (1915); 1939–45 Star; Atlantic Star; France Star with Clasp; Burma Star; Defence Medal; Canadian Volunteer Service Medal with Clasp; 1945 Medal; Commander of the Order of the British Empire (CBE), 1944; Bronze Star (USA), 1944; Mention-in-Dispatches, 1944; Distinguished Service Order (DSO), 1946; and the Canadian Forces Decoration with 3rd Clasp.

Courses and Qualifications

Courses for the rank of Lieutenant, 1920–1921; Navigation Specialist, 1924; First Class Ship Course in Navigation Qualification, 1927; Completed RN Staff Course, 18 December 1936.

Ships and Appointments

HMS *Leviathan*, 9 February 1917; HMS *Carnarvon*, 1 March 1917; HMS *Roxburgh*, 6 March 1917; HMS *Vivid II*, 18 July 1917; HMCS *Minotaur*, 10

August 1917; HMS *Canada*, February 1919; HMS *Victory*, 15 May 1919; HMS *Warwick*, 18 October 1919; HMS *Vivid*/HMCS *Aurora*, 14 September 1920; HMS *Dryad*, 17 September 1921; HMS *Excellent*, 16 October 1921; HMS *Ramillies*, 24 December 1921; HMCS *Patriot*, 4 September 1923; HMS *Dryad*, 4 February 1924; HMS *Victory*, 22 June 1924; HMS *Woolwich*/HMS *Saumarez*, 10 July 1924; HMS *Victory*, 14 August 1924; First Lieutenant and Navigating Officer, HMCS *Patrician*, 1 December 1924; RCNVR Training Officer, HMCS *Naden*, 1 September 1926; HMS *Dryad*, 14 March 1927; HMS *Victory*, 23 July 1927; HMS *Warspite*, 1 August 1927; Assistant Navigator, HMS *Queen Elizabeth*, 1 December 1927; HMS *Hood*/HMS *Tiger*, 2 April 1929; HMS *Victory*, 6 April 1929; Staff Officer (Intelligence), 24 June 1929; Navigating Officer, HMCS *Saguenay*, 1 May 1931; Executive Officer and Navigating Officer, HMS *Saguenay*, 7 June 1932; Executive Officer, RCN Barracks, Halifax, 1 January 1933; Staff Officer (Intelligence), 27 June 1934; Director of Naval Reserves, 1 July 1935; Staff Course, RN Staff College, HMS *Victory*, 5 January 1936; RN Staff Officer (Movements) Home Fleet, 25 March 1937; Commanding Officer, HMCS *Skeena*, 1 May 1938; Staff Officer (Operations) to Commanding Officer Atlantic Coast, 1 December 1939; Director of Naval Personnel, 26 August 1940; Captain (Destroyers) Newfoundland, 23 October 1942; Commanding Officer, HMS *Diomede*, 1 April 1943; Commanding Officer, HMS *Enterprise*, 1 June 1943; HMCS *Niobe*, 3 July 1944; NSHQ, 15 September 1944; HMCS *Niobe*, 17 March 1945; Commanding Officer, HMCS *Minotaur*; Commanding Officer, HMCS *Ontario*, 26 April 1945; Chief of Administration and Supply, 1 February 1946; Deputy Chief of Naval Staff and Chief of Naval Administration and Supply, 28 February 1946; Chief of Naval Staff, 1 September 1947.

Honourably discharged from service on 26 August 1952.

VICE-ADMIRAL EDMOND ROLLO MAINGUY, OBE, CD

Promotions

Entered the Royal Naval College of Canada as a Cadet on 3 August 1915; Midshipman, 15 February 1918; Sub-Lieutenant, 15 December 1919; Lieutenant, 15 July 1921; Lieutenant-Commander, 15 March 1929; Commander, 1 January 1937; Captain, 1 June 1941; Commodore, 1 July 1946; Rear-Admiral, 1 July 1947; Vice-Admiral, 1 December 1951.

Decorations, Campaign Stars and Medals
Awarded the Order of the British Empire (OBE) "for gallantry and distin-guished services before the enemy;" Mention-in-Dispatches in 1941 and again after the war while in command of *Uganda* in the Far East; Defence Medal; Canadian Volunteer Service Medal with Maple Leaf; War Medal 1939–45; 1939–45 Star; Atlantic Star; Pacific Star; King George VI Coronation Medal (1937); Officer of the Legion of Merit; Canadian Forces Decoration (CD) with 2nd Clasp.

Courses and Qualifications
Signal and W/T Specialist qualifications; RCAF Artillery Co-operation Course; Staff Course, Royal Naval College, Greenwich, England; Watch-Keeping Certificate; Gunnery Course; Tactical Course, 2 December 1944.

Ships and Appointments
HMS *Canada*, 24 February 1918; HMS *Barham*, 1 April 1919; HMS *Dryad*, 1 October 1920; HMS *Excellent*, 30 January 1921; HMS *Victory*, 1 July 1921; HMS *Pembroke II* 21 July 1921; HMS *Blake/Melton*, 10 August 1921; HMCS *Aurora*, 30 August 1921; HMCS *Guelph*, 2 July 1921; HMCS *Patriot*, 4 October 1922; RN Signals School, HMS *Victory*, 22 September 1923; HMCS *Naden*, 7 March 1925; Supervising Officer, Western Divisions, 1926; International Staff, RN Signals School, HMS *Victory*, 16 January 1928; HMS *Frobisher*, 10 September 1928; Flag Lieutenant-Commander, Squadron Signal and W/T Officer, HMS *London*, 4 April 1929; HMS *Victory*, 12 April 1930; Executive Officer and Signal Officer, HMCS *Vancouver*, 20 May 1930; W/T Experimental Officer, HMS *Delhi*, America & West Indies Station, May 1931; Staff Officer Intelligence, 29 July 1932; Executive Officer, HMCS *Saguenay*, 1 December 1934; Commanding Officer, HMCS *Vancouver*, 13 May 1936; Director Naval Reserves, 1 January 1937; RN Staff College, HMS *President*, 10 January 1939; Commanding Officer, HMS *Kempenfelt*, 19 October 1939; Commanding Officer, HMCS *Assiniboine*, 1 January 1940; Commanding Officer, HMCS *Ottawa*, 3 April 1940; Commanding Officer, HMCS *Sambro* and Captain (Destroyers) Halifax, 1941; Captain (Destroyers) Newfoundland, 8 November 1941; Chief of Naval Personnel, 15 November 1942; Commanding Officer, HMCS *Uganda*, 15 August 1944; Commanding Officer Pacific Coast, 1 August 1946; Flag Officer Atlantic

Coast and Senior Officer in Chief Command, 1 October 1948; Chairman of the Mainguy Commission, 1949; Flag Officer Commanding Canadian Special Service Squadron, 19 September 1950; Chief of Naval Staff, 1 December 1951.

Honourably discharged from service on 6 October 1956.

Vice-Admiral Harry George DeWolf, dso, dsc, cbe, CD

Promotions

Entered the Royal Canadian Navy as Cadet, 22 September 1918; Midshipman, 1 September 1921; Acting Sub-Lieutenant, 1 January 1921; Sub-Lieutenant, 1 July 1924; Lieutenant, 1 April 1926; Lieutenant-Commander, 1 April 1934; Commander, 1 July 1940; Acting Captain, 1 December 1941; Commander, 30 September 1943; Captain, 1 July 1944; Commodore I/C, 12 May 1945; Acting Commodore, 15 October 1945; Commodore, 1 January 1947; Rear-Admiral, 8 September 1948; Vice-Admiral 16 January 1956.

Decorations, Campaign Stars and Medals

Awarded psc Qualification, 1937; Mention-in-Dispatches, 1 January 1941; Mention-in-Dispatches (Operational), 1 January 1943; Star (1939–43), 3 February 1944; Companion of the Distinguished Service Order, 3 May 1944; Distinguished Service Cross, 29 August 1944; Canadian Volunteer Service Medal with clasp, 9 September 1944; Mention-in-Dispatches, 10 October 1944; Mention-in-Dispatches, 14 November 1944; Commander of the Order of the British Empire (cbe), 1 January 1946; Legion of Merit, 6 May 1946; Officer, *Croix de la Légion d'Honneur*, 29 September 1947; Canadian Forces Decoration with clasp, 11 August 1950; Canadian Forces Decoration with second clasp, 31 August 1953; Queen's Coronation Medal, 3 June 1953.

Courses and Qualifications

Attended Royal Naval College of Canada, 22 September 1918; 1st/Cl. Cert. in Anti-Gas Course, June 1922; 2nd/Cl. Cert. in Pilotage, May 1923; 1st/Cl. Cert. in Seamanship, December 1923; Royal Naval College, Greenwich, 10 April 1924; Royal Naval College, Greenwich, 25 September 1924; 3rd/Cl. Cert. in

Torpedo and 2nd/Cl. Cert. in Gunnery, 26 June 1925; Long "N" Course, 16 April 1928; Gunnery for Command of Destroyer, 9 September 1936.

Ships and Appointments

HMS *Resolution*, 14 October 1921; HMCS *Stadacona*, 26 February 1924; HMS *President*, 22 August 1924; HMS *Excellent*, 19 December 1924; HMS *Victory*, 11 July 1925; HMCS *Patriot*, 30 April 1927; courses in UK, 17 September 1928; HMS *Argus*, 29 September 1928; HMCS *Champlain*, 14 December 1928; HMCS *Stadacona*, 7 June 1929; HMCS *Naden*, 25 July 1929; Commanding Officer, HMCS *Festubert*, 14 April 1930; HMCS *Vancouver*, 27 April 1932; HMCS *Skeena*, 1 April 1934; HMS *President*, 3 January 1937; Staff Officer (Operations) HMS *London*, 20 December 1937; appointed Staff Officer to Captain (D), 1 December 1938; Commanding Officer, HMCS *St. Laurent*, 6 October 1939; Staff Officer Operations, Atlantic Coast, 9 March 1940; Chief Staff Officer, Atlantic Coast, 1 January 1942; Director of Plans, 25 May 1942; Commanding Officer, HMCS *Haida*, 30 August 1943; Assistant Chief of Naval Staff, 1 December 1944; Commanding Officer and SCNOA, HMCS *Warrior*, 18 January 1947; Commanding Officer and SCNOA, HMCS *Magnificent*, 7 April 1948; Flag Officer, Pacific Coast, 8 September 1948; Vice-Chief of the Naval Staff, 11 September 1950; Principal Military Advisor to the Canadian Ambassador in Washington; Chairman, Canadian Joint Staff (Washington); Representative, Chiefs of Staff (Washington); Representative, Representatives Committee of NATO; Canadian Liaison Representative to SACLANT, 15 December 1952; Chief of the Naval Staff, 16 January 1956.

Honourably discharged from service on 25 May 1961.

VICE-ADMIRAL HERBERT SHARPLES RAYNER, DSC AND BAR, CD

Promotions

Entered the Royal Canadian Navy as Paymaster Cadet, 7 September 1928; Cadet, 26 September 1928; Midshipman, 1 January 1930; Acting Sub-Lieutenant, 1 May 1932; Lieutenant, 1 April 1933; Acting Lieutenant-Commander, 14 July 1940; Lieutenant-Commander, 1 April 1941; Commander, 1 July 1944; Captain, 1 July 1948; Commodore, 1 July 1951; Rear-Admiral, 27 May 1955; Vice-Admiral, 1 August 1960.

Decorations, Campaign Stars and Medals
Awarded the Distinguished Service Cross (DSC), March 1941; Bar to Distinguished Service Cross, August 1944; *Croix de la Légion d'Honneur avec Rang de Chevalier*; *Croix de Guerre avec Palme*; 1939–1945 Star; Atlantic Star with France and Germany Clasp; Canadian Volunteer Service Medal with Clasp; War Medal 1939–1945; Mention-in-Dispatches; Queen Elizabeth II's Coronation Medal, 1953; Canadian Forces Decoration with First Clasp, 1950; Second Clasp, 1960.

Courses and Qualifications
Attended Royal Naval College, Greenwich, 28 April 1932; Senior Officer's Technical Course, 27 August 1949; Imperial Defence College Course, 10 January 1950.

Ships and Appointments
Commanding Officer, HMCS *Skeena*, 28 February 1940; Commanding Officer, HMCS *St. Laurent*, 14 July 1940; Staff Officer Operations, Atlantic Coast, 25 February 1942; Commanding Officer, HMCS *Huron*, 1 May 1943; Director of Plans, Naval Headquarters, 30 September 1944; Captain (D) Halifax, 17 December 1945; Commanding Officer, HMCS *Nootka*, 7 August 1946; Commanding Officer, HMCS *Nootka* and Commander (D), 8 October 1946; Officer in Command, Naval Air Section Dartmouth; Commandant, Canadian Services College, 29 July 1948; Secretary, Chiefs of Staff Committee, 15 January 1951; Co-ordinator Joint Staff, Chiefs of Staff Committee, 1 July 1951; Commanding Officer, HMCS *Magnificent*, 11 March 1953; Naval Assistant to the Chief of the Naval Staff, 1 February 1955; Chief of Naval Personnel, 27 May 1955; Flag Officer, Pacific Coast, 14 August 1957; Chief of the Naval Staff, 1 August 1960.

Honourably discharged from service on 29 April 1965.

Rear-Admiral William Moss Landymore, OBE, CD

Promotions
Entered the Royal Military College in September, 1934 and became Temporary Naval Cadet in the RCNVR, 14 June 1935; appointed Temporary

Midshipman, 10 June 1936; Appointed Naval Cadet in the RCN, 28 August 1936; Midshipman, 1 May 1937; Acting Sub-Lieutenant, 1 March 1939; Sub-Lieutenant, 6 March 1940; Lieutenant, 1 May 1940; Acting Lieutenant-Commander (G), 1 March 1945; Lieutenant-Commander (G), 1 May 1947; Commander, 1 July 1949; Acting Captain, September 1951; Captain 1 January 1953; Commodore, 1 October 1959; Rear-Admiral, 1 November 1962.

Decorations, Campaign Stars and Medals
Mention-in-Dispatches, 1 January 1946 and again on 9 June 1953; received the Order of the British Empire (OBE), Military Division, 20 February 1954; Canadian Forces Decoration (CD) with 2nd Clasp; Queen Elizabeth II's Coronation Medal, 1953.

Courses and Qualifications
Attended HMS *Excellent* and HMS *Victory* for various training in 1938, 1939 and 1942; Short Gunnery Course, 14 November 1939; Long Gunnery Course, 30 April 1942; Royal Navy Staff Course and the RN Tactical Course, 12 September 1948–April 1949; Royal Navy Joint Services Staff College, 23 May–2 December 1949 (granted qualification, 12 December 1949); Imperial Defence College, 29 December 1953–January 1955.

Ships and Appointments
Under training, HMS *Frobisher*, 9 September 1936; HMS *Emerald*, 1 May 1937; HMS *Glasgow*, 12 October 1938; as Watch Keeper and Ship's Officer, HMCS *Fraser*, 27 February 1940; sent to HMCS *Restigouche* in British waters as Navigating Officer, 19 July 1940; HMCS *Margaree*, 6 September 1940; for Gunnery training aboard HMS *Belfast*, January–June 1943; HMS *Grenville*, June–November 1943; HMS *Uganda*, 5 June 1944; HMCS *Uganda*, 21 October 1944; Staff Gunnery Officer, Directorate of Weapons Training, 15 October 1946; Director of Manning and Personnel Statistics, 23 January 1950; Commanding Officer, HMCS *Iroquois*, 21 October 1951; in Command (HMCS *Iroquois*) and Commander of Canadian Destroyers Far East, 18 June 1953; Assistant Chief of Naval Staff (Plans) as Director of Naval Plans and Operations, 21 January 1955; Commanding Officer, HMCS *Bonaventure*, 17

January 1958; Chief of Staff to the Flag Officer Atlantic Coast and the Maritime Commander as well as NATO Chief of Staff to the Commander Canadian Atlantic Sub-Area, 1 October 1959; Senior Canadian Officer Afloat, Atlantic, 6 September 1962; Flag Officer Pacific Coast, Senior Officer in Chief Command and Maritime Commander Pacific, 1 November 1962; Flag Officer Atlantic Coast, Senior Officer in Chief Command, Commander Atlantic Sub-Area and Canadian Maritime Commander Atlantic, 16 November 1964.

Honourably discharged from Service on 5 April 1967.

VICE-ADMIRAL HENRY ALLAN PORTER, CD

Promotions

Entered the RCNVR as an Ordinary Telegraphist on 20 November 1939; transferred to RCN, May 1940; promoted Able Seaman, August 1941; Leading Seaman, November 1941; course for commission, 1941; commissioned as Acting Sub-Lieutenant, August 1942; Sub-Lieutenant, September 1942; Lieutenant, October 1943; Lieutenant-Commander, December 1950; Commander, July 1954; Acting Captain, September 1958; Captain, January 1960; Commodore, August 1966; Rear-Admiral, September 1969; Vice-Admiral, January 1971.

Decorations, Campaign Stars and Medals

Awarded the 1939–45 Star; Atlantic Star with France and Germany Clasp; Defence Medal; Canadian Volunteer Service Medal (CVSM) with Maple Leaf; War Medal 1939–45; Canadian Forces Decoration.

Courses and Qualifications

Telegraphist and Seaman Courses, HM Ships *Collingwood* and *Excellent*, May 1940; Course for Commission, 1941; Sub-Lieutenant's Course, 1943; Watch-Keeping Certificate, 18 October 1943; Long Signals (S) Course, 1944; Royal Navy Pilot Training, 2 April 1946–5 March 1947; Royal Navy Staff College, 1950; Senior Officer's Atomic Biological Chemical Warfare Course, 1955.

Ships and Appointments

HMS *Prince Robert*, 8 April 1941; HMS *Excellent*, 23 August 1942; Signals/Plotting Officer, HMCS *Kootenay*, 12 April 1943; Executive Officer, HMCS *Kootenay*, 9 January 1944; W/T Technical Instructor, HMCS *St. Hyacinthe*, 28 June 1944; Royal Navy Service Flying Training School, 2 April 1946–5 March 1947; Royal Navy Air Station *Culdrose* 11 September 1947; Royal Navy Air Station *Eglinton* in 17th Carrier Air Group, October 1947; Staff Officer Operations and Communications to the Flag Officer Atlantic Coast, 28 June 1948; Officer in Charge of Communication School (Halifax), 14 November 1949; Royal Navy Staff College, 25 September 1950; Communications Officer, HMCS *Magnificent*, 30 April 1951; Commanding Officer, HMCS *La Hulloise*, 28 November 1952; Commanding Officer, HMCS *Lauzon*, 12 December 1953; Officer-in-Charge, Communications School (Cornwallis), 16 October 1953; Director of Naval Communications, 2 September 1955; B.C. Centennial Co-ordinator, on Staff of the Flag Officer, Pacific Coast, 26 August 1957; Commander 4th Canadian Escort Squadron, 3 September 1958; Director of Naval Training, 6 September 1960; Naval Assistant to Chief of Naval Staff, 20 August 1962; Commanding Officer, HMCS *Bonaventure*, 2 April 1965; Director General Maritime Forces, Director General Equipment requirements and Chairman, NATO Naval Advisory Group (NNAG), 2 August 1966; Senior Canadian Naval Officer Afloat, August 1968; Commander, Canada's Operational Fleet (CANCOMFLT), 1 September 1968; Commander Maritime Forces Pacific and Deputy Commander Maritime Command, August 1969; Commander Maritime Command and Commander Canadian Atlantic Sub Area, July 1970; Comptroller General, Canadian Forces, November 1971; Assistant Deputy Minister (Evaluation) on NDHQ Restructuring, November 1972.

Honourably discharged from service on 17 August 1975.

REAR-ADMIRAL ROBERT WALTER TIMBRELL, CMM, DSC, CD

Promotions

Entered the RCN as Cadet on 20 August 1937; promoted Midshipman, 1 September 1948; Sub-Lieutenant, 1 May 1940; Lieutenant, 15 August 1941;

Lieutenant-Commander, 15 August 1949; Commander, 1 July 1952; Captain, 1 July 1958; Commodore, 1 July 1965; Rear-Admiral, 1 September 1967.

Decorations, Campaign Stars and Medals

Awarded Commander of the Order of Military Merit (CMM); Distinguished Service Cross (DSC); Special Service Medal (SSM); Canadian Forces Decoration (CD) with 2nd Clasp; 1939–45 Star; Canadian Volunteer Service Medal (CVSM) with Clasp; Atlantic Star; Africa Star; War Medal; Mention-in-Dispatches; Defence Medal with France and Germany Clasp; Canadian Centennial Medal.

Courses and Qualifications

Sub-Lieutenant's Course, April 1940; Watch-Keeping Certificate, 1941; Long Anti-Submarine (A/S) Course, January 1942; PSC Qualification; 2nd Certification in Navigation and Pilotage; TAS Conversion; SACLANT Atomic Warfare Information Course; USN ASW Tactical Commander's Course; General Officer's Management Course.

Ships and Appointments

HMS *Erebus*, 7 September 1937; HMS *Vindictive*, 11 January 1938; HMS *Barham*, 1 September 1938; HMS *Afridi*, June 1939; HMS *Victory*, 16 September 1939; HMS *Hood*, January 1940; HMS *Warspite*, 16 March 1940; HMS *Excellent*, 4 April 1940; Commanding Officer, HM Yacht *Llanthony* at Dunkirk, May 1940; HMCS *Margaree*, 6 September 1940; A/S Officer and as Executive Officer, HMCS *Annapolis*, 3 January 1941; A/S Instructor, HMS *Osprey*, 15 February 1942; Commanding Officer, Anti-Submarine School, 15 March 1943; Staff Officer A/S, HMCS *Ottawa*, 9 May 1944; Staff Officer A/S, HMCS *Qu'Appelle*, 19 May 1944; Executive Officer, HMCS *Micmac*, 12 September 1945; Commanding Officer, Anti-Submarine School, 1 April 1946; Commanding Officer, HMCS *Iroquois*, 8 March 1948; Commanding Officer, HMCS *Swansea*, 12 April 1948; Staff Officer Torpedo Anti-submarine (TAS), to Director of Weapons and Training, 27 July 1949; Training Officer, HMCS *Ontario*, 12 February 1951; Vice-Commandant and Officer-in-Charge, Cadet Wing, HMCS *Royal Roads*, 25 March 1952; Royal Naval Staff Course, 27 September 1954; Commanding Officer, HMCS *St. Laurent* and Commander, 3rd Canadian Escort Squadron, 29 October 1955; Executive Officer, HMCS *Shearwater*, 23 January 1957;

Director, Undersea Warfare, 18 September 1958; Assistant Director Plans, Defensive Operations (SACLANT) 10 August 1960; Commanding Officer, HMCS *Bonaventure*, 7 August 1963; Director of Cadets, April 1965; On Staff Commander Designate Training Command, July 1965; Deputy Chief of Plans, August 1967; Commander, Canadian Defence Liaison Staff & Canadian Forces Attaché (Washington), June 1970; Commander, Maritime Command & Commander Canadian Atlantic Sub Area, October 1971.

Honourably discharged from service on 19 October 1973.

VICE-ADMIRAL JAMES ANDREW FULTON, CMM, CD

Promotions

Entered the Royal Canadian Navy in Victoria, British Columbia, on 3 July 1946; Promoted Acting Sub-Lieutenant, 3 November 1947; Lieutenant, 18 February 1950; Lieutenant-Commander, 18 February 1958; Commander, 1 January 1963; Captain, 1 July 1966; Commodore, 27 July 1973; Rear-Admiral, 15 July 1976; Vice-Admiral, 15 July 1978.

Decorations, Campaign Stars and Medals

Awarded Commander of the Order of Military Merit (CMM), Order of St. John of Jerusalem (OSJ), Canadian Forces Decoration (CD) with 2nd Clasp. Commendation for Outstanding Achievement from the Supreme Allied Commander Atlantic, Admiral E.P. Holmes, USN.

Courses and Qualifications

Military Occupation (MOC): 11A GOL (CF: 71C MARS SM) TARTAR Systems Course, Dam Neck Virginia 1 July 1963–8 September 1963; Senior Officers Anti-Submarine Warfare Tactical Course, Norfolk, Virginia; JSC 141, Londonderry, Northern Ireland; SOSP, JMWS, Nowra, Australia.

Ships and Appointments

Training Officer, HMCS *Haida*, 10 August 1949–13 January 1950; Gunnery Officer, HMCS *Huron*, 28 February 1950–23 September 1951; Flag Lieutenant to CANFLAGLANT, 28 September 1951–8 September 1952; Instructor, HMS *Excellent*, Portsmouth, England, 12 March 1954–16 December 1954;

Squadron Gunnery Officer, HMCS *Athabaskan*, 7 February 1955–28 October 1955; Squadron Gunnery Officer, HMCS *Crescent*, 1 November 1955–5 October 1956; Staff Officer (Guided Missile), 14 October 1957–15 February 1961; Commanding Officer, HMCS *Outremont*, 8 March 1961–6 September 1962; Project Officer (Programme Manager Missile Systems), 25 September 1962–30 September 1963; Director of Naval Operations (DNO), 13 January 1964–2 August 1965; Commanding Officer, HMCS *Gatineau*, 11 August 1965–7 September 1966; Deputy SACLANT Representative, Europe (SACLANTREPEUR), 19 September 1966–30 May 1969; Commanding Officer, HMCS *Provider*, 2 September 1969–30 June 1972; National Defence College, 27 August 1972; Commander, Northern Region Headquarters (NRHQ), 15 August 1973–4 July 1975; Assistant Deputy Minister (Policy), 5 July 1975–5 July 1976; Chief of Personnel Careers and Senior Appointments (CPCSA), 15 July 1976–November 1977; Canadian Military Representative, NATO Military Committee in Permanent Session (MCPS), Brussels, Belgium, 31 July 1978–April 1980; Commander, Maritime Command, 6 August 1980.

Honourably discharged from service on 3 March 1984.

Vice-Admiral Charles M. Thomas, CMM, CD

Promotions

Enrolled in the RCN as Officer Cadet, September 1954; promoted Midshipman, September 1956; Acting Sub-Lieutenant, September 1957; Sub-Lieutenant, July 1958; Lieutenant, 11 August 1960; Lieutenant-Commander, 1 July 1966; Acting Commander, 1 July 1969; Commander, 15 September 1969; Captain, 18 July 1975; Commodore, 6 July 1981; Rear-Admiral, 15 July 1984; Vice-Admiral, 22 July 1987.

Decorations, Campaign Stars and Medals

Awarded Commander of the Order of Military Merit (CMM); Canadian Forces Decoration (CD) with 2nd Clasp.

Courses and Qualifications

Military Occupation MOC: 44A MARE, 71B MARS and eventually GOL 11A. Received a Bachelor of Science in Mechanical Engineering, University of

Toronto; Auxiliary Machinery Operators Certificate; Basic Engineering Course, Royal Naval Engineering College; Mechanical Engineering Sub-Specialization Training, Royal Naval Engineering College; Engineering Certificate of Competency II; Joint Maritime Warfare Course (Standard); Astro Navigational Course; Network Planning Course; Staff Course, Canadian Forces Staff College; Master of Arts in Business Administration, Dalhousie University; French Language Training, Canadian Forces Language School.

Ships and Appointments

ROTP (University of Toronto), September 1954; Royal Naval Engineering College, July 1957; HMCS *Margaree*, 11 September 1959; Royal Naval Engineering College, May 1960; HMCS *Saguenay*, 21 May 1961; Engineer Officer, HMCS *Antigonish*, 11 September 1961; Cadet Training Officer and Operations Officer, 4th Canadian Escort Squadron, HMCS *Jonquière*, 18 December 1961; Engineer Officer, HMCS *New Glasgow*, 28 October 1963; Engineer Officer, HMCS *Saskatchewan*, 6 March 1964; Staff Officer, Postings and Careers (Sub-Lieutenants), 31 January 1966; Canadian Forces Staff College, September 1967; Staff Officer, Planning, HMC Dockyard (Halifax), 8 July 1968; Executive Officer, HMCS *Preserver*, 1 July 1969; Commanding Officer, HMCS *Fraser*, 1 June 1971; Senior Staff Officer, Training, MARCOM HQ, April 1973; Senior Staff Officer Combat System Readiness Sea, 1 August 1973; Command Personnel & Training Officer, 30 June 1975; Commander, Training Group Pacific, 5 August 1976 and Commander, 4th Canadian Escort Squadron, July 1977; National Defence College, 18 August 1978; Director Maritime Requirements Sea, 21 July 1979; French Language Training, August 1981; Director General Maritime Doctrine and Operations, 17 May 1982; Chief of Maritime Doctrine and Operations, 25 July 1984; Commander Maritime Command, July 1987; Vice-Chief of the Defence Staff, 1 September 1989.

Honourably discharged from service on 10 March 1992.

VICE-ADMIRAL ROBERT EARL DOUGLAS GEORGE, CMM, CD

Promotions

Entered the RCN on 30 January 1961; promoted Sub-Lieutenant, 1 May 1962; Lieutenant, 19 August 1965; Lieutenant-Commander, 5 May 1969; Commander, 7 January 1974; Captain (N), 2 July 1979; Commodore, 1 July 1984; Rear-Admiral, 13 July 1987; Vice-Admiral, 21 July 1989.

Decorations, Campaign Stars and Medals

Awarded Commander of the Order of Military Merit (CMM); the Canadian Forces Decoration (CD) with 2nd Clasp. Queens Silver Jubilee; Special Service Medal (SSM) with NATO Bar; and the Chief of Defence Staff Commendation.

Courses and Qualifications

Military Occupation (MOC): GOL 11A (CF: 71B MARS-SSQ). Obtained Bachelor of Science Degree, University of British Columbia, 1962; Cadet Under Training, HMCS *New Glasgow*, 18 May–11 August 1961; Cadet Under Training, HMCS *Ste. Thérèse*, 4 May–13 July 1962; Pre-Fleet Course "Kilo," 3 January–27 June 1963; 1st Sea Phase, HMCS *Saskatchewan*, 28 June 1963–18 December 1964; 4th Operations Officer Sub-Specialty Course, October 1965; AN/USQ-20 Basic Programming Course, USN Fleet Anti-Air Warfare Training Centre Atlantic, 15 November 1968; CS-1 Programming Course, USN Fleet Anti-Air Warfare Training Centre Atlantic, 22 November 1968; Canadian Forces Command and Staff College (CFCSC), 25 July 1972; Royal Navy Maritime Tactical Course, 22 February 1974; ASW Course, USN Fleet Anti-Submarine Warfare Training Centre Atlantic, 24 October 1975; Maritime Warfare Tactical Course, Maritime Warfare Training Centre (MWTC), 9 October 1975; Maritime Warfare Senior Seminar, 21 November 1975; Japanese Language Training, Canadian Forces Language School (CFLS), 9 July 1979; French Language Training, Canadian Forces Language School (CFLS), 5 August 1986.

Ships and Appointments

Watch Keeper, HMCS *Saskatchewan*, 18 December 1964–7 January 1965; Assistant Operations Officer, HMCS *Mackenzie*, 7 January–4 October 1965;

Operations Officer, HMCS *Saguenay,* December 1966; Executive Officer, HMCS *Saguenay,* August 1967; Operations Officer, HMCS *Nipigon,* December 1967; Tactical Data System Programming Officer, Directorate Maritime Combat Systems, September 1968; Executive Officer, HMCS *Skeena,* February 1971; Co-ordinating Officer, Combined Support Division, Canadian Forces Fleet School, 18 June 1973; Commanding Officer, HMCS *Margaree,* 7 January 1974; Senior Staff Officer, Combat Systems, MARCOM HQ, 22 December 1975; Commanding Officer, HMCS *Iroquois,* 18 April 1977; Canadian Forces Attaché, Tokyo, Japan, 6 August 1980; Squadron Commander, 2nd Canadian Destroyer Squadron aboard HMCS *Restigouche,* 12 July 1982; Director General Maritime Doctrine and Operations (DGMDO), 16 July 1984; Commander, Maritime Forces Pacific, 22 July 1987; Commander, Maritime Command, 1 August 1989; Deputy Chief of the Defence Staff (DCDS), 19 July 1991; Canadian Military Representative, NATO Military Committee in Permanent Session (MCPS), Brussels, Belgium, 8 August 1992.

Honourably discharged from service on 6 October 1995.

Admiral John Rogers Anderson, CMM, CD

Promotions
Entered under the Regular Officer's Training Plan (ROTP) as Officer Cadet, 1 September 1959; Sub-Lieutenant, 1 May 1963; Lieutenant, 29 April 1966; Lieutenant-Commander, 1 July 1971; Commander, 2 July 1976; Captain (N), 22 February 1982; Commodore, 20 June 1986; Rear-Admiral, 7 July 1987; Vice-Admiral, 1 July 1991; Admiral, 29 January 1993.

Decorations, Campaign Stars and Medals
Awarded Commander of the Order of Military Merit (CMM); Special Service Medal (SSM) with NATO Bar; Canadian Forces Decoration (CD) with 2nd Clasp.

Courses and Qualifications
Military Occupation (MOC): 11A General Officers List (CF: 71B MARS); completed Bachelor of Science at the University of British Columbia, 31 May 1963; Pre-Fleet Training HMCS *Stadacona,* 1 July 1963; Upper Deck

Watch Keeping Certificate, 24 September 1965; 5th Operations Officer Course, 1 October 1966; CF Staff School Course, 5 January 1968; Command Qualification, July 1970; USN Programming Digital Computer Course, Dam Neck Virginia, 20 November 1970; DDH 280 Combat Control Officer's Course, 9 August 1971; DDH 280 Engineering Officer's Familiarization Course for COs and Watch Keeping Officers, 22 November 1971; Standard Maritime Warfare Course; Canadian Forces Command and Staff Course, 18 August 1975; Communications Security, Specialist Course, 1976; ADP, GP, Programming and Analysis Qualification.

Ships and Appointments

HMCS *Discovery* while at UBC, 1959; Officer Cadet Summer Training in HMC Ships *New Glasgow* and *Fraser*, 1960–62; Sea Phase Training, HMCS *Saskatchewan*, 6 January 1964; First Sea Phase Appointment, HMCS *St. Croix*, 30 November 1964; Second Sea Phase Appointment, HMCS *St. Croix*, 1 April 1965; Instructor, HMCS *Venture*, 13 June 1966; AIO Officer, HMCS *Bonaventure*, 17 April 1968; CFHQ/CTS/DGMS/DMCS, 19 August 1970; Programmer CCS 280 Combined Support Division CFFS Halifax, 5 July 1971; Operations Officer, HMCS *Iroquois*, 15 March 1972; Executive Officer, HMCS *Iroquois*, 10 June 1974; Canadian Forces Command and Staff College, 18 August 1975; Senior Staff Officer Operations, National Defence Operations Centre, 9 July 1976; Commanding Officer, HMCS *Restigouche*, 24 July 1978; Commanding Officer, Naval Officer Training Centre *Venture*, 3 October 1980; Commanding Officer, First Canadian Destroyer Squadron, 27 February 1982; Director Maritime Requirements Sea, 22 August 1983; Canadian Forces Language School (Ottawa), 22 July 1985; Director General Maritime Doctrine and Operations, 23 June 1986; Chief Submarine Acquisition, 20 July 1987; Chief Maritime Doctrine and Operations, 14 July 1989; Commander Maritime Command, 12 July 1991; Vice-Chief of Defence Staff, 15 July 1992; Chief of Defence Staff, 29 January 1993.

Honourably discharged 1 May 1994.

ABBREVIATIONS AND ACRONYMS

AECL — Atomic Energy of Canada Limited

AEW — Aerial Early Warning

AGM — Admiralty General Message

AJAG — Assistant Judge Advocate General

AOR — Auxiliary, Oiler, Replenishment

ASW — anti-submarine warfare

BPF — British Pacific Fleet

CANCOMFLT — Commander of the Canadian Fleet

CANFORGEN — Canadian Forces General Message

CANLANT — Canadian Atlantic [SACLANT sub-area]

CANUS — Canadian-United States

Captain (D) — Captain ([of] Destroyers)

CAS — Chief of the Air Staff

CBE — Companion of the Order of the British Empire

CCNF — Commodore Commanding Newfoundland Force

CDS — Chief of the Defence Staff

CFAO — Canadian Forces Administration Order

CFHQ — Canadian Forces Headquarters

CGS — Canadian Government Ship

C-in-C — Commander-in-Chief

CNA — Canadian Northwest Atlantic Command

CNAS — Chief of [Naval] Administration Services

CNMO — Canadian Naval Mission Overseas

CNS — Chief of the Naval Staff

CO — commanding officer

COAC — Commanding Officer Atlantic Coast

COPC — Commanding Officer Pacific Coast

CPF — Canadian Patrol Frigate

CR-90 — Critical Review 90

CSC — Chiefs of Staff Committee

CTF — Commander Task Force

CUSRPG — Canada-US Regional Planning Group

CVL — Light Fleet Carrier

CVS — Anti-Submarine carrier

CWM — Canadian War Museum

DATAR — Digital Automatic Tracking and Remoting System

DDE — destroyer escort

DDG — guided-missile destroyer

DDH — helicopter-carrying destroyer

DDP — Department of Defence Production

DGMF — Director General Maritime Forces

DHH — Directorate of History & Heritage

DMAC — Deputy Minister's Advisory Committee

DND — Department of National Defence

DNPO — Director Naval Plans and Operations

DNS — Director of the Naval Service

DRB — Defence Research Board

DREA — Defence Research Establishment Atlantic

DSC — Distinguished Service Cross

DSO — Distinguished Service Order

EASTLANT — eastern Atlantic NATO sub-area

FONF — Flag Officer Newfoundland

FPS — Fisheries Protection Service

HF/DF — high frequency direction finding

HMCS — Her/His Majesty's Canadian Ship

HMS — Her/His Majesty's Ship

ICBM — Inter-continental Ballistic Missile

IRBM — Intermediate Range Ballistic Missile

LAC — Library and Archives Canada

LOFAR — Low Frequency Acoustic Ranging

MARCOM — Maritime Command

MARLANT — Maritime Forces Atlantic

MARPAC — Maritime Forces Pacific

MCC — Military Cooperation Committee

mfm — microfilm

MID — Mentioned-in-Despatches

MOPS — Maritime Officer Production Study

MORPS — Maritime Other Ranks Production Study

NATO — North Atlantic Treaty Organization

NCMS — *Navire canadienne de sa Majesté* [Her Majesty's Canadian Ship]

nd — no date

NEF — Newfoundland Escort Force

NHS — Naval Historical Section

NPIQ — Naval Presence in Quebec

NPRC — National Personnel Records Centre

NSHQ — Naval Service Headquarters

NTDS — Naval Tactical Data System

OBE — Order of the British Empire

OGD — Other Government Department

PANS — Public Archives of Nova Scotia

PJBD — Permanent Joint Board on Defence

PPCC — Policy and Project Coordination Committee

PRO — Public Records Office

RCAF — Royal Canadian Air Force

RCN — Royal Canadian Navy

RCNC — Royal Canadian Naval College

RCNR — Royal Canadian Naval Reserve

RCNVR — Royal Canadian Naval Volunteer Reserve

RN — Royal Navy

RNC — Royal Naval College

RNCC — Royal Naval College of Canada

SACEUR — Supreme Allied Commander Europe

SACLANT — Supreme Allied Commander Atlantic

SOSUS — Sound Underwater Surveillance System

SSBN — nuclear-powered ballistic missile firing submarine

SSN — nuclear-powered attack submarine

STANAVFORLANT — Standing Naval Force Atlantic

Sustops — Sustained Operations

TAS — Torpedo/Anti-Submarine

UK — United Kingdom

USN — United States Navy

VCDS — Vice Chief of the Defence Staff

VCNS — Vice Chief of the Naval Staff

VDS — variable depth sonar

WA — Western Approaches

WESTLANT — western Atlantic NATO sub-area

WRCNS — Women's Royal Canadian Naval Service

CONTRIBUTORS

R.H. Caldwell

R.H. Caldwell served in the Canadian Army for thirty-five years. He completed technical and general staff courses at the Royal Military College of Science at Shrivenham, the British Army Staff College at Camberley and the Joint Warfare Establishment at Old Sarum. He passed the master of arts program in War Studies at the Royal Military College at Kingston in 1987, and thereafter was employed as a researcher and historian at the Operational and Research and Analysis Establishment, followed by the Directorate of History and Heritage, in National Defence Headquarters, Ottawa.

Mr. Caldwell has been a member of the DHH naval history team for thirteen years, and he has written more than a dozen narratives on various aspects of the RCN in the Second World War. He has completed several studies on the RCN and unification for the official postwar naval history to be published in 2010. He is currently the Canadian representative on the first naval history project to combine the efforts of historians from the United States, Britain and Australia. Caldwell is concentrating on the Canadian navy in the Arabian Sea and Gulf from 1991 to 2002. This four-power project will publish its findings in 2007.

Richard Gimblett

Richard Gimblett is an independent historian and defence policy analyst. After graduating from the Royal Mililtary College (1979) and Trent University (1981), he served for twenty-seven years with the Canadian Navy in ships of various classes on both coasts, including as combat officer of HMCS *Protecteur* in the Persian Gulf during the war of 1991. He subsequently co-authored the official account of Canadian participation in that conflict, published under the title *Operation Friction* (1997). His last appointment was to the Directorate of Maritime Strategy, as lead writer of *Leadmark: The Navy's Strategy for 2020*. His doctoral dissertation (Laval, 2000) examined the cruise of HMCS *Crescent* to China in 1949. He is a designated co-author of Volume I (1867–1939) of the official history of the RCN. He has prepared naval analyses for the Conference of Defence Associations and the Council for Canadian Security in the Twenty-First Century. His most recent book is *Operation Apollo: The Golden Age of the Canadian Navy in the War Against Terrorism* (Magic Light, 2004). He is a research fellow with the Centre for Foreign Policy Studies at Dalhousie University, is on the visiting faculty of the Canadian Forces College, and is president of the Canadian Nautical Research Society.

WILLIAM GLOVER

William Glover is a maritime historian. His areas of interest include the RCN to the end of the Second World War and the history of navigation and hydrography in Canadian waters. He has been a frequent participant at Maritime Command historical conferences. His recent contributions include "The RCN: Royal Colonial or Royal Canadian Navy?" published in Hadley, Huebert and Crickard's *A Nation's Navy*, and a commentary on papers by Captain (N) Dan McNeil and Stuart Soward in Haydon and Griffiths' *Canada's Pacific Naval Presence: Purposeful or Peripheral*. He is currently working on the navigation and hydrography of Hudson Bay as seen through Hudson's Bay Company trading voyages. His preliminary findings have been published as "The Navigation of the *Nonsuch*, 1668–69" in *The Northern Mariner/Le marin du nord* and "Early Trading Voyages in Hudson Bay, 1700–1750," in *The Age of Sail*, edited by Nicholas Tracy (Conway Maritime Press, 2002). He organized the historical program for the conference marking the centenary of the Canadian Hydrographic Service. The papers were published in *Charting Northern Waters*, edited by William Glover (McGill Queen's University Press, 2004). He is the editor of *The Northern Mariner* and is a vice-president of the International Commission for Maritime History.

PETER TREVOR HAYDON

Peter Haydon is a former career officer in the Canadian Navy and reached the rank of commander before taking early retirement in 1988 to pursue a second career as an academic. He is now a senior research fellow with the Centre for Foreign Policy Studies at Dalhousie University in Halifax, and an adjunct professor in the Department of Political Science at the same university, specializing in naval and maritime security issues as well as in Canadian naval and defence policy during the Cold War. He has taught undergraduate courses in Maritime Strategy and Civil-Military Relations for the Department of Political Science at Dalhousie. He is also a part-time faculty member of the Royal Military College's War Studies Department, teaching postgraduate courses in War Studies and Maritime Strategy to students in the Halifax area. He is the author of *The 1962 Cuban Missile Crisis: Canadian Involvement Reconsidered* (1993) and *Sea Power and Maritime Strategy in the Twenty-First Century: A Medium Power Perspective* (2000). In the past decade he has been a frequent contributor to naval history conferences and to international conferences and workshops on contemporary maritime security.

WILFRED G.D. LUND

Captain (N) Dr. Wilf Lund was born in Victoria in 1941 and educated at University School. He entered the RCN through HMCS *Venture* in 1959 and became a submarine specialist in 1965, training with the USN. He passed the Royal Navy's Submarine Commanding Officer's Course, "The Perisher," in 1976 and took command of HMCS *Onondaga*. Subsequently, he commanded the destroyers *Nipigon* and *Assiniboine*. Captain (N) Lund served on the directing staff of both the Canadian Forces Command and Staff College and the National Defence College, retiring from NDC as the deputy commandant in 1993. He holds diplomas from the United States Naval War College and National Defence College, and degrees from Queen's University and the University of Victoria. Captain (N) Lund was awarded his Ph.D. in 1999; the title of his dissertation is "The Rise and Fall of the Royal Canadian Navy, 1945–64: A Critical Study of the Senior Leadership, Policy and Manpower Management." His most recent publication is the chapter entitled, "Vice-Admiral Harold Grant: Father of the Post-War Royal Canadian Navy" in *Warrior Chiefs: Perspectives on Senior Canadian Military*

Leaders. He is an instructor in the continuing studies program at RMC and a visiting professor during the naval phase at the Canadian Forces College. Captain (N) Dr. Lund has also conducted numerous interviews in support of the official history of the RCN.

RICHARD MAYNE

After receiving the Graduate Gold Medal for his MA at Wilfrid Laurier University, Richard Mayne has published extensively on the politics of naval expansion during the Second World War, as well as admiralship during the same period. His articles have been published in *The Northern Mariner, Canadian Military History* and *The American Review of Canadian Studies*. A serving officer in the Canadian naval reserve, he is a member of the Directorate of History and Heritage's postwar naval history team, and is currently pursuing his Ph.D. at Queen's University, where his focus will be on the procurement of the Canadian navy's DDH-280 class destroyers. He has also prepared a manuscript that explores the dismissal of Vice-Admiral Percy W. Nelles in January 1944.

MARC MILNER

Marc Milner attended the University of New Brunswick, where he earned a BA in 1977, an MA in 1979 and his doctorate in 1983. His dissertation was published by the University of Toronto Press in 1985 as *North Atlantic Run: The Royal Canadian Navy and the Battle for the Convoys*. From 1983 to 1986, Dr. Milner was a historian with the Directorate of History, where he wrote portions of Volume II of the RCAF's official history dealing with maritime air operations, and the first narrative of the official history of the RCN. Dr. Milner joined the History department at UNB in 1986 and since then has also been director of UNB's Military and Strategic Studies program. Among his other chores he was formerly chairman of the Canadian Military Colleges Advisory Board, he serves as an editor for the journal *Canadian Military History* and has conducted student study tours of battlefields in Europe on behalf of the Canadian Battlefields Foundation, of which he is a member of the board of directors. In July 2002 Dr. Milner took over as chair of the UNB History department.

Since the appearance of his first major book in 1985, along with numerous articles, he has published *The U-Boat Hunters: The RCN and the Offensive against*

Germany's Submarines (1995); *Corvettes of the* RCN (co-authored with Ken Macpherson in 1993); a novel, *Incident at North Point* (1998); a popular history, HMCS *Sackville 1940–1985* (1998), for the Canadian Naval Memorial Trust; and *Canada's Navy: The First Century* (1999). He has also edited *Canadian Military History: Selected Readings* (1993), and co-edited, *Military History and the Military Profession* (1992). His latest work, *Battle of the Atlantic*, was published by Tempus Publishing in 2003.

Roger Sarty

Roger Sarty became interested in maritime history during his childhood in Halifax, Nova Scotia, where he accompanied his father, a television producer, on research trips for historical documentaries. After studies at the University of Toronto (BA and Ph.D.) and Duke University (MA), he joined the Directorate of History at NDHQ in 1981. He worked on the official history of the RCAF as a specialist in maritime air operations during the Second World War, and in 1987 became a founding member of the team established to produce a new operational history of the RCN. From 1991 he was senior historian at the Directorate of History, with responsibility for all English-language publications, and in 1998 moved to the Canadian War Museum. As deputy director, in 2000–2003 he headed exhibition and public programming development for the war museum's new building in Ottawa. In 2004 Dr. Sarty became a professor of military and Canadian history at Wilfrid Laurier University. He has written or co-authored eight books, including, with W.A.B. Douglas and Michael Whitby, *No Higher Purpose: The Official Operational History of the Royal Canadian Navy in the Second World War, 1939–1943, Volume II, Part I* (2003) and the forthcoming Part II, *A Blue Water Navy*.

Michael Whitby

Michael Whitby is senior naval historian at the Directorate of History and Heritage, National Defence Headquarters, Ottawa, where he heads the team responsible for producing the three-volume official history of the RCN, covering 1867–1968. Besides co-authoring the two Second World War official histories, *No Higher Purpose* (2003) and *A Blue Water Navy* (2005) with Alec Douglas and Roger Sarty, he has co-authored two studies on Canada's experience in the

European theatre during the Second World War: *Normandy 1944* (1994) and *Liberation* (1995); co-edited a technical history of Canadian naval aviation, *Certified Serviceable* (1995); and written numerous articles on naval history for international journals. In 2002, the Society of Military History awarded him the Moncado Prize for his article on the 1943 mutiny in HMCS *Iroquois*. His edited volume *Commanding Canadians: The Second World War Diaries of Commander* AFC *Layard, RN*, will be published in 2005 by the University of British Columbia Press and the Canadian War Museum, and he is currently working on a biography of Vice-Admiral Harry DeWolf. In 2003, with Alec Douglas and Roger Sarty, he was awarded the Maritime Command Commendation for his contribution to the RCN official histories project.

ACKNOWLEDGEMENTS

This manuscript and the conference that sparked it could not have been carried out without the enthusiastic assistance of many people. At the conference itself, Admiral Robert Falls, Vice-Admirals Nigel Brodeur, Bob Stephens and Hugh MacNeil, and Rear-Admirals Fred Crickard and Glenn Davidson chaired sessions, and often added keen insights that increased the value of the papers and the discussion that ensued. Professor Jack Granatstein reluctantly stuck his toe into the puddle of naval history and presented a superb summation to the conference in a lively closing session chaired by Dr. Steve Harris, Chief historian at the Directorate of History and Heritage. Peter Haydon and Wilf Lund acted as "academic ADCs" to the former Commanders, MARCOM who gave papers, assisting them in defining common themes and in fleshing out ideas.

Rear-Admiral Glenn Davidson, Commander Maritime Forces Atlantic, hosted the conference, and members of his staff, particularly Lieutenant-Commander F.G. Rasmussen, Lieutenant-Commander Denise Laviolette, Lieutenant (N) Pat Jessup, Lieutenant (N) A.R. Ralph and Lieutenant (N) Dave Benoit, ensured that all ran smoothly. Captain (N) Dave Sweeney and the staff of the CF Maritime Warfare Centre, particularly, Lieutenant-Commander Doug Thomas, Major Brad Baker, Michael Dolliver and Barry Lake, provided an ideal site for the event. The Lieutenant-Governor of Nova Scotia, the Honourable Myra A. Freeman, Commodore Bruce Oland, Marilyn Gurney and the MARCOM Museum, and Cdr.Commander Bill Gard, commanding officer of HMCS *Sackville*, all hosted receptions that made the conference even more enjoyable for the participants. Lieutenant-Commander (LCdr) Richard Gimblett arranged approval of the conference through the Maritime Staff, while Lieutenant-Commander (LCdr) Graeme Arbuckle provided his usual effective and enthusiastic support.

A number of people helped to bring the conference proceedings to publication. Bob Caldwell prepared the list of Canada's naval leaders in Appendix I, while Lieutenant (N) Jason Delaney painstakingly prepared the career summaries in Appendix II. Lieutenant (N) Richard Mayne selected the images, and with Richard Gimblett, Peter Haydon, Isabel Campbell and Captain Gil Lauzon (USN, retired), commented on the introduction. Finally, Major-General P.R. Hussey, Commander of the Canadian Defence Academy, and Colonel Bernd Horn, Director of the Canadian Forces Leadership Institute, appreciated the importance of this volume and agreed to see to its publication.

BIBLIOGRAPHY

The following is a list of selected published secondary sources pertaining to the history of the Canadian Navy, as used in the preparation of this volume. Detailed citations of primary sources such as archival records, interviews, and media articles are given in the endnotes to the chapters.

Armstrong, John G. "The Dundonald Affair." *Canadian Defence Quarterly*, XI:2 (Autumn, 1981), 39–45.

Armstrong, John G. *The Halifax Explosion and the Royal Canadian Navy: Inquiry and Intrigue.* Vancouver: University of British Columbia Press, 2002.

Audette, Louis. "The Lower Deck and the Mainguy Report of 1949," in Boutilier (ed.), *The RCN in Retrospect.*

Bercuson, David. *True Patriot: The Life of Brooke Claxton, 1898–1960.* Toronto, 1993.

Bishop, Arthur. "Save Our Navy: Walter Hose, Rollo Mainguy," in *Salute: Canada's Great Military Leaders from Brock to Dextraze.* Toronto: McGraw-Hill Ryerson, 1997.

Bland, Douglas. *The Administration of Defence Policy in Canada 1947–1985.* Kingston: Ronald P. Frye, 1987.

Bland, Douglas. *Chiefs of Defence: Government and the Unified Command of the Canadian Armed Forces.* Toronto: Canadian Institute of Strategic Studies, 1995.

Boutilier, James A. (ed.). *The RCN in Retrospect, 1910–1968.* Vancouver: University of British Columbia Press, 1982.

Brock, P.W. "Commander E.A.E. Nixon and the Royal Naval College of Canada, 1910–22," in Boutilier (ed.), *The RCN in Retrospect.*

Brodeur, Commodore N.D. "The Naval Service of Canada — The End of the Beginning," in Boutilier, RCN in Retrospect.

Burke, David. "Hellyer and Landymore: The Unification of the Canadian Armed Forces and An Admiral's Revolt," American Review of Canadian Studies, VII:2, 1978.

Byers, R. "Reorganization of the Canadian Armed Forces: Parliamentary, Military and Interest Group Perceptions." Unpublished doctoral dissertation, Carleton University, 1970.

Caldwell, R.H. "The VE Day Riots in Halifax." The Northern Mariner 10/1 (January 2000), 3–20.

Cameron, James M. Murray the Martyred Admiral. Hantsport, Nova Scotia: Lancelot Press, 1980.

Canada. Department of the Naval Service. The Navy List. Ottawa: King's/Queen's Printer [various dates].

Chalmers, W.S. Max Horton and the Western Approaches. London: Hodder and Stoughton, 1958.

Chance, P.G. Before It's Too Late: A Sailor's Life, 1920–2001. Victoria: 2001.

Corbett, Julian S. England in the Seven Years' War: A Study in Combined Strategy [2 vols.]. London: Longmans, 1907.

Cuthbertson, Brian. Canadian Military Independence in the Age of the Superpowers. Toronto: Fitzhenry & Whiteside, 1977.

Davis, S. Mathwin. "The St. Laurent Decision: Genesis of a Canadian Fleet," in Douglas (ed.), The RCN in Transition.

Dixon, Norman F. On the Psychology of Military Incompetence. New York: Basic Books, 1976.

Douglas, W.A.B., Roger Sarty and Michael Whitby. No Higher Purpose. The Official Operational History of the Royal Canadian Navy in the Second World, Part One, 1939–43. St. Catharines, Ontario: Vanwell, 2003.

Douglas, W.A.B. "Conflict and Innovation in the Royal Canadian Navy, 1939–1945," in Gerald Jordan (ed.), Naval Warfare in the Twentieth Century. London: Croom Helm, 1977.

Douglas, W.A.B. (ed.). The RCN in Transition, 1910–1985. Vancouver: University of British Columbia Press, 1988.

Eayrs, James. In Defence of Canada, Volume 1: From the Great War to the Great Depression. Toronto, University of Toronto Press, 1964.

———. In the Defence of Canada, Volume 3: Peacemaking and Deterrence. Toronto: University of Toronto Press, 1972.

———. Northern Approaches: Canada and the Search for World Peace. Toronto: Macmillan, 1961.

Edwards, Kenneth. Seven Sailors. London: Collins, 1945.

Fisher, Robert. "'We'll Get Our Own': Canada and the Oil Shipping Crisis of

1942," *Northern Mariner*, III:3 (July 1993), 33–39.

Norman Friedman. *Fifty Year War: Conflict and Strategy in the Cold War.* Annapolis, Maryland: Naval Institute Press, 2000.

German, Tony. *The Sea Is at Our Gates: The History of the Canadian Navy.* Toronto: McClelland and Stewart, 1990.

Gimblett, Richard H. "The Postwar 'Incidents' in the Royal Canadian Navy, 1949," in Christopher Bell and Bruce Elleman (eds.), *Naval Mutinies of the 20th Century.* London: Frank Cass, 2004.

———. "What The Mainguy Report Never Told Us: The Tradition of Mutiny in the Royal Canadian Navy Before 1949" (*Canadian Military Journal*, I:2, Summer 2000).

———. "Reassessing the Dreadnought Crisis of 1909 and the Origins of the Royal Canadian Navy," in *The Northern Mariner/Le Marin du nord*, IV:1 (January 1994), 35–53.

Gordon, Andrew. *The Rules of the Game: Jutland and British Naval Command.* London: John Murray, 1996.

Goodspeed, Lieutenant-Colonel D.J. *The Armed Forces of Canada: 1867–1967: A Century of Achievement.* Ottawa: Queen's Printer, 1967.

Gough, Barry M. HMCS *Haida: Battle Ensign Flying.* St. Catharines, Ontario: Vanwell, 2001.

Gow, Jean Donald. *Alongside: The Navy, 1910–1950, An Intimate Account.* Quyon, Quebec: Chesley House Publications, 1999.

Granatstein, J.L. *The Generals: The Canadian Army's Senior Commander in the Second World War.* Toronto: Stoddart, 1993.

———. "Unification: The Politics of the Armed Forces," in the Canadian Centenary Series, *Canada 1957–1967: The Years of Uncertainty.* Toronto: McClelland and Stewart, 1986.

———. "When Push Came to Shove: Canada and the United States," in Thomas G. Paterson (ed), *Kennedy's Quest for Victory–American Foreign Policy 1961–1963.* New York: Oxford University Press, 1989.

Great Britain. Admiralty. *The Navy List.* London: Her/His Majesty's Stationary Office [dates various].

Hadley, Michael. *U-boats Against Canada.* Kingston and Montreal: McGill-Queen's University Press, 1985.

Hadley, Michael L., Rob Hubert and Fred W. Crickard (eds.) *A Nation's Navy: In Quest of Canadian Naval Identity.* Kingston, Ontario, and Montreal: McGill-Queen's University Press, 1996.

Hadley, Michael, and Roger Sarty. *Tin-Pots and Pirate Ships: Canadian Naval Forces and German Sea Raiders, 1880–1918.* Kingston, Ontario, and Montreal: McGill-Queen's University Press, 1991.

Haydon, Peter T. *The 1962 Cuban Missile Crisis: Canadian Involvement*

Reconsidered. Toronto: Canadian Institute of Strategic Studies, 1963.

Hellyer, Paul T. *Damn the Torpedoes: My Fight to Unify Canada's Armed Forces.* Toronto: McClelland and Stewart, 1990.

Hennessy, Michael. "Fleet Replacement and the Crisis of Identity," in Hadley et al (eds.), *A Nation's Navy: In Quest of Canadian Naval Identity,* 131–53.

———. "The Rise and Fall of a Canadian Maritime Policy, 1939–1965: A Study of Industry, Navalism and the State." Unpublished Ph.D. dissertation, University of New Brunswick, 1995.

John Holmes. *The Shaping of Peace: Canada and the Search for World Order 1943–1957, Vol. 2.* Toronto: University of Toronto Press, 1979.

Horn, Bernd, and Stephen Harris (eds.). *Warrior Chiefs: Perspectives on Senior Canadian Military Leaders.* Toronto: Dundurn Press, 2001.

Jones, Colin. "'The View from Port Phillip Heads: Alfred Deakin and the Move Towards an Australian Navy," in David Stevens & John Reeve (eds.), *Southern Trident: Strategy, History and the Rise of Australian Naval Power.* Crows Nest, NSW: Allen & Unwin, 2000, 160–73.

Kemp, Peter (ed.). *The Oxford Companion to Ships and the Sea.* London: Oxford University Press, 1976.

Knox, J.H.W. "An Engineer's Outline of RCN History: Part II," in Boutilier (ed.), *The RCN in Retrospect.*

Knonenburg, Vernon J. *All Together Now: The Organization of the Department of National defence in Canada 1964–1972.* Wellesley Papers 3/1973. Toronto: Canadian Institute of International Affairs, 1973.

Lamb, James. *The Corvette Navy.* Toronto: Macmillan, 1977.

Lay, Horatio Nelson. *Memoirs of a Mariner.* Stittsville, Ontario: Canada's Wings, 1982.

Lund, Wilfred G. "Rear Admiral Leonard Warren Murray, CB, CBE, RCN: A Study of Command and Leadership in the Battle of the Atlantic," in Yves Tremblay (ed.), *Canadian Military History Since the 17th Century.* Ottawa: NDHQ/DHH, 2001, 297–308.

———. "The Rise and Fall of the Royal Canadian Navy, 1945–1964: A Critical Study of the Senior Leadership, Policy and Manpower Management." Unpublished Ph.D. dissertation, University of Victoria, 1999.

———. "The Royal Canadian Navy's Quest for Autonomy in the North West Atlantic," in Boutilier (ed.), *The RCN in Retrospect.*

———. "Vice-Admiral Harold Grant: Father of the Post War Royal Canadian Navy," in Horn and Harris (eds.), *Warrior Chiefs.*

MacFarlane, John M. *Canada's Admirals and Commodores.* Maritime Museum of British Columbia: Maritime Museum Notes No 8, August 1992.

Macintyre, Donald. *U-Boat Killer.* London: Weidenfeld and Nicholson, 1956.

Macpherson, Ken, and Ron Barrie. *The Ships of Canada's Naval Forces, 1910–2002: A Complete Pictorial History of Canadian Warships*. St. Catharines, Ontario: Vanwell, 2002.

Macpherson, Ken, and Marc Milner. *Corvettes of the Royal Canadian Navy 1939–1945*. St. Catharines, Ontario: Vanwell, 1993.

Maginley, Charles D., and Bernard Collin. *The Ships of Canada's Marine Services*. St. Catherines, Ontario: Vanwell, 2001.

Maloney, Sean. "General Charles Foulkes: A Primer on How to be CDS", in Horn and Harris (eds.), *Warrior Chiefs*.

Mayne, Richard Oliver. "A Covert Naval Investigation," in *The Northern Mariner*, X:1 (January 2000), 37–52.

———. "A Political Execution," in *The American Review of Canadian Studies*, 29 (Winter 1999), 577–93.

———. "Bypassing the Chain of Command: The Political Origins of the RCN's Equipment Crisis of 1943," in *Canadian Military History*, IX:2 (Summer 2000), 7–22.

McKee, Fraser, and Robert Darlington. *The Canadian Naval Chronicle: 1939–1945*. St. Catharines, Ontario: Vanwell, 1998.

Middlemiss, Dan W. "Economic Considerations in the Development of the Canadian Navy since 1945," in W.A.B. Douglas (ed.), *The RCN in Transition*.

Milner, Marc. *Canada's Navy: The First Century*. Toronto: University of Toronto Press, 1999.

———. "A Canadian Perspective on Canadian and American Naval Relations Since 1945," in Joel J. Sokolsky and Joseph T. Jockel (eds.), *Fifty Years of Canada–United States Defense Cooperation: The Road From Ogdensburg*. Lewiston, New York: Edwin Mellen Press, 1992.

———. "HMCS *Somers Isles*: the Royal Canadian Navy's Base in the Sun," in *Canadian Defence Quarterly*, XIV:3 (Winter, 1984/85).

———. *North Atlantic Run: The Royal Canadian Navy and the Battle for the Convoys*. Toronto: University of Toronto Press, 1985.

———. "The Royal Canadian Navy and 1943: A Year Best Forgotten?" in Paul Dickson (ed.), *1943: the End of the Beginning* (Waterloo, Ontario: Laurier Centre for Military, Strategic and Disarmament Studies, 1995).

———. *The U-Boat Hunters: The Royal Canadian Navy and the Offensive against Germany's Submarines*. Toronto: University of Toronto Press, 1994.

Morgan, Henry J. *The Canadian Men and Women of the Time: A Handbook of Canadian Biography*. Toronto: W. Briggs: 1898 [1st ed.] and 1912 [2nd ed.].

Munton, Donald, and Donald Page. "The Operations of the Post-War Hostilities Planning Group in Canada, 1943–1945." Paper presented to the 55th Annual Meeting of the Canadian Historical Association, Laval University, 2 June 1976. DHH 76/188.

Naval Officer's Association of Canada (Ottawa Branch), *Salty Dips, Vol 4: "Well, All But One."* Ottawa: privately printed, 1993.

————. *Salty Dips, Vol 6: "Ready Aye Ready."* Ottawa: privately printed, 1999.

Nicholls, Bob. "William Rooke Creswell and an Australian Navy," in T.R. Frame, J.V.P. Goldrick and P.D. Jones (eds.), *Reflections on the Royal Australian Navy*. Kenthurst, NSW: Kangaroo Press, 1991.

Pedlow, Gregory W. *NATO Strategy Documents, 1949–1969*. Brussels: NATO, 1997.

Pickerskill, J.W., and D.F. Forster. *The Mackenzie King Record, Vol. 3, 1945–1946*. Toronto, 1970.

————. *The Mackenzie King Record, Vol. 4, 1947–1948*. Toronto, 1970.

Polmar, Norman, *et al. Chronology of the Cold War at Sea 1945–1991*. Annapolis, Maryland: Naval Institute Press, 1998.

Preston, Richard A. *Canada and "Imperial Defense": A Study of the Origins of the British Commonwealth's Defense Organization, 1867–1919*. Durham, N.C.: Duke University Press, 1967.

Pullen, Hugh Francis. "The Royal Canadian Navy between the Wars," in Boutilier (ed.), *The RCN in Retrospect*.

Rawling, Bill. "A Lonely Ambassador: HMCS *Uganda* and the War in the Pacific," in *The Northern Mariner*, VIII:1 (January, 1998).

Report of Admiral of the Fleet Viscount Jellicoe of Scapa on Naval Mission to the Dominion of Canada (November–December, 1919) (3 vols.). His Majesty's Stationary Office, 1919.

Report on certain "Incidents" which occurred on board H.M.C.S. ATHABASKAN, CRESCENT AND MAGNIFICENT and on other matters concerning The Royal Canadian Navy. Ottawa: King's Printer, 1949.

Sarty, Roger. *Canada and the Battle of the Atlantic*. Montréal: Art Global, 1998.

————. "The Ghosts of Fisher and Jellicoe: The Royal Canadian Navy and the Quebec Conferences," in David B. Woolner (ed.), *The Second Quebec Conference Revisited: Waging War, Formulating Peace: Canada, Great Britain, and the United States in 1944–1945* (The Franklin and Eleanor Roosevelt Institute Series on Diplomatic and Economic History/New York: St. Martin's Press, 1998), 143–70.

————. *The Maritime Defence of Canada*. Toronto: Canadian Institute of Strategic Studies, 1996.

————. "The Origins of Canada's Second World War Maritime Forces, 1918–1940," in *Maritime Forces in Global Security: Comparative Views of Maritime Strategy as We Approach the 21st Century*, Ann L. Griffiths and Peter T. Haydon (eds.). Halifax: Centre for Foreign Policy Studies, Dalhousie University, 1995.

————. "The Origins of the Royal Canadian Navy: The Australian Connection," in T.R. Frame, J.V.P. Goldrick and P.D. Jones (eds.), *Reflections on the Royal*

Australian Navy. Kenthurst, NSW: Kangaroo Press, 1991.

Simkoff, Daniel Theodore. "The Opposition of the Progressive Conservative Party, the Tri-Service Identities Organization and Senior Officers to Bill C–243, The Canadian Forces Reorganization Act." Unpublished MA thesis, University of Manitoba, February 1974.

Schurman, Donald M. *The Education of a Navy: The Development of British Naval Strategic Thought, 1867–1914*. Chicago: University of Chicago Press, 1965.

Smith, Kevin. *Conflict Over Convoys: Anglo-American Logistics Diplomacy in the Second World War*. Cambridge: Cambridge University Press, 1996.

Sokolsky, Joel J. *A Question of Balance: Canada and the Cold War at Sea, 1945–1968*. Kingston, Ontario: Queen's Centre for International Relations, 1987

———. "Canada and the Cold War at Sea, 1945–68," in Douglas (ed.), RCN *in Transition*.

Soward, Stuart. *Hands to Flying Stations: A Recollective History of Canadian Naval Aviation, Vol 1*. Victoria, B.C.: 1995.

Sutherland, R.J. "Canada's Long Term Strategic Situation," *International Journal*, XVII (Summer 1962), 199–223.

Tucker, Gilbert Norman. *The Naval Service of Canada: Its Official History, Volume I: Origins and Early Years*. Ottawa: King's Printer, 1952.

———. *The Naval Service of Canada: Its Official History, Vol. II: Activities on Shore During the Second World War*. Ottawa: King's Printer, 1952.

Wallace, W. Stewart (ed.). *The Macmillan Dictionary of Canadian Biography*. Toronto: Macmillan, 1963 [3rd ed.].

Whitby, Michael. "Matelots, Martinets, and Mutineers: The Mutiny in HMCS Iroquois, 19 July 1943," in *The Journal of Military History*, 65 (January 2001), 77–103.

———. "Masters of the Channel Night: The 10th Destroyer Flotilla's Victory off Ile de Batz, 9 June 1944." *Canadian Military History* II/1 (Spring 1993), 5–21.

———. "Instruments of Security: The Royal Canadian Navy's Procurement of the Tribal-Class Destroyers, 1938–1943." *The Northern Mariner*, II:3 (July 1992).

———. "In Defence of Home Waters: Doctrine and Training in the Canadian Navy During the 1930s." *The Mariner's Mirror* 77/2 (1991), 167–77.

———. "The 'Other' Navy at War: The RCN's Tribal Class Destroyers 1939–1944." Unpublished MA thesis, Carleton University, 1988.

Zimmerman, David. *The Great Naval Battle of Ottawa: How Admirals, Scientists, and Politicians Impeded the Development of High Technology in Canada's Wartime Navy*. Toronto: University of Toronto Press, 1989.

INDEX

Abbott, Douglas: 24, 146-7, 158, 164-5
Acts of Parliament:
    National Defence Act, 1950: 196, 278, 316
    Naval Service Act, 1910: 55, 79
Adams, Commodore K.F., RCN: 159
Admiralty, The: 33, 35, 38-45, 56, 61-2, 74-5, 78-9, 81-4, 88-91, 102, 104-5, 111, 116, 141-2, 144-5, 161, 187, 192, 200, 223-4
Agnew, Captain Ronald I., RCN: 100-1, 110, 128-130
Aid to the Civil Power: 313
Allen, Rear-Admiral J. "Jock": 16
Anderson, Admiral John R., RCN: 11, 16-7
    as Maritime Commander: 349-55
    and CR90: 352
    and new defence policy, 1991: 350
    Naval Reserve and NPIQ project: 351
    and helicopter replacement programme: 352
    and social issues: 352
Assistant Judge Advocate General: 331
Atomic Energy of Canada Limited: 223
Audette, Louis C.: 105, 119, 173-4, 194-5
Australia: 37-8
    and Queensland Maritime Defence Force: 38
Awards and Decorations:
    American Bronze Star: 168
    Companion of the Order of the British Empire (CBE): 169
    Distinguished Service Cross: 248-9
    Distinguished Service Order (DSO): 168
    Legion of Merit: 190
    Order of the British Empire (OBE): 169, 190, 277

Victoria Cross: 145, 192
Baffin Island: 114
Baker, Captain Roland, RN: 175, 232
Ball, Commodore E., RCN: 336
Ballantyne, Charles, C.: 46, 55-8
Barron, Frederick William: 34
Barron, John: 34, 47
Battle of the Atlantic:
    general references: 84-7, 89, 104-6, 109, 111-2, 116-7
    and U-Boat campaign 1941-1945: 78
    use of Ultra: 115
    and 25th Anniversary: 119
Battle of Coronel: 98
Battle of the Nile: 34
Battle of Trafalgar: 34
Belfast, N. Ireland: 159
Bennett, Richard B.: 64-6, 133
Benson, the Hon. Edgar: 318
Bermuda: 71-4, 78-9, 116, 141, 324
Bidwell, Rear-Admiral Roger S., RCN: 105, 118, 279
Bidwell, Mrs.: 279
Bland, Douglas: 223
Boyle, Vice-Admiral Douglas Seaman, RCN: 16, 19, 346
Brand, Captain Eric, RCN: 125, 135-7
Brantford, Ontario: 69, 276
Brayley, Jack: 291-2
Bridgeman, Admiral Sir Francis, RN: 43
Bristol, Rear-Admiral A.L., USN: 106-8
British Army:
    66th Regiment of Foot: 33
British Columbia Centenary: 250
British Columbia, University of: 351
British Commonwealth: 12, 89, 159, 281

Boards:
    Canada-United States Defence Board: 137
    Defence Research Board: 233-4, 236-7, 258
    Naval Board: 132, 135, 140, 142, 146-8, 159, 163-4, 169, 171, 232, 247, 251-2, 256, 262, 279, 319, 337, 351-2, 354
    Permanent Joint Board on Defence (PJBD): 18, 104, 161, 163
    Treasury Board: 66, 197, 221, 336
Borden, Sir Robert: 43-6, 55-6
Brock, Rear-Admiral Jeffry V., RCN: 22, 193, 228, 230-1, 259, 265, 279, 283
Brock Report: 257-8, 266, 283, 287
Brockington, Leonard: 154
Brodeur, Louis-Phillippe: 40, 42, 71
Brodeur, Vice-Admiral Nigel: 336
Brodeur, Rear-Admiral Victor-Gabriel: 71, 75, 89, 118, 135, 139
Brown, Chief Petty Officer "Buster": 353
Brown, Captain Tom, RCN: 337
Budge, Commander P.D., RCN: 193
Burke, Admiral Arleigh, USN: 19-20, 22, 238

Cadieux, the Hon. Leo: 317
Cairns, Vice-Admiral Peter: 353
Campney, Ralph: 202, 204, 224
Canada:
    and post-war strategic development: 165
    and defence policy issues: 231, 239-40, 251, 257, 260-1, 263-4, 268, 270, 280-2, 287, 295, 350
    and tri-service Mobile Force Planning Group: 266, 284-5
    and Forces Mobile Command: 285, 293-5
    and White Paper on Defence, 1964: 260, 264, 267-9, 278, 284-5, 295, 293
    and White Paper on Defence, 1987: 336, 346
    and White Paper on Defence, 1994: 338
Canada Steamship Lines: 234
Canada-U.S. Regional Planning Group (CUSRPG): 203
Canadian Armed Forces Council: 354
Canadian Army:
    and the Bobcat fighting vehicle: 234
    and unification: 16, 260-1, 268-9, 275-6, 278, 285-99, 310, 314-6, 321-2, 325, 328
    Camp Borden: 322
    regiments:
        Royal Canadian Dragoons: 70
        PPCLI: 343
        R22eR: 343
Canadian Fisheries Protection Service: 40-4
Canadian Forces Headquarters (CFHQ): 269, 278-9, 285, 287, 291, 298, 310
Canadian Joint Mission, Washington: 218, 240
Canadian Manufacturers Association: 80

Canadian Naval Mission Overseas (CNMO): 142-3, 145
Canadian Naval Service: 31, 33, 37-8, 41-2, 70-1
Cann, Midshipman, RCN: 98
CANUS defence of North America Agreement: 311
Chalk River, Ontario: 231
Chance, Commander Peter, RCN: 219
Charles, Rear-Admiral John, RCN: 167, 175, 189
Chemainus, B.C.: 188
Cherbourg, France: 168
Chicoutimi, Québec: 352
Churchill, Gordon: 263
Churchill, Sir Winston: 223
Classes and types of ships:
    Bangor class minesweepers: 81, 103
    Barbel class (U.S.) conventional submarines: 235, 256, 258
    Basset class minesweepers: 76, 80-1
    Canadian National Prince class passenger ships: 81
    Coastal Defence Vessel: 351
    Corvettes: 83-4, 86-88, 90-1, 103-4, 117, 140-2, 351
    Crescent class destroyers: 144, 217
    DDH-280: 315, 324, 336, 340
    Essex class aircraft carriers: 225-6
    Frigates: 87, 89-90, 116-7, 175, 196, 199, 227-31, 235, 252-3, 256-9, 263-6, 324, 328-9, 331-3, 335-6, 340, 351
    Helicopter-carrying destroyers (DHH): 310
    Light Fleet Carriers: 18, 24, 142, 144-5, 158, 217
    Mackenzie class destroyer escorts: 227, 230, 263
    Minesweepers: 78, 80, 142, 311, 324
    Oberon class submarines: 258, 266, 310
    Operational support ships: 213, 310, 315, 324
    Prestonian class frigates: 196, 227
    Restigouche class escorts: 176, 226, 263, 267, 329
    Repeat Restigouche class escorts: 239, 253
    River class destroyers: 83, 100, 116, 215, 276
    River class frigates: 141, 196
    Skipjack class SSN: 213, 232, 235
    St. Laurent class destroyer escorts: 175-7, 196, 203, 205, 213, 218, 253, 267, 329
    Thresher class SSNs: 259
    Tribal class destroyers: 77-8, 81, 91
    "Whale-catcher" anti-submarine vessels: 81
    Vancouver class frigates: 203-4
    Yankee-class ballistic missile firing submarines: 328
Claxton, Brooke: 24, 160, 165-6, 169-75, 194-7, 199-202, 204, 261

Cobourg, Ontario: 34
Coke, Sir Charles Henry: 35
Cold War:
general references: 11, 15, 47, 175, 196, 202, 249, 283, 310, 327-8
Cuban missile crisis: 252, 259-60, 280
and strategic revolution: 281
and Berlin Crisis, 1961: 172, 283
and changing realities: 295
and fall of the Berlin Wall: 350
Collins, Lieutenant D.A., RCN: 162, 165
Comox, B.C.: 310
Conferences:
Colonial Conference of 1887: 38
Colonial Conference of 1907: 39
Commander's Conference, 1992: 352-3
Imperial Conference of 1917: 55
Imperial Conference of 1923: 64
Imperial Conference, 1937: 215
Québec Conference, 1943: 142, 223
Québec Conference on Pacific strategy, 1944: 143
Connolly, John Joseph: 134-6, 140, 143, 145
Convoys:
Allied losses: 83, 86, 89, 110-1
designations:
BX 141: 117
HX 1: 79
HX 300: 117
SC 42: 106
Corbett, Sir Julian: 37
Cornwall, Ontario: 331
Cowichan Valley, B.C.: 188
Craddock, Admiral Sir Christopher, RN: 98
Creery, Rear-Admiral Wallace B., RCN: 190
Creswell, Captain W.R., RN: 38
Crow's Nest Club, St. John's: 190
Cuba: 260, 345
Cunningham, Admiral of the Fleet Andrew Browne, RN: 21, 57, 61
Curtis, Air Marshal W.: 175

Damn the Torpedoes: 21, 261
Dartmouth, Devon: 34
Dartmouth, N.S.: 103, 249
de Chastelain, General John: 343
Defence Committees:
Cabinet Defence Committee: 24, 226, 235, 258
Cabinet War Committee: 217
Chief of Defence Staff Advisory Committee: 314
Chiefs of Staff Committee (CSC): 175, 216, 220, 225, 233, 235-40, 249, 251, 256, 267, 281-2
Defence Management Committee: 354

Deputy Minister's Advisory Committee (DMAC): 139-40, 146-7, 159
DND Rank Structure Committee: 221
Military Cooperation Committee: 163
Policy and Projects Co-ordinating Committee: 202, 225, 227
Seaward Defence Committee: 203
Defence Council: 65, 261, 288, 313, 323
Department of Defence Production: 234
Department of Marine and Fisheries: 41
Department of National Defence (DND): 58-9, 63, 65, 196, 258, 295, 332, 336 350, 353-4
Desbarats, George: 55-6, 58-9, 64-5
DeWolf, Vice-Admiral Harry G., RCN:
Assessment: 214-5
state of RCN under DeWolf: 214
childhood and early career: 215
wartime career: 216-7
post-war career: 217-8
personality: 219
Naval Comptroller issue, 1956: 220-3
as CNS, 1956-1960: 223-40
policies regarding NATO: 223
problems regarding naval aviation: 224-6
policies regarding naval construction: 226-31
policies regarding nuclear submarines: 231-5
relations with superiors: 235-9
retirement: 240
other references: 17, 19-21, 147, 159-60, 163, 169, 172, 174, 177, 197-8, 201, 204-5, 247, 250, 256, 259, 262
Dextraze, Lieutenant-General Jacques: 317-8
Diefenbaker, John: 240, 252, 259-61
Dillon, Rear-Admiral Charles, RCN: 171
Dixon, Norman: 35-6
Dobratz, Kapitän-zur-See Kurt: 117
Donovans' rest camp, St. John's: 190
Douglas, Dr. W.A.B.: 113, 174
Dreadnought Crisis: 42
Drury, C.M.: 202
Dyer, Vice-Admiral Kenneth L., RCN: 16, 169, 259, 265, 269, 288-9, 291-2

Eayrs, James: 198
England and The Seven Years War: 37
Esquimalt, B.C.: 40, 100, 199, 310-1, 344-5
Falklands War 1982: 25, 327-8, 333, 343
Falls, Admiral Robert H.: 333
First World War:
outbreak of: 44, 72
Western Front: 70
Fisher, Admiral Sir John, RN: 41-2
Fishery Protection Service: 40-4, 70

Flags:
White Ensign: 279
Foster, Sir George: 46
Foulkes, General Charles: 175, 235-40, 259, 281-2, 285
Fraser, Admiral Sir Bruce, RN: 21, 192
Fulton, Vice-Admiral Andrew, RCN:
review of world situation in early 1980s: 327
and composition of fleet: 329
as Maritime Commander: 329-34
and women serving in HMC ships: 332
and CPF programme: 332
other references: 11, 16-7

Gander, Newfoundland: 345
George, Vice-Admiral R.E., RCN:
MARCOM and social and policy changes of the 1980s: 341-3
RCN public image and public relations in the 1980s: 343-4
MARCOM and the Gulf War: 344
and the changing international scene 1980s-1990s: 345
and assessment of naval operations in the 1980s: 345
and government's agenda for defence, 1980s: 346
other references: 11, 16-7, 338-9, 349, 354
German Navy:
High Seas Fleet: 44
ships:
Hannover: 189
U-boats:
U 30: 78
U 501: 106
Germany:
and seizure of Austria, 1938: 76
and offensive in western Europe, 1940: 82, 218
and shifting offensive to the Mediterranean, 1941: 86
Gibraltar: 83, 89-90, 107
Gironde River, France: 276
Glassco, J. Grant: 281
Glassco Commission: 281, 284
Globe and Mail: 289, 292
Goolden, Captain Massey, RN: 125, 138-9
Gordon, Andrew: 33, 35-6
Graham, George P.: 59, 64
Granatstein, Jack: 235
Grand Banks: 84, 106, 108-9, 114, 116
Grand River, Ontario: 70
Grant, Vice-Admiral Harold T.W., RCN:
childhood and early career: 167-8
wartime record: 168-9

policies as CNS, 1947-1950: 169-71
personnel policies: 171-2
ship construction: 172, 175
and Korean War: 176
assessment: 177
other references: 17, 19, 21, 190, 192-8, 201, 205, 218
Grant, John: 167
Grant, MacCallum: 167
Granton, N.S.: 92
Gray, Lieutenant Robert Hampton, RCNVR: 192
Greenock, Scotland: 189
Greenwood, N.S.: 310, 328
Groos, Captain David, RCN: 291
Guelph, Ontario: 31
Gulf of Maine: 114
Gulf of St. Lawrence: 88, 99, 102, 110, 112-3
Gulf War, 1990: 19, 213, 342-5

Hadley, Michael: 31
Halifax, N.S.: 11, 15, 22, 26, 36, 40, 44, 55, 58, 72-3, 78-80, 83-5, 88, 90, 98, 100-11, 114, 116-9, 130-2, 138, 146-7, 159, 161, 167-8, 188-90, 194-5, 199, 216-7, 221, 248-9, 265, 278, 291-3, 310, 312, 314, 324, 333, 338, 343, 345, 349-50
Halifax Chronicle: 118
Halifax explosion, 1917: 36, 188
Halifax VE-Day Riot, 1945: 22, 105, 118-9, 146-7, 159, 194
Hands to Flying Stations, 278
Harbron, John: 198
Harkness, Douglas: 259-60
Hathaway, Midshipman, RCN: 98
Healey, Rear-Admiral Ed, RCN: 346
Heeney, Arnold: 217
Hellyer, Paul T.: 16, 251, 253, 258, 260-70, 275-6, 278-80, 284, 287, 289-93, 296-7, 316, 321-3
Hennessy, Vice-Admiral Ralph L.: 16, 279, 291
Hibbard, Commodore J.C., RCN: 193, 200
Hibbard, Professor: 344
Holland, Rear-Admiral L.E., RN: 79-80, 161
Holmes, John: 282
Hong Kong: 169
Hope, Commodore A., RCN: 118
Horton, Admiral Sir Max, RN: 110-1, 115, 120
Hose, Commodore Walter, RCN:
appointed DNS: 55
career in RN: 57
assessment: 57-8
preserves existence of RCN, 1921: 57-8
policy for RCN: 59-65
preserves existence of RCN, 1933: 65-6
other references: 17, 19, 38, 46-7, 72-5, 77, 101, 129-30

Houston, Edith (Mrs. Reid): 161
Howard-Johnston, Captain C.D., RN: 116
Hurcomb, Commander P.R., RCN: 195

Iceland: 84-6, 89-90, 106
Imperial Defence College: 73, 101-2
Imperial Defence Course: 130
Ireland: 33, 83, 117, 189
Irish Sea: 219
Isley, J.R.: 118
Italy:
    and invasion of Ethiopia, 1935: 75

Japan:
    invasion of north China, 1937: 76
    attack on Pearl Harbor, 1941: 87, 108
    offensives in the Pacific: 87
Jellicoe, Admiral of the Fleet, Sir John, RN: 34-5, 44-6, 56
Jellicoe Report, The: 45
Joint Services Staff College: 277
Jones, Vice-Admiral George C., RCN:
    assessment: 125-7
    childhood and career to 1939: 127-8
    rivalry with Murray: 128-31, 146-7
    disliked by subordinates: 131
    health: 132, 148
    bureaucratic manoeuvres: 132-3
    equipment crisis: 133-7
    as CNS: 137-47
    relations with politicians: 137
    and Pacific Fleet: 142-5
    and postwar fleet: 145-6
    and Halifax Riots: 146-7
    other references: 17, 19-21, 61, 85, 88, 98-104, 107-10, 114-6, 118-20, 158-60, 162, 216-7

Keenleyside, Professor: 344
Keighly-Peach, Commodore C.L., RN: 201
Kellock, Justice R.L.: 118
Kellock Commission: 118-9
Kemp, Edward: 100
Kennedy, President John F.: 259, 283
King, Admiral Ernest J., USN: 89
King, William Lyon Mackenzie: 24-5, 40, 47, 58, 63-4, 72-3, 75, 78-9, 85, 132, 137, 142-5, 158, 164-5, 191, 223, 248
King George VI, His Majesty: 215
Kingsmill, Admiral Sir Charles Edmund, RCN:
    Assessment: 32
    destruction of personal papers: 32
    childhood and early life: 34
    career in RN: 34
    officer personality profile: 34
    attends RN College: 35, 37

transfers to Fishery Protection Service: 41
as commander of the Fishery Protection Service: 41
as Director, RCNS: 43-7
direction of Canadian naval war effort: 44
planning for postwar navy: 45-6
other references: 17, 19, 22, 25, 55-7, 70, 72-3
Kingsmill, John Juchereau: 33
Kingsmill, Nicol: 39, 41
Kingsmill, William: 33
Kingston, Ontario: 278, 388
Knowlton, Rear-Admiral J.G., RCN: 204-4
Korean War:
    invasion of South Korea: 174
    outbreak of war: 176
    and resulting rearmament programme: 249

Labrador: 85
La Citadelle, Québec: 343
Lakefield Preparatory School: 70
Landymore, Rear-Admiral William M., RCN:
    assessment: 275-6
    early life and naval career to 1964: 276-8
    personality: 279-80
    policies of Hellyer: 280-1, 285, 289
    NATO policies: 281-4
    the "Admirals' revolt" 1965-1966: 289-92
    forced retirement: 292
    actions after retirement: 292-3
    criticisms of unification: 293-5
    other references: 16, 17, 20, 316
Landymore Report: 199
Laurier, Sir Wilfrid: 39-41, 43, 47, 56, 70, 77
Lay, Rear-Admiral Horatio Nelson, RCN: 22, 132-3, 143, 145, 161, 163, 197, 202-5, 225-6, 231, 241
Lee, Group-Captain William: 290, 296
Liverpool, England: 84-5, 115
London, England: 39-40, 42, 64, 71, 119, 134, 276
Londonderry, N. Ireland: 134
Longueuil, Québec, 332
Lund, Dr. Wilf: 98, 214
Lynch, Charles: 239-40

MacBrien, Major-General J.H.: 63-5
Macdonald, Angus L., 3/26, 5/8-5/25
MacDonald, the Hon. Donald: 90, 131-46
Macdonald, E.M.: 65
MacLean, Lieutenant-Commander A.D., RCNVR: 133-5
Maclean's Magazine: 265
McNamara, Robert: 262, 322
Mahan, Alfred Thayer: 37
Mainguy, Daniel Wishart: 187

Mainguy, Vice-Admiral Daniel: 188, 335
Mainguy, Vice-Admiral Edmund Rollo, RCN:
  assessment: 187
  early life: 188-9
  naval career to 1939: 189
  wartime career: 189-91
  command of Uganda: 191
  personnel policies in wartime: 191
  postwar career: 191-6
  postwar personnel problems: 193-5
  work with Mainguy commission: 194-5
  as CNS: 196-206
  strengths as CNS: 205
  weaknesses as CNS: 205
  policies as CNS: 196-205
  other references: 17, 19, 131, 157, 177, 220, 224
Mainguy Inquiry and Report: 170-1, 173-4, 176-7
Maitland-Dougal, Midshipman, RCN: 99
Maloney, Dr. Sean: 235
Massachusetts Institute of Technology: 232
Masse, the Hon. Marcel: 350-2
Matelot naval personnel newsletter: 334
McNaughton, Major-General Andrew: 65-6
Meech Lake Accord: 343
Merchant Ships:
  Arandora Star: 218
  Athenia: 78, 103
  Bonsurf: 131
  Lusitania: 35
  Melrose Abbey: 189
  Port Fairy: 277
Merrick, Rear-Admiral S. RN: 100, 102
Mexican Civil War, 1914: 71
Middlemiss, Professor Dan: 165
Miller, Captain D.: 337
Miller, Air Vice-Marshal Frank: 236-40, 260, 287, 291
Minister of Marine and Fisheries: 39-40, 55, 70-1
Mitchell, Christian:, 168
Monk, F.D.: 43
Montreal: 56, 88, 105, 161
Mosiyev, General: 345
Mountbatten, Admiral Lord Louis: 20, 238
Munich, Germany; 78
Munitions and Supply, Department of: 87, 91, 135
Murdoch, Rear-Admiral Robert: 276
Murray, Rear-Admiral Leonard W., RCN:
  assessment: 97
  childhood and career to 1939: 97-102
  rivalry with G.C. Jones: 100-2, 118
  involvement with RCN expansion, 1939-1941: 103-4
  wartime commands, 1940-1941: 105-6
  involvement in ASW, 1940-1941: 105
  as CCNF and FONF, 1941-1942: 105-6
  problems with Allied command: 110-12
  concerns about operational training: 108, 111
  problems in the North Atlantic: 110-12
  establishment C-in-C CNA: 113-4
  relations with superiors: 114
  late war ASW: 116-8
  Halifax Riot and retirement: 118-9
  post-service career: 119-20
  other references: 16, 17, 19, 20, 22, 61, 84-6, 88, 90, 128-31, 146-7, 190
Nantucket, Massachusetts: 117
National Defence College (NDC): 169, 175, 354
National Defence Headquarters, (NDHQ): 15, 166, 309, 314-8, 335, 338, 346, 352
National Research Council: 66
Naval Information Organization: 163
Naval Militia scheme: 43
Naval Officers' Association of Canada: 318
Naval Operational Research Group: 266
Naval Secretariat: 163, 171
Navy League of Canada: 41, 318
Navy List, 129
Nelles, Charles Meklam: 69-70
Nelles, Admiral Percy Walker, RCN:
  assessment: 69
  early life and career: 69-71
  service in RN: 72-3
  service in RCN: 72-74
  appointed CNS: 74
  prepares RCN for war: 75-8
  oversees expansion of RCN, 1939-1942: 77-8
  and command situation in North Atlantic: 79-80, 83, 85-6
  policies on postwar fleet: 82
  and the Battle of the Atlantic: 83-4
  and ship construction: 80-2
  and establishment of CAN: 90
  removal from command: 90-1
  other references: 17, 20, 22, 32, 47, 57, 66, 101-2, 105, 158-9, 161, 168, 215, 223
Nelles, Mrs.: 215
Nelson, Admiral Lord Horatio: 187
Newfoundland: 38, 57, 84-90, 93, 97, 104-5, 107-8, 110-11, 113, 154
Newman, Captain Peter C.: 346
New York: 88, 99, 117
Nichol, Maraquita (Mrs. Mainguy): 188
Nichol, the Honourable Walther: 188
Nixon, Commander A.E.A., RCN: 160, 188
Nixon, Captain C.P.: 216, 219

Nixon, Lieutenant-Commander C.R.: 233-4
Noble, Admiral Sir Percy, RN: 99, 105-6, 111, 120
Norfolk, Virginia: 260, 324
North American Air Defence Command (NORAD): 281
North Atlantic Treaty Organization (NATO):
  general references: 12, 19-20, 172, 174-6, 195, 197-8, 201-2, 204-5, 210, 214, 218, 223, 239, 254, 256-8, 261-7, 282-6, 293-4, 309, 312, 314, 323-4, 327-8, 352, 354
  EASTLANT: 283
  "Flexible Response": 281, 283-6, 295, 327
  "New Look" strategy and plan (MC 48): 202, 223
  need for dual-purpose forces: 286
  SACEUR: 323
  SACLANT: 202-3, 223, 252, 256, 259, 262, 266-7, 284, 286, 293, 298, 323
  and Canada-U.S. Regional Planning Group: 203
  Standing Naval Force Atlantic (STANAVFORLANT): 19, 329
  WESTLANT: 283, 286
Northwest Rebellion, 1885: 70
Nova Scotia: 87, 98, 167
Nova Scotia Liberal Association: 296
Nova Scotia Tattoo: 353

Oliphansfontein: 70
On The Psychology of Military Incompetence: 35-6
Ottawa: 12, 43-4, 55-6, 64, 72, 75, 85, 89, 94-5, 98-100, 102-3, 105, 111, 113-4, 116, 118, 120-1, 130-1, 138-9, 143, 147, 151-2, 154
Ottawa Citizen: 232

Palmer, Midshipman, RCN: 98
Parliamentary Bills and Charters:
  Charter of Rights and Freedoms, 1982: 332, 340
  Naval Bill debate, 1909: 41-3
  Naval Aid Bill, 1912: 43
  Naval Militia Bill, 1904: 40
  Bill C-90: 278
  Bill C-243: 292, 316-7
Parliamentary Committees:
  Parliamentary Committee on National Defence: 315
  Sauvé Committee: 260
  Standing Committee on National Defence: 286-7, 290-1, 293
Pearkes, Major-General George: 250
Pearson, Lester B.: 162, 252, 260-1, 291
Phillips, Commander Geoffrey, RCN: 231
Phillips, Captain Ray, RCN: 219

Pictou, N.S.: 98
Piers, Rear-Admiral D.W., RCN: 195
Point Pleasant Park, Halifax: 119
Pollard, Captain (N) Dave: 338
Porter, Vice-Admiral H.A., RCN:
  appointment as Maritime Commander: 309
  previous career: 309-10
  experience and concerns as MARCOM: 309-10
  NATO: 314-5
  government policies towards the navy: 315-6
  unification versus integration: 316
  the effect of unification: 316-8
  conclusions on period of command: 318-9
  other references: 11, 16-7, 354
Portsmouth, England: 100-1, 277
Plomer, Commodore James, RCN: 219, 231, 265-6
Pope, General M.: 161-2
Portage-du-Fort: 160
Port Hope, Ontario: 70
Pound, Admiral of the Fleet Sir Dudley, RN: 79, 84, 105
Préfontaine, Raymond: 39
Prentice, Captain James D., RCN: 104-9, 111-2, 114, 116, 120
Progressive Conservative Party: 43, 56, 65, 71, 167, 252, 292, 346
Pullen, Rear-Admiral Hugh Francis, RCN: 160
Purvis, Vice-Admiral C.E. Kennedy, RN: 216
Puxley, Captain W.L., RN: 117

Qualicum, B.C.: 207
Quamichan Lake, B.C.: 188
Québec: 43, 99, 160, 332, 351-2
Québec City: 39, 42, 142-4, 223
Queen Elizabeth II, Her Majesty, 278
Quidi Vidi, Newfoundland: 344

Ralston, Colonel J.L.: 63, 65, 103, 112
Rawling, William: 191
Raymond, Commodore D.L., RCN: 203, 205
Raymont, Colonel R.L.: 235
Rayner, Vice-Admiral Herbert Sharples, RCN:
  assessment: 247
  early career to 1939: 248
  wartime career: 248-9
  postwar career: 249
  as CNS: 250-69
  during Cuban missile crisis, 1962: 252, 259-60
  relations with Paul Hellyer: 260-6
  policies on ship construction: 256-9; 265-7
  and composition of fleet: 253-5, 265-7

and personnel: 267
retirement: 269
other references: 17, 108, 177, 203, 217, 230, 284
Reid, Vice-Admiral Howard E., RCN:
assessment: 160
background and planning for postwar fleet: 157-9
early life and career to 1946: 160-2
personality: 162
as CNS: 162-7
other references: 17, 19, 79-80, 85, 110, 118, 134, 139, 193, 206
Richardson, James: 318
Rietfontein, South Africa: 70
Rogers, Norman: 80
Roosevelt, President Theodore, 40
Rowland, Captain J.M., RN: 134
Royal Australian Navy: 33, 38
Royal Canadian Air Force:
and the Avro Arrow: 233, 239, 280
and unification: 275
acquisition of specialized search and rescue aircraft: 239
and role in continental air defence: 221, 225, 239
stations:
Dartmouth: 249
Royal Canadian Naval Air Service: 44
Royal Canadian Naval Reserve: 138
NCSM Montcalm: 351
and forced retirements, 138
Royal Canadian Naval Volunteer Reserve: 66, 82, 133
Royal Canadian Navy:
early years:
creation: 34, 38, 42
east coast patrols: 35, 44
emergency expansion 1917-1918: 72
near collapse, 1921-1922: 72, 99
expansion of the fleet 1936-1939: 24, 77-8
Second World War:
mobilization for Second World War: 78, 102
wartime expansion of the fleet: 77-8, 85, 89, 103, 111-2, 115
west coast establishment: 100
establishment of Canadian Northwest Atlantic Command, 1943: 113-5
shipbuilding programme, Second World War: 80-81, 87
wartime training: 86-7, 89, 106-9, 111-2, 116-7, 132, 141
first victory over an enemy warship: 189

and Canada-U.S. Defence Plan ABC-22, 1941: 161
Corvette modernization: 91, 115, 133-7, 140
plans to create Pacific Fleet: 142-5, 157
plans for inshore offensive, 1943: 112, 114-5
need for consolidation and modernization in home waters: 113
separate identity within the alliance structure: 163
commitment to Pacific force, 1944: 142-4
postwar:
state of, and plans for, postwar navy: 142, 148, 157-8
new postwar role: 145-6, 163-4, 169, 171, 174, 177, 201, 218, 223-5
inadequate funding: 146, 159
strategic policy: 169-70, 175, 198
need for improvement in conditions of service: 166-7, 16974, 192-5
restructuring: 249
postwar Canadian-American cooperation: 162-3, 311
personnel problems: 163-4, 199, 172-4
composition and redistribution of fleet: 198-9
role of naval aviation: 175, 225-6
participation in Korean War, rearmament programme and period of expansion: 172, 176-7
Naval Defence Act, 1950: 196
role and commitments within NATO: 175, 201, 203, 218, 223, 252, 259, 262, 268, 284
fiscal mismanagement: 220
introduction of Naval Comptroller: 220-3
decline in naval expenditure 1955-1960: 222
increased political and bureaucratic control of the RCN: 251-2
technology and weapons: 77, 171, 175, 201, 214-5, 252, 257, 262, 282, 337
expansion of fleet, 1956-1960: 256
ship replacement needs and programmes: 225-231
nuclear submarine project: 231-5
submarine programme and training requirements: 252
personnel issues of the 1960s: 252, 254-5, 258
and the Cuban Missile Crisis: 252, 259-60

and Paul Hellyer's campaign for structural reform: 260-1
the RCN and Canadian armed forces unification: 261, 268-9, 275-6, 278, 285-94, 296-7, 310, 314-7, 322, 325, 328
the green uniform: 310, 325, 328
and Critical Review 90: 350, 352
and impact of new defence policy: 1991: 350
Naval Presence in Québec Project: 351
and Canadian Forces Official Language Plan: 353
and smoking policy: 353
and impact of funding reductions of early 1990s: 353
Maritime Command:
    operational resources during Cold War: 310
    Arctic surveillance: 313
    personnel and morale, 1970-1982: 309, 314-5
    petition for women to be admitted to the "Combat Arms": 332
    and lessons learned from Falklands War: 327-8, 343
    and work of MARCOM, 1990-1991: 350-1
    and contribution to the Gulf War, 1990: 342-5
    and effect of changing international scene: 344-5
escort and support groups:
    EG 11: 116
    EG 16: 116
    EG 27: 117
    "C" Groups: 190
    lst Canadian Escort Group: 199
    Newfoundland Escort Force (NEF): 86-7, 105-9, 190
establishments:
    Admiral Stephens Engineering Facility: 345
    Defence Research Establishment Atlantic: 315
    Maritime Warfare Centre: 15, 345
    Naval Operational Research Group: 266
    Naval Secretariat Branch: 171
    Naval Service Headquarters (NSHQ): 44-5, 72, 85-6, 88-90, 102, 106-7, 111, 114, 116, 126, 130, 132-5, 139, 141, 144, 147, 161, 166-9, 171-2, 188, 190-2, 194, 197, 215-7, 249, 252
    Training Command Headquarters, Winnipeg: 332

squadrons:
    lst Canadian Carrier Support Squadron: 203
senior appointments:
    Captain Commanding Canadian Ships: 110
    Chief of Maritime Doctrine and Operations: 349
    Chief of Naval Administration Services: 163, 169
    Chief of Naval Technical Services: 203-4
    Commander of Fisheries Protection Service: 41
    Commander of Maritime Command: 16, 354
    Commander-in-Chief, Canadian North-West Atlantic: 113, 117-9, 146-7
    Commander-in-Chief Atlantic Fleet: 85
    Commander Maritime Forces Pacific: 309, 338
    Commanding Officer Atlantic Coast: 79, 85, 104, 109-10, 112, 131, 138, 141, 147, 161, 168, 216, 249,
    Commanding Officer Pacific Coast: 192
    Commodore Commanding Halifax Force: 131
    Commodore Commanding Canadian Ships: 104
    Commodore Commanding Newfoundland Escort Force: 97, 105, 161
    Deputy Chief of Naval Staff: 100, 102
    Director General Maritime Forces: 310, 315
    Director of Naval Operations and Training: 102
    Director Naval Plans and Operations: 198, 201
    Flag Officer Newfoundland Force: 107-9, 140, 190
    Flag Officer Atlantic Coast: 194-5, 259, 278-9
    Flag Officer Pacific Command: 218
    Flag Officer Pacific Coast: 250, 278
    Maritime Commander: 16, 19, 309, 313, 315, 324, 327, 330, 334, 338
    Rear-Admiral Third Battle Squadron: 85, 161
    Senior Officer of the Canadian Destroyer Flotilla: 73
    Senior Officer, Halifax Force: 103
ships:
    HMCS *Annapolis*: 226

HMCS *Assiniboine*: 78, 80, 101, 103-4, 131, 189
HMCS *Athabaskan*: 21, 82, 172, 194, 219
HMCS *Aurora*: 58-9, 99
HMCS *Bonaventure*: 196, 213, 224-5, 253, 256, 259, 277-8, 280, 309, 314, 316, 323
HMCS *Bras D'or*: 313, 324
HMCS *Champlain*: 22, 74-5, 248
HMCS *Cormorant*: 332
HMCS *Crescent*: 172, 194
HMCS *Fraser*: 75, 83, 161, 276-7, 279
HMCS *Haida*: 19, 21, 82, 218-9, 277
HMCS *Halifax*: 349
HMCS *Huron*: 82, 249, 277; (second of name) 344
HMCS *Iroquois*: 82, 277; (second of name) 333
HMCS *Magnificent*: 19, 25, 159, 172, 194-5, 198, 203, 223-4, 249
HMCS *Margaree*: 83, 276, 279
HMCS *Niobe*: 43-4, 46, 49, 71, 99, 102
HMCS *Nipigon*: 226
HMCS *Nootka*: 166, 194, 249
HMCS *Okanagan*: 333
HMCS *Ontario*: 166, 169, 172-3, 193, 224
HMCS *Ottawa*: 75, 130-1, 189
HMCS *Patrician*: 58, 63, 100, 128, 129
HMCS *Patriot*: 58, 63, 100, 128, 161
HMCS *Preserver*: 239, 310
HMCS *Protecteur*: 239, 310, 342-3
HMCS *Provider*: 239, 254, 310, 342, 345
HMCS *Québec*: 202, 223-4
HMCS *Rainbow*: 43-4, 46, 56, 99
HMCS *Restigouche*: 75
HMCS *Sackville*: 354
HMCS *Saguenay*: 73-5, 83, 101; (second of name) 329
HMCS *Saskatchewan*: 291
HMCS *Sioux*: 157, 175
HMCS *Skeena*: 74-5, 216, 218-9, 248
HMCS *St. Laurent*: 75, 216, 218-9, 248; (second of name) 177, 205
HMCS *Uganda*: 191-2, 277
HMCS *Vancouver*: 22, 74-5, 100, 188; (proposed name for aircraft carrier) 225
HMCS *Warrior*: 19, 159, 169
training centres and shore establishments:
HMCS *Cornwallis*: 172, 174, 200, 331
HMCS *Discovery*: 351
HMCS *D'Iberville*: 200
HMCS *Naden*: 322
HMCS *Shearwater*: 172, 310, 323, 333

HMCS *Stadacona*: 276, 322
Royal Canadian Navy Benevolent Trust Fund: 189
Royal College of Defence Studies: 354
Royal Commission on Government Organization: 280
Royal Military College of Canada: 70, 270, 276
Royal Naval College of Canada: 47, 97, 127, 160, 188, 250
Royal Navy:
general references: 17-20, 31, 40, 61, 71-3, 75, 98, 140, 144, 200, 233, 249, 279-80, 295, 297-8
Second World War:
escort system: 104
escort duties: 82, 84-5, 88, 107
Norwegian campaign, 1940: 82
opinions and attitude towards RCN: 139, 161
commitment to Far East theatre: 142-3
postwar:
continued influence on RCN: 164, 174, 187, 248
development of air defence system: 237-8
and anti-submarine warfare ships: 171
loan of submarines to the RCN: 231, 254
and defence reforms: 280
and Falklands War: 25, 327-8, 333, 342
senior appointments:
Commander-in-Chief, Western Approaches: 84, 90, 105-6, 109, 111
Commander-in-Chief, Americas and West Indies station: 189
Commander-in-Chief, British Pacific Fleet: 192
Commodore (D) Western Approaches: 134
commands:
Western Approaches Command: 84, 90, 105-6, 109, 111, 115, 189-90, 248
fleets:
Grand Fleet: 35, 44-5, 99
Mediterranean Fleet: 20, 35, 216
British Pacific Fleet: 191
squadrons:
1st Cruiser Squadron: 216
1st Escort Squadron: 259
3rd Battleship Squadron: 79
America and West Indies Squadron: 98, 189
stations:
Americas and West Indies: 98, 189
Australia: 37
escort groups:
EG 10: 189

establishments:
HMS *Excellent*, gunnery school: 35, 277
HMS *Vernon*, anti-submarine warfare: 248
Nuclear Engineering establishment, Harwell: 232
Royal Naval Staff College, Greenwich: 35, 37-8, 61, 100, 189, 215-6, 277
ships:
HMRY *Victoria and Albert*: 35
HMS *Agincourt*: 99
HMS *Antrim*: 72
HMS *Attack*: 160
HMS *Belfast*: 277
HMS *Berwick*: 98
HMS *Britannia*: 34
HMS *Calcutta*: 99, 105, 276
HMS *Charybdis*: 38
HMS *Diomede*: 168
HMS *Dominion*: 38-9
HMS *Dragon*: 73
HMS *Dreadnought*: 71
HMS *Dunedin*: 189
HMS *Emerald*: 276
HMS *Empire Audacity*: 189
HMS *Enterprise*: 21, 168
HMS *Frobisher*: 276
HMS *Glasgow*: 21, 168, 276
HMS *Goldfinch*: 37
HMS *Good Hope*: 98
HMS *Harvester*: 189
HMS *Iron Duke*: 101
HMS *Kempenfelt*: 189
HMS *Leviathan*: 99, 102
HMS *Majestic*: 37
HMS *Mildura*: 37
HMS *Nabob*: 143
HMS *Nelson*: 248
HMS *Queen Elizabeth*: 100
HMS *Powerful*: 196
HMS *Revenge*: 100, 102, 248
HMS *Rodney*: 248
HMS *Seaborn*: 161
HMS *Sepoy*: 161
HMS *Scylla*: 38
HMS *Suffolk*: 71-2, 98
HMS *Tiger*: 100
HMS *Vanquisher*: 99-100, 127
HMS *Warspite*: 248
Rotary Club of Canada: 354
Royal Canadian Legion: 339
Royal Canadian Mounted Police: 331

Sarty, Roger: 31
Saskatchewan, University of: 198

Sauvé, Maurice: 260, 265
Scapa Flow: 34, 277
Sea Cadet units: 324
Seaward Defence Plan: 203
Second World War:
outbreak: 69, 248
and Canadian mobilization: 78, 102
Dunkirk evacuation of BEF: 83, 218
the Blitz: 276
and Operation Torch: 88-9
and Canadian naval development: 31, 33, 42, 62, 64, 71, 85, 88, 114, 163
D-Day landings: 168
and atomic bombs on Japan: 192
Seignory Club, Ottawa: 197
Sharp, General: 317-8
Shawnigan Lake School: 188
Shearwater, N.S.: 172, 310, 323, 333
Skrimshire's School: 188
Smallwood, Joey: 313
South African War, 1899-1902: 70
Soviet Union:
and post-war military and maritime threat: 163-4
and first atomic bomb test: 174
and Soviet navy's rise to major maritime power: 310
developing maritime strategy, 1970: 311
and submarine fleet: 262, 311
and increase in merchant marine: 311
and "spy ships": 312
composition of Soviet navy 1982-1983: 328
and disintegration of the Soviet bloc: 344-5
future of the Russian Navy, early 1990s: 345
Sailor's Memorial, Halifax: 119
Saint John, N.B.: 332
Saint John Shipbuilding and Dry Dock Company: 332
SCAN Marine Incorporated: 332
Scott, Jean Chaplin (Mrs. Murray): 99
Sherman, Commander Forrest, USN: 162
Silver, Midshipman Arthur, RCN: 98
Simpson, Commodore G.W.G., RN: 134
Skelton, Dr. O.D.: 64
Slade, Rear-Admiral: 349
Soward, Stewart: 225, 278
Spanish Civil War: 216
Spencer, Commodore B.R., RCN: 231, 234
Stalin, Joseph: 202
Stevens, Captain E.B.K., RN: 107
Stephens, Admiral R.S., RCN: 232, 234
St-Jean-sur-Richelieu, Québéc: 352
St. John's, Newfoundland: 84, 104, 109, 134
St. Lawrence River: 88, 110, 113, 352
St. Paul's Church, Halifax: 119

Storrs, Rear-Admiral A.H.G., RCN: 74, 195, 197-9, 205, 225
Strange, Lieutenant-Commander William, RCNVR: 133-4
Sutherland, Lieutenant-General Fred: 352
Sutherland, Dr. R.J.: 263-4, 266, 268

Taylor, Rear-Admiral Cuthbert, RCN: 103, 147, 194
Thacker, Major-General H.C.: 65
"The Continuing Royal Canadian Navy", policy paper: 158, 249
The Rules of the Game: Jutland and British Naval Command: 33, 35
Thomas, Vice-Admiral Charles M., RCN:
    and "replace the navy" capital equipment programme: 335-6
    and personnel training for new ships and equipment: 337
    as Maritime Commander:
        command and personnel issues: 337-8
        naval public relations: 339
    other references: 11, 16-7, 349-50, 352, 354
Tin Pots and Pirate Ships: 31-2
Timbrell, Rear-Admiral Robert W., RCN:
    reflections on political background of unification, 1965-1970: 321-2
    command positions prior to becoming CNS, 1970: 322
    problems as CNS, 1970-1973: 321-6
        personnel: 324
        fleet composition: 324
        research and development: 324
    other references: 11, 16-7, 169, 220, 270-1
Toronto: 33, 41, 133
Toronto Globe: 41, 289, 292
Tory Island: 117
Trinity College School, Port Hope: 70
Tri-Service Identities Organization: 292-3
Trois Rivières, Québec: 352
Trudeau, Pierre: 318, 332-3
Tupper, Sir Charles: 167

United States of America:
    entry into Second World War: 86
United States Navy:
    general references: 18-20, 72, 106, 146, 163-4, 171, 191, 195, 231, 254, 260, 295, 297-8
    Second World War:
        and convoys: 85-9, 107, 113
        involvement in Northwest Atlantic operations: 89, 113, 115, 162
        involvement in U-boat campaign: 116
        U.S. base at Argentia, Newfoundland: 86

Anglo-American Western Support Force: 109
postwar:
    as a model for the RCN: 170-1, 195, 221
    Bureau of Ships: 175
    promoting nuclear propulsion: 198, 234
    development of air defence system: 237-8
    and anti-submarine warfare ships: 171
    Naval Tactical Data System: 238
    and defence reforms: 280
fleets:
    CINCLANT (U.S. Atlantic Fleet): 85
    appointments:
        Commander Task Force 24: 86, 108
    ships:
        USS Seawolf: 233-4
        USS Burrfish: 254
United Nations:
    and Canadian role and support: 254, 257, 261
    and increasing international role, early 1990s: 345-6
Upper Canada College: 34
Upper Canada Rebellion, 1837: 33

Valencia, Spain: 216
Vancouver, B.C.: 40, 161
Vancouver Daily Province: 188
Vancouver Island: 188-9
Victoria, B.C.: 34, 40, 188, 194, 291, 343
Victoria Times Colonist: 233
von Spee, Admiral Graf: 98
Warsaw Pact:
    and deterrent power, 1959: 281
War Supply Board: 81
Warwick, Dr. Nina Sergeivma Shtetinin Seaford: 119
Washington, D.C.: 71, 89, 113, 115, 137, 162, 176, 218, 240
Welland, Rear-Admiral R.P.: 276
Western Approaches Convoy Instructions: 109
West Indies: 79
Westmount, Québec: 99
Whitby, Michael: 172
Windsor, University of: 344
Winnipeg: 322
Withers, General Ramsey: 332-3
Women's Royal Canadian Naval Service: 200-1, 293
Wood, Vice-Admiral James: 335-8
Worth, Captain Sam, RCN: 154
Wright, Commodore R.A., RCN: 222-3